THE DEATH OF A THOUSAND CUTS

CORPORATE CAMPAIGNS
AND THE ATTACK ON THE CORPORATION

JAROL B. MANHEIM
The George Washington University

2001

LAWRENCE ERLBAUM ASSOCIATES, PUBLISHERS

MAHWAH, NEW JERSEY   LONDON

Lawrence Erlbaum Associates, Inc., Publishers
10 Industrial Avenue
Mahwah, NJ 07430

Cover design by Kathryn Houghtaling Lacey

Library of Congress Cataloging-in-Publication Data

Manheim, Jarol, B., 1946-
The death of a thousand cuts: corporate campaigns and the attack on the
    corporation / Jarol B. Manheim.
        p. cm.
        Includes bibliographical references and index.
ISBN 0-8058-3831-7 (cloth : alk. paper)
1. Corporations–Public relations. 2. Labor unions–Public relations.
    3. Corporate image. 4. Social pressure. 5. Demonstrations. 6. Nega-
    tive goodwill. 7. Social responsibility of business. 8. Business ethics.
    9. Industrial relations. 10. Strategic communication.   I. Title.
HD59.M257   2000
659.2—dc21   00-034780
                                                            CIP

Books published by Lawrence Erlbaum Associates are printed on acid-free
paper, and their bindings are chosen for strength and durability.

Printed in the United States of America
10 9 8 7 6 5

CONTENTS

[A corporate campaign includes a] wide and indefinite range of legal and potentially illegal tactics used by unions to exert pressure on an employer. These tactics may include, but are not limited to, litigation, political appeals, requests that regulatory agencies investigate and pursue employer violations of state or federal law, and negative publicity campaigns aimed at reducing the employer's goodwill with employees, investors or the general public.

Judge Patricia Wald
In *Food Lion v. United Food and Commercial Workers International Union*

We will use old fashioned mass demonstrations, as well as sophisticated corporate campaigns, to make worker rights the civil rights issue of the 1990s.

John Sweeney
President
AFL–CIO

Corporate campaigns swarm the target employer from every angle, great and small, with an eye toward inflicting upon the employer the death of a thousand cuts rather than a single blow.

Richard Trumka
Secretary—Treasurer
AFL–CIO

PREFACE

Although it sounds like a charity drive or an advertising effort, *corporate campaign* is actually a term of art that refers to an assault on the reputation of a company that has somehow offended a union or some other interest. These campaigns are often long-running and wideranging affairs conducted without rules and constrained primarily by the knowledge and imagination of the campaigners, the availability of resources, and the prospects of success. Sometimes they are, at core, economic exercises, and sometimes they are inherently political or ideological, but corporate campaigns are always about power—who has it and what they are free to do with it. They are solidly based in sophisticated research—into the network of interests that sustain a corporation and give it power, into the public image of the corporation, into its strengths and vulnerabilities—but they are conducted not in an ivory tower or a research institute, but in the real world of political and economic struggle.

It is the argument of this book, and one of its principal objectives to demonstrate, that corporate campaigns are a distinctive phenomenon whose manifestations are today ubiquitous in both the marketplace and the media. This is not the conventional wisdom. In fact, among the general public, scholars, and journalists, corporate campaigns are little known and less understood. Even among those in the business community, who may find themselves on the receiving end of a campaign, there is little comprehension of the breadth and dynamics of these tightly coordinated efforts. But those companies that have experienced such campaigns—and, as is documented in two appendices, their numbers at this writing were approaching 200—are painfully familiar with the immense pressures that corporate campaigns can generate.

Some of those pressures are generated directly, through strikes or demonstrations or activities in the workplace. Still others are generated through third parties—stakeholders of the corporation who are mobilized to bring pressure against the company's management, typically by acting in their own self-interest. Indeed, it is this systematic exploitation of key stake-holder relationships through communication and other strategies that de-fines the corporate campaign and sets it apart from other forms of economic, political, or social pressure. If a union or some other advocacy group pursuing a grievance against a company can turn the company's cus-tomers, suppliers, shareholders, or some other group on whose goodwill it depends against it, that stakeholder group becomes a *de facto* supporter of the campaign. If enough such supporters can be mobilized in this manner, the pressure on the company may well be irresistible. Management may be willing to do almost anything to make the pain disappear. That is, at least, the theory of the corporate campaign.

Labor began developing the strategies and tactics of the corporate cam-paign—or, more correctly, adapting them to its own purposes—as struc-tural changes eroded the power of the unions in a growing number of industries and markets. Of particular importance was the movement during the 1950s and 1960s of the garment trade out of New York—principally to the American Southwest—in order to escape the grip of the unions. One beneficiary of this movement was the city of El Paso, Texas, which had an ample supply of low-wage, largely immigrant labor. By the late 1960s, sev-eral well-known firms were either based in the city or had major manufac-turing facilities there. The most prominent of these was Farah Manufacturing, an emerging darling of Wall Street that was capturing a large share of the men's trouser market. Farah was a publicly held com-pany, but was nevertheless controlled by the founding family and most es-pecially by its patriarch, William (Willie) Farah. Arguably the leader of the city's business community, and certainly the dean of the local garment trade, Willie Farah was rabidly anti-union, for which he was despised by the labor movement.

In the early 1970s, the Amalgamated Clothing Workers Union (ACWU) launched an organizing campaign at Farah's massive new factory in El Paso, accenting it with a series of new strategies that were destined to evolve into what is known today as the corporate campaign. It was at Farah that many of the most common techniques—personalization, coalition building, reliance on social justice themes, media management, and the like—were first woven together into a unified strategic whole. As is seen in the discussion of this campaign in chapter 2, this was an intense effort that effectively brought the company to its knees.

One of the mechanisms by which pressure was generated was through shareholders. As the price of Farah's stock declined and the company lost its Wall Street luster, shareholders joined the ranks of those pressuring the company to solve its problems and get on with its business. Together with a vigorous and widely publicized boycott, this was a highly effective strat-egy. In retrospect, it was also an object lesson in how a corporate campaign is designed to work—by giving people who are otherwise uninvolved a reason or impetus to do what they are naturally inclined to do, regardless of whether they might share in the goals of the campaign or even be aware of them. This is a classic communication strategy developed to perfection in the corporate campaign.

I confess to having had a special interest in the company's problems at the time because I held a small number of Farah shares myself, and I was among those in the chorus of complainers mobilized by the union's efforts.

Still, it was not until almost 20 years later, in the early 1990s, that I began to understand what had happened to Farah Manufacturing—and to me, one of its shareholders. The insight came, I must confess, not through a personal *eureka* experience, but from one of my students who, in the course of completing a research project on the communication strategies of the United Mine Workers, observed that there was something unusual occurring in the labor movement. There were, he suggested, some sophisticated communication strategies being deployed in support of striking coal miners in West Virginia—techniques that went far beyond traditional public relations. As I subsequently discovered, he was describing what is now recognized as the archetypal corporate campaign against Pittston Coal.

It was at about that point in time that I became convinced that something new, unique, and worthy of examination was developing, and I began to look more seriously at the corporate campaign phenomenon.

By then, the conventional wisdom—strongly supported, I would add, by the facts—was that labor was in decline and corporations were in the ascendancy—not only as economic players, but as wielders of political power. Those were the Reagan–Bush years—the years of the PATCO strike and consequent dismissal of all of the nation's air traffic controllers, the years of the Democratic Party's dive toward the center, the years of globalization and downsizing and of permanent replacement workers. They were the years—and I chronicle them statistically as well as anecdotally in chapter 2—of organized labor's virtual collapse as a locus of influence or even of public respect. For the labor movement, they were the years in the wilderness. Labor was in retreat on all fronts ... well, on all fronts but one.

For even as the movement confronted one of its darkest hours of the century, there were those in the unions who thought they saw a panacea—a new approach to organizing workers and flexing their collective muscles that would solve all their problems. Where traditional labor leaders were focused on the politics of labor organizing, with its heavy dependence on representation elections conducted by the National Labor Relations Board and on gains made primarily at the bargaining table, this new approach was genuinely outside the box and, by the old rules of the game, even off the board. It drew life not from the debate over rates of pay and bundles of benefits, but from an alternative emphasis on understanding the corporation as a social institution, and a potentially vulnerable one at that. The new game, which came to be known as the corporate campaign, was grounded more in the growing body of expertise regarding human motivation and behavior that had been developed by social scientists during the 20th century than it was in the narrow legalities of labor agreements, and it was conducted in the media much more than on the shop floor. It was the ultimate outside game, in which the fundamental social acceptability of the corporation—individually, but also collectively—was put into play.

As is seen here, this was not an idea that sprang forth whole within the labor movement. The strategy and tactics of the game were borrowed, in fact, from the New Left of Todd Gitlin and Tom Hayden, whose colleagues in the early Students for a Democratic Society actually developed them as much to subvert the unions (whose leaders they saw as corrupt and out of touch) as to empower them. They were adapted to meet the needs of organized labor by visionary activists like Ray Rogers and Michael Locker. Nor are these strategies and tactics employed only by unions engaged in corporate campaigns. To the contrary, we find similar approaches being used by progressive advocacy groups who have their own reasons for engaging in anticorporate politics, by political operatives on the right to carry their attacks against progressive groups and policies, and even by corporations as they seek competitive advantage. But it is organized labor that has most extensively, most effectively and, importantly for purposes of study and analysis, most openly exploited these strategies and tactics, and that is their foremost practitioner.

Moreover, these same strategies and tactics lie at the heart of the new internationalism that has manifest itself in the labor movement. Over the past decade, the international labor movement has coalesced, first around individual campaigns against multinational employers, then around the corporate campaign concept per se, and finally around a unifying policy agenda expressed, for example, through the coordinated international protests against the World Trade Organization. It is fair to say that the politics of labor in the early 21st century has been shaped by these developments.

That is true not only because corporate campaigns now constrain the relationship between labor and management, but because they have also provided the bridge by which organized labor and other progressive groups are newly finding their long-lost common ground. Largely as a product of its acceptance of the assumptions and techniques of the corporate campaign, which are based in the demonization of a target corporation, labor has moved back within the ideological comfort zone of the Left. In the process, it has effectively validated a core anticorporate sentiment that unites many progressive advocates. This in turn, is helping legitimize and move into the mainstream a distrust of corporations per se that is likely to have significant economic and political consequences in the years ahead. In short, organized labor is moving from an era of labor–*management* relations to one of labor–*capital* relations—a change that is far more than semantic in character.

All of that makes the phenomenon of the corporate campaign worth studying, both in its own right and as a gateway to understanding the use of similar communication-driven pressure strategies by others.

This volume examines in considerable detail the history, strategy, tactics, effects, consequences, and likely future directions of the corporate campaign and its nonlabor-based cousin, the anticorporate campaign. The book is based on a wide variety of sources and methods, among them an extensive review and analysis of media coverage, news releases, previous scholarship, union publications, campaign materials such as handbills and white-paper reports, interviews and conversations with a diversity of individuals who have experienced corporate campaigns, public presentations by labor leaders and others, correspondence, Internet postings, case law summaries, documents, videotapes, and other materials. Many of these materials are in the public record, and many campaign-related events are in the news almost daily. What this book adds, through original data and interpretation, is the context and integration that will give these seemingly isolated observations meaning.

ACKNOWLEDGMENTS

Any work of this magnitude reflects the intellectual debt of the author to many sources, and that is surely the case in this instance. In particular, I learned important lessons from the writings of Saul Alinsky, Charles Perry, and David Vogel, a rather disparate lot whose works I have tried to draw together here in what I hope is a comprehensible manner. Indeed, this troika of the community organizer, the business scholar, and the political scientist is symbolic of the topic—because these are the three legs on which the campaign stands—and of the treatment of it you find in these pages.

Although I have spoken in the course of this research with many individuals who have had experience in or with corporate campaigns, and their candid comments and reports have greatly shaped my understanding of the phenomenon, for which I express my heartfelt gratitude, none of them is identified by name or position in the text. Even as it fulfills my promise to some to preserve their anonymity, this clearly places the burden for accuracy and interpretation on my own shoulders, where it belongs. Over the years, too, I have had the opportunity to share my analysis of the corporate campaign with various industry associations, companies, and others who have their own views and interests with respect to this phenomenon. In these exchanges, I am always mindful of an aphorism first brought to my attention by my daughter: A professor is a person who talks in someone else's sleep. They are not responsible for my views, nor I for theirs.

Beyond that, I would like to express my appreciation in particular to Christian Downs, my former student, for sharing his insights into the communication strategies of the UMWA and, in the process, stimulating my interest in the subject; to Richard and John for their unending cynicism and for teaching me that in a corporate campaign there is no such thing as a coincidence; to David Vogel for the courtesy that he so graciously extended; to Norma Manheim for her superior indexing; to the students in my corporate campaign course at The George Washington University, on whom many of the ideas expressed here were first tested; to Lane Akers, Robin Weisberg, Heather Jefferson, Clare Romeo, and everyone else at Lawrence Erlbaum Associates who helped to make this book a reality; to Mark Siegel and Paul Dickson for their sage advice; and especially to Steve Bear for sparking the thoughts that in the end allowed me to develop what I believe is a complete and symmetrical argument. Thanks, too, to all those who have provided support and encouragement, or just plain patience, over the 2 years this book has been in the works. I hope that everyone who contributed to the enterprise in some way finds something in these pages they did not already know.

—Jarol B. Manheim

Introduction

This book tells the story of one of the more pervasive but least known elements of the contemporary business environment—the corporate campaign. *Corporate campaign* is a term of art referring to a coordinated, often long-term, and wide-ranging program of economic, political, legal, and psychological warfare usually, but not exclusively, initiated by a union or by organized labor in general. It is directed against a corporation that has opposed unionization, declined to accept contract terms a union deems critical, or in some other way refused to yield on some issue of great importance to the organization launching the campaign. It is warfare waged in such disparate venues as Wall Street, Capitol Hill, the regulatory agencies, the courts, and the marketplace. Most of all, it is warfare waged in the media, where the unions or other groups seek to redefine the image and undermine the reputation of the targeted company through systematic and unrelenting pressure … to cause so much pain and disruption that management is forced to yield to their will.

Corporations build their reputations by engendering trust and confidence among their key stakeholders. One analysis suggests, for example, that the components of these images include such elements as the company's emotional appeal, its aura of social responsibility, impressions of its workplace environment, the quality of its products and services, the vision and leadership of its management, and its financial performance.[1] Corporate campaigns attack these bedrock perceptions and, in the process, attempt to put companies into play—laying them open to attack from a variety of sources, many of them unexpected.

We see evidence of these attacks in the news, on the so-called news magazine programs, on tabloid television, and, increasingly, on the Internet. They come in many guises—anecdotes about corporate failings that endanger the public interest or safety, allegations of corporate greed, white papers, and other research reports claiming some form of corporate malfeasance. They come from many directions—not merely from unions, but from religious, consumer rights, environmental, human rights, civil rights, and other groups and coalitions that are more or less closely allied with labor. Not all such anecdotes, allegations, and reports arise from a corporate campaign, nor are all such items that are in fact associated with a campaign necessarily false. Rather, a corporate campaign is designed precisely to locate, exploit, exaggerate, and spin some act, event, or circumstance that is, in some measure, true—or can be made to appear to be true—in such a way as to take advantage of the natural inclinations and behaviors of journalists and news organizations (i.e., to fit campaign attacks into the natural order of the news so that they are perceived to be credible). In other words, corporate campaigns employ all of the techniques of strategic political communication.

However, they do much more. At a more fundamental level, corporate campaigns attack the viability of the essential relationships on which any corporation depends—relationships with its customers, shareholders, bankers, regulators—in summary, with all of its key stakeholders. At their heart—and, as we will see, at their philosophical origin—corporate campaigns are attacks on the very *corporateness* of their targets. They are attacks on the corporation as a social form and as a locus for organizing economic activity. They are invariably constructed around a myth that the corporation is a social outlaw, and they are designed to appeal to an underlying popular distrust of big business.

The stakes in a corporate campaign are real economic goods. The public face of the campaign, which tends to be heavily symbolic in character, is but a mask. Behind it are vested interests competing either for direct economic advantage or for some measure of economic restructuring. We will come to see these as the competing forces of pragmatism and ideology.

But pragmatists and ideologues alike have recognized that the broader public has little interest in, and probably even less sympathy for, their particularized objectives. If the public—as consumers, voters, citizens—is to be mobilized against a company and its weight manipulated to advantage, that can only be accomplished by appealing to values, perceptions, and preferences that are already widely held. The strategic communication component of the campaign is designed to portray a given dispute in terms that resonate with these preconceptions to such a degree that the public is prepared to understand, tolerate, or even praise actions that it might otherwise find uninteresting, unappealing, or altogether unacceptable.

In effect, then, although the core of the corporate campaign is a struggle for economic and/or political power, the public face of the campaign generally takes on the characteristics of a dramatic morality play in which the objective is to define and claim the moral high ground. Whoever holds that ground has the power to decide what is "true" about the behaviors and motives of the target company or industry. Whichever truth prevails sets the limits of the attack. If it is "true" that the company in question is a corporate outlaw, then, from a campaigner's perspective, all things are possible. If it is "true" that the company is a model corporate citizen, the freedom of action available to any antagonist is far more limited; in fact, the likelihood that a campaign will succeed is greatly reduced.

Some notion of truth, then, is the touchstone of the corporate campaign, and a key strategic consideration in defining that truth is the outline of the objective facts available to the campaigners. Some companies behave in ways that make them easy targets. Others may behave more responsibly, but may nonetheless be vulnerable because of their particular line of business or some other circumstance. In general, the likelihood of success in these campaigns is inversely related to how far the truth *needs* to be stretched and directly related to how far it *can* be stretched.

Those who want the unions to succeed in rejuvenating themselves, or who are otherwise concerned about the power of corporations, will judge this to be a worthy enterprise. Those who view such a rejuvenation less favorably, or who are more at ease with the shape of the contemporary political economy, will decry it. For my part, I believe it is important simply to understand the phenomenon of the corporate campaign so that, whatever subsequent judgments one may care to render, they are informed by thoughtful consideration. My purpose in writing this book is thus to shine a light into what has to date been a relatively dark corner of the contemporary political economy.

Although they draw on ancient antagonisms between labor and management, corporate campaigns are a distinctly latter-day phenomenon. Most histories trace their origin to an organizing campaign conducted by the Amalgamated Clothing and Textile Workers Union against textile giant J.P. Stevens, Inc., in the mid-1970s. For our part, we suggest that they took form at least a decade earlier and in a somewhat different setting. However, even such an extension of the roots of the family tree yields a life span (at this writing) of perhaps 35 years. Indeed, corporate campaigns as we know them today could not have occurred any earlier because their development required the confluence of four relatively recent social forces.

The first of these was, in Thomas Kuhn's terms, a *scientific revolution* in the study of human behavior. Over the course of the 20th century, this revolution produced, first, the notion of a *social* science and then an everexpanding body of knowledge and understanding of the factors that lead people and social institutions to think and act as they do. Today we possess theories, data, and methodologies of a sophistication and thoroughness that were not even conceived a 100 years ago. This knowledge base gives us the ability to measure, explain, and predict human behavior and, more particularly, the ways that people and institutions will respond to particular sets of stimuli, including the kinds of actions and messages that can be generated during a corporate campaign. It is a significant social technology.

The second force was the emergence of a class of professionals who are schooled in this new knowledge and who employ it in behalf of their own interests and/or those of clients whom they may choose to serve. These campaign professionals include researchers, financial analysts, media specialists, and others who inhabit such realms as election campaigns, public policy, and other so-called grassroots lobbying initiatives, the representation of foreign governments and interests, and the corporate campaign. They are the social engineers who move the new knowledge out of the laboratory and into the streets. Together, they constitute an industry—and a rather large one—that did not exist as recently as 50 years ago.

The third force was the development of a new left—in fact, *the* New Left—in the United States, particularly during the 1960s, but with influence that continues to the present day. The Old Left—the left of the overt Marxists, the Trotskyites, and the rest—was rooted in the politics of labor and class struggle and looked backward to European philosophy and experience for its essence. As a result of such factors as the assault of the McCarthyites and the revelation of Stalin's excesses, by the 1950s it was in disarray. The New Left was rooted in American sociology—most especially in the work of C. Wright Mills—was distrustful of labor, and was, in its formative years, inventive, experimental, and forward-looking. For the Old Left, the enemy was capital in all its guises. For the New Left, the enemy was far more particularized—the corporation as a social actor. It was this movement that provided the ideological perspective that underlies much of the corporate campaign.

The fourth and final force was the decline of organized labor over the second half of the 20th century. At the time of World War II, nearly half of the American labor force belonged to unions, and labor enjoyed tremendous prestige and power. By the end of the century, fewer than 1 in 10 Americans employed in the private sector was a union member, and distrust and disinterest had replaced prestige in defining the movement's image among the public. Along with the steady decline that produced that result came a loss of resources and influence that, by the early 1980s, led some serious observers to proclaim the demise of organized labor in the United States. By the 1970s, the movement's leaders, or at least a rising generation of new leaders, felt a growing sense of alarm at this turn of events and began casting about for some means of reversing the trend. The solution they hit on was the corporate campaign—an alternative to traditional labor organizing to which they now devote substantial resources. Probably the best marker of the influence of this new style of labor activity was the 1995 election of John Sweeney as president of the American Federation of Labor–Congress of Industrial Organizations (AFL-CIO). Sweeney was an early advocate and practitioner of the corporate campaign, and his election amounted to a changing of the guard between the proponents of strikes and union elections and those of pressuring management through the public and other stakeholders. The decline of labor's influence and the rise of a new generation of leaders with a new vision for reinvigorating their movement, then, became the engine that powered the emergence of the campaign as a factor in—and eventually as a routinized component of—labor–management relations.

The first chapters of this book tell the story of how these forces developed and how they came together to produce the corporate campaign phenomenon. These are followed by an examination of the theory of the corporate campaign and a conceptual and chronological review of how that theory has been developed by the campaign activists. Then, in the balance of the book, we explore the nature of the campaign—strategies, tactics, objectives, and effects. Along the way, we meet a diverse cast of characters, including student activists, social activists, journalists, financial analysts, labor leaders, and senior executives of some of America's leading companies. We explore theories, methods, and perspectives on the campaign phenomenon, but also cases and other examples that illustrate their application. Our objective is to provide a comprehensive understanding of this increasingly significant and visible form of political and economic conflict.

ENDNOTE

1. For an example of the rankings of major U.S. corporations on these criteria, which have been identified by the Reputation Institute, see Ronald Alsop, "Corporate Reputations Are Earned With Trust, Reliability, Study Shows," *The Wall Street Journal*, September 23, 1999.

1

FROM ANN ARBOR, WITH LOVE

Although the provenance of a social movement or broad stratagem is often difficult to detail with confidence, we can say with reasonable assurance that the corporate campaign was born in Ann Arbor, Michigan, circa 1965. It was sired by leading social scientists of the era in such fields as sociology, political science, and the sciences of persuasion; conceived by leaders of the Students for a Democratic Society (SDS); and, on delivery, nurtured in a religious home provided by the National Council of Churches. From there, the corporate campaign found its way into the labor movement, where it was developed over time into a finely tuned instrument of conflict.

As an intellectual exercise, the corporate campaign embodied the interaction between two parallel and contemporaneous developments—one ideological and one technological—that came together to provide the motivation, direction, and means for an effective attack on the corporation and its role in American society. Although each was carried forward through outposts elsewhere, both developments, as it happened, were centered at the University of Michigan in Ann Arbor. Let us consider each in turn.

THE NEW LEFT AND THE *ANTI*CORPORATE CAMPAIGN

Most histories of the corporate campaign, including Charles Perry's semi-nal work on the subject, *Union Corporate Campaigns,*[1] look to labor as the source of the corporate campaign. To be sure, because of its evident need, its particular objectives, and its political ties, all of which are explored in chapter 2, organized labor quickly assumed the role of prime mover in this new form of attack. However, labor was not the true point of origin of the campaign phenomenon. Rather, the ideological underpinnings, the critical understanding of the target, and the fundamental strategy of the corporate campaign trace to the emergence of the so-called New Left during the early 1960s and especially to the intellectual framework that shaped the worldview of one key organization—the SDS.

Barbara Ehrenreich, who serves as an honorary chair of the Democratic Socialists of America, writing with her husband, John, defined the New Left as:

> the consciously anti-racist and anti-imperialist (and later, anti-capitalist) white movement, centered initially in the universities but ultimately expanding well beyond them (e.g., it came to include underground newspapers; organizations of teachers, social workers and medical workers; theater groups; community or-ganizing groups; etc.). Students for a Democratic Society (SDS) was its most important organizational expression from 1964 to 1969. The New Left inter-acted with or was part of most of the other movements of the sixties, but it was not identical to them. To take two examples, the anti-war movement was far broader than the New Left; and the women's liberation movement emerged in part in opposition to the practices of the New Left.[2]

What made the New Left *new* was that it traced its birthright to neither la-bor nor international socialism in its various guises, as was the tradition on the American Left, but rather to a distinctly American sociological critique of dominance by an elite industrial class. It was this sociological perspec-tive that generated the key insights leading to the concept of a corporate campaign, the essence of which is to leverage a target corporation's social network against it.

The 1950s and 1960s were a period of considerable ferment and instabil-ity within the American Left. As we just noted, the Left was held in place by two roots—support for radical elements within organized labor and support for the international socialist movement, including, for some, communism. In the postwar years, however, the political ground began to shift and these roots were torn loose. First came the overwhelming pressure of the political inquisition conducted in the late 1940s and early 1950s by the House Un-American Activities Committee and by Senator Joseph McCarthy. This was followed in 1956 by Nikita Khruschev's denunciation of Stalinist excesses and by the Soviet invasion of Hungary, the collective result of which was sharply to divide the Left over the acceptability of those espousing sympathy with the communists.[3] Then during that same period, and in response to the same pressures, the Congress of Industrial Organizations (CIO) purged itself of its most radical constituent unions in preparation for a merger with the more politically and socially conservative American Federation of Labor (AFL), which occurred in 1955. This combination of events left the Left adrift and rudderless.

It was against this background that a new generation of Left activists arose in what seemed to many at the time an unlikely setting—the nation's colleges and universities. It was one of these activist student groups, the SDS—with the funding and initial encouragement of an old-line labor-left group, the League for Industrial Democracy—that emerged as the preeminent voice of the new, student-based Left. Based in Ann Arbor, populated at first largely by students at the University of Michigan, and grounded less in the ideas of Marxism–Leninism than in the analysis of class and society of C. Wright Mills, this student-based movement began by reconstructing the intellectual roots of the Left and then addressing specific policy concerns.[4]

Unlike their predecessors, the leaders of the New Left distrusted labor or, more correctly, the contemporaneous group of labor leaders whom they saw, in the phrase of the day, as more a part of the problem than of the solution. Unlike their predecessors, these new activists, most especially SDS leaders Alan Haber and Tom Hayden, were more committed to dialogue and consensus-building than to dogma and directives in the formation of their agenda—a process they characterized as *participatory democracy* and that was important to them as both a method and an outcome. Hayden drafted, SDS adopted, and a generation of activists has since worked directly or indirectly to implement a program for social and political change codified in a document known as *The Port Huron Statement*.

The Port Huron Statement, named for the United Auto Workers campsite where the document was discussed and affirmed, stands as a cogent manifesto of the worldview and objectives of the New Left circa its adoption in 1962. Beginning with an analysis of student apathy, the document calls on students to:

> look beyond the campus, to America itself.... The apathy here is, first, *subjective*—the felt powerlessness of ordinary people, the resignation before the enormity of events. But subjective apathy is encouraged by the *objective* American situation—the actual structural separation of people from power, from relevant knowledge, from pinnacles of decision-making.... The American political system ... frustrates democracy by confusing the individual citizen, paralyzing policy discussion, and consolidating the irresponsible power of military and business interests.[5]

We can see from this passage that the New Left, embodied in the SDS, arrived at the same destination as the Old, but by a very different route.

It is not surprising to find in this manifesto language critical of business. "It is not possible to believe," says the *Statement*,

> that true democracy can exist where a minority utterly controls enormous wealth and power.... We can no longer rely on competition of the many to assure that business enterprise is responsive to social needs.... Nor can we trust the corporate bureaucracy to be socially responsible or to develop a 'corporate conscience' that is democratic.... We must consider changes in the rules of society by challenging the unchallenged politics of American corporations.[6]

Perhaps more surprising, but revealing of the changing nature of the Left—and significant in the light of subsequent events—the document is equally critical of labor. Consider the following passage:

> Today labor remains the most liberal "mainstream" institution—but often its liberalism represents vestigial commitments, self-interestedness, unradicalism. In some measure, labor has succumbed to institutionalization, its social idealism waning under the tendencies of bureaucracy, materialism, business ethics. The successes of the last generation perhaps have braked, rather than accelerated, labor's zeal for change.... "Union democracy" is inhibited not simply by labor-leader elitism, but by the related problem of rank-and-file apathy to the tradition of unionism.[7]

Today many remember the SDS as a rock-throwing rabble from the Vietnam era that eventually morphed into a more radical subgroup, the Weathermen, and even into a terrorist organization known as the Weather Underground. All of that happened. However, before it did, a different and more socially constructive SDS existed—a sort of philosophical debating society with a radical viewpoint and an activist bent. As ably chronicled by James Miller in his book, *Democracy Is in the Streets*, this earlier SDS was a vibrant, if disorganized, intellectual community of social critics; it was a community that produced a core bibliography on which its philosophy was grounded and that sought to advance a new normative and pointedly radical theory of society.

More than that, the SDS was to social change something like what the contemporary university research park is to economic development. Today, universities nationwide operate special campuses where their research faculties are brought together with business entrepreneurs to form new ventures for the commercial exploitation of the latest discoveries. These business *incubators* have played a major role in the development of such technology-driven new industries as computer software and biotechnology. In much that same way, the SDS was an incubator for generating and experimenting with new ways of managing society.

This was accomplished not through new business ventures, which would, of course, have been precisely contrary to the SDS philosophy, but through the creation of what were termed *projects*.[8] Examples included the Peace Research and Education Project (PREP), a nascent foreign policy think tank formed by Richard Flacks and Tom Hayden in February 1963;[9] Students and Labor, undertaken in summer of that year;[10] the Economic Research and Action Project (ERAP), a community-organizing project begun in September 1963 with funding from the United Auto Workers;[11] and the short-lived Political Education Project (PEP),[12] which organized support for the election of President Lyndon B. Johnson in 1964 under the slogan, "Part of the Way with LBJ." ERAP, in particular, had far-reaching influence. Its program, which ranged from organizing renters to organizing voters, later influenced the formation of the National Welfare Rights Organization in 1966,[13] which, in 1970, spun off the Association of Community Organizations for Reform Now (ACORN), an organization that is active in confronting corporations to this day.[14] Its *modus operandi*, which centered on living in and serving communities of the poor and disadvantaged, influenced the development of VISTA, the domestic version of the Peace Corps, and its leaders exercised considerable influence within VISTA through such agencies as the Midwest Academy. The Midwest Academy, with a curriculum based on the work of activist guru Saul Alinsky, was established by Heather Booth, an SDS alumna, as a training school for community activists.[15] Other ideas incubated in SDS during this period eventually found their way into the feminist movement, the civil rights movement, and, of course, the antiwar movement.

Two generic ideas developed in SDS during this period (one philosophical and the other at least in part strategic) are of particular significance in the present context. First, and most fundamentally, SDS accepted as an essential component of its core philosophy a view of the corporation, per se, as the critical actor in contemporary American society and as a target of opportunity to force social change. This view was ably and repeatedly espoused by Tom Hayden, who emerged by 1962 as the group's principal theorist and spokesperson. Second, as a derivative of this emphasis on the corporation and as a natural outgrowth of its Mills-based view of political sociology—but also as a direct result the experience of the several ERAP communities that were established in such cities as Cleveland, Chicago, and Newark—SDS during this period came to appreciate the importance of extensive community research leading to the building of effective alliances with labor unions, religious organizations, and other activist groups. This theme was explored in detail during a week-long ERAP Summer Institute that preceded the 1964 SDS convention in Pine Hill, New York.[16]

In 1966, SDS and the National Council of Churches—along with other activists, some academics and returning Peace Corps volunteers—joined forces to establish the North American Congress on Latin America (NACLA)—a project headed by Michael Locker, Fred Goff, and John Gerassi that embodied precisely the sort of alliance anticipated in the Pine Hill discussions and that, despite its name, in all likelihood served as the incubator for what we know today as the corporate campaign. The Council of Churches provided office space and start-up funds for the project, which immediately began generating the data required to support attacks on American corporations by groups in the social change movement.[17]

A few years later, in 1975, Locker and two of his NACLA colleagues left that organization to establish the Corporate Data Exchange (CDE), whose sole objective was to "discover, document, and publicize the ownership and control of American corporations." Ironically, CDE relied on marketing this material to the business community to generate funds for its anticorporate research effort.[18] In the words of CDE founder Locker,

> The level of understanding of the corporate structure is just too low. Individual businessmen can only be made accountable if they become real human entities and not just a "street name." We see our role complementary to that of shareholder activists. Those filing shareholder resolutions can only devise a strategy to influence votes after they know who the shareholders really are.[19]

Both the CDE and Locker soon came to play important roles in the adoption of the corporate campaign by organized labor, a topic to which we return in chapter 3.

Yet another NACLA spin-off, also created to manage the increasing data and documentation needs of the movement, was The Data Center in Oakland, California, described by its founder, Fred Goff, as "a library for people involved in social change." The Data Center maintains files—many dating back to its establishment in 1977—on more than 7,000 U.S. corporations.[20]

All of this is of particular interest in the present context because it appears to have been NACLA that first developed the concept of the corporate campaign or, as the group termed it at the time, the *anticorporate campaign*. It also produced the earliest manual on how to conduct the extensive research that is essential to achieving the goals of such campaigns.

The focus of this particular volume was on what was termed *power-structure research*, which was aimed at

> identifying the people and institutions which make our lives and the lives of so many others intolerable,... locating weak points in the system,... suggesting a

strategy for resistance,... [and] propelling ourselves and others into a higher consciousness of where the nodes of power lie and how they function.

The logic of this research effort, stated succinctly in the following passage, points directly back to the ERAP sessions at Pine Hill and directly ahead, like a flashing arrow, to the contemporary corporate campaign:

> Knowledge of such points gives us the leverage to challenge the system effectively with the means at our disposal. Sometimes even an apparently insignificant weakness can be effectively exploited. The public image of a corporation, for instance, can be important to its continued prosperity—investment, government contracts, employee recruiting, etc., can all be affected by a change in this image.[21]

The NACLA manual was based on 10 basic tenets about how best to conduct power-structure research in American society. We can summarize these as follows:

- Because modern society is so complex, it is dependent on a continuous flow of data about itself. It follows that such data will exist. Every sector of American society incorporates an information infrastructure composed of government agencies, professional and trade associations, journals and newspapers, research centers, and the like that produce and distribute this information and serve as repositories.
- The first task of the researcher is to identify this infrastructure. The second task is to penetrate the infrastructure, which can be accomplished in part by projecting an aura of legitimacy. The third task is to master the jargon and style of the infrastructure and the key personnel and use this information to best advantage.
- In undertaking this effort, the researcher should take advantage of any access or legitimizing credentials possible. The document states at one point that "access to newspaper or magazine credentials will be particularly helpful in this regard," and later suggests employing the proxy of someone with stock in a corporation to gain access to shareholders' meetings.[22]

The volume then proceeds to identify a number of institutions as targets for such penetration and research. Among others, these include corporations, labor organizations, and organized religion.

In the words of the NACLA manual, "Wherever one starts studying U.S. power they end up investigating corporations." One investigates a corporation beginning with the identification of its owners—especially where those owners include universities, churches, foundations, banks, insurance companies, and pension funds. One also identifies government agencies that regulate the company, members of its Board of Directors, and any interlocks that may exist among the companies officers and directors, on the one hand, and other companies or institutions, on the other.[23] All of this information, of course, is useful primarily for identifying potential pressure points that can be turned against the company. As we see in a later chapter, it is precisely this information that constitutes the core of a *vulnerabilities assessment*, the first stage of the corporate campaign.

With that in mind, it is particularly interesting to note that this section of the NACLA manual was written by Michael Locker, who subsequently became an advisor to the Amalgamated Clothing and Textile Workers Union. In that capacity, he helped to conduct the financial and stakeholder analysis that lay at the heart of the J.P. Stevens campaign—the first full-fledged union corporate campaign.[24] It was also Locker and his colleague, Steven Abrecht, who were brought in by the International Association of Machinists to analyze the books of Eastern Air Lines in 1983, when then-CEO Frank Borman offered to open the company's finances to the union in the hope of obtaining labor peace.[25] Before long, a corporate campaign would drive Eastern out of existence. Locker now heads a firm that provides financial analysis, primarily of the steel industry, and serves as an advisor to the Steelworkers and other unions.

The NACLA manual's chapter on researching unions to determine how they can be mobilized to serve the interests of the activist was drafted by Paul Booth, at the time a member of the NACLA staff. Booth became active in SDS in 1961 when he was a student at Swarthmore College. When Tom Hayden was elected president of the group at the same 1962 meeting that adopted *The Port Huron Statement*, Booth was elected vice president. He later served as national secretary—a post he left under pressure in 1966 in the wake of a divisive debate over the SDS position on the draft. Booth settled in Chicago, where he was active in the antiwar movement and a variety of grassroots community movements. He took part in abortive efforts to form, first, an adult equivalent of SDS, then later a radical political party. Eventually he became a labor organizer. By the 1990s, he was serving as director of organizing for the American Federation of State, County, and Municipal Employees (AFSCME).[26]

In 1970, the same year the NACLA manual was published, Booth took the unusual step—for a former SDSer—of coordinating student support for the UAW's strike against General Motors, in which role he organized nearly 2,000 students in the Chicago area. Steve Max wrote to Booth, pointing out that "the labor folks are all unhappy that there is no one from the youth to carry on in the labor movement," and Booth reportedly believed that top labor officials would secretly support an effort to build a rank-and-file reform movement.[27]

The emphasis in the chapter he wrote for the NACLA manual is on what Booth termed *tactical intelligence*—data on the shape and structure of trade unionism. Among the topics of interest were the size and power of individual unions, the identification of those that either had militant traditions or internal characteristics that make militancy possible, and the analysis of how the various unions "[we]re tied into the system through politics and industrial statesmanship."[28] In effect and in context, in this volume, the future organizing director of one of the nation's most influential unions set out an initial strategy for penetrating the labor movement.

In yet another chapter of the manual, NACLA observed that the church, as an institution, "propagates an ideology which tends to shore up the established interests." In fact, the manual argued, through their substantial investments in corporate shares, through their interlocking directorates, and through their dependence on corporate largesse, the churches are actually partners in the corporate culture. However, the argument continued, churches are especially vulnerable to criticism because they "pose as the conscience and faith of society." By exposing the contradictions between word and deed, the strategists argued, activists could turn the churches against their corporate benefactors.[29] This argument not only anticipated the general strategy of attacking corporations through legitimizing third parties, but even identified a primary cluster of such organizations that plays an important role in today's corporate campaigns. It is also especially interesting, and somewhat ironic, of course, because it was the church itself, specifically the National Council of Churches, that provided NACLA with its first office space and much of its financial support.[30] In the same year that NACLA published the *Research Methodology Guide*, the Council of Churches established the Interfaith Center for Corporate Responsibility, which has since mobilized and represented segments of the religious community in pursuing precisely the strategies and objectives set forth in the manual.[31]

Although SDS fell victim to its own radicalism during the Vietnam period, having been infiltrated and effectively taken over by the Progressive Labor Party, a Marxist group, many of its leaders from this earlier period are influential in national life today, where they continue to help define the terms of debate. At least one—Hayden—entered electoral politics, while others—Bob Ross, Heather Booth—have served on the staff of the Democratic National Committee or Democratic candidates and office holders. Others became university professors—Richard Flacks, Todd Gitlin, Bob Ross—or publishers—Michael Lerner. Some became labor activists—Paul Booth—consultants with union clients—Michael Ansara, Michael Locker—or grassroots organizers with labor-friendly organizations like Citizen Action—Ira Arlook, Heather Booth, Steve Max.[32]

In summary, what we find is not only that the New Left, and most especially the SDS and NACLA, provided much of the original thinking behind the corporate campaign concept, but that some of the people who did this thinking later moved into the labor movement and associated groups, where they helped implement their ideas. Their influence is most evident in the emphasis on research—the structural analysis—that underlies the typical campaign: the assessment of stakeholder relationships, corporate structure, and finances that points toward potential pressure points. No campaign can succeed absent such an analysis, and many campaigns take their direction based on its findings. In that sense, the contribution of the New Left to the corporate campaign was a necessary one, but it was not sufficient.

SAUL ALINSKY: BUILDING A BRIDGE TO THE 21ST CENTURY

By 1970, then, the intellectual foundations of the corporate campaign were in place, the first research manual for such campaigns had been published, and an organizational infrastructure to conduct these attacks on corporations had been established under the protective and legitimizing umbrella of the National Council of Churches. It was also the case that, by 1970, the nascent anticorporate movement had begun to test strategies and tactics. Between 1966 and 1968, for example, Dow Chemical, which manufactured napalm for use in Vietnam, was the target of 183 major demonstrations on college campuses.[33] In 1969, Staughton Lynd wrote an article entitled "Attack War Contractors' Meetings" in the radical news weekly, *The Guardian*, in which he listed the annual meeting dates of 21 of the largest defense-related corporations and urged antiwar protestors to attend the sessions. In Lynd's words,

> We need to find ways to lay siege to corporations.... We need to invent anti-corporate actions which involve masses of people, not just a dedicated few.... By journeying next time, not to the White House ... but to the General Electric stockholders' meeting in Beverly Hills.[34]

Shortly afterward, a project of the American Friends Service Committee, National Action/Research on the Military-Industrial Complex (NARMIC), published an 18-page *Movement Guide to Stockholders Meetings*, which explained the securities laws as they pertained to annual meetings and suggested tactics that attendees might employ to disrupt the meetings or otherwise express themselves. These tactics were then implemented in demonstrations at the 1970 meetings of United Aircraft, AT&T, Bank of America, and Honeywell. The Honeywell campaign, in particular, was a harbinger of things to come. It included not only demonstrations on campuses designed to impede recruiting, but also boycotts of Honeywell products and a proxy campaign to place antiwar resolutions on the agenda for the meeting. The campaign continued into the early 1970s and even included an 8-day "Corporate Crimes Hearing" in which the company's antagonists suggested that Honeywell executives might be liable for prosecution as war criminals under the Hague Convention of 1907 and the precedents set by the Nuremberg Military Tribunals.[35]

But for all of these theories, experiments, advances, and lessons learned, the anticorporate movement lacked a cohesive strategy for organizing broad-based support once the Vietnam War ended. That was true on two levels. First, the movement was not yet prepared to create and organize activists to carry forward its agenda. Second, it did not yet have the means to generate the base of support and legitimacy among the broader public that would permit and, in some cases, facilitate the achievement of its objectives. The solutions to both problems were readily at hand. One came from the streets of Chicago and Rochester, the other from the hallowed halls of the University of Michigan and MIT. We examine each in turn.

One of the contemporaries who recognized precisely the first problem we have just stated—the absence of a coherent organizing strategy—was a Chicago-based, life-long radical organizer by the name of Saul Alinsky. Trained in criminology at the University of Chicago, Alinsky emerged in the 1930s as the nation's preeminent community organizer. By 1940, he had established the Industrial Areas Foundation, which carried on his work after his death in 1972 at the age of 63. By 1970, when the anticorporate campaign of the New Left was charting its direction, Alinsky was widely regarded as the elder statesman of community organizers.

In 1971, he published a book, *Rules for Radicals: A Pragmatic Primer for Realistic Radicals*, that was explicitly intended to pass the torch of radicalism to a new generation. As Alinsky wrote in the Prologue to the book,

> The revolutionary force today has two targets, moral as well as material. It's young protagonists are one moment reminiscent of the early Christians, yet they also urge violence and cry, "Burn the system down!" They have no illusions about the system, but plenty of illusions about the way to change our world. It is to this point that I have written this book. These words are written in desperation, partly because it is what they do and will do that will give meaning to what I and the radicals of my generation have done with our lives....

> Remember we are talking about revolution, not revelation; you can miss the target by shooting too high as well as too low.... [T]here are no rules for revolution ... *but* there are rules for radicals who want to change their world.... To know these is basic to a pragmatic attack on the system. These rules make the difference between being a realistic radical and a rhetorical one....[36]

Alinsky very clearly had the coming attack on the corporation in mind as he wrote these words, and he had in mind a specific model as well. In 1964, following a wave of race riots in their city, a group of local African-American and White church organizations in Rochester, New York, had invited Alinsky to come to their city to organize the African-American community to articulate the needs of the poor. After raising $100,000, mostly from local and national church groups, these leaders signed a 2-year contract with Alinsky's Industrial Areas Foundation. Under Alinsky's guidance, in the spring of 1965, a coalition of 134 local African-American organizations came together under the acronym FIGHT (Freedom-Integration-God-Honor-Today) to mobilize and represent the city's poor. In June 1966, the group settled on one local employer—Eastman Kodak—as a special target. Kodak was selected, not because it was a bad corporate citizen, but precisely because it was a *model* corporate citizen. Alinsky believed that the company's pivotal role in the local economy, combined with its inherent corporate liberalism, made it at once important and susceptible to influence. His idea was to push to the company's value structure to its very limits and then use Kodak's example as a way to pressure such other local employers as Xerox, Bausch and Lomb, General Dynamics, and General Motors.

The mechanism Alinsky hit on, which has subsequently been employed by ACORN and other community activist groups, was to demand that Kodak agree to hire 600 minority employees over an 18-month period, with these employees to be selected and referred by FIGHT. This would greatly enhance the group's standing in the community and make it into a force of some weight in the local economic and political structure. After protracted negotiations, two mid-level Kodak executives signed an agreement with FIGHT to implement a modified version of the original proposal. This agreement was immediately repudiated by the company's executive committee, which saw it as tantamount to a labor agreement that was contrary to the company's long history of opposing unionization.

The repudiation of the agreement transformed the conflict, which moved from the local to the national arena. In an innovative move, Alinsky had FIGHT ask its supporters to withhold their proxies from supporting management at the company's 1967 annual meeting. Church organizations and other investors controlling approximately 40,000 shares responded by withholding their votes in protest of management's dealings with the group. On the day of the meeting, 700 demonstrators marched outside carrying signs—"Kodak Is Out of Focus"—while one shareholder confronted the company's chairman inside the meeting before leading a walkout of FIGHT supporters. The dispute was settled some weeks later, with Daniel P. Moynihan serving as mediator.[37]

In the seventh chapter of *Rules for Radicals*, Alinsky set forth a series of tactical rules—13 in all—that amount to social and economic judo, using the overwhelming weight of the target company as a weapon against it. Among Alinsky's rules are the following:

1. Power is not only what you have, but what the enemy thinks you have.
2. Never go outside the experience of your people.
3. Whenever possible go outside the experience of your enemy.
4. Make the enemy live up to their own book of rules.
5. Ridicule is man's most potent weapon.
6. A good tactic is one that your people enjoy.
7. A tactic that drags on too long becomes a drag.
8. Keep the pressure on.
9. The threat is usually more terrifying than the thing itself.
10. Maintain a constant pressure upon the opposition.
11. If you push a negative hard and deep enough it will break through into its counterside.
12. The price of a successful attack is a constructive alternative.
13. Pick the target, freeze it, personalize it, and polarize it.[38]

We can see in these tactics many of the elements that have since come together under the banner of the corporate campaign. With that in mind, we return to many of them later in this book. Quite aside from that, however, there is direct evidence of Alinsky's influence on precisely the audience he had in mind. Heather Booth's Midwest Academy, for example, after some hesitation, came to base its curriculum explicitly on Alinsky's teachings. Then there is the establishment of the Corporate Data Exchange. Recall that this NACLA spin-off was established to create and maintain a computer database on the ownership of American corporations. That would seem a rather direct response to one of the less-often quoted passages from Alinsky's book. Toward the end of his volume, in the course of speculating on ways he might confront corporations, Alinsky tells of receiving two letters that revealed to him the path to organizing the middle class to rise up against corporate power—through large-scale, organized proxy wars in which the holdings of like-minded individuals can be pooled for maximum effect as one corporation is leveraged against another. "What will be required," he stated,

> is a computerized operation that will quickly give (1) a breakdown of the holdings of any corporation, (2) a breakdown of holdings of other corporations that own shares in the target corporation, and (3) a breakdown of individual stock proxies in the target corporation and in the corporations that have holdings in the target corporation.[39]

Can you spell CDE?

THE AMERICAN VOTER AND THE RISE OF STRATEGIC POLITICAL COMMUNICATION

If the early SDS and its organizational offspring were setting out to attack the corporation as a social form, and if Saul Alinsky was purposefully pointing the way, the final element requisite to success came from an altogether different direction and was never intended by its developers to serve this particular purpose. That element was the development of a new science of political behavior—one that was grounded in social psychology and (in some incarnations) the sociology of media effects and that focused initially on the study of the most routine of American political behaviors, voting. Led by such social scientists as Angus Campbell, Philip Converse, Warren Miller, and Donald Stokes, this new, survey research-based, quantitative approach to understanding why and how people voted as they did formed the basis for what has developed into a commonplace of American political life—the management of political perceptions. Its bible, a purely—one might even say, intensely—academic tome by the name of *The American Voter*, had little in common with the core teaching of the SDS, *The Port Huron Statement*, except that both issued forth from Ann Arbor, where the intellectual ferment of the 1960s took many and varied forms.

Campbell and his colleagues were not the first to undertake a quantitative study of electoral behavior, but they were destined to be, for many years, the most influential. Beginning in the 1920s and gaining pace in the 1940s and 1950s, political scientists, social psychologists, and sociologists had developed important new ways of understanding human behavior, including voting. They developed new and more scientific research methodologies, including systematic survey research based on truly representative samples, and many new theories to explain their observations. By the end of the 1950s, this new knowledge base had achieved critical mass. The publication of *The American Voter* in 1960 marked the maturation of this effort.

Perhaps the first genuinely empirical study of the factors that might predict and explain voting behavior was Harold Gosnell's 1924 experiment in Chicago's ethnic wards, in which he paired up various areas by the principal language spoken by their respective immigrant residents and then sent voting reminders to one ward in each pair to determine the effect of such messages on turnout.[40] This was followed in the 1930s by the development of professional public opinion polling organizations and in the 1940s by a series of community-specific case studies by Paul Lazarsfeld, Bernard Berelson, William McPhee, and others, many of which also focused on the effects of campaign communication.[41] Then in 1948, the center of gravity of the research shifted to Ann Arbor. In that year, a group of Michigan social psychologists was conducting the first nationwide survey of attitudes, perceptions, and beliefs using a sampling method—random sampling—they had borrowed from the agricultural sciences. Because it was a presidential election year, the researchers decided to include a question on presidential preference. In a year when all of the less scientific polls—including those of the professional pollsters—badly missed with their predictions, the Michigan survey was precisely accurate.

In 1952 and 1956, the Michigan social psychologists brought in some of their political scientist colleagues as collaborators, and employed the same random sampling technique in a pair of national studies that focused much more directly on voting behavior. The results of those studies, which formed a core of knowledge about the psychology and, to a lesser extent, the sociology of voting behavior that would shape scholarship for many years to come, were published in *The American Voter*.

This work was followed closely by other political scientists and especially by the scholars who had performed the earlier voting studies. A number of them came together in 1960 under the rubric of the Simulmatics Project. This was a collaborative undertaking of a group of political scientists and psychologists headed by MIT's Ithiel de Sola Pool, on the one hand, and several Democratic Party activists headed by New York businessman Edward Greenfield, on the other, all assisted by an advisory board composed of such social scientific luminaries of the day as Morris Janowitz, Harold Lasswell, and Paul Lazarsfeld. This group set out to represent for the first time the sum of accumulated knowledge about issue-driven voting behavior in a computer simulation model. The model was designed to predict the effect that the positioning of a candidate on a given issue would have on turnout and party preference in an election. By today's standards, neither the model nor the theory was especially sophisticated, but in contemporaneous terms it was quite remarkable—if it worked.

Convinced of the efficacy of their model, the development team offered its services to the Kennedy campaign and was commissioned to prepare recommendations on three issues: civil rights, foreign policy, and religion (i.e., how to address Kennedy's Catholicism, which was a subject of some controversy at the time). The purest test of the computer simulation appears to have come on the religion issue, where the data pointed toward confronting the matter directly. This analysis was generally regarded as a key factor that led Kennedy to his campaign visit to the Southern Baptist Convention in Houston that year, where he took the issue head on, apparently to some advantage.[42]

For Kennedy and his supporters, this was one of many decisions they made during the course of a closely contested campaign and by no means the most important. But for the social scientists, this was something of a Eureka moment—a moment of discovery—because at this moment they realized that their theory and research had reached the point where they might actually have applications in the real world.

Albert Einstein is quoted as having said, "Politics is harder than physics." It is, at the very least, different. Had the Simulmatics Project been relegated to a basement laboratory and managed by a team of white-coated, bespectacled academicians, its impact on the political process might have been minimal or at least long-deferred. However, because the project was a collaboration between theorists and partisans, social scientists and political activists, its impact moved quickly out of the laboratory and into the real world.

The simulation model itself did not long survive (although more sophisticated econometric models built on some of the same assumptions have been developed in recent years).[43] Rather, the lasting effect of the project was an appreciation among political practitioners that matched that among the scholars: Not only did polling data, statistical analysis, database management, and the other tools of the emerging sciences of human behavior provide useful information in real time, but the theories that social scientists had developed to explain and predict behavior were now serviceable as well. With a solid predictive theory and good data, a political campaigner—or any would-be persuasive communicator—could be far more effective than an opponent lacking those resources. As the theory and data became evermore sophisticated, so could the strategies built on them. A new class of political operatives, working in the streets but trained in the classroom, was born.[44]

These were not, at the outset, the campus radicals who gravitated to SDS or the community-based organizers of the Alinsky mold. They were the new generation of middle-of-the-road advocates of the two major parties. Like those in SDS, many of them were interested in power, but they saw the electoral process as the avenue to achieve it and were comfortable as Democrats or Republicans. Above all, they were technocrats. They saw the new technology of political campaigning as a novel and promising means to a traditional end. From the 1960s forward, they emerged as a new class of political operatives, one capable of blending polling, demographic analysis, content analysis, biofeedback research, and the like with such traditional political skills as organizing, writing, and public relations.

These skills—perhaps best described as perception management—turned out to have a variety of potential applications. Although many of these early practitioners plied their trade primarily in the electoral arena, as their numbers grew, some began to find outlets in other nonelectoral yet nonetheless highly political settings. For example, some developed an interest in public policy and used their skills to organize grassroots support for or opposition to a variety of issues. Others used the same skills to represent the interests of foreign governments seeking some advantage in American foreign or trade policy through the management of domestic political processes. Still others began to apply their skills in the service of organized labor.[45] In that setting, as we see here, this skill set provided the final requisite component of the corporate campaign.

TECHNOLOGY MEETS IDEOLOGY

In the 40 years since the emergence of perception management in politics, the body of social scientific knowledge underlying the practice has continued to grow even as the base of practical experience in applying it has expanded. Today we have a fairly comprehensive understanding of how the behavior of people and organizations can be managed through communication to enhance the chances of achieving a desired outcome. We refer to this process as *strategic communication*. This is a term of art that refers to the use of sophisticated knowledge of such attributes of human behavior as attitude and preference structures, cultural tendencies, and media-use patterns, as well as knowledge of such relevant organizational behaviors as how news organizations make decisions regarding news content and how legislatures and government agencies form their agendas, to shape and target messages so as to maximize their desired impact while minimizing collateral damage. It is set apart from other forms of communication—not by its messages, or media, or objectives, none of which is unique, but by the systematic manner in which it integrates theory, research, and practice to manage perceptions, preferences, and behaviors.

Viewed through the lens of the corporate campaign, strategic communication provides the social technology through which many of the objectives of the campaign can be achieved. To the extent that power-structure analysis identifies groups of stakeholders whose members' perceptions, preferences, and behaviors must be shaped if the campaign is to achieve its objectives, strategic communication provides the means by which this can best be accomplished.

In a strategic communication campaign, each element of the communication setting, each stakeholder, each prospective medium, and each prospective message is systematically evaluated for its potential contribution—either positive or negative—to the achievement of the campaign's objectives. Every action taken by any of the parties is seen as a communication. In some circumstances, *in*action also communicates.

Campaign settings include everything from the specific perceptions of the participants held by key audiences to the underlying cultural dynamics of the society and the general tenor of the times. They can vary in terms of such factors as the differing degrees of legitimacy accorded to various communicators, the broad themes that are socially acceptable or unacceptable for use in the campaign, the types of behaviors that will be tolerated or rejected, the social goals with which the campaigners might wish to associate themselves, and the like. To the extent that a campaign relies for its success on defining, mobilizing, demobilizing, or in some way representing public opinion or the public interest, the campaigners must have a solid understanding of the range of freedom of action available to them. The campaign setting defines that range. To the extent that a given campaign can be portrayed as consonant with the essential elements of the setting in which it occurs, it has the opportunity, in effect, to roll downhill—to take advantage of gravity in gaining speed and momentum. However, the campaign that struggles against the grain faces a much more difficult and costly task and is less likely of success.

Campaign stakeholders are those who, in the normal course of events, have an interest in the subject matter of the campaign. In electoral politics, this would include partisans, allies, voters, and coalition partners, among others. In the public policy arena, it would include industries, interest groups, policy consumers, and others with an interest in a given issue. In the corporate campaign, it includes all of the constituencies on whom a target corporation relies in some way—its employees, customers, shareholders, bankers, suppliers, regulators, and the like—precisely those groups that would be identified through a NACLA-type power-structure analysis. The communication strategist examines each of these constituencies or stakeholders in turn, first with an eye toward understanding the ways in which a given relationship is critical to the target company, second to assess the degree to which each relationship is vulnerable to disruption, and third to consider the most effective means by which that disruption can be accomplished and evaluate the associated costs.

Campaign media are quite diverse. In a political campaign, practitioners generally speak of two classes of media: paid and free (or earned). Paid media include campaign advertising or any other channel through which the campaign purchases the right to distribute its message. Free or earned media are those, like the news media, where the campaign is the subject of a distribution of information originated by some other, presumably neutral, third party (e.g., journalists). Political campaigners long ago realized that these two classes of media had countervailing strengths and weaknesses. Paid media could be totally controlled. Their content, format, style, distribution, and timing could be directly managed by the campaign. Unfortunately, for this very reason, paid media tended to lack credibility. They were seen as mere propaganda and had little persuasive value except to reinforce those already committed to a given cause. In contrast, free media, controlled primarily by journalists and news organizations, were, from the campaigners' perspective, communication wildcards. Everything about them was created by outsiders, and they might as easily harm the campaign as help it. Of course, that meant that these free media had much higher credibility and proportionately more persuasive power.

Although paid media play a modest role in some corporate campaigns, it is the free media that drive campaign communication strategies. This is the case for a single, critical reason. As we see in chapter 2, labor unions do not have a particularly strong claim on the public's affections. To the contrary, they are objects of considerable distrust. Hence, to the extent that they can channel their allegations and other campaign-related messages through third parties that are more highly regarded by the public—churches and religious organizations being one example already noted, and journalists and news organizations being a second—they are able to disassociate their own negative image from their message. For this reason, virtually all of the public aspects of the corporate campaign are designed to take advantage of free-media opportunities, and news *management* is an essential skill for an effective campaign team.

This reliance on making news while masking its source provides the context for understanding the fourth element of strategic communication in a corporate campaign—the message(s). In strategic communication terms, messages can be understood to be operating at two levels: symbol and meaning. A symbol is a simple, shorthand way of conveying a more or less complicated meaning. When demonstrators from the Rainforest Action Network climb the office-tower headquarters of a lumber company and hang a banner, much to the annoyance and embarrassment of the company, they are engaged in a symbolic act of communication—sending a message. This action conveys different meanings to different audiences. To the company's management, it expresses deep concern about the company's business practices and conveys a threat of future irrational acts. To the general public, it expresses commitment to the protection of the environment and, perhaps, concern about the inappropriateness of certain models of economic behavior. To RAN members, it denotes the depth of the group's commitment to shared objectives. None of those meanings need be made explicit to be communicated. They arise from the campaign setting and from the known or perceived characteristics of the players in this particular little drama.

Generalizing from this example, actions—whether in the form of demonstrations, boycotts, litigation, releases of correspondence, issuance of white-paper reports, staged media events, or any other similar maneuvers—are symbols, and symbols are the stuff of news. Symbols carry the message of the campaign and, if well chosen, draw journalists like magnets draw iron filings. Symbols are developed and controlled by the campaigners for the primary purpose of manipulating the media and the general public—or any other audience that is dependent on them for information or guidance. In contrast, meanings derive not from the communicators, but from their audiences. Meanings are the link to the preexisting storehouse of attitudes, beliefs, perceptions, and preferences that every individual brings to every communication situation. The effective strategic campaign, then, is the one that selects and markets through the news those symbols that most effectively resonate with the most relevant perceptions and expectations of the highest priority audiences.

So here we are in the early 1970s, with a group of aging "student" radicals committed to their New Left philosophy but largely alienated from a general public tired of all the shouting; with a newly formed anticorporate infrastructure neatly nestled in the arms of a legitimizing cluster of reli-

gious organizations; with a plea and a burst of tactical advice from the leading community organizer of the departing generation; with an emerging
ability effectively to predict and shape human behavior through communication; and with a new class of professional strategic communicators eager
to put this new social technology to work. All of the pieces for the corporate
campaign—save one—are now in place. Someone—and organized labor
was the logical choice—had to implement them.

This marriage of theory and technique with political and economic purpose did not occur instantaneously. There was a period of courtship; there
were objections from the relatives; there was even a spate of jealousy on the
part of those—the old-line labor leaders—who were jilted. But in the end,
the marriage did occur. The corporate campaign is its progeny.

In the next two chapters, we look at the state of organized labor by the
1970s and the forces that led its leaders to begin developing the corporate
campaign. Then we look more closely at the early history of union corporate campaigns and the stages of development through which these efforts
have evolved. Then, in the balance of the book, we examine the various elements of the campaign in considerable detail.

ENDNOTES

1. Charles R. Perry, *Union Corporate Campaigns* (Philadelphia: Industrial Research
   Unit of The Wharton School, University of Pennsylvania, 1987).
2. Barbara Ehrenreich and John Ehrenreich, "The New Left and the Profes-
   sional-Managerial Class," *Radical America*, Vol. 11, No. 3 (1977), p. 10.
3. James Miller, *Democracy Is in the Streets: From Port Huron to the Siege of Chicago* (New York: Simon and Schuster, 1987), p. 27.
4. The emergence of the SDS is chronicled in Miller, op. cit., passim.
5. From *The Port Huron Statement* as reproduced in Miller, op. cit., pp. 334–336.
6. Ibid., p. 363.
7. Ibid., p. 344.
8. Ibid., pp. 173–223, passim.
9. Ibid., p. 173.
10. Ibid., p. 179.
11. Ibid., p. 187.
12. Ibid., p. 223.
13. Ibid., p. 212.
14. Gary Delgado, *Organizing the Movement: The Roots and Growth of ACORN* (Phil-
    adelphia: Temple University Press, 1986), pp. 39–43.
15. Basil Talbott, " 'Outsider' helps lead Machine to victory," *Chicago Sun Times*,
    November 11, 1996, p.12.
16. Miller, op. cit., p. 194.
17. William T. Poole, "How big business bankrolls the left," *National Review* 41
    (March 10, 1989), pp. 34ff.

18. David Vogel, *Lobbying the Corporation* (New York: Basic Books, 1978), p. 139; and R.M. Moore, "Terrorism: The Environment," *The International Lawyer* 16 (Washington: American Bar Association, Winter 1982), p. 135ff.

19. From an interview reported by Vogel, loc. cit.

20. Fred Setterberg, "A library for dissenters: Oakland's Data Center," *American Libraries* 20 (July 1989), pp. 702ff.

21. North American Congress on Latin America, *NACLA Research Methodology Guide* (New York, 1970), pp. 2–3.

22. Ibid., pp. 3–4.

23. Ibid., pp. 14–19.

24. Wendy Cooper, "Labor's New Drive To Learn About The Bottom Line," *The New York Times*, July 24, 1983, p. 3:8.

25. Robert Kuttner, "Sharing Power at Eastern Air Lines," *Harvard Business Review* (November/December 1985), pp. 91ff.

26. Miller, op. cit., pp. 258, 323.

27. Peter B. Levy, *The New Left and Labor in the 1960s* (Urbana: University of Illinois Press, 1994), pp. 153–155. The quote appears on p. 155.

28. *NACLA Research Methodology Guide*, pp. 21–24.

29. Ibid., p. 42.

30. Frawley, op. cit.

31. Jennifer Loven, "Combining Share Votes with Virtue," *Los Angeles Times*, September 6, 1995, p.D6.

32. Parenthetically, both Ansara, who was Ron Carey's principal fundraiser, and Citizen Action were implicated in the 1998 campaign finance scandal that ended Carey's reformist leadership of the Teamsters Union.

33. Vogel, op. cit., p. 44.

34. Quoted in Vogel, op. cit., p. 51.

35. Ibid., pp.51–65.

36. Saul Alinsky, *Rules for Radicals: A Pragmatic Primer for Realistic Radicals* (New York: Vintage Books, 1989), pp. xiii–xviii. (Original edition published in 1971 by Random House.)

37. Ibid., pp. 170–175; Vogel, op. cit., pp. 30–35.

38. Alinksy, op. cit., pp. 127–130, quoted selectively.

39. Ibid., p. 180.

40. Harold F. Gosnell, *Getting Out the Vote* (Chicago: University of Chicago Press, 1927).

41. See, for example, Paul Lazarsfeld, Bernard Berelson, and Helen Gaudet, *The People's Choice* (New York: Columbia University Press, 1944); Bernard Berelson, Paul Lazarsfeld, and William McPhee, *Voting* (Chicago: University of Chicago Press, 1954); and Angus Campbell, Gerald Gurin, and Warren E. Miller, *The Voter Decides* (Evanston, IL: Row, Peterson, 1954).

42. Ithiel de Sola Pool, Robert P. Abelson, and Samuel Popkin, *Candidates, Issues & Strategies: A Computer Simulation of the 1960 and 1964 Presidential Elections* (Cambridge, MA: MIT Press, 1964), pp. 1–24.

43. Randall G. Chapman and Kristian S. Palda, "Econometric Models of Voting and Campaigning," in Michael Margolis and Gary A. Mauser, eds., *Manipulating Public Opinion: Essays on Public Opinion as a Dependent Variable* (Pacific Grove, CA: Brooks/Cole, 1989), pp. 116–136.

44. The rise of this new class has been well chronicled by political scientists in such books as Dan Nimmo, *The Political Persuaders: The Techniques of Modern Election Campaigns* (Englewood Cliffs, NJ: Prentice-Hall, 1970); David Lee Rosenbloom, *The Election Men: Professional Campaign Managers and American Democracy* (New York: Quadrangle Books, 1973); and Larry Sabato, *The Rise of Political Consultants: New Ways of Winning Elections* (New York: Basic Books, 1981).

45. These and other examples are developed more fully in Jarol B. Manheim, *All of the People, All the Time: Strategic Communication and American Politics* (Armonk, NY: M.E. Sharpe, 1991).

2

THE STATE OF THE UNIONS

To say that the ground has been laid for a wide-ranging attack on the corporation—whether by unions or any other set of interests—is not the same as saying that such an attack will be initiated. After all, there are many issues to be considered, not least of which is that organized labor shares with corporate management a vested interest in preserving the economic viability of the company. At least that is true in certain circumstances. In others, however, the union may be willing to risk, or may even place a positive value on, killing off an employer in the pursuit of some larger objective. To understand why the corporate campaign came to be adopted by the unions and implemented on a large scale, one must first examine the circumstances in which these events came to pass. A broad-brush look at the last 100 years of labor history is a good place to start.

The 20th century provided a veritable roller-coaster ride for the leaders of organized labor. It was a period divided almost perfectly into thirds. In the first third of the century, labor lacked legitimacy and any meaningful representation within the social and political establishment. Labor leaders were generally seen as thugs, miscreants, or, worse, anarchists. Accordingly, the movement's strategy—continuing from the late 1800s—was to engage its corporate foes in bloody confrontations partly to raise the cost of maintaining the status quo and partly to create a wave of public sympathy for martyred workers. This activity, coupled with the rising threat of Bolshevism in the wake of World War I, eventually convinced the nation's political leaders to bring labor within the capitalist fold.

This was accomplished in the 1930s with passage of the Wagner Act, establishment of the National Labor Relations Board (NLRB), and through other labor-friendly legislation that lay near the heart of the New Deal. Very quickly, labor emerged as a central component of the new Roosevelt–Democratic Party coalition. Finding itself suddenly inside the tent, labor promptly turned its attention during the middle third of the century to constraining its own most radical voices, as through the merger of the nation's two leading labor federations, and to expanding and using its newly found legislative and regulatory prerogatives in addressing a series of bread-and-butter issues—wages, hours and working conditions, restrictions on child labor. With legitimacy came genuine political influence, especially among Democrats, who came to rely on labor's ability to mobilize armies of campaign volunteers and voters. The NLRB, collective bargaining, and, especially, the strike became the instruments of choice.

However, with legitimacy came growing complacency. Labor began to lose its edge as a movement. Union members came to feel disassociated from their leaders, and those leaders came less and less to resemble or truly represent their respective members. In effect, as the century neared its eighth decade, labor's successes began to take their toll. As the wage and hour battles were won, as workplace conditions improved, and as workers came to share more or less fully in achievement of the *American Dream*, labor's agenda shifted to social and other issues that divided its members rather than united them, and the fundamental source of the movement's legitimacy—the need to establish the rights of workers—lost its power to generate broad public support. By the late 1960s, when many activist movements—civil rights, consumerism, environmentalism—found new or renewed vigor and emerged as powerful forces for change, labor was seen—even among its leaders—as a bulwark of the status quo. More and more, organized labor lost touch with key sectors of the public on whose acceptance, its leaders belatedly came to realize, much of its influence depended. It was this very embracing of the status quo that Tom Hayden and the SDS attacked in *The Port Huron Statement* and that Paul Booth sought to overturn through the research plan set forth in his chapter on unions in the NACLA *Research Methodology Guide*.

By the mid-1970s, an emerging generation of labor leaders recognized that their movement faced a crisis. Membership had begin to decline, strikes failed more often than not to achieve their objectives or simply proved so costly that unions could not afford them, public support was waning, and the ability to rely on government for support and assistance in organizing and representing workers—the very prize their predecessors had fought so hard and at such a price to achieve—had begun to lose its value. Management—never a passive opponent—had, with time, developed new and more effective tools of its own that were proving effective at thwarting labor's initiatives. With its resources and influence under great pressure, labor began to develop its strategic response—the corporate campaign.

In the balance of this chapter, we explore each of these three periods briefly. Our objective is to establish an historical basis for understanding the contemporary dynamics of the labor movement, the strategies and tactics by which it has come to confront its corporate adversaries, and the perspectives that guide the current generation of labor leaders.

1900–1932: THE ERA OF CONFRONTATION

The first third of the 20th century can be aptly characterized as an era of confrontation. In this, it was no different than the several decades immediately preceding. Strikes were commonplace—especially in mining, manufacturing and transportation, what we today refer to as the Rust Belt industries. In those years, the so-called Rust Belt was, in fact, the cradle of American industrial development, and its labor- and capital-intensive industries were the primary engines driving the nation's economy. But neither labor unions nor capitalists were yet afforded much acceptance by a public that came of age in a largely agrarian society. Capitalists were seen as greedy, self-interested exploiters, a view best represented in the efforts of Teddy Roosevelt and his *trust-busters*, whose highly popular objective was to use the power of government to protect the people from the excesses of corporations and the wealthy class that controlled them. Unions were seen as quasicriminal syndicates and extremist political organizations devoted to the overthrow of an economic and political system that was by then beginning to generate a level of prosperity unmatched in human history. Neither side had public support, and neither side garnered much sympathy.

All of that notwithstanding, working conditions in the nation's factories were, even by contemporaneous standards, genuinely appalling. Safety and sanitation were seldom primary concerns of management; hours were long, wages were low, and the rights of workers were routinely abused, if they existed at all. Unions were anathema to management, and they were opposed when proposed, suppressed when manifest, and destroyed when deployed. None of this made the American workplace unique; it was a commonplace of industrialization worldwide. However, it did set the stage for the violent and bloody confrontations that eventually forced a new order on labor–management relations.

To be sure, there was ample precedent for the labor violence of the early 1900s. One need point only to the Great Railroad strike of 1877, in which a single volley of shots from Pennsylvania militiamen killed 16 strikers and in which that state's governor ordered his troops to seize Pittsburgh, for which purpose he dispatched a train protected by sharpshooters and a Gattling gun.[1] Furthermore, one could point to the Homestead Strike of 1892, again near Pittsburgh, where, according to a contemporaneous account, Pinkerton guards allied with local law enforcement officials waged a 4-month war with locked-out workers at Carnegie Steel, complete with cannons and an assassination attempt on Carnegie Chairman H. C. Frick by a Russian anarchist. In the end, 8,000 militiamen were required to restore the peace.[2] The Pullman strike of 1894, with its own wave of rioting, death, and massive property destruction is yet another example.

The turning of the century was not accompanied by the turning of a new leaf. In 1910, violent streetcar strikes swept through Philadelphia, Columbus, and other cities, and unionists were blamed for a massive explosion that destroyed the building housing the *Los Angeles Times*, a staunchly anti-union newspaper in a city undergoing large-scale organizing efforts and the threat of a general strike. This latter event was dubbed, with a measure of hyperbole that would make a contemporary journalist proud, the "Crime of the Century."[3] In 1913, migrant workers on the Durst hop ranch in Wheatland, California, rioted to protest unsanitary working conditions and, in the process, killed a local deputy sheriff and a district attorney.[4] Indeed, so commonplace was such violence that, at one point, a dispute raged in the popular magazine *Outlook* as to which constituted the appropriate statistics on labor-related violence for the period from January 1, 1902 to June 30, 1904, a period of relative calm. Was it 180 killed (including 116 strikebreakers, 51 strikers, and 13 peace officers), 1,651 injured (1,366 strikebreakers, 151 strikers, and 134 officers), and 5,553 arrested—apparently management's view—or was it 904 killed, nearly 1,500 children orphaned, and 672 women widowed, as claimed by the editor of the *United Mine Workers Journal*?[5]

The most potent symbol of labor–management warfare of the 20th century was probably the Ludlow Massacre of 1914. The culmination of a 30-year running battle between miners and mine owners in Colorado, "Bloody Ludlow," resulted when miners walked off the job at the Colorado Fuel and Iron Company (40% owned by Rockefeller interests), which controlled approximately one third of the coal in the state. The September 1913 strike was immediately extended to two other mining interests in the region. The miners issued a series of demands—among them an 8-hour day, the right to trade in any store, a 10% wage increase, the hiring of *check weighmen* to ensure they were not being cheated by the company, abolition of the mine guards system, and recognition of the United Mine Workers union as their bargaining agent. The companies announced that they would meet every one of these demands except that for union representation.[6]

With the issue thus joined, there followed a period of skirmishes between the striking workers on the one hand and a combination of

Baldwin-Feltz strikebreakers and state militiamen on the other. As the dispute wore on for several months, the militia, whose members served without pay, began to experience significant desertions and vacancies. These positions were filled by mine guards and "detectives" provided to a grateful state by the mining companies—at their own expense. In April 1914, not quite 2 weeks after John D. Rockefeller, Jr., testified before a congressional committee that his companies would lose all their assets before they would agree to unionization, the "militia" trained a machine gun on the strikers' camp near Ludlow and opened fire. The camp was burned, and 33 strikers and members of their families were killed.[7] The next day, the strikers issued the following call to arms in the region's newspapers:

Organize the men in your community in companies of volunteers to protect the people of Colorado against the murder and cremation of men, women and children by armed assassins in the employ of coal corporations, serving under the guise of state militiamen.

Gather together for defensive purposes all arms and ammunition legally available. Send name of leader of your company and actual number of men enlisted at once by wire, phone or mail to W. T. Hickey, Secretary of the State Federation of Labor.

Hold all companies subject to order.

People having arms to spare for these defensive measures are requested to furnish same to these local companies, and where no companies exist, send them to the State Federation of Labor.[8]

In the end, open warfare was averted when, following a march by 1,000 women on the state capitol in Denver, Colorado's governor appealed for federal troops and President Woodrow Wilson complied. The U.S. Army entered the area at month's end and restored calm.[9]

By the 1910s, the need to rethink the role of organized labor in the American economy was apparent, even to the most conservative political forces. Accordingly, in 1912, President William Howard Taft proposed to Congress the establishment of a Commission on Industrial Relations empowered to reexamine all state and federal laws, study arbitration and mediation methods, and investigate the condition of labor in the nation's principal industries. By year's end, after considerable political wrangling, especially between the American Federation of Labor and the National Association of Manufacturers, the Commission was established and set on its course. Although in the end it fell victim to inevitable discord within and without, it was this Commission that pointed the way toward the legitimization of organized labor and the second phase of 20th century labor–management relations.[10]

A second harbinger of labor relations to come was the Railway Labor Act of 1926, the first legislation to guarantee workers the right to organize and bargain over the conditions of their employment. This law, passed in the wake of World War I, in which government control had proved essential to ensuring the effective operation of the nation's most vital transportation system, established boards of adjustment to resolve grievances, provided voluntary arbitration for parties at an impasse, and authorized the president to appoint emergency boards to resolve contract disputes. The Railway Labor Act was, in many regards, the bridge between open conflict and collective bargaining and the gateway to modern labor legislation.[11]

1933–1980: THE ERA OF REGULATION

In 1933, the first New Deal Congress enacted the National Industrial Recovery Act (NIRA). Section (7a) of this legislation envisioned codes of fair competition across the various sectors of the economy—codes providing that "employees shall have the right to organize and bargain collectively through representatives of their own choosing, and shall be free from the interference, restraint or coercion of employers." Acting under this legislation, President Roosevelt created the National Labor Board and named then-Senator Robert Wagner as its chair. In 1935, a divided Supreme Court, ruling in the *Schlecter Poultry* case, invalidated the statute on grounds that Congress had improperly used its authority to govern *inter*state commerce as a basis to regulate *intra*state commerce. Thereupon, Senator Wagner introduced the National Labor Relations Act (NLRA), which Congress approved on July 5, 1935. The NLRA further codified and legitimized the rights of workers to organize and established the National Labor Relations Board (NLRB) to administer its provisions. To the surprise of employer groups, in its 1937 decision in *NLRB v. Jones & Laughlin Steel*, the Supreme Court declined to extend its *Schlecter* reasoning to the NLRA and the legislation was allowed to stand.[12] This case had the effect of legalizing the New Deal and, in so doing, eased the political pressure on the Supreme Court itself, and the Roosevelt administration's impetus to pack the Court by enlarging it. The second phase of labor–management relations—the Era of Regulation—was at hand.

We could as easily have named this second period the Era of Big Labor because it was during these years at mid-century when organized labor blossomed into a potent economic and political force, shaping, if not controlling, the destinies of political parties, politicians, and many of the nation's leading corporations. As an organizationally unified, publicly legitimate, politically influential and economically powerful force, America's unions and their allies literally defined the terms of industrial relations for nearly 50 years.

The years from 1935 to 1955 were something of a golden age for organized labor. Union membership soared—from 3.6 million workers (13.2% of the nonagricultural workforce) in 1935 to more than 17 million workers (35% of the nonagricultural workforce) in 1954[13]—and the movement's preeminent weapon, the strike, was wielded with both alacrity and great effect. Conservative leaders emerged to steer labor through the Red baiting of the early 1950s, and the merger of the American Federation of Labor (AFL) with the more radical Congress of Industrial Organizations (CIO) to form the AFL–CIO in 1955 provided both a symbolic statement of the fundamental trustworthiness of American labor and a genuine mechanism for controlling its most radical elements.

During these same years, but especially after the conclusion of World War II in 1945, the U.S. economy expanded rapidly and the nation emerged as the world's preeminent economic power. Labor came along for the ride, with rising expectations in such areas as wages and benefits. Labor–and its members–came to claim a larger and larger slice of the economic pie, even as that pie was growing. Partisan politics and the strike were the two tools wielded ever more forcefully by labor leaders as they raced to keep pace with workers' expectations and, in truth, with their own self-aggrandizing needs as well. The key to building power, they clearly believed, was to flex their collective muscle from time to time.

Unfortunately, the set of assumptions and political relationships that was forged in the New Deal and that had served organized labor so well during the years when Democrats dominated the nation's politics, controlling both the Hill and the White House, brought labor up short when Republicans began to reassert themselves, tentatively at first in the Eisenhower years, then more forcefully from the Nixon administration forward. The close ties between labor and the Democratic Party, and between labor and its traditional allies on the Left, came under great stress, even to the point where, eventually, many of these ties were broken. But we are getting ahead of our story.

One scholar has characterized the period from the late 1940s to the late 1960s—the heart of our designated Era of Regulation—as one of *workplace contractualism*. In his words:

> There is no argument about the essential characteristics of that system: first, that the shop-floor rights of industrial workers would be specified rather than be left undefined; second, that specification of those rights would occur through the process of collective bargaining and take contractual form; and finally, that the contractual rights of workers so achieved would be enforced through a formal grievance procedure … with arbitration by a neutral third party normally as the final and binding step.[14]

Toward the end of this period, Gallup and other polling services reported widespread support for the principal of unionism. In 1967, for example, 92% of Americans believed workers should be free to join unions, more than 60% of Americans indicated that they approved of unions (a figure that had held more or less steady since Gallup began asking the question in 1935), and 52% said they believed that companies had to be forced to pay higher wages when they prospered. At the same time, 58% favored stricter regulation of unions, 66% believed union growth should be capped, and a mere 8% listed labor leaders (as opposed to leaders of other institutions) as those they would be most likely to believe.[15] Although it was not readily apparent at the time, these negatives were about to assume a dominant role in defining the public image of organized labor.

In a prescient 1970 analysis of the labor movement, Derek Bok and John Dunlop identified five emerging problems that were being laid at the feet of organized labor. These included:

1. Public concern with inflation was growing, with much of the responsibility for this trend being attributed to unions and collective bargaining.
2. Strikes—and especially those affecting vital industries or inconveniencing large numbers of people—were increasingly unpopular and were viewed by the public as proportionately more significant than they were viewed by either labor or management.
3. Restrictive work practices, widely perceived to be the result of protectionist union contracts, were seen by the public as contributing to economic inefficiencies and as contrary to the public interest.
4. The increasing rights of public-sector employees to organize and bargain were seen to represent an increasing threat to government sovereignty and to the public good, especially when public employees threatened to strike.
5. Collective bargaining was becoming less important to society at large and to union members, suggesting that unions would need to find alternative services to provide if they were to gain and hold members.[16]

The fact is that, by the late 1950s, labor's power had reached its zenith, although it would be more than a decade before the passage of this critical point became fully evident. Even as the number of union members continued to grow for several years, union membership as a percentage of the non-agricultural workforce peaked in 1954. There followed a lengthy period of slow, and then accelerating, decline. In large measure, this was attributable to shifting fundamentals—the changing demographics of the workforce, industrial and technological advances, global economic trends, and, it must be said, a growing sophistication on the part of employers seeking to limit their exposure to unions.[17] Other factors were at work as well, including both the labor movement's success in pressing its core agenda of wage and workplace reform as well as the growing arrogance of labor leaders who, arguably, lost touch with both their members and the public. This reversal of fortunes is evident in Fig. 2.1, which summarizes union membership as a percentage of the total workforce and the private-sector workforce.[18]

The bulk of the heavy lifting of labor–management relations during these years was accomplished in NLRB-certified elections, in the regulatory arena (again primarily NLRB proceedings), and in the courts as those decisions were subsequently tested. Figure 2.2 summarizes the number of certification elections held in representative years (the scale on the left) and the corresponding percentage of these elections won by the contesting union (the scale on the right). Here, too, we can see that, sometime during the 1950s, labor's success rate began a significant and sustained decline.[19] In the words of a study commissioned by the Departments of Labor and Commerce,

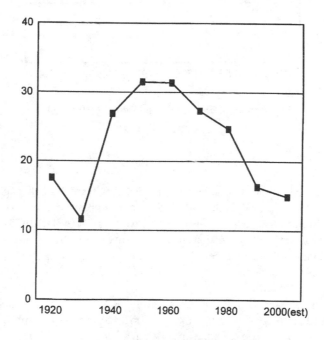

Percent of Workforce Unionized
Nonagriculture, 1920-2000, By Decade

—■— Percent of Nonagricultural Workforce

FIG. 2.1

Union Certification Elections
Number and Outcome, Selected Years

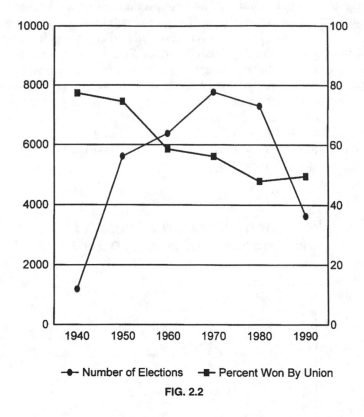

—●— Number of Elections   —■— Percent Won By Union

FIG. 2.2

The extent of NLRB election activity has trended downward through much of the post-World War II period. In the early 1950s, for example, the Board conducted nearly 6000 elections, involving over 700,000 workers. By the late 1970s, the total number of certification elections had risen to over 7500, but in smaller-sized units totaling 490,000 employees. From 1975 to 1990 the number of elections fell by 55 percent to 3,628 elections involving 230,000 workers.[20]

In addition to election procedures, the NLRA established a process for the filing and review of grievances by a union against a company (or by a company against a union). These are known as *unfair labor practice* claims (ULPs). Here the problem for the unions is somewhat different. Not only is their success rate in these filings modest, but the process can be slow and cumbersome.

Union elections and adjudication of ULPs were the heart of the New Deal approach to labor–management relations, but they were not the soul. That was to be found not in the hearing rooms of the NLRB, but in the streets and in the media because the Era of Regulation—the Era of Big Labor—was also the Era of the Strike. Big strikes, small strikes—size was not an issue. As the right to strike became ever more firmly established in law, regulation, and judicial decision, the exercise of that right became ever more frequent. Figure 2.3 summarizes the frequency of major strikes on an annual basis.[21]

At the outset of World War II, leaders of both the AFL and the CIO agreed that their member unions would not strike until the war was concluded. That did not prevent strikes altogether—wildcat strikes and other job actions did occur although when they did, unions and management worked together to end them—but, except for a series of strikes by the United Mine Workers in 1943, it did produce an extended period of production without disruption. As is clear from the figure, however, that era of rel-

Number of Major Strikes
By Year, 1947-1999

—■— Number of Strikes

Figure 2.3

ative labor peace did not last into the postwar years. Indeed, it appears to have generated a measure of pent-up demand as unions sought to reclaim what they regarded as a fair share of the wartime corporate profits.[22]

> With the end of the war, the expected strike wave began. In September 1945, the first full month after the Japanese surrender, the number of workdays lost to strikes doubled. It doubled again in October. Forty-three thousand oil workers struck in twenty states on September 16. Two hundred thousand coal miners struck on September 21.... Forty-four thousand Northwest lumber workers, seventy thousand Midwest truck drivers, and forty thousand machinists in San Francisco and Oakland all struck. East Coast longshoremen struck for nineteen days, flat glass workers for 102 days, and New England textile workers for 133 days. These were but a prelude to the great strikes of 1945 and 1946.[23]

During the first 6 months of 1946, strikes were initiated that involved 2,970,000 workers. By the end of that year, as many as 4.6 million workers had been involved in a strike.[24] In reaction to these perceived excesses, in 1947, the Republican Congress passed the Taft–Hartley Act over President Truman's veto. Taft–Hartley restricted the actions of unions in dealing with workers and employers alike, and provided that workers could *decertify* a union that had been chosen to represent them.[25] Still, the strikes continued. In 1952 alone, as illustrated in Fig. 2.3, there were nearly 500 major strikes.

Among the principal targets of major strikes in the three decades following World War II were General Motors, U.S. Steel, Kohler, Southern Telephone, General Electric, East Coast ports, the railroads, and the coal mines. In 1970, the wave of strikes hit home—potentially *every* American home—when postal workers in more than 200 cities and towns staged a wildcat strike—the first significant strike against the federal government. Before it was over, as many as 200,000 postal workers in 15 states may have participated.[26]

But this frequent and seemingly indiscriminate use of the strike weapon was beginning to undermine labor's hard-won legitimacy.[27] Precisely as Bok and Dunlop had anticipated, it was the use of this weapon in the public sector that brought about the abrupt end of the second era of 20th-century labor relations. The year was 1981. The president was Ronald Reagan. The union was the Professional Air Traffic Controllers Organization (PATCO). The precipitating event was a strike. The outcome was the complete demoralization of the American labor movement.

After some fits and starts, PATCO first took form in January 1968 under the guidance of prominent attorney F. Lee Bailey, who promised that the group would "make noise" in Congress and the media to tell the controllers' story. Bailey helped guide the framers to adopt a constitution that placed an attorney as chief executive in each of the nascent group's eleven regions, these leaders to be selected by and report to PATCO's general counsel—a post filled by Mr. Bailey. At its constitutional convention, the group—not yet identified as a union—also served notice on the FAA that it saw little commonality of interest with the agency's management when it rejected a request to allow a delegation of FAA supervisors to remain as members. The convention closed with a vote for a work-to-rule slowdown, which PATCO then implemented between July 4, 1968, and late August of that year. PATCO issued three demands as a condition of calling off this initial job action. By November 1968, the last of these demands had been met.

The next year there was a rather confusing incident in which Mr. Bailey, appearing on *The Tonight Show* on NBC, may or may not have uttered a phrase that PATCO had advised its members would be the trigger for a sick-out intended to wring still further concessions from the FAA and Congress. In the event, controllers in Denver and Kansas City claimed to have heard Bailey utter the phrase, and they began a new job action. PATCO was summoned to a meeting with the FAA, where it was represented by Bailey. He then returned with assurances that participating controllers would be given immunity from prosecution (strikes against the federal government are illegal) and that controllers' GS ratings would be upgraded—all contingent on ending the sick-out. Regardless of whether this deal was actually placed on the table, when the job action ended it was not implemented by the government. This led to an escalating of tensions between the FAA and PATCO that grew in bitterness year by year. A subsequent sick-out, in March 1970, brought the Air Transport Association (ATA), which represents the airline industry, into the conflict on the side of the FAA. Citing airline losses, ATA sued PATCO for $100 million.[28]

In 1970, PATCO took three steps that set its direction for the next decade. It elected John Leyden as its president and ended its association with F. Lee Bailey; it affiliated with the Marine Engineers Beneficial Association, a wealthy AFL–CIO union; and it filed with the Department of Labor (DOL) for official recognition as a union. The FAA petitioned to bar this recognition. A DOL Hearing Examiner held PATCO responsible for the 1970 sick-out and set conditions for its recognition: The group was to disclaim any right to strike and was required to post a notice at all work sites that it had committed an unfair labor practice and would not strike again. Shortly afterward, in the ATA litigation, PATCO agreed, in return for a token financial settlement, to be placed under a permanent injunction never again to violate the ban on work stoppages by federal employees. Then, in 1971, PATCO applied to be the sole collective bargaining agent for all of the FAA's air traffic controllers. In a subsequent election conducted by DOL, 87% of the controllers voted in support of their new union.[29]

The rest, as they say, is history. The 10-year relationship between PATCO and the FAA was rocky at best and sometimes intensely confrontational. Then at 7 a.m. on Monday, August 3, 1981, some 85% of PATCO's

membership—approximately 13,000 controllers—honored a strike call issued by their leaders. More than 6,000 flights were suspended immediately,
and the president ordered the strikers back to work. When this order was
largely ignored, President Reagan fired 11,345 striking air traffic controllers, blacklisting them from future federal employment. Even before that,
federal courts found the union to be in contempt of court and in violation of
the 1970 injunction, in the first instance fining PATCO nearly $5 million
per week and in the second $100,000 per hour that the work stoppage con-
tinued. Nor did organized labor rush to PATCO's rescue. The AFL–CIO issued some words of support, but there was no concerted support from other
unions. Finally, PATCO was literally vilified in the media.[30] In the end, it
was more than the union could bear. It ceased to exist. With its demise came
both a demonstration of precisely how weakened organized labor's position had become by 1981 and the symbolic end of the Era of Regulation.

Two years later, in 1983, mining giant Phelps Dodge locked out and replaced its striking workers at the Morenci open-pit copper mine and other
facilities in Arizona, who were represented by the Steelworkers union. This
was followed by an election that decertified the union. By some accounts,
this election marked the beginning of a systematic reliance by management
on permanent replacement workers as a means to defeat unions. In effect,
Phelps Dodge was to the private-sector unions what PATCO was to those in
the public sector—a symbol of weakness so fundamental that the legitimacy, and perhaps the survival, of the labor movement was called into
question.[31]

1981 TO THE PRESENT: THE ERA OF "COMMUNICATION"

Some would call the PATCO strike and its aftermath a watershed event in
the history of the American labor movement. However, for those in the
movement, it surely felt more like going over the falls in a barrel. Labor's
principal political allies had lost power, replaced by a regime that was not
only ideologically opposed to its agenda, but extraordinarily aggressive
and effective in achieving its contrary goals. Labor's principal economic
weapon—the strike—had been turned against it.

The mood among labor's supporters during this period may have been
captured best by labor lawyer Thomas Geoghegan in his candid and personal book-length essay, *Which Side Are You On?*, especially when he
wrote that:

> [l]abor gives off now an almost animal sense of weakness. Concessions,
> de-certs, shutdowns. It's like the Italian army in 1918: cars breaking down,
> baggage getting lost, officers getting fired on by their own troops. I joined or-
> ganized labor, and we just started retreating.[32]

A second look at Fig. 2.3, with its precipitous decline in the frequency of strikes after 1981, makes the magnitude of the change strikingly clear. And those strikes that did occur were increasingly costly. One analysis by the Employment Policy Foundation of 18 major strikes between 1985 and 1996 in which wages were the principal issue, for example, found that in only one would workers recoup their losses during the course of their new contract.[33] If organized labor was to survive as a significant political and economic force, its leaders would need to undergo an adjustment in their thinking.

As it happened, such an adjustment was already underway. Historically, the unions had relied on grassroots organizing efforts and certification elections to extend their reach. As we saw in Fig. 2.2, however, by 1980 their success rate in elections had dropped from nearly 80% in the postwar period to around 50%. As a primary instrument of growth, the certification election was at best a risky undertaking and could hardly be considered cost-effective. Some unions—most notably the Amalgamated Clothing and Textile Workers Union (ACTWU)—had recently begun experimenting with an alternative approach to pressuring employers and gaining members, a series of techniques they variously termed *comprehensive campaigns*, *coordinated campaigns*, or, in the phrase widely attributed to then-ACTWU staffer Ray Rogers, *corporate campaigns*. The emergence of the corporate campaign as an instrument of union power ushered in the third period of 20th-century labor–management relations, which we term the *Era of Communication*.

The Era of Communication—really the era of *strategic* communication—derives its name from the introduction into labor–management relations of a wholly new set of objectives, assumptions, strategies, and tactics, the origins of which we have already explored and the collective purpose of which was to reposition organized labor and its component unions as the defenders of the public interest against the evils of big business. Through this repositioning, it was hoped, labor could reclaim its lost legitimacy, resume its growth, and restore its influence. At the same time, by bringing new and sustained forms of pressure on corporate management not trained to recognize, let alone respond to them, labor leaders believed they could circumvent the risky NLRB election process and organize workers at the wholesale, rather than the retail, level. That is a difference worthy of some consideration.

Traditionally, unions have organized workers from the bottom up—workplace by workplace and bargaining unit by bargaining unit. That is what we mean by retail-level organizing. As we have seen, such organizing is costly and entails risk. Having expended substantial time and money in campaigning for workers' votes, unions lose half of all NLRB-conducted elections. Would it not be better to organize from the top down, pressuring management, in effect, to turn its workers over to the union without an election? This idea was perhaps most clearly expressed in 1991 by Joe Crump, at the time Secretary Treasurer of Local 951 of the United Food and Commercial Workers (UFCW), when he said, "Employees are complex and unpredictable. Employers are simple and predictable. Organize employers, not employees."[34] This is what we mean by wholesale-level organizing.

By the 1990s, the need for wholesale organizing was crystal clear. The unions' share of the private-sector workforce was dropping below 10%, about half its level as recently as 1983, and labor's share of the total civilian workforce was only marginally higher at around 14%. In 1995, newly elected AFL–CIO President John Sweeney—a long-time advocate of the corporate campaign—set an ambitious goal for the rejuvenation of the labor movement and the restoration of its influence: increase union membership by 3% each year. The Employment Policy Foundation, an industry-based research group, has estimated that, to meet this goal while offsetting normal attrition, AFL–CIO unions would need to recruit as many as 600,000 new, previously nonunion members annually for the foreseeable future. Only wholesale-level organizing could allow the federation to accomplish that.

How might this be achieved? How could employers be encouraged to recognize a union when their employees had not voted one in? The answer was twofold. First, the unions developed a set of bargaining objectives that was closely tuned to the objective of wholesale organizing. Three of these were of primary importance: neutrality, card check, and master agreements.

Neutrality refers to a promise on the part of management that it will remain neutral as a union seeks to organize its employees. From the unions' perspective, this is an especially important objective. The unions believe that there exists a population of labor relations consultants—lawyers, economists, and others—who are effective *union busters*, in that they can advise companies in ways successfully to defeat union organizing initiatives. They believe further that many companies have developed effective union-avoidance strategies and tactics. The neutrality agreement is a device designed to freeze this capability—the labor-relations equivalent of unilateral disarmament.

Card check refers to a procedure other than an election by which a union demonstrates its support among workers. In this procedure, workers are encouraged to sign cards expressing their desire to be represented by the union; the company agrees to recognize the union when a majority of workers has signed such cards. Card check, when successfully employed, legitimizes recognition of the union without the need for an election. In that way, it eliminates much of the cost and risk of an organizing campaign. More than that, it takes such a campaign out of the public view. Elections must be conducted according to certain rules, the violation of which can constitute a ULP. In a card check procedure, these rules do not generally apply. The union's representatives can visit employees in their homes or elsewhere and can obtain signatures under a variety of circumstances that might not be permitted in an NLRB-conducted procedure. Thus, the union can avoid delays and faces fewer barriers in contacting workers, although management often claims that such procedures lead to intimidation of workers, especially recent immigrants. Whatever one's view of the dynamics, card check generally enhances the prospect that the organizing campaign will succeed. One study prepared by the AFL–CIO's George Meany Center found, for example, that the success rate for organizing campaigns conducted through card check was more than 70%—a considerable improvement over NLRB election results.[35] In at least a few instances, however, this approach can be problematic. That was the case, for example, when the Teamsters union organized workers at Basic Vegetable, a California-based processor of onions and garlic, using card check. The union then staged a strike, during the course of which some workers began to mount a decertification drive. The union was then forced to call on the NLRB to hold a recognition election as a way to prevent such a vote.[36]

Master agreements, the third element of the bargaining strategy, represent a consolidation of collective bargaining. Rather than dealing with individual workplaces and multiple negotiations, the unions typically seek to bring all of their negotiations with a company under a single, overarching agreement. This is efficient for both union and management. However, as a component of a bargaining and organizing strategy, it can also create a single pressure point on management—the expiration of the master agreement—that carries far greater risk than any of the lesser agreements *and* that can be used as leverage to extend union representation to nonunion segments of the company's workforce.

In concert, these three objectives, when achieved, simplify the union's organizing efforts and greatly enhance its power vis-à-vis a particular employer. The reasons a union might pursue such a wholesale-level strategy are clear, but the reasons a company might concur are hardly evident. That is where the second part of the strategy—the corporate campaign—enters the scene. The corporate campaign is designed to create incentives for management to agree to these or other demands of the unions. The idea is a simple one—create great pain and disruption through the campaign and then offer to make it go away in exchange for certain considerations. That was the idea of the early anti-corporate ideologues of the New Left, and it was the idea that attracted the attention of the new generation of labor leaders who found their power and base of support on the wane.

There were reasons this approach could be expected to bear fruit for labor. Just as labor leaders were distrusted by the general public, so, too, were the leaders of the business community. Indeed, the underlying value system of American society still afforded more sympathy to hard-toiling workers than to greedy capitalists. Of course, far more Americans were workers rather than industrialists. Moreover, an aggressive repositioning of labor as public-regarding would offer the movement opportunities to restore its historical alliances with other "progressive" interests—alliances that had fallen into disrepair during the social upheavals of the 1960s and 1970s. Indeed, it was the clear objective of at least some of those interests, as represented by NACLA, to bring about this precise end.

Most of all, the new techniques of social marketing, image management, and media manipulation had proved their effectiveness in the political arena—they were, in fact, largely responsible for Ronald Reagan's rise to power and, in that sense, for the unions' plight. They could, it was believed, be easily adapted to serve the unions' interests instead. The unions—or at least these new union leaders—no doubt saw the corporate campaign as a delightful irony, a way to turn the weapons of their economic and political adversaries against them.

We reserve a discussion of the nature and development of these techniques for the next and subsequent chapters. For the moment, let us simply assert that, by the mid-1970s, such new and effective instruments of influence were available; by the 1980s, an increasing number of labor leaders had reason to both appreciate their effectiveness and employ them for their own purposes.

Labor's adoption of the strategies and tactics that we now associate with the corporate campaign began, somewhat tentatively, in the campaign waged by the Amalgamated Clothing Workers Union (ACWU) against Texas-based Farah Manufacturing in the early 1970s and were refined during the same union's 1976 campaign against textile giant J.P. Stevens. These early campaigns showed some of the elements that have since become commonplace—intense personal attacks on top management; wild allegations about poor corporate citizenship; contacts with financial analysts as part of a concerted effort to undermine the valuation of the target company's equities; secondary pressure on the target through its banking, distribution, or other essential relationships; regulatory and political pressure; and the like. They showed labor's newfound willingness to innovate, experiment, and learn. Most of all, these campaigns demonstrated the seeming reckless abandon with which the unions would henceforth attack their adversaries. It was as if the unions felt they had nothing to lose. As the prior data indicate, in a real sense that was true. At its inception, the corporate campaign comprised a set of desperate measures for desperate times.

As we show later, the corporate campaign has evolved in the past quarter century from an experimental collection of new and unexpected challenges to a mature and predictable strategic platform; it has emerged from relative obscurity into the mainstream of labor's organizing efforts. It is now fully developed, fully institutionalized, fully funded, and widely used. Whether it is fully effective is a question we may be able to answer as we proceed.

The corporate campaign is intended to substitute for—or supplement—two of the three legs on which labor's power rested during its heyday—the organizing election and the strike. It is worth noting before we move on, however, that the unions have not ignored their third base of power and influence—partisan political support. Although they have flirted with the Republicans from time to time, even as far back as the Nixon administration, labor leaders still find their home—and their greatest influence—in the Democratic Party. During the waning years of the last century, they have bestowed considerable support on their Democratic friends. The effectiveness of these contributions in enhancing the power of organized labor is thus far unclear. On the one hand, it did not prevent the Republicans from capturing control of both houses of Congress in 1994. On the other, it played an important role in both of President Clinton's successful campaigns for the White House and has put labor at the table with any Democratic presidential hopeful likely of success. In that sense, at least, the unions have restored a key political alliance.

With the new era has come true globalization and a fundamental restructuring of the American economy. Responding to these new pressures—and learning to define for itself a role as an agent of change rather than an adversary—has been part and parcel of labor's own restructuring. In such a circumstance, political influence, in the narrow electoral sense, cannot suffice. Instead, labor must find ways to exercise effective influence on the nation's social and economic policies, both foreign and domestic. Here, too, the themes, approaches, tactics, and alliances that lie at the heart of the corporate campaign have been brought to bear, not on companies or the business community per se, but on policies and the process of making them. In the Era of Communication, labor's agenda has broadened to match its new perspective.

In the chapters that follow, we examine in great detail the adoption of anticorporate strategies by organized labor, the tactics and techniques of the corporate campaign, instances in which they have been employed, their contextual significance and implications, and, most recently, the adoption of corporate campaign-style activities by interests other than organized labor. Our objective is to provide the most comprehensive look to date at this phenomenon of great and growing consequence.

ENDNOTES

1. James Ford Rhodes, "Railroad Riots of 1877," *Scribners Magazine*, July 1911, pp. 86–96. Much of the discussion of labor violence in this portion of the chapter draws on Jarol B. Manheim, *Déjà vu: American Political Problems in Historical Perspective* (New York, St. Martin's Press, 1976), pp. 18–28.

2. Arthur G. Burgoyne, *The Homestead Strike of 1892* (Pittsburgh: University of Pittsburgh Press, 1979. Reprint of the 1893 edition).

3. Harold J. Howland, "War in Philadelphia," *Outlook*, March 5, 1910, pp. 522–525; "Anarchy in Columbus," *Outlook*, August 27, 1910, pp. 908–911; and Graham Ad-

ams, Jr., *Age of Industrial Violence, 1910–15* (New York: Columbia University Press, 1966), pp. 1–24.

4. Carleton H. Parker, "Wheatland Riot and What Lay Back of It," *Survey*, March 21, 1914, pp. 768–770.

5. Slason Thompson, "Violence in Labor Conflicts," *Outlook*, December 17, 1904, pp. 969–972; and S.M. Sexton, "Strike Violence," *Outlook*, January 21, 1905, pp. 198–199.

6. Helen Ring Robinson, "War in Colorado," *Independent*, May 11, 1914, pp. 245–247.

7. W.T. Davis, "Strike War in Colorado," *Outlook*, May 9, 1914, pp. 67–73; "Tent Colony of Strikers Swept by Machine Guns," *Survey*, May 2, 1914, pp. 108–110.

8. Davis, "Strike War."

9. Robinson, "War in Colorado"; "Industrial War in Colorado," *Review of Reviews* 49 (June 1914), pp. 732–734.

10. Adams, *Age of Industrial Violence*, passim.

11. Charles B. Craver, *Can Unions Survive? The Rejuvenation of the American Labor Movement* (New York: New York University Press, 1993), pp. 25–26.

12. Craver, pp. 26–27.

13. Craver, p. 34.

14. David Brody, *In Labor's Cause: Main Themes on the History of the American Worker* (New York: Oxford University Press, 1993), p. 221.

15. Reported in Derek C. Bok and John T. Dunlop, *Labor and the American Community* (New York: Simon and Schuster, 1970), pp. 12–19.

16. Bok and Dunlop, pp. 38–40.

17. Craver, pp. 34–51.

18. Derived from data reported in Marick F. Masters, *Unions at the Crossroads: Strategic Membership, Financial, and Political Perspectives* (Westport, CT: Quorum Books, 1997), p. 44.

19. Derived from data reported in Masters, p. 55.

20. Commission on the Future of Worker–Management Relations, *Fact Finding Report* (Washington: U.S. Department of Labor and U.S. Department of Commerce, 1994), p. 67.

21. Derived from data reported on the Bureau of Labor Statistics web site, January 5, 1999.

22. Jeremy Brecher, *Strike!*, revised and updated edition (Cambridge, MA: South End Press, 1997), pp. 237–242.

23. Ibid., p. 245.

24. Ibid., p. 246.

25. Daniel V. Yager, *Has Labor Law Failed?* (Washington: National Foundation for the Study of Employment Policy, 1990), pp. iii–iv.

26. Ibid., pp. 258–261. For a chronology of major strikes and other significant events relating to organized labor, see www.uniononline.com/html/history.

27. Thomas Geoghegan, in *Which Side Are You On?* (New York: Penguin, 1992), pp. 30-31, argues that the Supreme Court's 1969 decision in *Boys Markets*, in which the Court indicated its intention to issue injunctions enforcing no-strike clauses in

labor contracts—a major change in judicial policy—actually brought about the end of the strike as a viable union weapon. However, if that was the case, the data in Fig. 2.3 indicate the effect was delayed by several years.

28. Arthur B. Shostak and David Skocik, *The Air Controllers' Controversy: Lessons from the PATCO Strike* (New York: Human Sciences Press, 1986), pp. 48–57.
29. Shostak and Skocik, pp. 58–62.
30. Shostak and Skocik, pp. 103–122.
31. Jonathan D. Rosenblum, *Copper Crucible: How the Arizona Miners' Strike of 1983 Recast Labor–Management Relations in America* (Ithaca, NY: ILR Press, 1995), See especially pages 48, 217.
32. Geoghegan, op. cit., p. 4.
33. Cited in Jonathan Marshall, "Labor Strikes Are Becoming Rare as Unions Turn Cautious," *San Francisco Chronicle*, May 4, 1998, p. B1.
34. Joe Crump, "The Pressure Is On: Organizing Without the NLRB," *Labor Research Review* (1991/92).
35. Adrienne E. Eaton and Jill Kriesky, "Organizing Experiences Under Union-Management Neutrality and Card Check Agreements," Report to the Institute for the Study of Labor Organizations, George Meany Center for Labor Studies, February 1999, pp. ii–iii. The study also assessed the effectiveness of various phrasings of card check and neutrality agreements. An interesting case related to this practice is that arising from the Hotel Employees and Restaurant Employees International Union (HERE) against MGM Grand Hotel in Las Vegas. In this instance, in 1996, the company agreed to card check in exchange for an end to the union's 3-year corporate campaign. The union produced a sufficiency of cards and was recognized by the company. Within the next year, however, as contract negotiations dragged on, three employee petitions, collectively signed by a majority of employees, were filed with the NLRB asking for the right to vote on whether HERE should represent them. This would effectively be, by implication, a decertification election. The Labor Board rejected these petitions in favor of the card check procedure. *MGM Grand Hotel, Inc., 329 NLRB No. 50 (1999)*.
36. Eric Brazil, "Teamsters ask NLRB for election at processing plant," *San Francisco Chronicle*, January 29, 2000, p. A3.

3

The Learning Curve

Although finding effective ways to oppose the Vietnam War was the primary business of the December 1964 meeting of the SDS National Council—at least one observer traces the origins of the antiwar movement to this very meeting[1]—the group's two top officers, president Todd Gitlin and vice president Paul Booth, had much of their attention on a different project. They asked for and received the endorsement of the Council for a demonstration against Chase Manhattan Bank in New York. Chase Manhattan was a leading lender to the Apartheid regime in South Africa; by protesting at Chase, Gitlin and Booth hoped to bring pressure on that regime.[2]

In selecting a bank as the symbol of de facto American support for Apartheid and as a point of leverage against South Africa, the SDS leaders were applying two lessons learned from the civil rights movement of the day. First, by sitting in at segregated Woolworth lunch counters in the South in 1960 and then pressuring the company through a nationwide boycott to alter its policies, civil rights activists had demonstrated that public policies might be attacked through their implementation in the private sector.[3] Second, by pressing the Bank of America, among other companies, in 1963 and 1964 to recognize the legitimacy of the Congress on Racial Equality (CORE) by reporting to it regularly on the racial diversity of the bank's employees, the movement made the point that, in the words of political scientist David Vogel, "Business was viewed less as an institution which had the responsibility for immediately improving the economic condition of blacks, and more as an integral part of the national and local structures of power that oppressed them."[4]

Gitlin and Booth chose March 19, the anniversary of the 1960 Sharpeville Massacre in South Africa, as the date for their protest.[5] On that day, 41 well-mannered and well-dressed SDSers sat in on the sidewalk outside the Chase Manhattan headquarters in the Wall Street area, where they were arrested in what Gitlin described as a "not ungentle" manner.[6] Although the antiwar demonstrations of the era attracted far more attention than this isolated and peaceful sit-in, it was the action at Chase Manhattan that more clearly presaged the coming war on the corporation.

Beginning with the SDS sit-in, corporations became the primary point of leverage for Americans opposed to the South African regime. SDS itself was swept up in opposition to the Vietnam War and never again played a direct role on this issue. But it is likely that some of its members did (e.g., Booth and Locker, through their involvement in NACLA, which was formed at that time and represented a sort of partnership between SDS and the National Council of Churches [NCC] that hosted it). In any event, the NCC became a leading player in pressuring companies to break their ties to South Africa.

The National Council of Churches, founded in 1950, was the successor organization to the Federal Council of Churches of Christ, which had been formed in 1908 under a charter commissioning it to address the problems of modern industrial society through the teachings of the New Testament. The ninth article of this charter, the so-called *Social Creed*, stated the council's economic and social agenda:

> We deem it the duty of all Christian people to concern themselves directly with certain practical industrial problems. To us it seems that the churches must stand—
>
> For equal rights and complete justice for all men in all stations of life.
>
> For the right of all men to the opportunity for self maintenance, a right ever to be wisely and strongly safeguarded against encroachment of every kind.
>
> For the right of workers to some protection against the hardships often resulting from the swift crises of industrial change.
>
> For the principle of conciliation and arbitration in industrial dissension.
>
> For the protection of the worker from dangerous machinery, occupational disease, injuries and mortality.
>
> For the abolition of child labor.
>
> For such regulations of the conditions of toil for women as shall safeguard the physical and moral health of the community.

For the suppression of the "sweating system."

For the gradual and reasonable reduction of the hours of labor to the lowest practical point, and for that degree of leisure for all which is a condition of the highest human life.

For a release from employment one day in seven.

For a living wage as a minimum in every industry, and for the highest wage that each industry can afford.

For the most equitable division of the products of industry that can ultimately be devised.

For the abatement of poverty.[7]

This document stated quite succinctly not only the positions of the Federal Council, but the objectives of the labor movement of the day—all in terms that retain a remarkable degree of similarity to both the substance and rhetoric extant nearly a century later.

According to Vogel's comprehensive analysis of early efforts to motivate business toward "socially responsible" behaviors, the NCC had become interested in the issue of corporate accountability per se as early as 1947, when it created a unit on Church and Economic Life. Then in 1963, the organization's governing board broke new ground, suggesting that the churches' equity holdings in public corporations could be used to pressure management on social and ethical issues. The board recommended that churches divest themselves of holdings in companies that practiced racial discrimination if they were unable to persuade the companies to change their policies. In 1966, the NCC board shifted the balance a bit, placing greater emphasis on influencing policy rather than divestiture. In 1968, it carried the logic of its position further, arguing that churches should take corporate responsiveness to these demands into account in selecting vendors for their own purchases of goods and services. Because, according to estimates at the time, the total wealth of all churches was approximately $160 billion—more than the combined assets of the 10 largest industrial corporations in the United States—including approximately $20 billion in holdings of corporate stocks, this NCC initiative was of potentially great significance.[8]

There was another important dimension to the NCC's actions as well. In the words of Frank White, who soon emerged as a leader of the effort,

We know from talking with many people in the corporations that of all the institutions and individuals that bring social concerns out into the limelight, they most fear the church. The real power of the church is in consciousness raising and in embarrassing the corporation into doing what it ought to be doing.[9]

Between 1969 and 1971, the governing bodies of four major Protestant denominations took initiatives to monitor the social impact of their respective investments. In 1971, the Episcopal Church went so far as to file a shareholder resolution calling on the management of General Motors to cease operations in South Africa. These developments led the NCC, in that same year, to establish the Corporate Information Center (CIC), headed by Frank White. CIC was housed in the NCC offices in New York, which also housed NACLA. It was created the year following publication of the NACLA *Research Methodology Guide* and charged with five research tasks: creating social profiles of corporations, exploring alternative investment opportunities, examining government policies toward business, outlining current corporate challenges, and conducting church economic research. Although CIC's initial emphasis was on establishing a social rating system that would allow churches easily to identify companies from which they might wish to divest, within a few years of its establishment the churches were actually employing a far wider range of tactics, including shareholder resolutions, shareholder lawsuits, public hearings, private meetings and correspondence with management, demonstrations, boycotts, leafleting retail outlets, attending annual meetings, research, critical publications, and fact-finding trips.[10] In 1974, the CIC merged with the Interfaith Committee on Social Responsibility, an ad hoc grouping of several Protestant and Catholic organizations, to form the Interfaith Center on Corporate Responsibility (ICCR), which was then formally separated from the NCC.[11] ICCR remains today one of the prime movers in pressuring corporations to adopt "progressive" policies.

In summary, during the early to mid-1970s, the churches, led by the NCC, developed many of the components we see today in union corporate campaigns, and they put in place an infrastructure to support both research and action targeted against corporations whose actions they wished to influence.

Then they put these tactics to work. In 1973, the CIC obtained confidential documents showing that, over the preceding 3 years, a consortium of 40 banks had loaned $210 million to the South African government. A church-led campaign produced pledges by several of these banks either to cancel their existing loans or cease making such loans in the future. Then in November 1974, the NCC conducted 2 days of "hearings" on IBM's commercial dealings with South Africa. The participating denominations owned 130,000 shares of IBM stock so they had management's ear, although in the end the company declined to accede to the NCC finding that it should end its activities in that country.[12] Nevertheless, the IBM initiative, and a similar effort aimed at Polaroid, helped the churches test and refine their methods.

The South Africa campaign also brought the churches together with labor activists in the context of an anticorporate campaign. In 1973, the Southern Company, an electric utility, agreed to purchase a large volume of coal from South Africa. This produced an outcry at home from the United Mine Workers and a demonstration by some 500 miners outside the company's 1974 annual meeting in Birmingham, Alabama. In 1975, the ICCR filed a shareholders' resolution, calling on the company to end its purchases of South African coal until the regime's Apartheid policy had been changed.[13]

CUE THE AMALGAMATED, CUE RAY ROGERS

At the time these events were transpiring, and just as labor and religious leaders began to find a commonality of interest in pursuing what was, in effect, the agenda of the SDS and the New Left, the Amalgamated Clothing Workers Union (ACWU) was beginning a major organizing drive among garment workers in the American Southwest, where much of the industry's manufacturing base had moved in recent years. One of the primary targets was a rapidly growing Texas company with a nonunion workforce—Farah Manufacturing. In the early 1970s, Farah had just opened a massive new facility in El Paso, where it employed about 9,000 workers. Beginning in 1972, the union orchestrated a campaign of consumer boycotts and corporate pressure to force Farah to recognize the ACWU as the bargaining agent for all the employees at its El Paso facility. This effort was, in effect, a dress rehearsal for a subsequent campaign by the same union against J.P. Stevens and for all that was to follow.[14]

The Farah campaign began in May 1972, when about 3,000 workers walked off their jobs and set up pickets outside the company's main plant. Issues in the strike included wages and the right to organize. For the union, it appears fairly clear that the latter was the key issue. The labor market in El Paso was exceptionally deep, which left the balance of power clearly in the hands of employers opposed to unionization. Among these employers, Farah Manufacturing was the corporate leader, and its outspoken chairman, William F. (Willie) Farah, was the leading executive voice. If the ACWU could organize the plants and silence Willie Farah, the union reasoned, it could then organize workers at many other companies across the city. However, the deep labor market, fed by a large Hispanic population seeking low-wage jobs and legal immigrant workers from nearby Juarez, Mexico, also permitted Farah to replace striking workers quickly and with relative ease. It was clear from the outset, then, that the strike would fail unless the union could find another way to pressure the management of the family-controlled company.

So it was that, within a few days of the beginning of the strike, the union initiated a boycott of Farah trousers by launching a tour of strikers to major cities around the country where they picketed outside stores selling the company's products. One such demonstration, on May 17, 1972, outside the main Macy's store in New York attracted particular attention. Two months later, in July 1972, Wisconsin Senator Gaylord Nelson announced the formation of the Citizens Committee for Justice for Farah Workers, whose purpose was to support the strikers and call for a nationwide boycott. The Committee immediately placed an advertisement in *The New York Times* urging consumers to support the strike.

By September 1972, prominent political, civic, and religious leaders had joined the campaign—among them presidential candidate George McGovern, Senator Edward Kennedy, and the Right Reverend S.M. Metzger. Each side was charging the other with violence and intimidation. G.H. McAlmon, chair of the Citizens Committee, claimed that the Anglo establishment in El Paso, which generally supported Farah in the conflict, was trying to keep local (Hispanic) workers unorganized to sustain its power. On September 13, vice presidential candidate R. Sargent Shriver picked up on this theme when he met with some of the strikers, telling them they were fighting not just for economic independence, but for human rights. For its part, the company told the NLRB that recognizing the union would be "ruinous" to its ability to compete with foreign manufacturers.

In December 1972, Santa Claus joined the fight when a department-store Santa at Higbee's, the large Cleveland retailer, walked off the job to join 500 workers in a pro-boycott demonstration outside the company's flagship store. At year's end, the union claimed that a number of major national retailers had stopped ordering or advertising Farah clothing.

In February 1973, Bishop Metzger wrote a letter to his fellow Catholic Bishops across the country citing workers' complaints about production pressures, noting suggestions that Willie Farah would rather close his company than recognize the union and asking that they endorse the boycott. The ACWU reprinted the Metzger letter as an advertisement in major newspapers. In May 1973, one year into the strike, the NLRB ordered Farah to stop harassing and intimidating pro-union workers.

At its October 1973 meeting, the AFL–CIO convention voted to support the Farah boycott. In the same month, the company filed a lawsuit against the union alleging that it had illegally threatened and coerced merchants into boycotting its products. Two months later, the company laid off one third of its supervisory personnel—a sure sign that the boycott was being felt. Finally, in February 1974, the two sides reached an agreement and the strike and boycott were called off.[15]

During the course of the ACWU campaign, the market price of Farah's stock fell from a prestrike high of $49 a share to a low of about $5. This created a new source of pressure on management—the company's shareholders. The boycott, which proved quite effective, was combined with a public relations campaign and the filing of unfair labor practice claims—a volatile mix that is today a corporate campaign commonplace.[16] In 1993, the Interfaith Committee for Social Responsibility (soon to merge into the ICCR) included Farah on a short list of publicly traded companies that were asked to provide the group with data about the composition of their workforces by gender, race, and job category. In February 1974, shortly before the company conceded defeat, the group submitted to Farah a shareholders' resolution requiring disclosure of these data.[17] This may well have been the proverbial straw that broke the camel's back.

Or perhaps not. Sometime during 1973, the ACWU hired a new staff member and assigned him to the Farah campaign. His name was Ray Rogers, and he was destined to become a legend as the guru—partly demonstrated and partly self-proclaimed—of the corporate campaign. As recounted in an early *New York Times* retrospective on Mr. Rogers' career,

he joined the then-flagging campaign mounted by the textile workers to organize employees at the Farah Manufacturing Company, a Texas-based firm that had fought unionization for more than a decade. In 1974, William Farah said that he would never sit down with the union. Three weeks later, after Mr. Rogers began his campaign, Mr. Farah showed up at the textile union's New York headquarters and asked that the fight be ended.[18]

Working mostly in Alabama, Rogers recruited other unions to support the boycott by picketing stores in their local communities. These stores then canceled their orders of Farah slacks rather than being drawn into the dispute.[19] It was shortly after this that the company gave up the fight.

The Farah campaign lasted 22 months. It cost the union an estimated $5 million and the company an estimated $8 million, not including shareholder losses. It succeeded, according to one contemporary analysis, "because it was endorsed by major church groups, including the National Council of Churches, the United Church Board for Homeland Ministries, and several Catholic bishops."[20] Indeed, in Farah, the union was heavily dependent on such support because the characteristics of the local labor market in El Paso rendered victory on its own all but impossible. The worth of such an alliance, and the value added to the campaign by the NCC and others, were thus very clearly established. More than that, Farah provided the first opportunity for organized labor to test the emerging tactics of what would become the union corporate campaign, and it served as an essential learning experience for the man who would emerge to lead labor, albeit briefly and controversially, into the new era of anticorporate warfare.

Raymond Franklin Rogers was born into a union household in Beverly, Massachusetts, in 1944. His mother was an assembler in an electronics plant, and his father was a lathe operator who had experienced a bitter strike at a General Electric plant in nearby Lynn. He was a guard on his high school football team, before attending the University of Massachusetts, where he graduated in 1967 with a degree in sociology. Rogers next served as a VISTA volunteer in Tennessee, where he organized teams of poor people and college students to demolish and replace housing for the poor. From there, he worked with Miners for Democracy, the group that toppled Tony Boyle from the presidency of the Mine Workers Union in 1972. Then it was on to the Appalachian Regional Commission in Washington, DC, where he was fired when he produced a graphic 15-page report on hunger and malnutrition in Appalachia and distributed his report after being told not to do so. After that came Human Love Action, a traveling series of seminars Rogers organized to stimulate the discussion on college campuses of the conditions under which Native Americans and poor people lived. It was serendipity that set the remaining course of his life, when political consultant Walter Clinton bought the building in which Rogers had an apartment and suggested that the two merge their skills—Clinton's in political campaigning and Rogers' in organizing.

It was while he was working as a VISTA volunteer that he began reading the writings of Saul Alinsky, which came to form the basis for his belief in the need to involve the middle class, with its political influence and economic power, in support of labor. Rogers describes his own objective as to "disorganize the power structure,"[21] or elsewhere as "organizing workers" and "disorganizing companies."[22]

Rogers was characterized in a 1985 profile by *The New York Times* as a barrel-chested man with a mustache who leads a "monkish" existence that some likened to Ralph Nader's. He lived at the time in an inexpensive bachelor apartment on New York's Lower East Side, spending his free time on his hobbies of running and lifting weights.[23] Today he lives in a Harlem coop apartment, and works from an office near NYU. One observer described Rogers as "a firebrand with a genius for publicity and motivation."[24] Although we do not wish to get too far ahead of our story, it is important to understand Ray Rogers and what he brought to the labor movement and, more particularly, to the J.P. Stevens campaign where he earned his reputation and set his life's course. This is best accomplished by considering his own words. Among them, in chronological order covering about two decades:

> We must confront giant corporate capital with workers' capital. We must confront interlocking corporate power with interlocking workers' power.[25]

> Workers' struggles are power struggles. Money is a tremendous source of power. They must have much greater control over it.[26]

Powerful institutions are both economic and political animals, and they must be attacked in both the economic and political spheres.[27]

The labor movement has the only real institutional power to pull off a nonviolent revolution.[28]

What I did is I took the power, all the power that Stevens had behind it, and I broke it down into segments that we could deal with, that we could confront and defeat.[29]

The goal of a corporate campaign is to polarize the entire corporate and financial community away from a primary target, thus pulling its most crucial underpinnings out from underneath it.[30]

We're moving from a time when [management] pits worker against worker to one where it's board member against board member and corporation against corporation.[31]

Anybody who is a stockholder is part owner of a company and is responsible for its actions.[32]

The only way to stop a corporate campaign is to create a dictatorship that wipes out workers' right to free speech.[33]

Ray Rogers scared ACTWU President Murray Finley, who was reluctant to bring him into the Stevens campaign and kept him on a tight leash, partly out of fear he would open the union to allegations it was engaged in an illegal secondary boycott.[34] But the struggle against the textile giant had been underway since 1963. Stevens was seen as the linchpin of the Southern textile mills and as vulnerable in part because its facilities were mostly concentrated in a relatively small geographic area.[35] When, in the wake of the Farah settlement, the small and weak Textile Workers Union merged with the ACWU to form the Amalgamated Clothing and Textile Workers Union (ACTWU), it was with the hope and expectation that the larger and more powerful union could bring the effort to a successful conclusion. Rogers turned out to have the keys to that kingdom.

In a contemporaneous interview, Rogers described himself as applying "political campaign technology" to labor–management relations. But as we can see in retrospect, it was the blending of campaign technology (i.e., strategic communication) with the perspectives and newly developing tools of Alinsky and the New Left that really accounted for the power of the new approach. In fact, the Stevens campaign brought Rogers together with one of the principal architects of the new anticorporate research, SDS veteran and

NACLA and CDE cofounder Michael Locker. The Corporate Data Exchange provided the ACTWU with a shareholder profile of Stevens, and Locker, along with Stephen Abrecht, with whom he would soon form a consulting partnership, advised the union on its attack strategy.[36] Rogers and Locker would join forces again in a later campaign against Eastern Air Lines. Rogers also met his own future partner, Ed Allen, during the Stevens campaign. In 1981, the year after Stevens settled, the two formed the first consulting firm devoted to the conduct of union attacks, Corporate Campaigns, Inc.[37]

The Stevens campaign was constructed around precisely the sort of power structure research that was anticipated in the ERAP Pine Hill discussions in 1964 and first codified in the NACLA *Research Methodology Guide*, to which Locker contributed the chapter on anticorporate campaigns. The outline of such an analysis was clearly captured by Rogers as he reflected on the Steven's campaign in a 1985 interview with William Serrin of *The New York Times*:

> For six weeks, he recalls, he studied his target, drawing a circle to represent Stevens and arrows pointing toward the center to represent every conceivable way to apply pressure. He wanted to make his attacks personal; that is, to single out Stevens's executives and supporters in the financial community, and embarrass them with the association.[38]

In effect, Rogers began by identifying all of the key stakeholder relationships of the target company, assessing the strengths and weaknesses of each, and devising ways to exploit the weaknesses. This is the classic model of the contemporary corporate campaign, and it was present in the very first truly comprehensive effort. In the years since, this model has been refined and tested, and new strategies and tactics have been developed to apply it. However, the basic conceptualization of the campaign as a confrontation with an interlocking corporate power structure has endured.

In the Stevens campaign, which began in earnest in 1976 and continued until the company agreed to recognize the ACTWU in 1980, the strategy played out much as advertised. Rogers first targeted Manufacturers Hanover Trust, on whose board James Finley, Steven's chairman, sat. Finley was forced to decline reelection to the board and also to resign from the board of New York Life. Shortly afterward, David Mitchell, chairman of Avon Products, resigned from both the Manufacturers Hanover board and the board of Stevens as well. "Ray was saying he would get this director and that director to resign, and everyone was skeptical," William Patterson, national field director of the textile union, said of the effort. "Then, all of a sudden, they started falling, and everyone was awed."[39] Rogers then turned his attention to Metropolitan Life, one of Stevens' principal lenders. The pressure against the insurer led its chairman, Richard Shinn, to play a central role in the backstage maneuvering that eventually produced a settlement.[40]

The events were not nearly as bloodless as this brief accounting might suggest. Manufacturers Hanover, for example, was threatened with the withdrawal of union and pension funds, which, by one estimate, might have totaled as much as $1 billion.[41] In dealing with Metropolitan Life, which held $111 million of Stevens debt, the union proposed an alternative slate of candidates for the company's board. In doing so, it cited a little-used New York state law under which the company would have had to conduct an election among all of its 23 million policyholders that was estimated to cost approximately $9 million.[42] Other companies in the line of fire, either of the union or consumers' groups that threatened sympathy boycotts, included Seaman's Bank for Savings, investment banker Goldman Sachs, and the Sperry Corporation.[43] Of particular interest in the context of our larger narrative is the role of the church in this effort. Five church organizations affiliated with ICCR filed a pair of proxy resolutions that closely resembled that sent earlier to Farah Manufacturing. The resolutions called on the company to report to shareholders on its labor policies and on its equal employment practices. ICCR sent a highly critical four-page report to 8,000 specially targeted shareholders. The company's 1977 annual meeting was attended by many church and labor activists, including Coretta Scott King. Meanwhile an estimated 3,500 people similar in composition to those who had demonstrated outside Manufacturers Hanover in 1965 marched outside the meeting.[44]

Vogel summarizes the Stevens campaign as composed of four elements: the aggressive use of the NLRB and the courts through the filing of unfair labor practice claims, the extensive consumer boycott organized by the AFL–CIO, a strike by the employees, and an elaborate campaign of proxy challenges. It was this latter component, as we have seen, that attracted most of Rogers' attention and that gave the campaign its unique character. Rogers saw the Stevens contest as one between quickness and cunning on the one hand and sheer brute force on the other. He once observed,

> It was like Muhammad Ali doing Sonny Liston. He jabbed him here and he jabbed him there, he danced around, and boom boom boom, weakened him, always knowing that he was going to come in with a final knockout blow, but he could not take his adversary head-on, he had to figure out ways to go in the back door before he could actually deal that knock-out blow.[45]

Edward Silver, an attorney whose firm represented Stevens against the ACTWU, acknowledged the power of the corporate campaign. "These new approaches can be very effective," he said, "especially if they embarrass the officers of the company or of the banks it does business with."[46] But the best indicator of the power of the corporate campaign from the point of view of the target is found in the contract that Stevens eventually signed with the union. That document contained what came to be known as the *Ray Rogers clause*; it prohibited the union from engaging in "corporate campaign-style activities" against the company for the duration of the agreement. Companies that felt Rogers' sting in later years—most notably Hormel—sought similar protections.[47]

In the longer view, the Stevens campaign may have been a significant victory for the ACTWU, but it nevertheless took a toll on the union. The drive to organize Stevens is estimated to have cost more than $13 million between 1963 and 1980, most of that in the final, corporate-campaign years. From June 1976 to the end of 1980, the union's assets dropped from $21 million to $13 million, and in 3 of those years, expenditures exceeded income. Membership in the ACTWU dropped from about 500,000 in 1976, when the merged union was formed, to 402,000 in 1982, two years after the Stevens settlement. Although the union gained the right to organize 3,500 workers in 12 Stevens plants—about 10% of the total Stevens workforce—it soon found itself losing more certification elections than it was winning.[48] The corporate campaign had yet to demonstrate that it had the power to reverse the long-term trends noted in chapter 2.

That did not deter Ray Rogers, however. Two months after resigning from the union in October 1980, he and fellow ACTWU campaigner Ed Allen formed a new consulting firm, Corporate Campaign, Inc., to carry forward their efforts. By August 1981, the company had a staff of 15.[49] In a 1992 interview, Rogers summarized the character of the firm and its mission:

> Corporate Campaign is set up as a team of professional troubleshooters. We're experts in all facets of political and community organization, communications, public relations, research, analysis, strategy development. We maintain a database of more than 70,000 organizations, including every labor union, religious, civil rights and other groups sympathetic to labor and progressive causes.[50]

Corporate Campaign's slogan is "Tools to Confront Power with Power." In effect, Rogers created a *company* that embodies the philosophy, perspective, methodology, and intent of the New Left as set forth a quarter century earlier.

Among the targets of Corporate Campaign's campaigns in behalf of unions over the years have been New York Air, Hormel, Campbell's Soups, A. E. Staley, International Paper, Brown and Sharpe, Texaco, Brown & Root, Eastern Air Lines, and Washington Gas Light Company. Union clients have included the Air Line Pilots Association (ALPA), the Transport Workers Union, the International Association of Machinists (IAM), the Oil, Chemical, and Atomic Workers (OCAW), the Farm Labor Organizing Committee (FLOC), the International Union of Gas Workers, and, famously as we shall see, Local P-9 of the United Food and Commercial

Workers (UFCW). In addition, the firm has assisted Greenpeace in a campaign designed to pressure DuPont to stop using ozone-depleting chemicals and another sponsored by the Fund for the Feminist Majority to force Roussell-Uclaf—a joint venture of the French firm Rhone-Poulenc and the German firm Hoechst—to release the drug RU486—the so-called morning-after pill—in the United States.

If Rogers sees himself as a trouble*shooter*, there are those in the labor movement who, even as they adopt his methods, view him instead as a trouble*maker*. Jay Foreman of the UFCW, whose union has had its own confrontation with Rogers, has said, "Ray acts as if he is a Messiah, and that worries me." Robert Harbrant, formerly president of the AFL–CIO's Food and Allied Service Trades Department (FAST) and a strong advocate of the corporate campaign, has also expressed some reservations. "I think some of his ideas are exciting. Some of his ideas, on the other hand, are suicidal."[51]

Rogers also ran afoul of a fellow labor consultant, Victor Kamber, and his company, The Kamber Group. After he founded the firm, Rogers filed with the Patent and Trademark Office to protect the term *corporate campaign* as a registered service mark. He said of the action, "I developed the corporate campaign concept. I even coined the phrase 'corporate campaign.'" In March 1984, however, Kamber protested the filing, in effect blocking Rogers' exclusive claim to the term until the matter was resolved in the courts. In Kamber's view, "It would be as ridiculous as me trying to trademark the title 'political consultant.' He'd like everybody to disappear so that he can have all the business." For its part, the AFL–CIO took a rather different view. Said one labor official of the dispute, the consultants "make it appear to be some sort of magic wand, which it is not—that just takes away credit from the workers who take the risks."[52] By the time the courts ruled in 1985, the term had come into such general use that the issue was moot.[53]

HORMEL: A DEFINING MOMENT FOR CORPORATE CAMPAIGNS AND FOR CORPORATE CAMPAIGN, INC.

As we have seen, Ray Rogers has proved a rather controversial fellow—not only in the eyes of the companies he has confronted, but within the labor movement. Part of that controversy is undoubtedly attributable to his role as innovator, which has marked him from the outset as a lightening rod for criticism. Even within the labor movement, there was, until the 1995 election of activist AFL–CIO president John Sweeney, a great reluctance to engage in the sort of fundamental economic warfare that Rogers routinely champions. Part of it is attributable to either jealousy or genuine dismay arising from the high visibility of Rogers' participation—which he certainly encourages. Many traditional laborites have seen this as detracting from the issues and the workers involved in the disputes that he enters. Part of the controversy is also at some level ideological. The top labor leadership of the 1970s, 1980s and early 1990s was, as we have seen, very mainstream in its politics. Ray Rogers is not. Rather, he is the embodiment of the early New Left, with its antagonism to the corporation as a social entity and its willingness to raise its issues in the streets, to which he has added the full toolbox of the strategic communicator. Just as the New Left spoke in the NACLA research manual of infiltrating the labor movement, which they saw as overly supportive of the status quo, Rogers has been willing to take on the labor establishment. There are those in organized labor who share this view, but there are many who regard it as impractical and counterproductive. This parting of the ways between what we might think of as the ideologues and the pragmatists in organized labor was exposed in the Rogers-led corporate campaign against George A. Hormel & Company, the Minnesota meatpacker.

Hormel was an unlikely target. Although there had been a bitter strike at the company's flagship Austin, Minnesota, plant in the 1930s, the next half century was marked by cooperation between Hormel management and Local P-9 of what eventually became the United Food and Commercial Workers union. The company provided a guaranteed annual wage, focused on quality, and, through the Hormel Foundation, which owned nearly half of the company's stock, channeled substantial money back into the Austin community. That began to change in 1978 when the company told the union that it needed concessions so that it could build a modern new plant in the town. A deal was worked out under which the union agreed to a 7-year no-strike contract, a 20% increase in production, and the creation of a fund from the workers' incentive pay that would loan Hormel $20 million to help finance the plant. In return, Hormel provided job guarantees and a promise that wages in the new plant would at least equal those in the old. In 1981, the company asked for a wage freeze, to which P-9 agreed, in part because the UFCW distributed a contract summary stating there would be no reduction in wage rates through 1985.

The new plant—the most efficient in the industry—opened in 1982 and produced record profits for Hormel. Nonetheless, even as the company reported profits of $29 million in 1984 and told *Business Week* that it was prepared to come up with $100 million for acquisitions, management went back to the workers seeking still more concessions, this time in the form of a 23% wage cut, which, it said, was permitted under the 1978 agreement because the industry-wide wage structure had changed in the interim. Local P-9 rebelled, but in arbitration the union was told the company's interpretation of the 1978 contract was correct. Then, adding fuel to the fire, the local learned that the protective language the UFCW had circulated in 1981 when it agreed to a wage freeze was not in the final contract the international union signed with the company. Seeing itself as betrayed by both parties, P-9 determined to take on the company and, in October 1984, hired Ray Rogers to help.[54]

In August 1985, with the reluctant approval of the international union, members of Local P-9 walked off the job, and Austin became a war zone reminiscent in some ways of the most bitter labor battles of earlier eras. There were pickets, demonstrations, and, when the company hired replacement workers, some violence. For a time, Governor Rudy Perpich mobilized the National Guard to maintain order. Members of P-9 tried to generate support, first by traveling to other Hormel plants to encourage job actions and later by traveling around the country to raise funds. Rogers, applying his power-structure analysis, targeted First Bank System, which had one seat on the Hormel Board and managed the company's pension system. In this instance, however, the effort yielded no results. Indeed, it led to the filing of an unfair labor practice claim by the company, which charged Local P-9 with staging an illegal secondary boycott. The NLRB ruled on February 28, 1986, that the union's actions were, in fact, illegal.[55]

Following this ruling, in March 1986, the UFCW withdrew its support for the strike and ordered the Local to return to work. That set off a highly visible legal and public relations battle, with Rogers and Local president Jim Guyette taking on the international union and, by extension, the decay in labor's strength that we noted in the preceding chapter. In many ways, the Hormel campaign became a symbol of the conflict within the labor movement.

Hormel also came in some measure to symbolize the relationship between labor and the Left. In the context of our discussion of the differences between New and Old Left in chapter 1, Rogers can be seen as embodying the perspective and approach of the New Left. Yet he has never presented himself publicly in expressly ideological terms. It seems reasonable to believe, then, that despite any compatibility of interests he might have had with the New Left worldview as we have defined it, he had no stake whatsoever in the internecine fighting within the Left against which the early SDSers rebelled. So it is perhaps not surprising that, once the schism between P-9 and the UFCW had occurred, Rogers and the P-9 leaders were willing to accept support from any source that offered it. In this case, there were several Old Left interests that did just that, among them two Trotskyist groups, the Socialist Workers Party and the Workers' League, and two Communist groups, the Communist Party and the Communist Labor Party.[56] As Hardy Green, who participated in the effort as a staff member of Corporate Campaigns, Inc., summarized the role of such groups,

> Local P-9 could not have done without the left, broadly defined. In Austin and in support groups around the country, left-leaning liberals, nonaligned socialists, and some members of leftist organizations made indispensable contributions to the cause....[57]

Although scattered Locals in various unions such as the United Auto Workers offered strong backing to Local P-9, this willingness to court groups that were far outside the mainstream drove a substantial ideological wedge between the Austin Local and most of the labor establishment—not just that of the UFCW, but the leadership of the AFL–CIO as well. Such ties were contrary to the entire thrust of the movement since at least the 1940s, and they were not to be tolerated. They also provided a convenient device for isolating Local P-9 and for isolating Ray Rogers. Rogers poured gasoline on these flames when he observed in an interview during the strike,

> No question there is a need for some sort of structure that can challenge situations where international unions are not doing the job or can be shown to be in collusion with companies to undermine rank-and-file workers.[58]

In the end, the UFCW placed the Local into receivership, and the pickets came down in June 1986. The union and Hormel agreed to a contract on August 28th of that year—a contract that did not guarantee that striking workers could return to their jobs. The agreement was announced at a news conference 100 miles away from Austin because the UFCW feared that P-9 militants, who opposed the agreement, would disrupt the event. Indeed, by then the displaced leadership of P-9 had already formed a new union, the North American Meatpackers Union, and announced plans to contest the certification of the re-established UFCW local at the Austin plant.[59] The coda was put on Rogers' own post-Hormel relationship with organized labor by UFCW spokesperson Alan Zack, who said of the consultant, "I don't see [him] as a threat except to the jobs of union members who pursue his all-or-nothing strategy."[60]

ENDNOTES

1. James Miller, *Democracy Is in the Streets* (New York: Simon and Schuster, 1987), pp. 226–227.
2. Todd Gitlin, *The Sixties: Years of Hope, Days of Rage*, revised edition (New York: Bantam, 1993), p. 179.
3. David Vogel, *Lobbying the Corporation: Citizen Challenges to Business Authority* (New York: Basic Books, 1978), pp. 24–25.
4. Ibid., pp. 27–30. The quoted statement appears on p. 30.
5. Miller, op. cit., p. 228.
6. Gitlin, op. cit., p. 317.
7. Quoted in C. Gregg Singer, *The Unholy Alliance* (New Rochelle, NY: Arlington House, 1975), p. 23.
8. Vogel, p. 162.
9. Quoted in Vogel, op. cit., p. 163.
10. Ibid., pp. 164 165.

11. Ibid., p. 167.
12. Ibid., pp. 171 173.
13. Ibid., pp. 173 174.
14. Robert McG. Thomas, Jr., "Murray H. Finley, Labor Leader for Textile Workers, Dies at 73," *The New York Times*, August 3, 1995, p. B11; and Robert D. McFadden, "2 Get Ready to Lock Horns at The Daily News," *The New York Times*, January 12, 1993, p. B3.
15. This account of the Farah strike and boycott is based on articles that appeared in *The New York Times* on the following dates: May 18, 1972 (p. 50), July 27, 1972 (p. 18), July 30, 1972 (p. 4:5), September 11, 1972 (p. 57), September 14, 1972 (p. 43), December 12, 1972 (p. 62), December 18, 1972 (p. 33), February 18, 1973 (p. 4:4), June 16, 1973 (p. 23), October 20, 1973 (p. 17), December 16, 1973 (p. 53), and February 25, 1974 (p. 36).
16. Charles R. Perry, *Union Corporate Campaigns* (Philadelphia: Industrial Research Unit of the Wharton School, University of Pennsylvania, 1987), p. 1.
17. Vogel, op. cit., pp. 153–154.
18. "Labor Takes Notice of Tactics by Organizer of J.P. Stevens Workers," *The New York Times*, November 30, 1980, p. 68.
19. Ibid.
20. "A Boycott Battle to Win the South," *Business Week*, December 6, 1976, p. 80.
21. William Serrin, "A Gadfly for Labor: Ray Rogers; Trying for a Comeback as a Union Hero," *The New York Times* (October 6, 1985), p. 3:6; William Serrin, "Labor Maverick: Ray Rogers; An Organizer Beset by Problems," *The New York Times*, September 19, 1982), p. 3:6; Alfred Siewers, "Labor Organizer Ray Rogers: 'Fighting Power With Power,'" *Christian Science Monitor*, August 13, 1981, p. B15; and Kenneth C. Crowe, "Contract Put Out on Zuckerman: Guild hires a labor guerrilla warrior to take on boss," *Newsday*, January 12, 1993, p. 33.
22. William Serrin, "Organized Labor is Increasingly Less So," *The New York Times*, November 18, 1984, p. 4:3.
23. Serrin, October 6, 1985, op. cit.
24. Hal Hinson, " 'American Dream': The Strike That Struck Out," *Washington Post*, April 27, 1992, p. D1.
25. Quoted in A.H. Raskin, "Show 'Em the Clenched Fist!" *Forbes*, October 2, 1978, p. 31.
26. During an appearance on the MacNeil–Lehrer NewsHour as transcribed in *The American Banker*, August 8, 1979, p. 4.
27. Quoted in "Labor Takes Notice of Tactics by Organizer of J.P. Stevens Workers," *The New York Times*, November 30, 1980, p. 68.
28. Ibid.
29. Quoted in Siewers, op. cit.
30. Quoted in Stephen Szkotak, "The Nation's Longest Running Major Strike Highlights New Labor Strategy, Industry Woes," *United Press International*, August 25, 1982.
31. Quoted in William K. Rashbaum, "Paperworkers' union: Don't answer when Avon's calling," *United Press International*, July 14, 1988.

32. Quoted in "Eastern Union Pickets Institutions," *Money Management Letter*, Vol. XIV, No. 17 (August 21, 1989), p.2.
33. Quoted in James L. Tyson, "As Strikes Lose Potency, Unions Turn to Tactics Outside the Workplace," *Christian Science Monitor*, February 16, 1996, p. 1.
34. "The ripples spreading from the Stevens pact," *Business Week*, November 3, 1980, p. 107.
35. Barry E. Truchill, *Capital-Labor Relations in the U.S. Textile Industry* (New York: Praeger, 1988), p. 139.
36. Vogel, op. cit., p. 139; and Wendy Cooper, "Labor's New Drive to Learn About the Bottom Line," *The New York Times*, July 24, 1983, p. 3:8.
37. Serrin, October 6, 1985, op. cit.
38. Ibid.
39. Quoted in Jonathan Tasini, "For the Unions, a New Weapon," *The New York Times*, June 12, 1988, 6:24, passim.
40. Truchill, op. cit., pp. 141–142.
41. Serrin, November 18, 1984, op. cit.; and Truchill, loc. cit.
42. "The Picket Line Gives Way to Sophisticated New Tactics," *Business Week*, April 16, 1984, p. 116; and Doug McInnis, "A New Chill on Organizing Efforts at Southern Textile Mills," *The New York Times*, May 30, 1982, p. 3:5.
43. McInnis, op. cit.
44. Vogel, op. cit., pp. 216–217.
45. Quoted in Siewers, op. cit.
46. Quoted in Aaron Bernstein, "The Unions Are Learning to Hit Where It Hurts," *Business Week*, March 17, 1986, p. 112.
47. Serrin, October 6, 1985, op. cit.
48. McInnis, op. cit.
49. Siewers, op. cit.
50. Quoted in Annette Fuentes, "Why 'Buy American' Sells Workers Short," *Newsday*, February 19, 1992, p. 39.
51. Quoted in William Serrin, October 6, 1985, op. cit.
52. Bill Keller, "For Union Ally, It's All in the Name," *The New York Times*, May 2, 1984, p. A24.
53. Perry, op. cit., p. 2.
54. Nicholas Mills, "Why Local P-9 is going it alone; the Hormel strike," *The Nation*, April 26, 1986, Vol. 242, p. 578.
55. Hardy Green, *On Strike At Hormel: The Struggle for a Democratic Labor Movement* (Philadelphia: Temple University Press, 1990), pp. 77–78, 101–106.
56. Ibid., pp. 111–115.
57. Ibid., p. 113.
58. Quoted in William Serrin, "The Hormel Strike: A Union Divided," *The New York Times*, April 21, 1986, p. A12.
59. Kenneth B. Noble, "Union Says Contract Does Not Guarantee Jobs for Strikers," *The New York Times*, August 29, 1986, p. A10.
60. Quoted in Kirk Victor, "Striking Out in the '80s," *National Journal*, January 7, 1989, Vol. 21, No. 1, p. 18.

4

THE CORPORATE CAMPAIGN
COMES OF AGE

By 1980, when the J.P. Stevens campaign ended, it was clear that this new phenomenon would become a commonplace of labor–management relations. Whatever their misgivings—and from Hormel we know that they were substantial—labor leaders could not afford to reject out of hand a technique that had demonstrated the potential to enhance their influence. Either with Ray Rogers or without him, labor would find a way to employ the corporate campaign. In the event, that is precisely what happened—the corporate campaign developed along two overlapping but relatively distinctive tracks: one with Rogers and one without him. In this chapter, we take a brief tour of some of the more noteworthy campaigns.

CORPORATE CAMPAIGNS ENTER THE MAINSTREAM

We can get a general idea of the extent to which campaigns have become commonplace from an examination of Fig. 4.1, which reports the number of references to *corporate campaign* (adjusted to minimize nonrelevant references, such as those to corporate campaign contributions) in a broad range of media from 1974, when the Farah campaign ended, through 1998, a period of 25 years. The figure shows three stages of development that generally correspond with the actual level of corporate campaign activity and

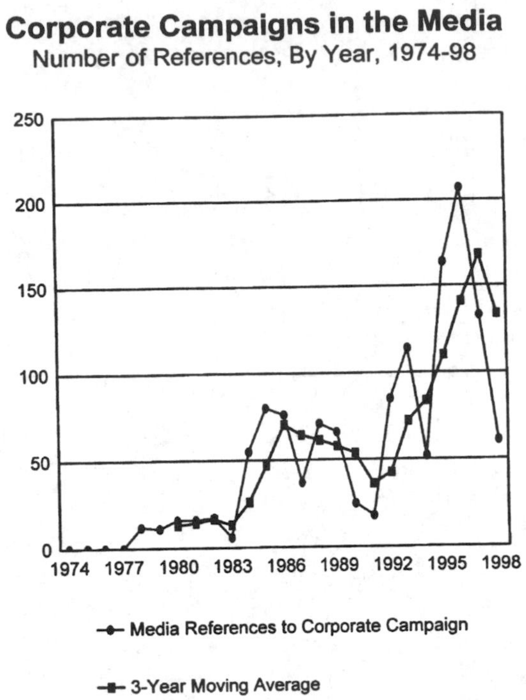

Corporate Campaigns in the Media
Number of References, By Year, 1974-98

-●- Media References to Corporate Campaign

-■- 3-Year Moving Average

Figure 4.1

that are most clearly evident in the relatively less volatile 3-year moving average. From 1977 to 1983—the period of the Stevens campaign and a few other early efforts—the references are quite minimal. From 1984 to 1991, the corporate campaign phenomenon becomes more visible, but remains of only modest interest to journalists. After 1992, however, the corporate campaign becomes far more visible partly, it would seem, because of the immense publicity given to one such campaign, which was waged by the UFCW against the Food Lion supermarket chain which was energized by a union-inspired expose' on ABC News' *PrimeTime Live* broadcast at the very end of 1992, and partly, especially after 1995, by the increasingly public commitment of the leadership of the AFL–CIO to the corporate campaign approach as a primary organizing strategy.

In truth, the corporate campaign rubric today may suggest that more is going on in any particular labor dispute than a detailed analysis would support. That is true because the term itself retains the power to frighten the management of targeted companies and is therefore bandied about by unions in an effort at intimidation that falls far short of a genuinely comprehensive campaign. It is also true because in public parlance the term has now come to take in a wide range of boycott, public relations, legislative,

and regulatory activities that may not rise to the level of an assault on fundamental stakeholder relationships. So there are genuine boundary issues to
be addressed. Moreover, even as some full-fledged campaigns are lengthy
and diverse, others are brief and narrow. There is, in fact, no mold for the
corporate campaign. Each one is different depending on its unique mix of
participants, objectives, and potentialities.

   That said, the corporate campaign is nevertheless a genuine and identifiable phenomenon if one has sufficient access to information about players
and events. There have been many such campaigns launched. Appendix A
represents an effort to list known corporate campaigns initiated by unions
that occurred sometime between 1974 and 1999. This listing (of 162 campaigns) is unlikely to be complete, either as to companies that have been targeted, unions that have employed these techniques, dates (which are
necessarily approximate or uncertain), or other information that is included. Corporate campaigns initiated by entities other than unions—and
the number of such actions is increasing—are not included in Appendix A,
but are addressed later in this book.

SELECTED EXAMPLES OF CORPORATE CAMPAIGNS

Little purpose would be served by reviewing all of the campaigns listed in
Appendix A in detail. However, it is a worthwhile exercise to review the
highlights of a few campaigns that serve as exemplars of particular dimensions of the phenomenon and that collectively can provide a sense of the enterprise—and of how it has developed over the years. In the balance of this
chapter, we undertake that review. We then return to some of these campaigns as well as others in later chapters to illustrate the strategies and tactics of the corporate campaign.

International Paper: Power Analysis in Play

When International Paper (IP) opened its plant in Androscoggin, Maine, in
the early 1960s, the company recognized three local unions: two Locals of
the United Paperworkers International Union (UPIU) to represent the
skilled and unskilled workers in the mill—Local 1939 and Local 14, respectively—and a non-UPIU Local to represent workers in the associated power
plant. Seeing themselves as distinctive from other IP unions because of the
modernity of their facility, the two UPIU Locals held themselves out of
multiple facility agreements negotiated between the international and the
company. Because these "multiples" helped build the union's power by
consolidating negotiations (the negotiating equivalent of what we have earlier referred to as organizing at the wholesale level), their refusal to join in
cast the Androscoggin Locals as loners. For a time, however, their separat-

ist approach was productive, because they were routinely able to bargain for compensation superior to that in the multiples.[1]

In 1983, in line with the general Reagan-era toughening of corporations' approach to dealing with unions, IP sought major concessions from the Androscoggin locals, which they resisted. But after several months and the first strike vote in the mill's history, the union agreed to a number of concessions in return for a small pay increase. Afterward, the two UPIU Locals merged into a successor Local 14, which was headed by William Meserve, who had previously presided over Local 1939. The Local then streamlined its structure, organizing new committees and expanding the numbers of shop stewards and union officers.[2]

IP continued to press the union for concessions on pensions and work rules at other facilities. When the company opened a new mill in Louisiana, it went so far as to campaign against the union in a representation election. This marked a significant change in the corporate culture. It also motivated the UPIU to call on Ray Rogers to conduct a corporate campaign against IP, even over the privately expressed objections of the ACTWU, which by then was feuding with its progeny. The short-lived campaign opened at the April 12, 1983, IP shareholders' meeting, where Rogers had arranged to provide proxies to a large number of unionists, environmentalists, and feminists who then peppered management with hostile questions about the company's labor policies. One speaker, noting CEO Edwin Gee's membership on the board of American Home Products, at the time under attack for selling infant formula in Third World countries, referred to IP officials as "baby killers." Two weeks later, the union and the company reached an agreement, and the campaign was called off. The union agreed to break up its multiple bargaining units—thereby weakening its bargaining position for the long run—to accept the closing of inefficient mills and to accept more flexible work rules. In return, the union believed, the company agreed not to attempt any further give-backs. However, the company denied having made such a commitment and soon began implementing new programs designed to speed production. The seeds of a more bitter conflict were sown.[3] By early 1987, in a conflict centered on the IP mill in Mobile, Alabama, they had begun to sprout. As the company continued to impose ever more restrictive terms on the union, on March 20, the UPIU once again turned to the corporate campaign to strike back. On March 21, the company locked out all of the union workers in Mobile, operating the mill with supervisors and replacement workers.[4] A new battle was joined.

Although some in the union wanted to bring in Ray Rogers once again, Rogers' dispute with the AFL–CIO establishment had deepened in the wake of the Hormel campaign. To maintain federation support, the UPIU decided to bring in the politically more acceptable Kamber Group instead. Kamber carried the explicit approval of the AFL–CIO's Industrial Unions Department. Indeed, Kamber had reportedly assisted the UFCW in its dealings with Local P-9 during the Hormel dispute. In support of the locked-out workers in Mobile, 98% of the members of Local 14 voted to walk off the job.[5] The strikes at Androscoggin and two other mills began in mid-June. In response, the company hired more than 1,000 replacement workers, whom it declared to be permanent employees.[6] IP was ready; it is not clear the same was true of the union.

In March 1987, the Maine AFL–CIO brought in yet another consultant, Peter Kellman, a friend of Ray Rogers, to assist Local 14. Kellman was what is known as a *red diaper baby*—a child of Old Left radicals who grew up in an activist family and worked in the civil rights movement in the 1960s, including a stint with the Student Nonviolent Coordinating Committee during the period when it was closely allied with the SDS. As an organizer with New England's environmentalist Clamshell Alliance, Kellman worked to increase the interaction between environmental and labor activists—a natural fit, as it turned out, for a corporate campaign against a paper company.[7]

The Local set up a picket line that saw its share of shouting, rock throwing, and the like, but proved ineffective at keeping out replacement workers and deliveries, was a source of negative publicity for the union, and drained the union's limited resources. Kellman argued that it should be limited to one or two pickets at a time. But Meserve and others in the union saw it as symbolically important. Members of other unions, college students, and politicians walked the line as a means to express support for the strikers.[8] But the picket line was never going to defeat IP. That was the job of the corporate campaign.

The campaign, however, was languishing—or at least that was the view of the strikers. While IP took the initiative in shaping public opinion, with a particular emphasis on picket-line violence, the Kamber Group worked quietly behind the scenes, issuing press releases, forwarding financial information about the company to reporters and financial analysts, and placing pro-union advertising. The firm also worked with the UPIU staff to produce a newsletter, *The Coordinated Bargainer*, that was distributed to the IP locals.[9] This relatively staid approach to the corporate campaign, which reflected Kamber's roots as a relatively traditional public relations firm with a labor and progressive clientele, differed sharply from that of the more confrontational Ray Rogers—precisely the difference the AFL–CIO leadership of the era desired. However, it was not what the leaders of Local 14 had in mind.

Matters came to a head in November 1987 when Meserve forged an agreement among the striking or locked-out Locals and then informed the international that, if it did not replace Kamber with Rogers, the Locals would hire him on their own. They saw his approach—with its systematic attack on the company's interlocking relationships and power structures—as far more likely to achieve success. Late in the month, with UPIU approval, Rogers traveled to the various Locals, where he gave a rousing speech and presented a plan of action based on an assessment of IP's financial position. By December, Rogers had displaced Kamber, in some measure it appears, to preserve the power structure within the UPIU itself, which was sharply divided by the decision.[10]

IP-2, Rogers' second effort at the company, had much more of a chance to develop than had its predecessor, but in the end it was less successful. The campaign opened in January 1988 with the announcement that Coca-Cola and the Bank of Boston—both tied to IP through Donald McHenry, a director of each company—would be targeted for action.[11] This was followed by a caravan through New England to enlist support. In Pennsylvania, workers from the Lock Haven mill lobbied the state legislature while others distributed literature door to door. Here, Hershey Foods and PNC Financial became secondary targets of the campaign.[12] More caravans traveled from Mobile through the South in February. In the meantime, Local 14 turned its attention to the Bank of Boston, where noisy demonstrations were conducted and where, at one point, an environmental group sympathetic to the strikers even placed dead fish in a safety deposit box to protest IP's pollution.[13] One Iron Workers Local withdrew $4.7 million from the bank in response.[14] The union sent a campaign flyer to Georgetown University where McHenry was a professor, while faculty members at Mt. Holyoke College, where he served as a trustee, invited him to the campus to debate representatives of Local 14.

The union also targeted Avon Products, on whose board IP board member Stanley Gault also served, calling for a boycott of the company's products. The bank and the soft drink maker were also subject to boycott calls, but IP was not. Roger attributed this strategy to his effort to leverage big players with limited stakes in a dispute, who would therefore be relatively easy to move, into points of pressure against the primary target, whose actions the union alone was powerless to influence.[15] It was the quintessence of the Rogers-style campaign.

The campaign was called to a halt in March 1988—just as consumer activist Ralph Nader was poised to add his support—at the insistence of the international, whose leaders had never been especially comfortable with Rogers. The impetus for this decision was an offer from the company to negotiate with the union if it would terminate Rogers. Although the striking Locals wanted to carry on, the UPIU leadership was adamant, and all of the campaign activities ceased.[16] The corporate campaign clearly put IP on the defensive. However, in the end, whether it was begun too late, ended too soon, or was simply not effective, it did not work.

In October 1988, the strike was called off without a vote of the workers, many of whom had been replaced in the interim. Even as some returned to jobs at IP, there was worse to come. During the winter of 1988, one of the replacement workers had filed a petition to decertify Local 14. After some delays by the union, which hoped in the interim to return more of its members to the company workforce and gain votes against the petition, the vote was finally held in 1992. Local 14 was decertified by a vote of 660 to 380. Subsequent representation elections in 1995 and 1996 failed to reinstate the union.[17] Perhaps the greatest irony of all is that, even as the striking workers at three IP mills were being replaced, the NLRB ruled that the company could not outsource work being done by the workers it had locked out in Mobile. Those workers, in sympathy with whom the other Locals had struck, returned to their jobs.[18]

Beverly Enterprises: The Never-Ending Story[19]

The granddaddy of ongoing corporate campaigns is that being waged by the Service Employees International Union (SEIU) and the UFCW against Beverly Enterprises, the nation's largest nursing home operator. The Beverly campaign went public in January 1983 when the two unions launched a nationwide organizing campaign at the company's then nearly 900 nursing homes and at this writing was still underway. At the outset, the SEIU represented workers at 21 Beverly facilities and the UFCW at 10. Beverly, however, was aggressive in its opposition to further unionization of its workforce and trained its executives in union-avoidance techniques. Furthermore, even at organized facilities, the unions believed Beverly was dragging its feet in contract negotiations.[20]

Although the early years of this campaign saw many initiatives in venues ranging from Wall Street to Capitol Hill, the power of the campaign came from an early test of what is now a common thematic in the health care industry—the juxtaposition of the quality of care with corporate economic values. From the start, this issue—defined as the "corporatization of healthcare"—threatened the company's image not only among the general public, but with the state and federal governments on which its business was heavily dependent. Initially it led the company to try to come to terms with the unions.[21] In March 1984, the parties reached an agreement to form a more positive relationship.[22] That agreement was not destined to last.

In the years since, Beverly and the unions have engaged in an enduring conflict peppered by allegations that the company abuses its clientele and its employees with equal ardor. The allegations filed between 1986 and 1994 were consolidated by the NLRB in a series of complaints known as Beverly I, II, and III.[23] The centerpiece of this campaign to date has been a report entitled *System Breakdown*, issued in behalf of the two unions by the AFL–CIO's Food and Allied Service Trades Department (FAST) in January 1995. A classic of its genre and, as we see elsewhere in this volume, a model for future reports, the white paper combined statistics on the performance of Beverly's nursing homes in Missouri with graphic accounts of residents tied to their beds for hours at a time, soaked in their own urine or excrement, and riddled with large bedsores. On publication of the report, the unions and FAST then undertook a campaign to bring the regulatory wrath of the states and the federal government to bear on the company, both by increased inspection of its records and facilities and by imposing higher staffing levels on its facilities. Although unionized facilities also came in for some criticism, the UFCW had a ready retort. Said a spokesperson, "We hear from workers we represent nearly every day that they want to give the best resident care possible, but Beverly isn't giving them the tools they need to do their jobs."[24] In February 1996, the union released another report, this time focusing on the state of Alabama, as part of a campaign that also involved mobilizing family members of nursing home residents.[25]

In addition, Beverly was employed as a test case for an SEIU ergonomics initiative. A series of complaints about back injuries related to lifting patients in nursing homes was consolidated and tried before an Administrative Law Judge in 1994. The decision was a setback for the union, however, because it found that effective standards for lifting had not been established and that such lifting had not been clearly linked to lower back pain among employees.[26] At this writing, the case was before by the OSHA Review Commission on appeal.

In 1996, the SEIU also weighed in against Beverly with a whistleblower campaign tied to organizing efforts in Pennsylvania. The union targeted Beverly and two other companies in full-page advertisements that appeared in several newspapers around the country. Its president, Andrew Stern, vowed "to use every means at our disposal to hold healthcare providers accountable to their patients and their workers."[27] In March of that year, the union filed 260 ULPs against Beverly homes in Pennsylvania and attacked the company in flyers and radio commercials.[28] Then in April, the SEIU staged a 3-day strike by some 800 workers at 15 Beverly facilities. Beverly responded by hiring 350 replacement workers to maintain needed patient care, then designated them permanent replacements, which generated yet another round of disputes in the courts and at the NLRB. In mid-April, Democratic members of the state's congressional delegation participated in a Capitol Hill news conference with the SEIU and more than 100 of the replaced workers and, referring to Beverly as a "Lawbreaker on the Loose," called on the company to reinstate them.[29] All of this activity produced the fourth consolidated complaint to be brought against Beverly by the NLRB during the course of the corporate campaign—Beverly IV.[30]

In June 1996, the UFCW and SEIU joined forces to call on Florida Governor Lawton Chiles to prevent Beverly from expanding in his state.[31] In January 1997, the unions issued another white paper—*Bad Care In Beverly's Back Yard*—targeting the company's operations in Arkansas and alleging a pattern of similar problems in nine other states. Against this backdrop, in a May 1997 mailing to all holders of at least 1,000 shares of

Beverly stock, the SEIU urged the company's shareholders to vote against management's slate of directors to "send a strong message to management that poor operating performance and inadequate resident care are closely related and cannot be tolerated."[32] Later that month, at the SEIU's initiative, a congressional town hall meeting was held in Pittsburgh to focus attention and further pressure on Beverly.[33] The Pennsylvania dispute was finally defused when Governor Tom Ridge intervened in late June 1997.[34] In the end, Beverly took back all the striking employees, but the union failed to achieve its three principal objectives—card check, neutrality, and a master agreement—and other terms of the agreement were little different from those available at the outset. Nor did the Pennsylvania agreement end the campaign. In July 1998, Beverly shares fell 41% in value in a single day when the company announced it was the subject of a Medicare-related federal investigation.[35] (That case was later settled when the company agreed to pay a fine of $175 million and to sell 10 of its nursing homes.[36]) A March 1999 article in *The Nation* resurrected the full panoply of anti-Beverly allegations.[37]

This long-running campaign has served as a proving ground for many of the themes, alliances, and strategies that are now typical of the campaign against a number of companies in the health care industry. That it continues nearly two decades after its inception is indicative of the perceived viability of these lines of attack and of the unions' endurance, even where, as in Beverly, they have been slow to advance their interests.

Nike: Attack of the 50-Foot Surrogates

In the early to mid-1980s, American manufacturers were in a race with their Japanese counterparts to establish manufacturing facilities in East Asia. The U.S. balance of trade with such countries as South Korea and Indonesia was pouring forth red ink, and it was clear that this region would be a net exporter of manufactured goods to the American market for many years to come. The choice, as the companies saw it, was either to control this flow of goods or be displaced by it. Their decision, reached in many different corporate boardrooms, was to establish their own East Asian operations even if it meant displacing the jobs of American workers to do it. Between 1980 and 1982, for example, American companies invested $4.8 billion in the region, increasing their stake by 71%. Still they were falling behind the Japanese, who invested $5.8 billion during the same period and held a 25% lead in the value of East Asian plant and facilities. Just as Asia had replaced Europe as the dominant trading partner of the United States over the preceding two decades, Asian countries around the Pacific Rim were coming to dominate the Asian trade, displacing Japan. The new interest in East Asia was encouraged by the Reagan administration through changes in tax and other policies. Among the companies riding this wave was the shoe manufacturer, Nike, which by 1984 had seven factories in China and others in South Korea.[38]

In 1979, Lucas Sasmito, who owned a factory on the outskirts of Jakarta, imported several pairs of Nike athletic shoes, paid the duty and registered the trademark for his company under Indonesian law, reverse-engineered the shoes, and began producing "Nikes", complete with the "swoosh" logo, in volume. Nike sued Sasmito for copyright infringement. In 1984, nearly 5 years later, Nike won a judgment in a lower court only to have the decision overturned on a technicality by the country's Supreme Court. The trademark, it seemed, had not yet been posted to the government's official records. The Court ruled that Nike could not sue until that had occurred. The case dragged on for several more years. Along the way, Nike declined an offer from Sasmito to become its official distributor in Indonesia.[39]

By 1990, the copyright situation had stabilized and labor and currency costs elsewhere in East Asia, especially in South Korea, had begun to rise. In an effort to benefit from these trends and from a wage differential that reached as much as 93% in comparison with Taiwan ($42 per month minimum wage vs. more than $600), the Indonesian government instituted development-friendly policies designed to attract new factories. As a result, Nike, together with its rivals Reebok and Adidas, had begun to shift manufacturing capacity to Indonesia. By the spring of that year, Nike was ordering 400,000 pairs of shoes a month from Indonesia—Reebok about the same—and the country was being described as a potential "power-house producer." Many of the contractors employed by Nike were themselves Koreans who were establishing facilities outside their own country to avoid the same soaring labor costs. Wages in South Korea had climbed some 20% in both 1987 and 1988, and the aggressive Korean unions were frequently threatening strikes.[40]

Nike's shift to Indonesia and other markets corresponded with a surge in the company's profitability. After several difficult years in the mid-1980s, Nike's profits rose sharply in 1989.[41] From that point forward, Nike began to dominate the market for athletic shoes, diversify its product line, and emerge as a Wall Street favorite.

It also attracted the attention of the unions back home. At the very moment that Nike was shifting its production contracting to Indonesia, the AFL–CIO dispatched Jeff Ballinger to that country. Assigned to the federation's Asia Institute, Ballinger, a young labor lawyer, was fresh from a labor organizing and education assignment in Turkey when he was sent to Jakarta, where he focused his attention—and his flair for publicity—on Nike. More specifically, he focused on what he regarded as the abuse of its Indonesian workers. Working through local social and religious groups, Ballinger began meeting secretly with many of the young, and mostly female, workers to collect anecdotes about abusive employers. He then combined his observations with those of various religious and human rights groups to produce a series of reports on working conditions in Indonesia, which he distributed widely to labor organizations, the media, Nike, and many of the athletes who endorsed its products.[42] These reports formed the thematic core of the corporate campaign that followed.

When Ballinger returned to the United States after 4 years in Indonesia, he set about establishing a one-man organization, Press for Change, to carry forward his attacks on Nike. He was not alone. In 1989, just as Ballinger was beginning his work in Indonesia for the AFL–CIO, the Made in the USA Foundation (MUSA) was setting up for business. Claiming a membership of 50,000 labor unions, corporations, and individuals at the time (and 60,000 today), MUSA had a budget in 1992 of approximately $10 million.[43] In November of that year, MUSA devoted an estimated $1 million to the opening shot of its own anti-Nike campaign—a series of full-page advertisements in 20 major newspapers pointing out the loss of 65,000 shoe manufacturing jobs in the United States during the 1980s and urging Nike to "come back home." The ads also urged consumers to send their smelly old shoes to Nike CEO Phil Knight with notes urging him to build a manufacturing facility in the United States. MUSA is headed by Joel Joseph, a former staff attorney for Consumers Union.[44] MUSA does not list its principals other than Mr. Joseph, but both Jack Sheinkman, president of the Amalgamated Bank, and Charlie Mercer, secretary treasurer of the AFL–CIO's Union Label Department, play an active role.[45] Sheinkman served as secretary treasurer of the Amalgamated Clothing (and Textile) Workers Union during the Farah and Stevens campaigns and later as the union's president before heading the union-affiliated bank. He also serves on the Board of Directors of the Council on Economic Priorities—an early player in the development of the generic anticorporate campaign.

The month before the ad campaign began, at the urging of the International Labor Rights and Education Research Fund along with the human rights group Asia Watch, the Office of the U.S. Trade Representative scheduled hearings on labor practices in Indonesia. Nike figured prominently in labor's allegations.[46]

The big hit of the campaign during that period came in 1993, when CBS' *Street Stories* magazine program invited Ballinger to accompany a crew to Indonesia, where they interviewed a number of Nike's contract workers. The resulting story, which ran in July 1993, began a drumbeat of media pressure that eventually threatened the company's brand image. It also marked the beginning of Nike's efforts to assuage its critics.[47] Correspondent Roberta Baskin opened the report with these words:

Jeff Ballinger, an American union activist, worked on a wage survey of Indonesian factories and found that last year most of the factories making Nikes

were paying some workers less than the legal minimum wage. We flew
Ballinger back to Indonesia to talk about Nike.[48]

From Nike's perspective, everything was downhill from there. The company was described as workers' worst nightmare, and the piece contrasted
the low wages in Indonesia with the large sums the company routinely paid
to such celebrity endorsers as Michael Jordan.[49]

In the years since, even as the campaign against Nike has been joined by
a variety of groups, much of the coordination has centered in the Campaign
for Labor Rights (CLR). CLR is a coalition of groups—some drawn from
labor and some more directly ideological—that have joined forces to conduct campaigns against several companies, including Starbucks, Guess?,
Disney, Philips Van Heusen, and Nike. (We examine CLR more closely in
a later chapter.) The CLR effort has included worker tours and various other
media events, as well as a personal attack on Nike CEO Phil Knight. CLR is
part of a broader coalition, the so-called *Working Group on Nike*, that includes, among others, the Coalition of Labor Union Women, Amnesty In-
ternational/USA, Global Exchange, the Interfaith Center for Corporate
Responsibility, the National Organization for Women, and the pension
board of the United Methodist Church.[50]

The campaign appeared to achieve its objective in May 1998, when
Knight, speaking at the National Press Club in Washington, issued an apol-
ogy for his company's practices and vowed to change the corporate culture.
He even agreed to a key demand of the Nike critics—independent
third-party review of the company's Indonesia facilities by labor and human rights groups. Within 10 days of his speech, however, AFL–CIO President John Sweeney renewed the attack in a talk at a public relations seminar
in Pebble Beach, California, calling Knight's concessions "meaningless."[51]
In the years since, the drumbeat has continued, perhaps suggesting that,
rather than the working conditions that represent the public focus of the
campaign, it is the simple *fact* that Nike manufactures its shoes abroad
rather than in the United States—which is to say, the core interest of the
American unions—that truly drives the effort.

Food Lion: The Media Are the Message

Food Lion, a nonunion, North Carolina-based supermarket chain, began to
attract the attention of the unions—specifically the United Food and Commercial Workers Union—late in the 1970s when it began expanding into urban markets in the Southeastern and Mid-Atlantic regions. As summarized
primarily in documents relating to two major lawsuits filed by the company,
in 1980, the union tried to organize Food Lion's workers, but without success. So in 1985, the UFCW called for a boycott of Food Lion stores ostensi-

bly to protest the fact that much of the company's stock was owned by a Belgian firm, Delhaize Le Lion. Between 1986 and 1988, a union advertising campaign accused the company of paying substandard wages and benefits to its employees—charges that were reinforced in a complaint filed with the Organization for Economic Cooperation and Development (OECD). The campaign escalated in 1990 through the filing of class action litigation claiming that Food Lion's management had systematically fired employees just before they vested in the company's profit-sharing plan—its most attractive benefit. Then in 1991, the union filed a complaint with the Labor Department alleging a pattern of wage and hour violations at the company. In March 1992, Congressman Tom Lantos held two hearings in which several workers selected by the UFCW testified against the company's practices and in which the Labor Department was pressured directly to take swift action against Food Lion. Eventually the OECD complaint was dismissed, the litigation was denied class standing, and the company agreed to a sizable settlement with the Labor Department.

In November 1992, the campaign hit a home run when the ABC magazine program *PrimeTime Live* ran a lengthy segment accusing Food Lion of selling outdated and contaminated food as part of a company-wide cost-cutting policy that included the requirement that employees work overtime without pay (so-called *off-the-clock* work). The broadcast employed ABC producers working undercover in Food Lion meat and delicatessen departments and using hidden cameras to capture the alleged violations. The product of this effort was a set of extraordinarily unsavory images that turned the stomachs of consumers and had an immediate and long-lasting impact on the company's sales. Shortly afterward, Food Lion was forced to close nearly 100 stores in Texas and Oklahoma—newly entered markets where the ABC broadcast had an especially devastating impact. The company alleged that the ABC broadcast was essentially manufactured by the union, working through an intermediary, the Government Accountability Project. ABC denied that, but acknowledged accepting the union's assistance in training its producers for their undercover assignments.

Whatever its role in the ABC story, the union clearly sought to capitalize on its good fortune—first through an extensive advertising campaign attacking Food Lion, and then through a newly established surrogate group, Consumers United with Employees (CUE). CUE staged news conferences accusing the company of selling outdated foods, including infant formula, and staged a regional caravan returning—in the glare of local media attention—outdated products it had claimed to have purchased at numerous Food Lion stores. CUE was eventually revealed to be a direct front for the UFCW—with a mail drop for an office and a telephone number that was answered at union headquarters—after which it ceased its activities.[52] The campaign appeared to lose momentum after the company filed a RICO lawsuit in July 1995 naming the union and several other participants as defendants.

Although the Food Lion campaign lasted for well over a decade and demonstrated a number of interesting union tactics, it is the ABC broadcast that will be remembered the longest, first for its impact on the company and later for its impact on television journalism. This is the case because Food Lion sued ABC for fraud, breach of fiduciary duty, and a variety of other alleged infractions arising from the production of the program. In February 1997, it was awarded damages in a federal court in North Carolina.[53] The damages were all but eliminated when the case was heard on appeal, but the breach of duty claim was sustained in principle and is likely to constrain newsgathering practices for many years.[54]

Catholic Healthcare West: A Higher Morality[55]

Catholic Healthcare West (CHW) is a system of hospitals, ancillary facilities, home care, and physician organizations operating in three states: California, Arizona, and Nevada. Sponsored by a consortium of nine orders of nuns and administered by a lay board of directors, it was, at the time of this writing, the largest and fastest growing hospital chain on the West Coast and the seventh largest in the nation. Its workforce was about 25% unionized, including contracts with the Laborers, Teamsters, Engineers and Scientists, AFSCME, and the California Nurses Association, as well as the SEIU.

The SEIU's campaign against CHW traces to the fall of 1996, when bargaining in the West Bay area of California produced an agreement that included labor-friendly language on standards of conduct. The union—SEIU Local 250—believed it had obtained this language by bringing pressure on CHW at the corporate level, pressure that was then transferred downward to the regional bargaining level. The pressure in question took the form of a new theme—challenging CHW to live up to the Church's teachings on the right to organize in the workplace. The Local seems to have concluded that a broader campaign of such pressure would help it organize the other bargaining units. This appears to have been a serious miscalculation.

According to industry sources, in June 1997, the AFL–CIO channeled $3 million to SEIU Local 399 in Southern California to turn the local into a major health care union. At the same time, Andrew Stern committed the SEIU to a massive organizing effort, and Local 250 reassigned its paid staff to organizing, largely turning contract administration responsibilities over to its stewards. Then in September of that year, District 1199 merged with the SEIU, in the process displacing Local 250 as the largest health care local. Local 250 apparently took that as a challenge. Among other things, it created, funded through increased dues, and staffed a "Patient and Health Care Worker Defense Program."[56]

The effort to turn up the pressure on CHW began in earnest at the 1998 assembly of the Catholic Health Association of the United States (CHAUSA), where a panel entitled "A Just Workplace: Seeking Greater Understanding" featured, among others, Mary Kay Henry of the SEIU and Kim Bobo, Director of the National Interfaith Committee for Worker Justice.[57] By some reports, during this session, Ms. Henry took the position that Catholic teachings require a just workplace and that it is not possible to have a just workplace without a union. The former argument was not in dispute, but the latter argument was contrary to the interpretation common within the Catholic health care community generally. In effect, she was taking on the entire Catholic health care system and the orders that run it over the implementation of their values.

In the meantime, the SEIU began working the religious communities and the bishops' offices, posing the question of how the Church can support unionization for farm workers but not for health care workers. In July 1998, West Coast editions of *The New York Times* carried an advertisement on this theme, headed "Where does CHW stand?" Late in that same month, the union published a white paper, *A Time to Break the Silence*, arguing that CHW was out of step with Catholic teachings on the right to organize, which it then distributed to local unions as an encouragement to open a "social justice dialogue" with local Catholic leaders.[58] On October 22, 1998, the issue was brought to congregations nationwide as part of the National Day of Prayer and Reconciliation. By far the most damaging publicity on this theme came in a lengthy article in the September 4, 1998, issue of *National Catholic Reporter*, which provided a sympathetic portrayal of the union's efforts accompanied by quotations from Pope John Paul II and other sources supporting unionization.[59]

During October 1998, the SEIU mailed videos to the various religious orders claiming that CHW was not showing good faith in its dealings, bought advertisements on cable television systems in several markets, and purchased a full-page advertisement in *National Catholic Reporter*, all focusing on the dispute with CHW. The issue came to a head in the fall of 1998 in a dispute involving a project of Mercy Charities Housing, a nonprofit organization sponsored by religious communities that partially overlapped CHW's sponsors. The SEIU announced plans to picket the groundbreaking for a San Francisco area low-income housing project despite the fact that it was funded in part with $7.5 million from the AFL–CIO Housing Trust and was to be built with union labor. The union tried to leverage its opposition to the housing project to bring pressure on CHW. The groundbreaking was deferred. However, after the city's mayor intervened, it was eventually held.[60]

By 1999, the SEIU's California organizing campaign had moved into the local political arena in such places as San Jose and the San Joaquin Valley. The general objectives varied with the circumstances, but included such items as passing local card check and living wage legislation, adopting union city contracting requirements, and, in the specific case of CHW, channeling local managed care contracts away from the company. Other tactics, more closely related to the rather unique religious theme of this particular campaign, included prayer vigils, candlelight rallies, passing out materials after church services, pilgrimages, and rallies when a Mother Superior visited a CHW facility. At one point, the National Organization for Women (NOW) chimed in to protest the merger of secular Glendale Memorial Hospital into CHW by holding a candlelight vigil on the anniversary of *Roe v. Wade*, a protest against the merger-related changing of policies on performing abortions.[61] The same issue was raised more generally in a report issued by Catholics for Free Choice, an advocacy group that decried the increasing rate at which Catholic hospital chains were absorbing non-Catholic hospitals.[62] In the spring of 1999, the SEIU brought suit against the company for resisting its organizing efforts.[63]

Sutter Health: Regulation, Regulation, Regulation[64]

California-based Sutter Health was, in 1999, the eighth largest health care company in the country. It operated 26 hospitals and 4 long-term care centers, as well as other facilities, and was the majority owner of Omni Healthcare HMO until that company ceased operations in 1999. Sutter employed more than 35,000 workers, of whom 26%, or approximately 9,200, were covered by union contracts.

Like CHW, Sutter operated through a decentralized structure that resembled, at least in its labor relations, a holding company rather than a single employer. And as was the case with CHW, that proved a source of frustration to the unions, most notably SEIU Local 250. In addition, Sutter actively pursued the consolidation and restructuring of its operations. Finally, Sutter's unified balance sheet included both its nonprofit and limited for-profit operations under one corporate umbrella, which, the union claimed, provided opportunities to shift resources from one type of balance sheet to the other. This emerged as a focal point of union attacks and, through the corporate campaign, as a potential regulatory vulnerability. Indeed, although the campaign had many salient features, including a survey asking employees to describe problems they experienced in providing patient care, a "care-a-van" led by the Reverend Jesse Jackson, picketing at the homes of board members and at charity events they attended, and a "Sutter Deception" video, it was this regulatory vulnerability that gave the campaign against Sutter its defining character. This campaign probably demonstrates the most comprehensive exploitation of the regulatory environment of any that has occurred in any campaign to date.

The allegations were set forth in a series of broadsheets that was launched by the SEIU in July 1997. These *Sutter Scam Sheets* detailed the union's claims that Sutter had routinely violated financial regulations, tax laws, and patient care requirements. They were distributed by broadcast fax to senior management for the apparent purpose of undermining morale, as well as to legislative leaders, the media, and other health care influentials. The thrust of the campaign was aptly summarized in the opening words of the first *Scam Sheet*:

[Sutter Health] pays its CEO $600,000, spends millions on political initiative campaigns, has been forced to pay $1.3 million in settlement of fraud charges, bullies local leaders and swallows up local community institutions, and then cuts staff and services to finance further corporate expansion. The company has terrible labor relations, and refuses to negotiate contracts with industry-standard provisions on subcontracting and union organizing.... Sutter's 1996 revenue: $2.2 billion. Taxes on most Sutter operations: $0.... What kind of care do patients get? Sutter was cited by the state 26 times for patient care violations in intensive care units.[65]

The union's objectives in Sutter were similar to those in the CHW dispute. Local 250 wanted Sutter to accept card check and neutrality and to impose system-wide standards on its bargaining units. In addition, the union wanted a total prohibition on subcontracting. Sutter resisted these demands. The essence of the campaign, too, was similar to the CHW experience in that the union was trying to work through external forces to bring pressure on the company. In the case of CHW, the external forces were those of the Church and the religious community. In the Sutter case, it was the regulatory authority of the federal and state governments that the union sought to exploit.

Local 250 argued that, by combining nonprofit and for-profit operations as it did, Sutter did the following: (a) violated the letter and spirit of the laws and regulations that favor and protect nonprofits, and (b) diverted the resulting revenue stream into its for-profit operations where it could pay higher executive salaries and in other ways pull money out of the system rather than reinvesting it in nonprofit operations. Along the way, the union claimed, almost incidentally, that patient care suffered because resources were drained from operations and staffing levels were reduced.

This line of argument opened to the union a remarkable variety of regulatory and political venues, which Local 250 showed considerable imagination in employing. Among these:

- Internal Revenue Service (audit of alleged violations of nonprofit status; union allegations of tax fraud)

- Department of Defense (investigation of billing practices)
- Department of Health and Human Services (investigation of billing practices)
- Health Care Finance Administration (allegations of Medicare fraud)
- Federal Trade Commission (antitrust investigation of a proposed merger)
- National Labor Relations Board (multiple ULPs)
- California State Assembly, Committee on Health (hearings on alleged breakdown in emergency services)
- California State Assembly, Committee on Revenue and Taxation (investigation of financial practices; hearing on tax-exempt status)
- California Fair Political Practices Commission (alleged campaign spending violations)
- California Franchise Tax Board (investigation of the regulatory framework for mixed-tax-status entities like Sutter)
- California Health Facilities Financing Authority (alleged transfer of proceeds of tax-exempt bonds to for-profit operations; effort to prevent approval of issuing tax-exempt bonds for new projects)
- California Department of Health Services (oversight and investigations)
- California Medical Assistance Commission (effort to divert state health care contracts away from Sutter's Omni Healthcare)
- California Department of Corporations (licensing proceedings)
- California Public Employees' Retirement System (effort to channel health care contracts for beneficiaries away from Sutter)
- Peninsula Health Care District–San Mateo (lawsuit for alleged conflict of interest)
- Encouraging several local jurisdictions to sue to break contracts with Sutter

It is not the success of these efforts—indeed, success was rare, and the listed agencies sided with the company more often than not—but their sheer breadth and magnitude and the attention they undoubtedly claimed from Sutter's management, which was forced to justify and defend each of its actions, that has given this campaign its unique character.

New Otani: Playing the "Race" Card

Six months before the Japanese-owned and styled New Otani Hotel & Garden opened in Los Angeles in 1977, Local 11 of the Hotel Employees and Restaurant Employees International Union (HERE) demanded that management sign a standard labor agreement mirroring those at all of the city's other major downtown hotels. The company indicated that it would sign if the union would agree to two changes—that employees could retain the medical insurance plan already provided by the company and that, consistent with the custom at all Japanese hotels, employees could be asked to perform any reasonable task (e.g., in the case of a front desk clerk who might be called on to assist a cashier). The union declined this offer, and the hotel commenced operations as a nonunion hotel except for its engineering staff, where it was from the outset a union shop.[66]

In 1981, the union petitioned for an NLRB-sponsored representation election. Of the 230 votes cast, only 24 favored representation by HERE. As a result, the union dropped its organizing efforts. Over the next 10 years, however, three more major downtown hotels opened and all remained nonunion. In addition, the leadership of Local 11 was replaced with a more activist team that determined to force one of the four hotels to accept the union's terms. Because of its foreign—Japanese—ownership and management, the New Otani emerged as the most viable target. In November 1991, the union put the hotel on notice that it was in the cross-hairs.[67]

Local 11 spent the next 2 years preparing for a corporate campaign, which it launched in March 1994 with a series of protests at the hotel and other tourist sites around the city. By that summer, the union was accusing New Otani of mistreating its employees, punishing those with pro-union attitudes, demonstrating bias and disrespect toward Hispanic and female workers, and unfairly manipulating the grievance process. In January 1995, students in an American Studies course at UCLA adopted the New Otani campaign as a class project and worked to assist the union organizers. That same year, Local 11 tried unsuccessfully to have Kajima Corporation, which owned the hotel, removed from a politically popular project to build a new high school west of downtown Los Angeles. In the fall of 1995, the union began a boycott of the hotel, pressuring local officials, Japanese merchants in the city, and major customers and suppliers to shun the facility. Reverend Jesse Jackson lent his weight to the effort with a news conference at Local 11's headquarters in February 1996. That summer, New Otani was included among the targets of the first "Union Summer" program, in which the AFL–CIO recruited college students to serve as labor organizers. In 1997, the union went after the hotel's core trade of Japanese visitors, printing flyers in Japanese claiming the hotel's food was infested with insects. The flyers were covered with pictures of cockroaches. The union also advised wedding and event planners that they risked embarrassment if their events happened to coincide with ongoing union demonstrations at the New Otani.

The campaign also had a significant international dimension. In 1996, for example, a delegation from the International Union of Food, Agricultural, Hotel & Restaurant, Catering, Tobacco and Allied Workers Association (IUF), an international labor federation with approximately 2.6 million members, went to Los Angeles to demonstrate support for the campaign. The Japanese member of the delegation subsequently recruited RENGO,

Japan's largest trade union, to support the effort. That same year, Jesse Jackson visited Tokyo, where he met with the top management of Mitsubishi—at the time embroiled in its own, nonunion corporate campaign—and of New Otani. In October 1996, the IUF met in Tokyo to discuss the dispute. In April 1997, AFL–CIO President John Sweeney led a delegation to Tokyo, where he met with RENGO, the IUF, and New Otani management, after which he agreed to support the boycott. The union also wrote a letter to Japan's Emperor asking him to intervene in the dispute.[68]

Perhaps the most distinctive aspect of the New Otani campaign has been the role played by race as an issue and a theme. This has taken two basic forms. The first is to divide the hotel's management from its workers and from the local community by emphasizing alleged injustices toward Hispanic employees. For example, when the hotel's general manager wrote to a city councilman to complain about union organizers' visits to the homes of immigrant employees, suggesting that these would be especially intimidating to unsophisticated persons from countries where such visits led to "disappearances," the union translated his words into Spanish so as to give the impression he had insulted the workers as "uneducated." When three Hispanic employees were terminated for blatant time-clock violations that were eventually sustained by the NLRB, the union presented the terminations as targeted at the Hispanic community.[69] In addition, the union attacked the former management of the Kajima Corporation as World War II war criminals who had run slave labor camps.[70]

A. E. Staley–Caterpillar–Bridgestone/Firestone: Inside, Outside, All Around the Town (of Decatur)

In 1993, the southern Illinois city of Decatur became, almost literally, a war zone—ground zero in a series of bitter labor disputes that were widely regarded as the front line in the battle over corporate downsizing. Three companies with major facilities in Decatur—corn starch and sweetener maker A. E. Staley, heavy equipment manufacturer Caterpillar, and tire maker Bridgestone/Firestone—were separately targeted for corporate campaigns by three different unions while their workers joined forces to support one another.

First in line was A. E. Staley, where the dispute traced to the acquisition of the Decatur-based company by the British conglomerate, Tate & Lyle, in 1988. When the last contract negotiated by the Allied Industrial Workers union before its merger into the United Paperworkers International Union (UPIU) expired in October 1992, the company moved to impose new work rules. The union responded by seeking outside help from two sources: Ray Rogers, of whom we have already spoken at length, and Jerry Tucker, a United Auto Workers (UAW) activist who had devised a strategy known as an *inside game*, by which workers could engage in antiemployer actions on the job without giving up their paychecks as they would in a strike. While Rogers began researching and planning the external corporate campaign, Tucker implemented a work-to-rule slowdown inside Staley's sprawling plant.[71] On June 27, 1993, the company locked out its 740 hourly workers to prevent what it described as sabotage, which included changing identification labels on tanks of chemicals, contaminating products, tampering with locks, and closing certain valves that then shut down equipment.[72] At that point, two things happened.

First, the external campaign heated up. The first target was First of America Bank, which drew Rogers' attention because Staley Chairman Robert Powers sat on its Board.[73] Literature sent to every home in Decatur, and then distributed more broadly pointed out that James Wogsland, Vice Chairman of Caterpillar, also served on the bank's Board.[74] Other targets included ADM, which had a sizable holding in Staley's parent company, Tate & Lyle, and which apparently also helped Staley, ostensibly a competitor, to fill orders during the lockout by building a pipeline joining the two neighboring plants. Consumer boycotts were also developed, targeting the Domino and GW brands of sugar, both Tate & Lyle products, and State Farm Insurance, which owned a substantial block of ADM stock.[75] Later boycotts were targeted at two of the company's biggest customers: Miller Brewing and Pepsico.[76]

Second, the religious community became involved in the dispute. Workers engaged in prayer vigils and symbolic fasts at a number of local churches, and in a series of demonstrations at the Staley facility, priests, nuns, and ministers were dragged off by police. At one point, Staley workers formed a "prayer chain" by linking hands and surrounding the company headquarters building.[77] Father Martin Mangan, a local Catholic priest who led much of this activity, said at the time, " I really hope Decatur can be the Stalingrad of the labor movement, where they dig in and say: 'Enough is enough is enough.' "[78] Mangan purchased a single share of Tate & Lyle stock and a plane ticket, and attended the company's 1995 shareholders meeting in London, where he read a statement signed by 400 U.S. religious leaders calling for an end to the lockout.[79]

While all of this was going on, workers at Caterpillar were having their own problems with management in a nationwide dispute that dated to the expiration of their last contract in October 1991. Cat workers had struck the company for 5 months—October 1991 to April 1992—but in the end had returned to work without a contract. A few days later, the UAW sent a letter to its members suggesting that they had not really ended their strike, but rather shifted their tactics. The union declared "war" on the company, its officers and managers, and workers who had crossed the union picket lines during the strike. Billboards, buttons, hats, banners, and rallies all employed warfare themes. The union also established and trained "Contract Action Teams" whose job was to carry on the conflict inside the company's plants.

Among the tactics employed by the UAW over the next 2 years were a flood of union apparel bearing hostile slogans ("In Your Plant and In Your Face"), chanting, extensive use of ridicule and disparagement that included putting pictures of the company's CEO on urinals and pistol targets, and organizing parking lot meetings of union supporters who formed a gauntlet through which others had to pass.[80]

On June 21, 1994, 1,800 workers again went out on strike. The company claimed the union was trying to impose pattern bargaining matching contracts at the major auto manufacturers, which were not in the same industry. The union claimed the company was trying to impose changes in work rules and in pay and benefits. To ensure that permanent replacement workers would not be hired, the union filed approximately 100 unfair labor practice claims with the NLRB shortly before striking.[81]

Less than a month later, on July 12, 1994, the Staley and Caterpillar strikers were joined by 1,250 members of the United Rubber Workers at the nearby Bridgestone/Firestone factory. Here, as at Caterpillar, the company wanted to implement work-rule changes—as well as 12-hour shifts, worker contributions to the health insurance program, and a linkage between pay and productivity—and here, too, the union wanted to establish industry-wide pattern bargaining.[82] Here, as at Staley, foreign owners had recently acquired the company—in this case, Japan's Bridgestone Tire Company. Indeed, the Japanese interest in the company contributed to a racist thematic that was employed in ways similar to its use in the campaign against the New Otani Hotel. For example, the union posted a sign outside the company's Decatur factory that read, "1941, Japan Attacks Pearl Harbor. July 12, 1994, Bridgestone/Firestone Attacks American Workers"[83]

Although Ray Rogers was a consultant to only one of the groups of strikers, it was with his encouragement that all three unions joined forces in a "Campaign for Justice" that, at its height, was capable of turning out 5,000 marchers for a demonstration or influencing the local mayoral race. The campaign sent emissaries to points from Chicago to MIT to raise funds—they reportedly brought back more than $2 million—and generated a million pieces of direct mail. The Campaign for Justice was strongly supported by the local clergy, especially the Catholic clergy, and provided an umbrella for much of the related activity in the Staley campaign in particular. At one point, amid charges of violence and the harassment of replacement workers, the unions hired veteran civil rights activist George Lakey to help them plan nonviolent acts of civil disobedience.[84]

In the end, the outcome of all three campaigns was the same—failure. Caterpillar workers again returned to work without a contract and carried on their campaign against the company well into 1998. The striking rubber workers at Bridgestone/Firestone returned to work as well. Finally, after 30 months off the job, the Staley workers replaced the leaders of the local union and, in December 1995, voted by a 56 to 44 margin to accept a contract that was essentially similar to the one they had refused to accept in 1992. Among its terms: a reduction in union jobs from 762 in 1992 to 250 by 1997, rotating 12-hour shifts, mandatory overtime, and a grant to the company of unlimited subcontracting rights.[85] The Staley agreement, in particular, also produced a measure of radicalism among the 44% of workers who opposed it. In the words of one,

> We won the national solidarity battle but we lost the struggle on the shop floor. We're all corn-fed Americans and at first didn't know how to counter the company. We would be forced to escalate our strategy in order to hold it back. But every time we did our people would get afraid. They were afraid of fasting, afraid of chaining themselves to the gate, afraid of working with supporters who were socialists. We lost fighting for democracy. The more progressive we got, the more separated we got from the rank and file. We couldn't keep our members up with what had to be done to win.[86]

CONCLUSION

From even this small sampling of campaigns and the selective treatment we have given each, four things should be clear. First, although all corporate campaigns share certain common elements, every campaign is different. There is no cookie cutter in use except this: Every well-conceived corporate campaign will probe for a potential weakness in the target company and then systematically exploit that weakness until the benefit of doing so declines. Second, in assessing the vulnerabilities of their targets and in selecting their tactics, union and other labor-based corporate campaigners are very imaginative. They seek out ways to apply the general themes and dynamics that unify all corporate campaigns in ways that are uniquely suited to the designated corporate target. Third, corporate campaigners are relatively shameless in the sense that they will exploit *any* vulnerability, and they will create vulnerabilities where none exist naturally. That is the implication of the supremacy of strategy in these exercises. As Robert Harbrant, former president of the AFL–CIO's Food and Allied Service Trades Department, once put it: "We think you can rewrite the rules of the game by creating circumstances and exploiting them."[87] Fourth, corporate campaigners are energetic, patient, and enduring. In the words of one union leader, "To be successful, I believe you have to be relentless."[88] Whether for ideological or pragmatic reasons, or simply as a matter of expressing bitterness over some situation or just discomfiting management, they often enjoy conducting the campaign and "sticking it to the bosses." The campaign, then, apart from the pressure it generates on the company, also serves as a rallying point for the workers and a symbol of the union's activism in their behalf.

ENDNOTES

1. Julius Getman, *The Betrayal of Local 14* (Ithaca, NY: Cornell University Press, 1998), pp. 10–11.
2. Ibid., pp. 16–17.
3. Ibid., pp. 18–21.
4. Ibid., pp. 23–24.
5. Ibid., p. 38.
6. Kenneth B. Noble, "Tough Labor Organizer Leading Strike in Maine," *The New York Times*, February 3, 1988, p. A14.
7. Getman, op. cit., pp. 25–43.
8. Ibid., pp. 47–54.
9. Ibid., pp. 65–69.
10. Ibid., pp. 109–111; and Noble, op. cit.
11. "Paperworkers Union Escalates Its Campaign," UPIU news release, January 6, 1988.
12. "Wisconsin Paperworkers Join National Union Campaign," UPIU news release, January 28, 1988.
13. Getman, op. cit., pp. 123–132.
14. Philip T. Sudo, "Iron Workers Union Boycotts Bank of Boston," *American Banker*, January 26, 1989, p. 12.
15. Getman, loc. cit.
16. Ibid., pp. 143–145.
17. Ibid., pp. 192–200.
18. Kirk Victor, "Striking Out in the 80's," *National Journal*, Vol. 21, No. 1 (January 7, 1989), p. 18.
19. An earlier version of this analysis appeared in Jarol B. Manheim, *Labor Pains: The Corporate Campaign Against the Healthcare Industry* (St. Michaels, MD: Tred Avon Institute Press, 1999).
20. Charles R. Perry, *Union Corporate Campaigns* (Philadelphia: The Wharton School, University of Pennsylvania, 1987), pp. 8–9.
21. Ibid., pp. 115–116.
22. Ibid., p. 104.
23. In Beverly I, the NLRB issued a company-wide "cease and desist" order that was subsequently reversed by the U.S. Court of Appeals for the Second Circuit. Beverly II and Beverly III have yet to be resolved.
24. "UFCW Sounds the Alarm on Care At Beverly Nursing Homes," *UFCW Action*, March–April 1995, p. 23.
25. "Community, Patient Advocate and Worker Organizations Rally Monday in Support of Quality Care Improvements at Birmingham Area Nursing Homes," UFCW press release, February 26, 1996; "United Food and Commercial Workers Care for Caregiver Campaign Wins Precedent Setting Nursing Home Contract with Beverly Enterprises," UFCW press release, April 2, 1996.

26. *Secretary of Labor v. Beverly Enterprises, Inc.* (OSHRC Docket Nos. 91-3344, 92-0238, 92-0819, 92-1257, and 93-0724).

27. Don Jacobson, "Union hits 'greed' in health industry," UPI, April 24, 1996.

28. These actions were the basis for a defamation lawsuit filed against the union by Beverly in Pennsylvania state court, the disposition of which was pending at this writing. The company also filed a similar lawsuit against the UFCW in Florida state court.

29. "SEIU Begins Three-Day Strike at Pennsylvania Nursing Homes, *Daily Labor Report*, April 2, 1996, pp. A1–A2; "Beverly Enterprises Permanently Replaces 350 of 800 Workers in Three-Day Strike," *Daily Labor Report*, April 5, 1996, pp. A7–A8; and "Sen. Simon, Pennsylvania Democrats Call On Beverly To Reinstate Its Employees," *Daily Labor Report*, April 18, 1996, pp. A20–A21.

30. Marilyn Alva, "NLRB investigation puts Beverly in the hot seat," *Contemporary Long Term Care*, July 1996, pp. 20–21.

31. Susan Lundine, "Union targets nursing home giant Beverly Enterprises," *Orlando Business Journal*, June 24, 1996.

32. "SEIU Calls for Beverly Shareholder Action," *Bold Action* (SEIU newsletter), May 6, 1997.

33. "Beverly Employment Practices Scrutinized During Lawmakers' 'Town Hall Meeting,' ", *Daily Labor Report*, May 22, 1997, pp. A9–A10.

34. Nancy Montwieler, "Beverly, SEIU Breakthrough Is Reached In Pennsylvania With Governor's Assistance," *Daily Labor Report*, July 1, 1997, p. AA1.

35. "Beverly in Medicare Probe," *CNN Interactive*, July 23, 1998.

36. Alice Ann Love, "Nursing Home Chain Must Sell Homes," Associated Press, February 4, 2000.

37. Eric Bates, "The Shame of Our Nursing Homes: Millions for investors, misery for the elderly," *The Nation*, March 29, 1999.

38. Bruce Stokes, "U.S. Lags Behind Japan in Competition Over Investing in East Asia Production," *National Journal*, Vol. 16, No. 7 (July 7, 1984), p. 1300.

39. Paul Charles Ehrlich, "When in Indonesia do as others do—run; athletic shoe copyright infringement," *Footwear News*, March 3, 1986, p. 2.

40. Paul Charles Ehrlich, "Indonesia seeks investors for footwear field," *Footwear News*, August 7, 1989, p. 98; Paul Charles Ehrlich, "Korea may act on shoemakers' exodus; footwear outsourcing shifting to Southeast Asia," *Footwear News*, August 24, 1989, p. 26; and Paul Charles Ehrlich, "Indonesia is moving up in export lineup; athletic shoe industry," *Footwear News*, April 23, 1990, p. 23.

41. "Shoemaker gets kick from fitness," *Journal of Commerce*, July 18, 1989, p. 4A.

42. Caroline Brewer, "From One Voice to a Roar for the Workers," *Bergen Record*, May 31, 1998, p. L1.

43. Steve Lohr, "New Appeals to Pocketbook Patriots," *The New York Times*, January 23, 1993, p. 37.

44. Jamie Beckett, "Dunk Nike Is Theme of New Ad Campaign," *San Francisco Chronicle*, November 2, 1992, p. C3; and Christy Fisher, "Made in USA Tells Nike: Come Home," *Advertising Age*, October 26, 1992, p. 3.

45. See the MUSA Web site at www.madeusa.org/cause.htm
46. Charles P. Wallace, "Doing Business: New Shots Fired in Indonesia Wage War," *Los Angeles Times*, September 22, 1992, p. 2.
47. Brewer, op. cit.
48. "Just Do It: Nike Cheap-Labor Factories in Indonesia," CBS News Transcripts, July 2, 1993.
49. Ibid.
50. The complete membership of this coalition is listed on a CLR Web site at home.inreach.com/mochi/nike/napp5.html.
51. "Big Labor rips Nike at Big PR's annual outing," *O'Dwyer's PR Services Report*, July 1998, p. 1.
52. Many of these events and allegations are summarized in the original complaint filed in *Food Lion, Inc. v. United Food and Commercial Workers, International et al.*, the company's RICO lawsuit against the union, which was entered in the U.S. District Court for the Western District of North Carolina, in 1995, passim. That case was still pending at this writing so these claims had yet to be tested in court. Other information has been drawn from documents relating to another lawsuit, *Food Lion v. ABC*, the outcome of which is discussed later.
53. Barry Meier, "Jury Awards $5.5 Million in ABC Case," *The New York Times*, January 23, 1997.
54. Lisa de Moraes, "ABC Won't Pay Food Lion's Share," *Washington Post*, October 20, 1999, p. E1.
55. An earlier version of this analysis appeared in Jarol B. Manheim, *Labor Pains: The Corporate Campaign Against the Healthcare Industry* (St. Michaels, MD: Tred Avon Institute Press, 1999).
56. This is documented in a 1998 job position posted by Local 250.
57. The agenda from the Assembly can be found on the CHAUSA Web site.
58. "Break the Silence of Catholic Healthcare," SEIU *Bold Action* newsletter, July 31, 1998.
59. Pamela Schaeffer, "Shared values clash in hospital-labor war," *National Catholic Reporter*, September 4, 1998.
60. Ken Garcia, "Far-flung disputes affect S.F. project," *San Francisco Chronicle*, November 14, 1998.
61. Jacqueline Fox, "NOW protests hospital merger," *Los Angeles Times*, January 22, 1999.
62. Deanna Bellandi, "Catholic Deals with Non-Catholics Grow," *Modern Healthcare*, March 15, 1999, p. 24.
63. Kristen Bole, "Catholic Healthcare West, union tangle in court," *San Francisco Business Times*, May 31, 1999.
64. An earlier version of this analysis appeared in Jarol B. Manheim, *Labor Pains: The Corporate Campaign Against the Healthcare Industry* (St. Michaels, MD: Tred Avon Institute Press, 1999).
65. *Sutter Scam Sheet*, No. 1, July 10, 1997, published by SEIU Local 250.

66. Ron Kipling, *The New Otani Hotel & Garden: A Corporate Campaign Case Study* (Washington: LPA, Inc., 1998), pp. 2–3.

67. Ibid., pp. 3–4.

68. Ibid., pp. 4–13.

69. Ibid., pp. 5–6.

70. "Boycott the New Otani Hotel," flyer issued by Local 11, HERE, July 1995.

71. Eric Jarosinski, "Labor War Zone in Illinois," *Progressive*, Vol. 58, No. 2 (February 1994), p. 30.

72. Herbert R. Northrup, "Union Corporate Campaigns and Inside Games as a Strike Form," *Employee Relations Law Journal*, Vol. 19, No. 4 (Spring 1994), pp. 526–527.

73. Robert B. Cox, "First of America's Illinois Unit Target of Labor Union's Boycott," *American Banker*, November 24, 1992, p.1.

74. "Union Launches Boycott of First of America Bank," AIW news release, November 20, 1992.

75. Eric Jarosinski, op. cit.

76. Marc Cooper, "Harley-riding picket-walking socialism haunts Decatur," *The Nation*, April 8, 1996, Vol. 262, No. 14, p. 21; Donald W. Nauss, "Labor Wars Hit Home in Decatur," *Los Angeles Times*, September 5, 1994, p. A1.

77. William Bole, "Priest carries corn workers' plea to CEO," *National Catholic Reporter*, Vol. 31, No. 15 (February 10, 1995), p. 9.

78. Kevin Clarke, "Dispatches from Decatur: Community is the first casualty in America's labor wars," *U.S. Catholic*, Vol. 61, No. 4 (April 1996), p. 20.

79. William Bole, op. cit.

80. Columbus R. Gangemi, Jr., *Inside Game Tactics: Understanding Work-to-Rule and Other Union In-Plant Campaign Strategies* (Washington: Labor Policy Association, 1997), pp. 10–14.

81. Steven Beaven, "Bitter division in Decatur: Effects of 3 labor disputes taking a toll," *State Journal-Register* (December 25, 1994), p. 1.

82. Beaven, op. cit.

83. Nauss, op. cit.

84. Christopher Carey, "Labor Strife Pits Unions Against Three Companies, City," *St. Louis Post–Dispatch*, September 29, 1994, p. 5C.

85. "Labor takes its lumps," *Progressive*, Vol. 60, No. 3 (March 1996), p. 8.

86. Cooper, op. cit.

87. Quoted in Bob Kuttner, "Can Labor Lead?," *New Republic*, March 12, 1984, p. 23.

88. Bruce Raynor, International Secretary-Treasurer of UNITE, in a presentation at the annual meeting of the American Political Science Association, Atlanta, GA, September 3, 1999.

5

NONLABOR-BASED
ANTICORPORATE CAMPAIGNS

Organized labor became the principal initiator of corporate campaigns from the mid-1970s on, but the unions have by no means been the only players in the game. Other groups—notably environmentalists, human and civil rights advocates, and feminists—have been active campaigners in their own right. In some measure, this may be attributable to learning from the unions as such groups—the National Organization for Women (NOW) seems a likely case in point—saw the value of such campaigns demonstrated through their participation in coalitions and partnerships with labor. It is also the case, however, that the same civil rights and New Left movements that dispatched anticorporate campaigning alumni into organized labor dispatched them elsewhere in what is now commonly termed the *progressive community* as well.

Although they can be brutal and damaging affairs, may labor-based corporate campaigns—those intended to influence a contract negotiation, for example, as opposed to those intended to punish a target company for some antilabor offense or to drive a nonunion competitor out of business—are actually likely to be relatively conservative in character. That is the case because, despite the evident conflict, there is a point at which labor and management share a common interest in preserving the company as a source of employment. Indeed, it is this clear sense of limits that best explains the enduring split between Ray Rogers, on the one hand, and the labor establishment, on the other, in dealing with companies like Hormel or International Paper. The international's driving concern in each instance was defending its membership, and the AFL–CIO's interest was in maintaining order within the labor movement. However, both saw Rogers as being driven primarily by the game itself and having no long-term stake in the outcome.

Once we move outside the labor movement, however, such constraints do not necessarily apply. Indeed, although lacking a self-interest-based economic motivation, some of these campaigns may have a much stronger anticorporate *ideological* basis than the typical labor campaign. They have economic objectives to be sure—that is why corporations are the targets—but they are often fundamentally motivated by politics. Their objective is to change the business practices of a targeted company—not just as a means to an end, but as an end in itself. In reality, it makes sense to think of these efforts, not as corporate campaigns, but as *anti*-corporate campaigns.

Campaigns initiated by nonlabor entities, then, are likely to have a stronger ideological dimension than is typically true of labor-based campaigns—not in the sense of liberal versus conservative, a range of opinion that does not really capture these groups, but rather of relying for their motivation and form on philosophical opposition to the corporation per se. This adds a certain distinctive edge to these campaigns. Although he has not been involved in many such efforts, at least in this particular sense nonlabor corporate campaigns really do take place in Mr. Rogers' neighborhood.

These efforts also tend to differ from their labor-based counterparts with respect to the level of resources available to the campaigners. With one exception to be noted later in this volume, the income streams of the groups engaging in such campaigns simply cannot match those of the unions. As a result, their efforts are more likely to be sporadic and almost entirely media-centric. It follows that in recent years they have benefited even more than have the unions from the low cost of Internet-based organizing, although such groups sometimes seem to equate the posting of material on the World Wide Web with genuine activism—a relationship that has yet to be proven.

If they are disadvantaged in financial wherewithal in comparison with the unions, however, these essentially political campaigners are strongly advantaged in another way. Recall from our discussion in chapter 2 that organized labor and its leaders are not generally held in high public regard. We argue later that this empirical fact represents a major potential constraint on the effectiveness of labor unions as corporate campaigners and, in turn, a principal reason that they devote so much of their campaign effort to forming coalitions and working through surrogates. Such partnerships and fronts have the advantage of masking the evident self-interest of a campaigning union behind a verbal veneer of acting in the public interest.

Groups that are perceived by the public as protecting the environment, human rights, the rights of consumers, religious values, and the like do not confront this problem. The unions are presumed guilty, whereas self-described "public interest" advocates are presumed innocent. The same logic that gives such groups value as allies of labor also enhances their standing when they choose to conduct a campaign on their own.

Yet for all the differences between labor- and nonlabor-based campaigns, these latter efforts bear a clear resemblance to the former. They are based on an analysis of the relationships between the targeted company and its stakeholders, and they seek to alter the company's behavior by attacking those relationships that appear most vulnerable. The substantive objectives are different (e.g., stop exploiting the forests rather than stop exploiting workers), but the methods are essentially the same.

Appendix B represents an effort to list known anticorporate campaigns initiated by entities other than unions and labor-related groups that occurred sometime between 1989 and 1999. Like that in Appendix A, this listing of 35 campaigns is unlikely to be complete, either as to companies that have been targeted, groups that have employed these techniques, dates (which are necessarily approximate), or other information that is included. Still, it probably represents the most complete listing of such efforts to date.

THE CAMPAIGNS

In the balance of this chapter, we review a small sampling of these nonlabor-based, and often predominantly ideological, anticorporate campaigns. As in chapter 4, our purpose is primarily to give them shape and to provide a sense of their similarities to and differences from their labor-based cousins.

Mitsubishi: RAN, NOW PUSH

Mitsubishi Industries, the Japanese conglomerate that controls Mitsubishi Motors, Mitsubishi Electric, Mitsubishi Heavy Industries, and a host of other subsidiaries and corporate cousins, has the distinction of having been targeted in three entirely separate corporate campaigns by political activists. The first of these—a decade-long affair that continues to this writing—is an attack on its lumbering practices by an environmental group, the Rainforest Action Network (RAN). The second, more visible but of shorter duration, was an attack on its diversity policies spearheaded by Jesse Jackson of the Rainbow Coalition and PUSH and by NOW. The third, an effort to stop development of a desalinization plant on the Pacific Coast of Mexico that ostensibly threatened a gray-whale breeding ground, was led by the Natural Resources Defense Council and ended after 5 years (and 700,000 protest postcards mailed to the company) with a decision in March 2000 to cease development.[1] We summarize the first two of these campaigns here.

The RAN campaign dates to August 1989, when RAN purchased a full-page advertisement in *The New York Times* declaring that Shinroku Morohashi, Mitsubishi's president, was one of eight men who held in their hands the fate of the world's rainforests. The group objected to Mitsubishi's importing of Penan wood from Indonesia and Malaysia, claiming that it would destroy the rainforest.[2] After publication of the advertisement, Mitsubishi was deluged with letters and boycott threats from environmentalists. The company responded by joining other Japanese firms in creating an environmental department. Still, an official of at least one of these firms characterized such developments as essentially a response to environmental extortion. "An increasing number of would-be environmentalists come to us for donations," he said. "If we refuse to contribute money, they cite us as a destroyer of the global environment. We have no option but to maintain dialogue with and contribute to them." Mitsubishi claimed that it was targeted not because it was it was the biggest Japanese importer of Southeast Asian lumber (it was actually ninth on the list), but simply because it was better known than other trading companies.[3] The company refused to meet with the environmentalists.

Indeed, in true corporate campaign style, RAN set about quite systematically to attack Mitsubishi brands in markets where timber harvesting was not an issue, but where consumer pressure could be effectively generated.

In 1993, RAN declared Mitsubishi to be the leading destroyer of the world's rainforests and promised a campaign of banner hangings, civil disobedience, national advertising, and the targeting of Mitsubishi's network of automobile and electronics dealers and business partners.[4] A month later, RAN launched a nationwide boycott of Mitsubishi products. It placed a second full-page advertisement in *The New York Times*, this time listing a toll-free number through which people could send telegrams to the company, to the Prime Minister of Japan, and to the Premier of Alberta, Canada, where a large Mitsubishi logging project was underway. The ad—headlined "Dying for a Mitsubishi? You're Not the Only One"—also carried a list of Mitsubishi products, including Nikon cameras and Kirin beer. The advertisement culminated a 6-month fundraising campaign. RAN also said it had developed a video presentation on Mitsubishi's logging operations and planned to canvass neighborhoods in 20 cities and form picket lines at Mitsubishi Motors dealerships as well as at such electronics retailers as Circuit City.[5] In June, RAN announced plans to extend its boycott into the newspaper industry, targeting the sale of printing presses and aiming informational campaigns at Mitsubishi's corporate customers as well as professional associations.[6] In 1994, RAN and Greenpeace supported a group of Filipinos who met with Japan's Export–Import Bank to ask that it rescind the financing for a Mitsubishi power-plant project on the island of Luzon.[7]

In 1996, the boycott effort was extended to Unionbancal, which was tied to Mitsubishi through its parent, Bank of Tokyo. According to one analysis, although not formally connected to Mitsubishi Industries, Bank of Tokyo, the world's largest with $820 billion of assets at the time, was part of the Mitsubishi informal collective, or *keiretsu*, and a key to financing the activities of its members.[8]

While the "corporate" aspects of the campaign were gearing up, RAN was also developing the media tactics that would soon become its hallmark. RAN members demonstrated noisily both inside and outside the 1992 International Auto Show in San Francisco, even using a 40-foot inflatable Godzilla balloon to gain attention.[9] Auto dealerships in Van Nuys and Santa Monica, California, were visited by pickets.[10] A RAN member in a Superman costume jumped off a Mitsubishi sign at the 1993 auto show in San Francisco, where 37 protestors were arrested after throwing chopsticks and sawdust at the Mitsubishi cars on display.[11]

At the Los Angeles auto show the following January, five RAN protestors handcuffed themselves to Mitsubishi cars while others unfurled a banner from atop the company's display tower that said "Welcome to the Show, Boycott Mitsubishi—World's #1 Rainforest Destroyer."[12] Three months later, an additional 15 protestors were arrested after chaining themselves to cars at the San Diego auto show and draping a banner in what a RAN spokesperson said was the fourteenth such incident of the year.[13] In April 1996, RAN activists climbed 80-foot palm trees in Beverly Hills to hang banners attacking the Mitsubishi-owned Bank of California, a Bank of Tokyo subsidiary. The banner read: "Mitsubishi banks on rainforest destruction. Withdraw your dollars from rainforest destruction." This and demonstrations in three other cities were timed to correspond with the merger of the bank with Union Bank. In San Francisco, RAN demonstrators attached themselves to half-ton cement blocks to barricade the entrance to the bank, while in New York City they scaled the Mitsubishi building to hang banners. In Portland, two climbers rappelled from the top of the 15-story Bank of California tower while unfurling yet another banner. One of the Beverly Hills climbers took time out, while hanging from a rope near the top of a Beverly Hills palm, to speak with reporters on his cell phone.[14] This followed an Earth Day 1995 media event in which RAN deposited supposedly blood-stained money in the bank.

The objective of the attacks on the bank, in particular, was to press the parent Bank of Tokyo to stop financing Mitsubishi projects that the group found objectionable.[15] In October 1996, seven demonstrators in Oregon were arrested for "vehicle prowling in the first degree" and "interference with owner's control" under an early 20th-century law intended to limit union activity after two of their number scaled the mast of a ship being loaded with logs for export to Japan.[16] In September 1997, the group received a $250,000 grant from the Richard and Rhoda Goldman Fund, a substantial portion of which was to be devoted to establishing a Japanese-language web site to help carry its anti-Mitsubishi campaign to Japan.[17]

Where did all of this activity lead? In the mid-1990s, Mitsubishi Motors and Mitsubishi Electric helped RAN open lines of communication with the trading company; it also provided start-up funds for a study of sustainable forest management. As a result, RAN stopped demonstrating at auto shows and electronics dealers, focusing instead on the company's bank.[18] In October 1996, officials of the trading company agreed to meet with RAN.[19] Those discussions have yet to lead anywhere. In the meantime, in February 1998, Mitsubishi Motors and Mitsubishi Electric did reach an agreement with RAN. In exchange for an end to the group's boycott activities and demonstrations, the companies agreed to curb pollution and help protect the rainforests. Specifically, they agreed to phase out the use of paper packaging by the year 2002 and to cooperate with RAN and other environmental groups in undertaking a complete environmental review of their businesses, including setting up a system of *ecological accounting*. The companies also agreed to create a fund to restore and preserve ancient forests and their indigenous residents.[20] The agreement, however, explicitly did not extend to any other Mitsubishi company, and the struggle between the companies and their environmental antagonists continues at this writing.

But Mitsubishi's troubles have not been limited to the environment. In a completely separate campaign, the company's hiring and other diversity practices have also come under attack, this time from a cluster of women's rights and civil rights groups headed by Jesse Jackson's Operation PUSH and NOW. Mitsubishi's difficulties in this arena were centered in its American auto manufacturing arm, Mitsubishi Motors Manufacturing of America, and sprang from the filing by 28 female employees in 1994 of a private lawsuit alleging sexual harassment that included verbal and physical abuse as well as sabotage of their work by male employees, some of it resulting in injury. This led to two distinct events.

First, it attracted the attention of the U.S. Equal Employment Opportunity Commission (EEOC), which began its own investigation—one that received complaints that male employees grabbed at the breasts and genitals of their female coworkers, scrawled humiliating graffiti on restroom walls, drew obscene pictures on the fender covers protecting cars from scratches during the assembly process, and routinely referred to the women as "sluts," "whores" and "bitches". After proposing a 10-point plan to address the issues that was reportedly turned down by Mitsubishi, in April 1996, the EEOC filed a massive sexual harassment lawsuit against the company, litigation that was independent of the private lawsuit. Potential damages were estimated at the time of filing at up to $200 million. The company responded in an extremely aggressive manner. After flatly denying all of the allegations in the EEOC lawsuit, it issued a warning to its workers that their jobs could be at risk if the lawsuit adversely affected sales. Then the company installed additional phone lines in its Normal, Illinois, plant so that those workers could call their Senators and Representatives in Congress to denounce the EEOC's action. Two weeks later, after being encouraged by the company's general counsel, bus loads of employees—2,600 in all—with paid time off, free transportation, and even a free lunch trouped to Chicago where they rallied in front of the EEOC's regional offices and demonstrated against the agency. The UAW Local at the plant may have agreed to this action, but the national UAW leadership condemned it.[21]

Second, the filing of the lawsuit attracted the attention of PUSH and NOW. Already supporting the private litigants, NOW and PUSH responded to the company's anti-EEOC initiative by announcing a boycott of all products carrying the Mitsubishi name, especially automobiles. They announced plans to conduct informational picketing at selected auto dealerships, partly to gain public attention, partly to leverage these independent dealerships against the company, and partly to raise yet another issue—the small number of Mitsubishi dealerships owned by women and minorities. Seven Congresswomen announced that they would no longer buy Mitsubishi products, and some went so far as to urge their constituents to join the boycott. In June 1996, senior managers from the company's American distribution unit—not the same company as the manufacturing unit—met with Jackson and NOW President Patricia Ireland to head off the boycott. They proposed changing the company's dealer investment program to attract more women and minority investors. Not satisfied, PUSH and NOW extended the boycott to include Chrysler dealers because some Chrysler cars included parts made by the factory in Normal. Then late in June, NOW Vice President Rosemary Dempsey went to Tokyo, where she joined with Japanese women's rights groups in protesting the company's response to the EEOC. She was followed in July by Jackson, who, after meeting with Mitsubishi executives during the same trip that he used to pressure New Otani management as described in chapter 4, announced plans to expand the boycott.[22] In advance of the visit, Mitsubishi had announced that, pursuant to a report from former Labor Secretary Lynn Martin, whom it had retained as a consultant, it would set aside more money as capital to assist minority owners in building dealerships, would train and educate those who lacked industry experience, and would establish a new position in the manufacturing company charged with the task of increasing purchases from minority vendors, but Jackson was not dissuaded.[23]

As the boycott continued through that summer, NOW established a special fund to lobby Congress to pay for the EEOC's litigation against the company, although there was no reason to think the case would not proceed in any event.[24] By September, Jackson was telling the National Association of Minority Automobile Dealers that he intended to step up the picketing in Michigan and elsewhere.[25] In the meantime, Mitsubishi's auto sales showed some impact from the picketing and publicity, and the threat of broadening the boycott to products other than autos apparently generated pressure on the parent company within the corporate group.[26] Then in January 1997, PUSH and NOW called off the boycott in exchange for the company's agreement to provide more than $200 million in potential business opportunities for women and minorities, especially in the form of dealership opportunities. The only link in this agreement to the sexual harassment litigation was a pledge by the company to rehire some of the litigants who had left their jobs. The EEOC made clear at the time that its pending case against the company was not affected.[27]

In February 1997, Mitsubishi released a second report from Lynn Martin, this one spelling out a 34-point plan to create a "model workplace." Among the points to which the company committed were changes designed to enhance accountability, workforce development and opportunity, communication, and quality of life in the workplace. The company clearly hoped this program of action would not only further assuage PUSH and NOW, but also help speed a settlement of the EEOC lawsuit.[28] However, it did not turn out that way.

In May 1997, NOW announced that it was resuming its campaign against Mitsubishi, which it now labeled a "Merchant of Shame," to protest what it termed the company's lack of good faith in settling both the private and EEOC litigation. NOW President Ireland said that plaintiffs in the lawsuits had faced retaliation, and that other women had been warned against joining the EEOC class action.[29] On August 29, 1997, the company finally settled with 27 of the 29 private litigants for an estimated $9.5 million.[30] On June 11, 1998, Mitsubishi and the EEOC also reached a settlement, and the class action was dropped. In exchange, Mitsubishi agreed to pay a fine of $34 million (the largest of its kind at that time), provide sexual harassment training at its plant, and investigate complaints of sexual harassment within 3 weeks of receiving them. The company also agreed to monitoring by a panel of outsiders.[31] In December 1998, Mitsubishi suspended its training program for minorities pending a review and enrichment of the curriculum.[32]

Smith Barney: A Merchant of Shame

On March 12, 1997, NOW President Patricia Ireland declared the investment firm of Smith Barney to be NOW's first "Merchant of Shame" (Mitsubishi earned a similar designation a mere 2 months later). Ten months earlier, the firm had been targeted in a class action lawsuit filed by 26 female employees at offices in 11 states.[33] The most notorious of the allegations in the complaint pertained to a branch whose manager maintained what was termed the "Boom Boom Room," a basement room where, according to the plaintiffs, male employees groped their female colleagues while drinking Bloody Marys dispensed from a trash can. The class included 22,000 female employees of Smith Barney and included allegations of sexual harassment and discriminatory patterns of compensation.[34] The March announcement placed NOW squarely behind the lawsuit, and was designed to generate pressure on the company to settle it quickly. Smith Barney CEO Jamie Dimon initially took a hard line in responding to this challenge. In a letter to Ireland, he wrote:

> We at Smith Barney continue to maintain that those allegations will and should be tested in court—the proper place to challenge such allegations—with a review of facts and law.... NOW has elected to parrot the views of lawyers involved in litigation against our firm. Through NOW's chosen course, you have reduced your role in an important debate and initiative to public grandstanding and publicity seeking.[35]

Later he took a somewhat more conciliatory approach, inviting the NOW president and *Ms.* editor Gloria Steinem to meet with him to discuss the firm's plans to improve employment opportunities for women and minorities. Steinem made the invitation public at a rally outside Dimon's New York office.[36]

In the course of the campaign, NOW chapters around the country picketed Smith Barney brokerage offices. Among the cities targeted were New York, Chicago, Washington, San Francisco, Seattle, Kansas City, Memphis, and Boston.[37] At least one of these demonstrations forced Smith Barney to move a scheduled conference on technology investments.[38] Pickets also appeared at the Hartford, Connecticut, headquarters of the firm's parent company, Travelers Group Inc.[39] The Equal Employment Opportunity Commission assumed an active role in the dispute when it began informing the media that it was looking into the allegations against Smith Barney, but, the Commission ominously noted, in the context of a larger inquiry into whether the firm's use of mandatory arbitration clauses in its standard employment contracts was inherently unfair to new workers and a violation of federal employment law.[40] This was, in fact, an issue that soon engaged NOW with the entire securities industry.

Jesse Jackson and his Rainbow Coalition/Operation PUSH provided additional pressure on Smith Barney and the industry in general with a January 1998 conference on diversity in the securities industry. President Clinton, Treasury Secretary Robert Rubin, Federal Reserve Chairman Alan Greenspan, and Securities and Exchange Commission Chairman Arthur Levitt were among the featured speakers, along with Jamie Dimon. Jackson had recently opened his own office on Wall Street following a class action settlement by Texaco.[41]

The most interesting series of events in this campaign occurred around the time of the settlement of the class action litigation. By then, 23 of the original plaintiffs had settled, and Smith Barney had proposed a novel plan under which employees could voluntarily take claims of harassment or discrimination to a mediator. The firm also agreed to pay several hundred thousand dollars in compensation and to establish a $15 million fund to provide antidiscrimination and antiharassment training.[42] However, the proposed settlement divided NOW, with the national organization supporting it but the New York City and State chapters in opposition.[43] Interestingly, at this point, Local 100 of the Hotel Employees and Restaurant Employees International Union (HERE), which had not been active in the campaign, tried to intervene to oppose the settlement. The union's interest proved to be secondary: Local 100 was conducting its own corporate campaign, not against Smith Barney, but against Aramark, a service firm whose employees worked in the cafeterias at both Smith Barney's headquarters in New York and that of its parent in Hartford. In typical corporate campaign style, the union was attempting to pressure the investment firms as a source of leverage against its primary target. Its leadership believed that opposing the settlement served that purpose, although the union later claimed to be protecting the interests of Smith Barney's female employees as well.[44] In the end, a settlement was reached only after the judged returned the original agreement with the suggestion that it be enhanced.

Roussell-Uclaf: Campaigning for the Pill

Our next example is provided by a modest and fairly obscure campaign made interesting primarily by the involvement of Ray Rogers and Corporate Campaigns, Inc.—one of the few nonlabor campaigns in which that consulting team has participated.

Roussell-Uclaf is the French pharmaceutical firm that manufactures RU-486, the so-called morning-after abortion pill. Although this drug had been available in Europe for some time, by 1992, the company was still reluctant to introduce it in the United States because it feared the reaction of the activists in the prolife movement. The Feminist Majority Foundation, headed by former NOW President Eleanor Smeal, had been pressing for some time in the political arena to have the drug distributed. Flush with a new $10 million endowment from one of its founders, Hollywood producer Peg Yorkin, the foundation decided on a new course in January 1992—a corporate campaign.

Roussell-Uclaf was a joint venture of two European firms—Germany's Hoechst, A.G., a $28 billion a year producer of chemicals and pharmaceuticals, which held a majority interest in the venture, and its minority partner, the French firm Rhone-Poulenc. Taking a new tack, the foundation decided to pressure the parent companies through their American subsidiaries, Hoechst Celanese, a producer of fiber for clothing, and

Rhone-Poulenc Rorer, a pharmaceuticals manufacturer. On January 21, the anniversary of the *Roe v. Wade* decision, the opening shot of the campaign was fired when Smeal, speaking at a meeting of the New Jersey Religious Coalition for Abortion Rights, called on women in New Jersey (Celanese's headquarters state) and elsewhere to turn their wrath on the company, which, she stated, had been pivotal in the decision of Hoechst management in Germany not to distribute the pill in the United States. "We must create a climate in the U.S. and New Jersey," said Smeal, "which will ensure that Hoechst Celanese will be more responsive to American women on RU-486."

According to Ray Rogers, the campaign was designed to attack the "whole network of power and support" surrounding Hoechst and its American subsidiaries, including pension funds that held large blocks of the companies' stock, unions, physicians, and consumer groups.[45] Rogers observed, for example, that 20% of Hoechst was owned by the Kuwaiti government, which, in the wake of the Persian Gulf War, suggested to him a potential political strategy.[46] As part of the effort, the foundation collected more than a quarter-million signatures on petitions supporting the release of RU-486 and secured endorsements from such groups as the American Medical Association (AMA), the American Association for the Advancement of Science, and the American Public Health Association.[47] It also launched a consumer information campaign and boycott of products made with fabric manufactured by Celanese. In June 1992, it contacted shareholders, including major pension funds, urging them to press management to seek FDA approval for the drug.[48] The following month, the foundation—together with NOW and the Abortion Rights Mobilization—coordinated the legal purchase of RU-486 in London by an American woman and the media events surrounding its seizure by Customs agents when she attempted to bring the pills into the United States. The objective was to duplicate the 1936 decision in which Planned Parenthood founder Margaret Sanger successfully challenged the ban on importing contraceptives.[49]

In July 1992, the House Small Business Committee on Regulation held a hearing on legislation sponsored by Democrat Ron Wyden to take the drug off the import-alert list.[50] Wyden, FDA Director David Kessler, the foundation, and other groups then joined in pressuring Hoechst, which was still unwilling to allow its own subsidiary to market the pills. However, it did agree in April 1993 to release a supply of the drug to the Population Council, a nonprofit organization that would administer its testing on 2,000 women in the United States. Kessler announced the beginning of an FDA review of the drug that was expected to last approximately 2 years, and the Population Council announced plans to find an American pharmaceutical firm willing to manufacture it.[51] Two months later, it seemed that Hoechst's fears were confirmed as angry anti-abortion activists organized by Operation Rescue and abortion supporters backed by the Feminist Majority Foundation and NOW confronted one another in angry demonstrations outside the French embassy in Washington. Other anti-abortion demonstrators targeted French consulates in Miami, San Francisco, and other cities, as well as the offices of Roussell-Uclaf and Hoechst Celanese. Demonstrations were also planned in several European cities for June 21, the day of the Rousell-Uclaf shareholders' meeting in Paris.[52]

Some argued at the time that anti-abortionists opposed RU-486 not only because it was a means to achieve an abortion, but also because it was a means to do so privately. Its widespread adoption would thus deprive the movement of the opportunity to demonstrate at abortion clinics.[53] It is equally possible that this positioning could have represented an effort to persuade Hoechst that its concerns about becoming embroiled in controversy missed the mark. In July 1996, three years after the embassy and consulate demonstrations, the FDA's Reproductive Health Drugs Advisory Committee voted 6 to 1 to approve RU-486, which was considered tantamount to agency approval.[54] In 1997, the Population Council arranged for the Danco Group in New York to manufacture and distribute the drug in the United States. However, by this writing, the FDA's approval, which had seemed assured, had yet to be issued.[55]

Pepsico and Unocal: A Close Shave in Burma

One of the more intriguing campaigns of recent years has been that waged by the Free Burma Coalition and a host of human rights and other groups against companies doing business under a military regime in Burma—now Myanmar. The regime is known by the acronym SLORC (for State Law and Order Restoration Committee); it took control of the country in 1988 and gained international notoriety when it ignored the results of a 1990 election that would have brought its political opposition to power. The campaign is of particular interest for two reasons. First, it is a campaign that operates on two levels. At one level, this is a corporate campaign against a *government*. It is grounded in a classic power and stakeholder analysis of the target, but the primary target is the regime. The companies that have been drawn in have attracted attention first and foremost because they offered points of potentially substantial leverage against that regime. At another level, this is also an anticorporate campaign per se and one firmly grounded in ideology. The campaign is also of particular interest because it has been waged to a significant degree on the Internet. For that reason, it provides a model for future politically motivated corporate campaigns. Indeed, a similar campaign is underway attacking companies doing business in Nigeria.[56]

Organized initially by a graduate student at the University of Wisconsin and proselytizing almost exclusively via the Internet, the Free Burma Coalition became the focal point for a network of immigrants and student groups. By 1996, it claimed chapters on 110 college and university campuses, as well as dozens of immigrant-based and human rights groups around the world, although few of them constituted the household names of the progressive movement. Seizing on corporations doing business in the country as levers, the Coalition organized product boycotts, campus demonstrations, embarrassing media events at annual meetings, and other shareholder-related actions all aimed at pressuring the target companies to withdraw from Burma/Myanmar as a means to bring economic pressure on the regime and deprive it of their legitimizing presence.[57]

Of particular note in this campaign has been the success of the Coalition in recruiting support from state and local governments in the United States in the form of economic sanctions—laws and resolutions preventing them from doing business with Burma or companies engaged in trading with Burma—a tactic borrowed from the early campaign against the Apartheid regime in South Africa. Among the governments signing on to this boycott have been those of Berkeley and San Francisco, California, Madison, Wisconsin, New York City, and the State of Massachusetts.[58] (In June 2000, the Massachusetts sanctions law was overturned by the Supreme Court on the grounds that it conflicted with the supremacy clause of the U.S. Constitution, though proponents vowed to continue their efforts.[59]) During the 1990s, a number of companies became entangled in the Burma campaign, among them Arco, Texaco, Mitsubishi, Pepsico, and Unocal. Of these, let us focus our attention briefly on Pepsico and more extensively on Unocal because these two companies illustrate the two defining aspects of the campaign.

Pepsico was targeted by the Free Burma Coalition because, in the words of one Coalition document,

Pepsi claims that its Burmese partner ... is a "private entrepreneur." In fact he is chairman of a joint venture with the military called JV3, and was chosen by Pepsi because of his close military connections.

Pepsi claims that it "compete(s) with the government" in the soft drink business. In fact, the military, which controls all aspects of business and the economy, has essentially granted Pepsi a monopoly in the Burmese market, where Pepsi now has a 90% market share. In return, Pepsi sponsors international trade fairs where the junta woos other foreign investors, and Pepsi funds youth and sports activities organized by the military. Pepsi's support of the military regime has been consistent and steadfast.

Pepsi is a major contributor to the Union Solidarity and Development Association (USDA), the junta-sponsored "patriotic organization." Nobel Peace Prize winning Burmese democracy leader Aung San Suu Kyi, whose NLD has been subject to rising violence and intimidation ... compared USDA thugs to "Hitler's

brown shirts," saying " I want the whole world to know that the USDA is being
used to crush the democratic movement."

Pepsi also purchases agricultural products in Burma to sell abroad, as a method of
repatriating its profits. With forced labor pervasive in the agricultural sector, activists are concerned that Pepsi's purchases are connected to forced labor.[60]

This statement is revealing on several levels. It reflects the power analysis that underlies the campaign. It ties Pepsico to the main themes of the
campaign—profiting from slave labor, supporting antidemocratic activity, general duplicity, and propping up an illegitimate regime. It demonstrates the sophistication of the campaigners. However, in some ways,
what is most revealing about the statement is the date when it was issued,
which was shortly *after* the company had announced its intention to pull
out of Burma.[61]

One graphic produced by this campaign is especially indicative of the sophisticated understanding of corporate operations that lay behind the effort. This figure, which appeared on the Free Burma Coalition web site,
illustrated what was at the time Pepsico's corporate structure in the form of
a tree with commercially identifiable branches and an underlying corporate
root structure. By this device, it suggested the connection between boycotting, say, a Pizza Hut restaurant (Pepsico owned this and other restaurant
chains at the time, but later spun them off) and attacking the regime in
Burma. Such devices—a commonplace in these campaigns—are especially
useful for creating a sense of direction and involvement among those at the
grassroots level of the movement—in this case primarily college students.

Eventually Pepsico did leave Burma, and eventually the Free Burma Coalition did leave Pepsico alone. Arco and Texaco made similar exits, although Texaco, for one, has attracted the attention of activists in other
causes. Unocal, however, has shown greater resistance to the pressure from
the activists and, as a result, has seen a substantial escalation of the corporate campaign. The core issues involving Unocal and Burma are not greatly
dissimilar to those stated previously against Pepsico. They center on a 1995
agreement under which Unocal was to develop an offshore natural gas field
and transport the gas via an underwater pipeline to Thailand, and on a second pipeline project, also involving Mitsui of Japan and the French oil company Total, that would traverse a tropical forest and end at a new power
plant that the consortium would construct.[62]

Like the Pepsico campaign, this one has involved shareholder actions,
boycotts, and other demonstrations, perhaps even contributing to Unocal's
1997 decision to sell off its "Union 76" service stations. Unlike the Pepsico
campaign, however, this one has attracted broad participation from a large
group of established human rights, civil rights, and environmental groups
and from the Oil, Chemical, and Atomic Workers Union (OCAW). With the

notable exception of OCAW, many of these groups—including, among others, such regular corporate campaign participants as the Feminist Majority Foundation, the Free Burma Coalition, Global Exchange, NOW, Project Underground, RAN and the Transnational Resource and Action Center (which maintains a web site known as Corporate Watch), and even California State Senator Tom Hayden, whose thinking nearly four decades earlier helped generate the anticorporate movement—have come together under the banner of HEED. HEED is an acronym for the International Law Project for Human, Economic & Environmental Defense, an activity of the National Lawyers Guild. In the words of the Guild's constitution,

> The National Lawyers Guild is an association dedicated to the need for basic change in the structure of our political and economic system. We seek to unite the lawyers, law students, legal workers, and jailhouse lawyers of America in an organization which shall function as an effective political and social force in the service of the people, to the end that human rights shall be regarded as more sacred than property interests.[63]

Critics on the Right have long characterized the Guild in somewhat different terms, including describing it as a communist front or even as "the chief legal bulwark of the Communist Party."[64] Our interest here is less in characterizing the Guild's ideology than in simply noting it and noting its role in the Unocal campaign.

In this instance, the Guild and its coalition partners in HEED have gone for Unocal's jugular by petitioning the Attorney General of California to revoke the company's corporate charter. Their petition includes a bill of particulars listing 10 charges against Unocal, among them environmental devastation, unfair and unethical treatment of workers, and complicity in crimes against humanity. Among the latter are specified aiding the oppression of women; aiding the oppression of homosexuals; enslavement and forced labor; forced relocation of Burmese villages and villagers; killings, torture, and rape; complicity in the gradual cultural genocide of tribal and indigenous peoples; usurpation of political power; and deception of the courts, shareholders, and the public.[65]

Robert Benson, the Guild's lead attorney on the petition project, has offered his own perspective on this initiative. "Corporate power," he has said,

> is subverting our democracy. Giant corporations—by participating in and therefore warping elections and lawmaking, by using wealth resulting from special privilege to influence political decisions in this and other countries, and by massive spending on propaganda to mold public debate—are routinely engaged in the mechanics of the civil governing of the state.[66]

In attempting to extricate itself from this quagmire or, from an alternative perspective, in recognizing its role in a truly global economy, Unocal has gone so far as to state in its 1994 annual report that it "no longer considers itself as a U.S. company."[67] The company subsequently sold off its West Coast refining and marketing operations to raise capital for further investments in Asia. In April 1997, it opened what it termed a "twin corporate headquarters" in Malaysia, to which it posted the company's president and several senior executives.[68]

CONCLUSION

In a sense, in this attack on Unocal, we see the corporate campaign coming full circle—from the Left to the Left and even from Tom Hayden to Tom Hayden. The assumption that drives this ideological attack on multinational corporations like Unocal and the others in Burma, or like Nike in Indonesia, is that inherent in international corporate capitalism is a dynamic that inevitably inhibits the development of human rights in host countries. As analyzed by Stephen Hymer in 1971, this dynamic literally requires that such corporations exploit the poorest segments of the local populations because doing so provides the rationale for their very multinationality. To accomplish this, they place themselves in league with repressive political regimes.[69]

More recently, political scientist Debora Spar has questioned this thesis, suggesting that:

> in the off-cited global economy, increased flows of information are starting to change the calculus facing firms and particularly the calculus surrounding their treatment of human rights issues. Specifically; the advent of the Internet has dramatically increased the reach and scope of even marginal activist groups. Using inexpensive electronic mailing campaigns, these groups can rapidly and broadly highlight corporate practices deemed abusive or exploitative. The result is to push multinational firms ever closer to the human rights camp. Over time (and perhaps even over their own objections) a concern for human rights might well work itself to the bottom line of multinational corporations.[70]

That argument, if validated, would add still another dimension to the circularity of events.

Yet we also see in these campaigns a more clearly linear pattern in the maturity and sophistication that these attacks on the corporation have developed, the way that one has built on another to add to their weightiness, and, in some cases, to the viability of the threat that they can represent. As we see in subsequent chapters, just as organized labor has produced a campaign-supportive infrastructure and a cadre of players experienced and ever more skilled in the techniques of the corporate campaign, so, too, have the progressive groups of the political left developed an institutional and conceptual grounding for continued anticorporate initiatives and honed their objectives, strategies, and tactics. Indeed, as noted earlier, precisely because these groups often have a more fundamental ideological objection to corporate business-as-usual—evident, for instance, in the Unocal campaign—and a greater willingness to test the limits of legal and political tolerance (e.g., in some of RAN's publicity-seeking antics), the potential threat they represent to a corporate management can be at least equal to that represented by a labor-based campaign, despite the usual disparity in campaign-available resources, and the range of their demands and expectations can be far greater.

ENDNOTES

1. For a summary of this latter campaign, see John Ward Anderson, "Environmentalists Persuade Mexico to Save the Whales," *Washington Post*, March 3, 2000, p. A30.
2. Mark McQuillen and Randy Ulland, "The coming of the greens; As the economy booms, Japan imports some heavy environmental pressure," *Japan Economic Journal*, December 23, 1989, p. 26.
3. Akihiro Tamiya, "Environmental action on corporate agendas," *Japan Economic Journal*, July 21, 1990, p. 1.
4. "Mitsubishi named as worst rainforest culprit," United Press International, April 13, 1993.
5. Pimm Fox, "Rainforest Group Calls for Boycott of Mitsubishi," *San Francisco Chronicle*, May 11, 1993, p. C1; "Environmental Group Aims at Mitsubishi," *The New York Times*, May 11, 1993, p. D6; and "U.S. group's ad hits Mitsubishi rain forest logging," *Japan Economic Newswire*, May 13, 1993.
6. Mark Fitzgerald, "Boycott; Rainforest group says it will target the newspaper industry in Mitsubishi boycott," *Editor & Publisher*, June 12, 1993, p. 77.
7. "Japanese bank urged to cancel Philippine power plant loans," *BBC Summary of World Broadcasts*, December 7, 1994.
8. Barton Crockett, "Unionbancal Faces Boycott Over Mitsubishi Ties," *American Banker*, May 10, 1996.
9. "Mitsubishi: Enviro Protestors Attack Firm's Logging Policy," *Greenwire*, November 25, 1992.
10. Jeff Schnaufer, "Rain Forest Group Pickers Auto Dealer," *Los Angeles Times*, October 20, 1993, p. B3.
11. "Protestors Drop In on S.F. Car Show," *San Francisco Chronicle*, November 23, 1993, p. A16.
12. "Activists handcuff themselves to Mitsubishi cars," *United Press International*, January 10, 1994; and "Activists Arrested in Auto Show Protest," *Los Angeles Times*, January 16, 1994, p. B3.
13. "Rain-forest activists seized at auto show," *San Diego Union-Tribune*, April 23, 1994, p. B3.

14. Karen Lowe, "Environmentalists urge Mitsubishi boycott over logging practices," *Agence France Presse*, April 1, 1996.
15. Crockett, op. cit.
16. "Environmentalists Get Pretrial Hearing," *The Vancouver (WA) Columbian*, December 17, 1996, p. B3.
17. "Three Awarded with Goldman Fund Grants," *Greenwire*, September 12, 1997.
18. Crockett, op. cit.
19. "Logging: Oregon Protesters Gain Audience with Mitsubishi," *Greenwire*, October 18, 1996.
20. Danielle Knight, "Truce Between U.S. Greens and Mistubishi," *Inter Press Service*, February 11, 1998; and Claudia H. Deutsch, "Group Ends Its Boycott of Mitsubishi Entities," *New York Times*, February 12, 1998, p. D4.
21. Barbara Wanner, "Mitsubishi Motors' Sexual Harassment Case, Part I," *JEI Report*, July 12, 1996.
22. Wanner, op. cit.; and Andrew Pollack, "Jackson Says He'll Expand Boycott Against Mitsubishi," *The New York Times*, July 18, 1996, p. D5.
23. Lindsay Chappell, "Mitsubishi Promises to Add Minority Dealers, Vendors," *Automotive News*, July 22, 1996, p. 3.
24. David Southwell, "Jackson, NOW push on with Mitsubishi boycott," *Chicago Sun-Times*, July 24, 1996, p. 20.
25. Larry Bivins, "Jackson's Rainbow Coalition to lead protests against Mitsubishi," *Detroit News*, September 10, 1996.
26. Wanner, op. cit.
27. Kirsten Downey Grimsley, "Jackson, NOW End Boycott As Mitsubishi Makes Pledge," *Washington Post*, January 16, 1997, p. E1.
28. Barbara Wanner, "Model Workplace Plan Unveiled for Mitsubishi Motors Manufacturing," *JEI Report*, February 21, 1997.
29. Yochi Dreazen, "NOW presses anti-Mitsubishi campaign," *Chicago Sun-Times*, May 22, 1997, p. 22.
30. De'Ann Weimer, "Slow Healing at Mitsubishi," *Business Week*, September 22, 1997, p. 74.
31. Kristin Downey Grimsley and Frank Swoboda, "Mitsubishi, EEOC Settle Lawsuit," *Washington Post*, June 11, 1998, p. C1; and Barnaby J. Feder, "$34 Million Settles Suit for Women at Auto Plant," *The New York Times*, June 12, 1988, p. A12.
32. Arlena Sawyers, "Minority Plan Suspended at Mitsubishi," *Automotive News*, December 21, 1998, p. 4.
33. "Now Targets Smith Barney as First 'Merchant of Shame,' " NOW news release, March 12, 1997.
34. Deborah Pines, "Judge Rejects Smith Barney Settlement," *New York Law Journal*, June 25, 1998, p. 1.
35. Marcia Vickers, "Smith Barney Chief Blasts NOW For Labeling Firm 'Merchant of Shame,' " *On Wall Street*, May 1, 1997.
36. Marcia Vickers, "Steinem and NOW Consider Smith Barney Chief's Offer, *On Wall Street*, July 1, 1997.

37. "NOW Chapters Refuse to Yield to Corporate Pressure, Plan Day of Pickets at Smith Barney Branches in Key Cities," NOW news release, March 21, 1997; Deborah Clubb, "NOW Joins March to End Parade of Abuses," *Memphis Commercial Appeal*, July 4, 1997, p. A8; "Brokerage target for picketing," *Kansas City Star*, March 26, 1997, p. B2; and Diane Lewis, "NOW Stages Protest Against Smith Barney," *The Boston Globe*, March 25, 1997, p. D2.

38. Marcia Vickers, "Smith Barney Moves Conference to Avoid NOW Demonstration," *On Wall Street*, July 1, 1997.

39. Andrew Julien, "Alleged Harassment Prompts Protest," *The Hartford Courant*, September 11, 1997, p. F2.

40. Darryl Van Duch, "Bad PR Spurs Cave-ins," *National Law Journal*, October 13, 1997, p. A1.

41. Royce T. Hall, "Jackson Leads Wall Street Push," *Newsday*, January 15, 1998, p. A46.

42. Steven Greenhouse, "Companies Set to Get Tougher on Harassment," *The New York Times*, June 28, 1998, p. 1:1.

43. Roland Jones, "Smith Barney Deal Opposed By NOW," *Financial Planning*, June 1, 1998.

44. James T. Madore, "Accord Raises Union's Ire," *Newsday*, March 13, 1998, p. A57.

45. "American feminists fight for new abortion pill," *New Scientist*, Vol. 134, No. 1818, p. 9.

46. Annette Fuentes, "Why 'Buy American' Sells Workers Short," *Newsday*, February 19, 1992, p. 39.

47. "Feminist Majority Foundation Announces Expanded Campaign for RU 486," foundation news release, January 21, 1992; and "American feminists fight," op. cit.

48. "Abortion," *Business Week*, June 29, 1992, p. 46.

49. Carol Polsky, "A Bitter Pill: Challenging import ban on abortion," *Newsday*, July 2, 1992, p. 5.

50. Tamar Lewin, "Abortion pill maker won't seek approval; Drug stays on FDA's import-alert list," *Houston Chronicle*, July 26, 1992, p. A2.

51. "German Firm Agrees to Allow Abortion Pill in U.S.," *Reuters*, April 20, 1993.

52. Jacqueline Frank, "Groups Clash in Vocal Battle Over Abortion Pill," Reuters North American Wire, June 18, 1993.

53. Howard Libit, "RU486 Advocates See Private Abortion Techniques Quieting the Public Debate," *Los Angeles Times*, July 6, 1993, p. A5.

54. Julia Duin, "Abortion pill gets panel OK: Final approval by FDA seen near," *Washington Times*, July 20, 1996, p. A1.

55. Judy Foreman, "'Compassionate use' of RU486 hits snag: Abortion politics blamed for threat to distribution," *Minneapolis Star Tribune*, January 3, 1999, p. 3E.

56. Although these campaigns are, in the author's judgment, political rather than economic in origin, it is well worth noting that the majority of companies being targeted are oil companies—Arco, Chevron, Shell, Texaco, Mobil, Unocal—and that the Oil, Chemical, and Atomic Workers Union (OCAW) claims membership in the

Free Burma Coalition. On the latter point, see "Oil, Chemical & Atomic Workers Union Blasts Oil Companies' Support for Burma's Narco-Regime in Wake of Peace Activists' Arrests," OCAW news release, August 12, 1998.

57. Agis Salpukas, "Foreign Energy, Domestic Politics; Burmese Project Tests Unocal Resolve," *The New York Times*, May 22, 1997, p. D1. The roster of members of the Free Burma Coalition as of October 1996 can be found at www.freeburmacoalition.org/old/onboard.html.

58. "US City Approves Anti-SLORC Curbs," *Emerging Markets Datafile*, July 10, 1997.

59. Linda Greenhouse, "State Law on Myanmar Boycott is Voided," *The New York Times,* June 19, 2000.

60. "Pepsi 'Burma Pull-Out' Called a Sham; Angry Activists Announce Hunger Strike Plans," Free Burma Coalition news release, April 25, 1996.

61. Ibid. For a look at the history and tactics of the Pepsico campaign, see Reid Cooper, "A Historical Look at the Pepsico/Burma Boycott," *Boycott Quarterly* (1997), found online at www.thirdworldtraveler.com/peo ... evetwt/Boycotts/Hx_PepsiBurmaBoy.html, December 7, 1999.

62. "UNOCAL: Making a Killing in Burma," posting by the International Rivers Network on the Corporate Watch Web site at www.corpwatch.org/trac/feature/humanrts/cases/b-unocal.html.

63. From the Preamble to the NLG Constitution, which can be found at www.nlg.org.

64. S. Steven Powell, *Covert Cadre: Inside the Institute for Policy Studies* (Ottawa, IL: Green Hill Publishers, 1987), pp. 11, 17, passim.

65. "Environmental, Human Rights, Women's and Pro-Democracy Groups Petition Attorney General of California to Revoke Unocal's Charter," news release from HEED, September 10, 1998, posted at www.heed.net/doc2.html.

66. Robert W. Benson, "Three Strikes, and the Company's Out," *Legal Times*, November 2, 1998, p. 23.

67. William Furlow, "Nationality changes for U.S. producers?" *Offshore*, June 1997, p. 86; and Sheri Prasso and Larry Armstrong, "A Company Without a Country?" *Business Week*, May 5, 1997, p. 40.

68. Prasso and Armstrong, op. cit.

69. Stephen Hymer, "The Multinational Corporation and the Law of Uneven Development," in J.W. Bhagwati, ed., *Economics and World Order* (New York: Macmillan, 1971), pp. 113-140. See also the insightful discussion of Hymer's thesis in Debora Spar, "Foreign investment and human rights; International lessons," *Challenge*, Vol. 42, No. 1 (January 1, 1999), pp. 57 et passim.

70. Spar, op. cit., p. 56.

6

LOOK FOR THE UNION LABEL

Although campaigns attacking the reputations of corporations are becoming evermore commonplace and the nature of the attackers more diverse, by far the greatest number and the most significant of these efforts have been spearheaded by organized labor. But that is not to say that corporate campaigns originate from a single, readily identified source. To the contrary, labor-based corporate campaigns arise from a diversity of origins, or at least that is the appearance that the attacks give. That this diversity is more apparent than real is itself an element of campaign strategy—a means to redefine the terms of conflict so as to circumvent the widespread popular distrust of organized labor.

There are a great many labor and labor-based organizations that become involved in corporate campaigns, ranging from union locals to women's groups to think tanks. A reasonable estimate would be that as many as 100 to 200 such groups have participated in campaigns over the years. In this chapter, we focus on four types of organizations—the national federation, international unions, international trade secretariats, and labor coalitions—and on selected groups or activities within each category. These examples have been selected for their relative importance and for their illustrative value, but they by no means represent a comprehensive listing of campaign-active labor organizations.

THE AFL–CIO: ORGANIZING FOR CHANGE, CHANGING TO ORGANIZE

As we saw in chapter 2, the 1995 election of John Sweeney to head the AFL–CIO marked a watershed in the organization's history. The AFL–CIO had already played a role in the evolution of the corporate campaign, especially through two of its departments—Food and Allied Service Trades (FAST) and Industrial Unions (IUD), each of which had published early how-to manuals that we discuss in more detail in chapter 8. But these activities were generally marginalized within the federation and, as we have seen, were somewhat controversial. Sweeney came in as the leader of a veritable rebellion in the ranks of organized labor, and his commitment to rebuilding the membership of the labor movement through aggressive and nontraditional tactics pointed to a new direction and a far deeper commitment to using every means at the movement's disposal—a commitment that would address not only the need to restore union membership, but the need to reestablish the legitimacy and primacy of organized labor per se.[1] These objectives were perhaps stated most succinctly in the new federation president's inaugural speech in October 1995, when he promised that "[w]e will use old fashioned mass demonstrations, as well as sophisticated corporate campaigns, to make worker rights the civil rights issue of the 1990s."[2]

It was a promise on which Sweeney has made good or at least toward the fulfillment of which he has made good progress. His tenure began with a sweeping reorganization of the labor federation and a reinvigoration of its organizing initiatives. In a formal statement issued in September 1995 and reflective of the new administration's views, the AFL–CIO Executive Council committed itself to the following objectives:

- Providing leadership, coordination, and support for a movement-wide effort to return unions to a dominant role in improving the lives of Americans;
- Promoting efforts to refocus unions at all levels on organizing and dramatically increasing spending on organizing;
- Helping develop the internal capacity of unions to increase the scale of organizing and membership education programs about the necessity to organize;
- Assisting in the development of strategic plans and leverage strategies;
- Assisting in recruiting and training a new generation of organizers;
- Promoting and coordinating the integration of political, legislative, and legal activity, bargaining strategies, and corporate strategies to increase unions' ability to organize;

- Raising the visibility and public profile of unions as the vehicle for improving the jobs, working conditions, and lives of American families; and
- Expansion of bargaining unit strength by increasing membership levels in existing units and by using bargaining leverage to create organizing opportunities, including neutrality and card check provisions.[3]

In this statement, we find a blueprint for much of the activity that has occurred in subsequent years—the framing of issues, the attention to coalition building, the recruitment of organizers and supporters, and the creation and allocation of resources.

One of the principal mechanisms through which the Council proposed to implement this new agenda was the Organizing Institute. The Institute actually predates the Sweeney era, having been established in 1989 to train union organizers. All participants, many of whom come from within the labor movement, undergo an intensive weekend-long classroom program. Some then go on to a 10-day orientation regime and a 3-month program of field experience working on an actual campaign. The Institute then helps place those who complete the program with participating unions, which include, among others, the Communications Workers of America (CWA), Hotel Employees and Restaurant Employees International (HERE), Service Employees International Union (SEIU), Teamsters, Union of Needletrades, Industrial and Textile Employees (UNITE), United Food and Commercial Workers (UFCW), and United Steelworkers of America (USWA), all of which are heavily involved in corporate campaigns. As of 1999, beginning organizers were paid between $20,000 and $30,000 per year. The Organizing Institute maintains offices in four cities—Washington; New York; Oakland, California; and Ypsilanti, Michigan—and conducts between two and three dozen training sessions per year in cities around the country.[4]

A second important component of the renewed commitment to organizing is the Union Cities program. Here the purpose is to forge coalitions *within* the labor movement but across union locals in specific communities and *between* these locals and their prospective allies among other local activists—religious leaders, environmentalists, and the like. These coalitions are designed to mirror in the communities the integration and outreach activities envisioned by the federation at the national level and to build momentum for policy changes and expressions of support for labor at the local level, where the problems are often more tractable and the political impediments more easily overcome. The emphasis in Union Cities is as much on mobilization as on organizing, but it is through this program that the federation has done the following: (a) built support in local legislative bodies for the living wage campaign and restrictive contracts requiring the use of unionized employers for all publicly funded jobs or procurement, and (b) recruited local civic and political leaders to intervene on labor's side in corporate campaigns and other disputes.[5]

A rather different enterprise—but one that plays an important role in building the infrastructure that supports corporate campaigns as well as other, more traditional, labor activities—is the George Meany Center for Labor Studies situated on a 47-acre campus in the suburbs of Washington, DC. Named for a long-time AFL–CIO president, the Meany Center offers bachelors'- and masters'-degree programs in labor studies (the latter in cooperation with the University of Massachusetts at Amherst), as well as a wide range of noncredit courses on such topics as

- Internet for Union Activists,
- Strategic Research for Organizers,
- Building a More Powerful Movement for Social Justice: Labor–Community–Religious Coalitions,
- Media Strategies for Unions, and
- Presentation Techniques for the Electronic Media.[6]

The 1999 description of the social justice course provides a good sense of the flavor of these offerings:

> Building broad-based coalitions with deep roots in the community is an important labor movement strategy for building power. We will examine coalition building from a number of different points of view and consider a variety of models, strategies and tactics. This institute will challenge participants to create a vision for building grassroots community support for workers' rights as well as union support for community struggles—building true partnerships.
>
> Participants should expect to explore: Workers' Rights Boards; Living Wage coalitions; community support for the Right to Organize; involving the religious community; building the labor movement using community organizing models; labor's role in 20th century social change movements; and history of community organizing.[7]

This particular course was cosponsored by Jobs with Justice, a group about which we have more to say later.

Similarly, the 1998 offering on media strategies included "framing issues for the media; developing contacts in the media; preparing news releases; planning actions to generate media interest; and other techniques that get labor's story in front of the public in a positive and professional way." The course on electronic media focused on "working with TV reporters and skills relating to the camera: gestures, postures, eye contact, dress and makeup, body language, relaxation techniques and visual aids. Participants will learn how to control the interview process...."[8]

In summary, participants in these and the other offerings of the Meany Center are taught all the basic skills required of an effective corporate campaigner, and the Center could be thought of as the "George Meany College of Corporate Campaign Knowledge."

All of this, of course, costs money, and one of labor's problems going into the 1990s was a shortage of money devoted to organizing. That has been addressed in two basic ways: redirecting existing resources and generating new money. Because most of the financial resources of organized labor reside not with the AFL–CIO but with the international unions that comprise its membership, the first of these approaches has centered mostly on persuasion, with the federation leadership pressing the leaders of the internationals to devote more of their own efforts to membership development. Some unions–notably the SEIU, UFCW, and a few others—have been responsive to this pressure, but others have not. Of course, the movement's principal approach to increasing its resources has been to increase its membership, the very circularity from which it has struggled to escape.

Now another, rather different approach has begun to pay dividends. This is the Union Privilege program, a package of benefits for union members offered through the AFL–CIO, and more particularly the affinity credit card that is part of the program. An affinity credit card is a card—typically a Visa or MasterCard—that is offered exclusively to the members of a particular organization and carries the group's logo. Such programs are attractive to credit card issuers because they provide built-in marketing advantages as the issuers seek to recruit participants and build their lending portfolios. They are attractive to the featured organizations because the issuers forward a portion of their revenues from the program to the sponsoring group. The AFL–CIO began an affinity credit card program through the Bank of New York in 1996, the year after Sweeney's election. Today the program is maintained by Household Bank (a Household Finance subsidiary) and has a lending portfolio of approximately $3.5 billion. In 1998, it provided the AFL–CIO with an estimated $20 million in *new* money, much of which it earmarked for organizing.[9]

It must be noted that the federation's credit card program has not been an unmitigated success. In fact, the program was implicated on the margins of the 1997 scandal in which the Teamsters and the Democratic Party were found to have illegally channeled funds amounting to some $700,000 to support the reelection of Ron Carey as president of the union. One of the central figures in the scandal was former SDSer Michael Ansara, whose company—Share Group—marketed the affinity credit card to union members.[10] The contract was then shifted to another company, Telespectrum Worldwide of Cambridge, MA. However, when the Communications

Workers tried to organize the company's workers, Telespectrum announced that it was closing immediately and moving to New Mexico. The
union then filed an Unfair Labor Practices charge with the NLRB.[11] Still,
for all its troubles, the Union Privilege card program has been both an imaginative and effective device for generating money for organizing, much of
which revolves around corporate campaigns.

THE INTERNATIONAL UNIONS: ON THE LINE AND IN THE TRENCHES

In the final analysis, of course, the AFL–CIO does not organize or represent
a single worker. Rather, it is the international unions, through their many locals, that do the heavy lifting in those areas. In the next section, we profile
five of these internationals, focusing on some of those most heavily committed to the corporate campaign.

Communications Workers of America (CWA)

As of 1999, the CWA represented 630,000 workers through more than
1,200 local chapters. Among the major employers of CWA members were
AT&T, GTE and the regional Bell telephone companies, the ABC and NBC
television networks, and many newspapers around the country.[12] The union
was the largest one representing customer service professionals, number-
ing 140,000 of them among its members, and engaged in large-scale representation campaigns at such employers as American Airlines. With its large
number of professional and skilled members, the CWA is one of the most
sophisticated practitioners of the corporate campaign, having produced an
extensive manual on their conduct, *Mobilizing for the 90s*, which we discuss in detail in a subsequent chapter, and having initiated campaigns
against such high-profile employers as Bell Atlantic, Sprint, Blue Cross,
and the Detroit newspapers the *Free Press* and the *Detroit News*.

In recent years, the greatest challenge confronting the CWA in organizing and bargaining has been the rapid development of new communications technologies and services, often by nonunion start-up companies or
newly created nonunion subsidiaries of companies with which the CWA
has agreements. Although it often lacks leverage in dealing with start-ups,
especially those in traditionally nonunion areas of the country, the union
has used, or at least threatened to use, corporate campaigns against unionized companies such as the so-called *Baby Bells*. They do so to pressure
management to agree to card check and neutrality provisions in contracts
for their organized workers that would apply to workers in their nonunion
subsidiaries.[13]

Since 1985, the CWA has been headed by Morton Bahr, who also serves
as chair of the AFL–CIO's Department of Professional Employees. Bahr

has been among the most politically active union presidents, serving on the Democratic National Committee and as one of President Clinton's appointees to the 21st Century Workforce Commission. Bahr also served on the Labor Advisory Committee to the National Administrative Office, charged with oversight of the labor side agreements to NAFTA, so it was no accident that the CWA campaign against Sprint served as the first test of these agreements.[14] The union, too, has been politically active, having contributed more than $1.2 million to candidates during the 1997–1998 congressional election cycle (of which $8,000 went to Republicans).[15]

Although the CWA's campaigns are interesting in their own right, two of the union's other related actions are more noteworthy still. The first was the founding by Larry Cohen, now the CWA's executive vice president, in 1987 of Jobs with Justice, an organizational structure under which local coalitions with religious and other leaders could be unified and through which workplace and organizing disputes could be framed as issues of social justice. We look more closely at Jobs with Justice later in this chapter. The second was a policy of growth and consolidation through mergers with other established unions, including the International Typographical Union in 1987, the National Association of Broadcast Employees and Technicians (NABET) in 1994, and the Newspaper Guild in 1997.

The NABET and Guild mergers are especially interesting because they give the CWA some measure of direct influence in the production and distribution of news. Most of the journalists, and virtually all of the production technicians, in the major news operations around the country are now members of the CWA. Although this fact does not necessarily mean that news is consciously slanted toward a prolabor or any other point of view, it is not without consequence. For example, during the NABET campaign against ABC and during the Newspaper Guild campaign against the Detroit newspapers, Democratic politicians have declined to be interviewed by these media, even during their 1996 National Convention, lest they offend striking union members.[16] An even more fundamental and widespread impact on the news may be taking shape as well.

The Newspaper Guild represents more than 31,000 employees of news organizations, many of them reporters and editors. Employees of newspapers in such diverse cities as Boston, Buffalo, Chattanooga, Cincinnati, Dayton, Denver, Detroit, Harrisburg, Knoxville, Los Angeles, Memphis, Milwaukee, New York, Philadelphia, Pittsburgh, Providence, Sacramento, San Jose, and St. Louis are Guild members. It is an affiliation in which many journalists feel a great sense of pride, reveling in stories of forming new chapters, forcing management to raise salaries and change working conditions, marching in solidarity with fellow unionists, and filing unfair labor practice claims. The October 9, 1998, issue of *The Guild Reporter*, the union's newspaper that is distributed to all members, for example, carried stories of three corporate campaigns, two (against Microsoft and the Detroit newspapers) being waged by the CWA through the Guild itself. Some sample content includes:

• On Microsoft: "Although they work for months at a time alongside full-time employees with health plans, paid vacations and stock options, the permatemps' employers technically are temporary agencies offering few, if any benefits. Job security is non-existent, and as fragile as the next illness or accident.... *Which, come to think of it, sounds like an invitation for a union organizing drive.*"[17]

• On the Detroit newspapers: "As a reporter for the Detroit News I covered some incredible stories.... Yet nothing ever affected me like the story in which I found myself playing a personal role: The strike by some 2,000 of my fellow workers at the News, owned by Gannett, and Knight Ridder's Free Press.... We've watched the newspapers deliberately slant news coverage of the strike against us; hire security goons who physically assaulted members (some have been physically disabled), and hire workers to 'permanently' replace us.... The story of the Detroit newspaper strike and lockout is personal for every member of the newspaper business.... It's personal because those companies made no secret of their willingness to use violence, lies, money and headlines to get what they wanted — a union-free newspaper where workers do as they're told and have no recourse, no voice in the workplace."[18]

• On Avondale: "Waving signs and wearing caps, T-shirts and buttons that identified them as belonging to the UAW, AFT, AFSCME, *CWA*, IBEW, IUE, SEIU and a score of other unions, the crowd of about 500 sang, chanted and heard speeches castigating a company described as one of the worst union-busting employers in the country."[19] (emphasis added)

Other stories in the same issue included "NLRB orders Knight Ridder to boost Monterey wages," a piece on anticipated OSHA regulations governing VDT users in the newsroom and elsewhere, a five-step guide to building union power in the workplace, and a commentary by a UAW official headlined, "Mamas, don't let your babies grow up to be columnist scabs." The point here is merely that members of the Newspaper Guild have a perspective and a measure of self-interest that is seldom disclosed in their reporting.

Perhaps the clearest example of this is provided by coverage of the extensive round of negotiations, posturing, and corporate campaign activity associated with industry-wide bargaining in the telephone and long-distance industry in the summer of 1998. During a period of just over 3 months, the CWA negotiated new contracts with seven major employers: Ameritech, AT&T, Bell Atlantic, Bell South, GTE, SBC, and US West. Using an electronic search service, I identified 2,074 news stories, news releases, and other entries (including overlaps) making a reference to one or another of these companies and to negotiation- or strike-related activities. I then search these items to find the number of news stories making reference to the fact that the author of the article was a member of the CWA or the Newspaper Guild. I did not find a single such reference.

Taken together, these observations suggest that the CWA has positioned itself as a filter through which news of labor and other issues must pass and by which the news may be conditioned in one direction or another. It is not that the union or a consciousness of their membership explicitly guides journalists in their reporting of any particular story, but simply that their own unionism gives them a particular perspective on labor and management just as where you sit in an arena determines what you see of the game. As we explore the strategies and tactics of the corporate campaign in later chapters, we see that the effective management of news is essential to defining the "reality" in which every campaign operates. The perspective to which the CWA, in particular, socializes its members, and especially its journalist members, provides a potentially significant strategic advantage, not merely to one union, but to all that engage in corporate campaigns.

Service Employees International Union (SEIU)[20]

That John Sweeney came to prominence through his leadership of the Service Employees International Union (SEIU) would, itself, be enough to explain the union's aggressive, campaign-based approach to organizing workers. However, it is the union's current leader, Sweeney protégé Andrew Stern, who has set the style for the SEIU in recent years, including its wide-ranging campaign to organize hospital, nursing home, and other health care workers and its aggressive "Justice for Janitors" campaign.

Stern, a graduate of the University of Pennsylvania, began his rise in the SEIU after becoming a social worker in 1972. Schooled in civil disobedience, he first attracted national attention when, as the union's organizing director, he led Los Angeles janitors in a late-1980s wave of protests and sit-ins, including a march on the Century City office complex in which police beat several dozen demonstrators. The resulting outcry led political and business leaders to press the city's janitorial companies to come to terms with the union. It also enhanced the stock of a man known as one of organized labor's major risk-takers. He was elected president of the SEIU in April 1996.[21] Aaron Bernstein of *Business Week* has characterized the SEIU president in the following terms:

> Stern's background as a bushy-haired young left-winger in the 1960s student movement era led him to experiment with the in-your-face tactics that first put the SEIU on the map.... Now [he] wants the whole union to adopt these high-profile methods.[22]

His reputation, together with the success of the SEIU in building its membership under his leadership, have marked Stern as a potential successor to Sweeney at the head of the AFL–CIO.

Altogether, the SEIU has a total membership of about 1.2 million workers—nearly 10% of the entire membership of AFL–CIO unions—including approximately 600,000 in the health care industry, making it the nation's largest health care union. The union devotes a large proportion of its resources to organizing, including 47% of the budget of the international as well as substantial local resources, and it employs approximately 400 full-time organizers.[23] In 1996, the union's Committee on the Future recommended that the SEIU "shift resources to industry organizing as opposed to 'hot shop' organizing."[24] In October of that year, the SEIU unveiled a "Dignity Campaign" that called for organizing 100 nursing homes a year and building a force of 1,000 member-organizers (volunteers) in that segment of the health care industry.[25] Elements of this ongoing program include, among others,

> organizing targeted nursing home corporations on a mass scale, researching and distributing patient care deficiency reports, working in coalition with nursing home reform advocates, and waging shareholder proxy fights on quality of care issues.[26]

Among the substantive issues raised in the campaign are staffing ratios, staffing standards, improved wages and benefits, improved training and supervision, and occupational safety and health.[27] In February 1999, the union scored one of its biggest victories—indeed organized labor's biggest single victory in 60 years—when it won the right to represent 74,000 Los Angeles County workers providing home health care.[28]

The SEIU is well versed in the strategies and tactics of the corporate campaign. In fact, as early as 1988, during the Sweeney era, the union published its own how-to guide, the *Contract Campaign Manual*. As we see in chapter 8, that manual includes extensive chapters on research and goal setting, organizing the campaign, pressuring the employer, and bargaining. An introductory chapter advises,

> Instead of relying only on old-style strikes, many locals have surprised employers with a combination of actions such as work site actions; jeopardizing the employer's relations with customers, investors, politicians or other sources of funds; rolling or selective strikes; legal or regulatory challenges to the way the employer conducts its operations; [and] media campaigns and community pressure based on the common interests of workers and the general public.[29]

In effect, this is the outline for a corporate campaign.

Over the years, the SEIU has undertaken campaigns against such compa-nies as Beverly Enterprises and a host of other nursing home and hospital operators, Somers Building Maintenance, Argenbreit Security, and Com-mercial Real Estate Developers. The latter three companies are not espe-cially well known, but the campaigns targeted against them have attracted considerable attention. For example, Somers provides janitorial and other services to buildings in Sacramento, California. The SEIU drew a major Somers client, Hewlett-Packard, into the campaign to gain leverage.[30] Argenbreit provides security services at O'Hare Airport in Chicago and at Los Angeles International Airport, and has been targeted as part of an SEIU drive to organize all service providers at the airports. Commercial Real Es-tate Developers, like Somers, provides janitorial and other services to com-mercial buildings in several major cities, including Washington, DC. In that campaign, one tactic, using a school bus to block access to the city on a major bridge during the morning rush hour, actually back-fired, generating great pressure on the union to moderate its tactics. Many SEIU campaigns are channeled through a subsidiary group, Justice for Janitors.

Union of Needletrades, Industrial and Textile Employees (UNITE)

As the successor to the Amalgamated Clothing and Textile Workers Union, which launched the first campaign against J.P. Stevens in the 1970s and sponsored the Amalgamated Bank to marshal the assets of the labor move-ment, UNITE has deep roots in the history of the corporate campaign and a tradition of innovative thinking. It also confronts some of the most difficult challenges of any American trade union because it is UNITE, more than any other union, that has seen the industries with which it deals (e.g., textiles, shoe manufacturing, assembling garments) and the jobs of the workers it would be positioned to represent move steadily off-shore. As a result, UNITE's corporate campaign activities have been closely integrated with labor's positions on immigration and international trade and closely allied with other groups, especially those on the political left and those with an in-terest in political development in Central America, Asia, and elsewhere in the Third World.

UNITE was formed in 1995 through the merger of two unions with long traditions—the ACTWU and the International Ladies Garment Workers Union, the latter perhaps best known for its catchy song, "Look for the Un-ion Label." At the time of the merger, the union had 350,000 members. The membership is divided among a large number of relatively small employ-ers, but includes 7,000 manufacturing workers at Xerox and, as a result of a 1999 victory in an NLRB election after a 25-year organizing campaign, 5,100 workers of Fieldcrest Cannon.[31]

Targets of UNITE campaigns have included Disney, GAP, Guess?, K-Mart, Nike, and Philips Van Heusen, among others. What the majority of companies attacked by UNITE have in common is that they either operate, or market goods produced by third-party contractors, in lesser developed countries. The union's interest here is twofold: to raise the cost of production overseas to a point at which domestic-based manufacturing becomes more competitive, thus saving or creating jobs within the United States, or, failing that, to support efforts by workers in the supplier countries to form their own labor unions affiliated with UNITE. Much of this activity is channeled through a coalition known as the Campaign for Labor Rights (CLR), the organization and activities of which we examine later in this chapter.

UNITE has been a leader in the use of overarching campaigns built around a single theme—a type we label in chapter 9 as *metacampaigns*. The Stop Sweatshops campaign begun in the 1990s and directed against Nike, Disney, and other companies is the quintessence of such efforts. UNITE guides and participates in that campaign primarily through CLR, of which it is a member, but also through the National Labor Committee, another participant in the CLR coalition. Another metatheme developed by UNITE and promulgated mostly through a surrogate organization is the "Made in the USA" campaign, promotion of which is spearheaded by the Made in the USA Foundation (MUSA). Elsewhere in this book, we document the connections between MUSA and UNITE. Through these high-moral-ground campaigns, and through its emphasis on workplace justice, UNITE has worked to build a strong symbolic position for its organizing efforts. To help cement this image, UNITE has its own media strategy: The union has created the Sidney Hillman Foundation named for the founding president of the ACWU. The Foundation, in turn, annually awards the Sidney Hillman Prize for journalists reporting on social justice issues. Among the recipients of the $2,000 prize in 1999 were three-time winners Donald Bartlett and James Steele of *Time Magazine* for their series entitled "Corporate Welfare."[32]

United Food and Commercial Workers International (UFCW)

Formed in 1979 through a merger of unions representing meat cutters and retail clerks, the UFCW today represents 1.4 million workers, or more than 1 in 10 under the AFL–CIO umbrella. Four out of five members work in food-related industries, although the union has been moving into the health care industry in recent years as well. Other members are in such industries as banking and chemical manufacturing. The UFCW is headed by Douglas Dority, a former supermarket clerk who was elected president in 1994 after a decade as the union's Director of Organizing. Under his aegis, the UFCW was the only private-sector union to increase its membership during the 1980s. Like other campaign-active unions, the UFCW has been generous in its political contributions, having distributed just over $1.5 million in the 1997–1998 congressional cycle. Like the other unions featured here, the bulk of that generosity—all but $37,000—was directed at Democrats.[33] Dority serves as chair of the AFL–CIO's Public Affairs Committee, where his charge is to enhance the public image of the labor movement.[34]

Among the companies targeted for UFCW corporate campaigns have been several supermarket chains—Albertson's, Food Lion, Publix—nursing home operator Beverly Enterprises (where the UFCW and the SEIU have waged a joint campaign since 1983), Nordstrom's, Perdue Farms, Seafirst Bank, Tyson Foods, and Wal-Mart. These campaigns typically center on allegations of off-the-clock work (hourly employees being required to work overtime without compensation), discrimination, and unsafe or unsanitary conditions in the workplace. They are often accompanied by private and/or class-action litigation that threatens employers with substantial financial penalties if they do not come to terms with the union.[35]

The UFCW has demonstrated considerable longevity in some of its campaigns, including those against Beverly and Food Lion, both of which trace to the 1980s. Among the more interesting of these efforts is the rather low-key assault on Mount Wal-Mart, which attracted the alarmed attention of the union when it began moving into the supermarket business in 1992 through development of its *supercenter* format (i.e., a gigantic store that includes a full-scale discount department store *and* a full-scale supermarket under one rather large roof).[36] By 1993, the union was developing the themes it would employ to attack the Arkansas-based megaretailer, focusing on the shift to low-wage jobs and the threat to local communities, and positioning Wal-Mart as the enemy of Main Street.[37] Wal-Mart was also tagged for advertising a buy-American program, even as it sold goods manufactured abroad, and harming the interests of women by employing many of them at what the union portrayed as substandard wages. Picketing and demonstrations at Wal-Mart stores began in earnest in 1995.[38] The Main Street thematic, in particular, resonated in a number of communities, where it offered local merchant's a symbolic hook on which to hang their own opposition to Wal-Mart's entry. This theme was reinforced and legitimized in a book issued by the National Trust for Historic Preservation, *How Superstore Sprawl Can Harm Communities*, which took on Wal-Mart quite directly while setting forth organizing, media, and legal strategies for opposing such development.[39] Arguably the anti-Wal-Mart campaign gave rise to the broader issue of urban sprawl to which Al Gore devoted considerable attention in the early stages of his presidential campaign effort in 1999–2000.

United Steelworkers of America (USWA)

In 1935, under the leadership of famed Mine Workers president John L. Lewis, eight unions broke away from the AFL to form the more radical Con-

gress of Industrial Organizations. Among their first actions was establishment of the Steel Workers Organizing Committee (SWOC). Steel workers
had played a central role in the early and tumultuous history of American labor, perhaps most notably in the violent Homestead Strike of 1892, but their
previous efforts at unionization had all either failed or been short-lived. By
January 1937, however, SWOC had signed up 125,000 members in 154 locals, and, in March of that year, U.S. Steel, the nation's largest producer
(known as "Big Steel"), recognized the union and signed a 1-year contract.
Seven other producers, however—together known as "Little Steel"—refused to negotiate, and the union struck. One result was the 1937 Memorial
Day Massacre in Chicago—a labor riot in which 13 strikers were killed.
The disputes lingered, but by 1942 the union had signed contracts representing 170,000 Little Steel workers, bringing its total membership to
700,000. In May of that year, SWOC renamed itself as the United Steelworkers of America (USWA).[40] For the next three decades, the USWA was
among the nation's most militant and strike-oriented unions. But as the
Rust Belt actually rusted and steel production shifted overseas, the union
found itself fighting a rear-guard action to preserve jobs. One of the tools it
has come to rely on in that fight is the corporate campaign.

Today the union is led by George Beckers, a second-generation Steelworker who led major corporate campaigns, most notably against Ravenswood Aluminum, during his years as USWA vice president between 1985
and 1993. As president, Beckers initiated a planned merger of the Steelworkers, United Auto Workers, and International Association of Machinists that promised to create a powerful new union with substantial
membership and resources, although at this writing the consummation of
the merger appeared to be in question.[41] In 1995, the rubber workers union
merged with the USWA and much of the union's corporate campaign activity for the balance of that decade focused on tire manufacturers, most notably Bridgestone-Firestone, Titan Tire, and Continental. Other recent
USWA campaigns have included those against Oregon Steel and Kaiser
Aluminum. In 1998, the union decided to boost the proportion of its budget
dedicated to organizing from 7% to 30%. This was expected to produce a total organizing fund of approximately $40 million annually.[42]

More than some other unions, the Steelworkers have stayed true to the
Rogers-style corporate campaign, particularly in their focus on a target
company's underlying financial dependencies. In both the Oregon Steel
and the Kaiser campaigns, for example, the union brought pressure on
Wells Fargo and other banks in an effort to gain leverage over its primary
target. Of perhaps greater interest for the future of the corporate campaign
is the Steelworkers' increasing participation in international coalitions of
unions designed to generate pressure against multinational employers. In
the Continental Tire campaign, for example, the campaign's point of origin was a strike at a plant in Charlotte, North Carolina, but much of the

campaign was carried forward by the International Federation of Chemical, Energy, Mine, and General Workers Unions (ICEM), 1 of 14 secretariats of the international labor movement. Similarly, in 1999, the USWA joined with 13 other domestic unions to form the Coordinated Bargaining Committee to consolidate labor's dealings with a major multi-union employer, General Electric. If divide and conquer has been a management strategy for weakening the unions, unify and confront seems to be emerging as labor's response. With its megamerger plans, its international campaigns, and its coalition bargaining, the USWA has been at the forefront in framing that response.

Other Unions

The fact that we have singled out these five unions for attention by no means suggests that they are the only ones significantly engaged in the conduct of corporate campaigns. Several other unions (e.g., the hotel workers, the Teamsters, the oil and chemical workers among them) might as easily have been selected. That is really the point. Today, many unions have had extensive experience in campaigning against corporations, and many have in place the infrastructure and resources to campaign effectively in the future. Where it was a radical experiment and very much a rarity as recently as 10 or 15 years ago—something to be employed as an act of desperation against a particularly recalcitrant employer—today the corporate campaign is a commonplace, routine element of labor–management relations and one with which increasing numbers of companies find themselves confronted. In a sense, the union that does not campaign is today's rarity.

INTERNATIONAL TRADE SECRETARIATS AND MULTI-UNION COALITIONS

As our discussion of the Steelworkers suggests, two of the most significant recent developments with implications for corporate campaigns are the increased willingness of U.S. unions to work cooperatively on such campaigns with their international counterparts and the increased significance of multi-union bargaining coalitions. In this section, we look a bit more closely at both phenomena.

In many areas of the world, and most notably in Western Europe, labor unions are held in considerably higher regard than they are in the United States, and they exercise commensurately greater influence. These unions, in turn, have traditionally worked together across national boundaries under a variety of umbrella organizations in an effort to establish international labor standards and practices. Historically, U.S. unions have maintained friendly, but distinctly arm's-length relationships with these various organizations, viewing them with distrust and some measure of disdain. However, as the global economy has become more integrated and as multinational employers have increasingly played one labor market against another, the American unions have begun to take these relationships more seriously.

One of the most influential of these international labor organizations is the International Confederation of Free Trade Unions (ICFTU), established in 1949 as a federation of national trade union federations, which is to say its members are such national-level groups as the AFL–CIO. The ICFTU currently claims 213 such affiliates in 143 countries around the world. The organization works closely with the International Labor Organization (ILO), a UN agency that deals with issues of international labor policy, and consults with other UN agencies as well.[43]

Much of the heavy lifting in the ICFTU is conducted through subsidiary groupings, known as International Trade Secretariats (ITSs). Each ITS is an industry- or sector-specific coalition of individual national-level unions, and these individual unions may belong to more than one ITS depending on the range of their interests. The cooperation between the Steelworkers and ICEM is an example of such a relationship. There are 14 ITSs in all, including:

- CI—Communication International
- EI—Education International
- FIET—International Federation of Commercial, Clerical, Professional and Technical Employees
- ICEM—International Federation of Chemical, Energy, Mine and General Workers' Unions
- IFBWW—International Federation of Building and Wood Workers
- IFJ—International Federation of Journalists
- IGF—International Graphical Federation
- IMF—International Metal Workers' Federation
- ITF—International Transport Workers' Federation
- ITGLWF—International Textile, Garment and Leather Workers' Federation
- IUF—International Union of Food, Agricultural, Hotel, Restaurant, Catering, Tobacco and Allied Workers' Associations
- MEI—Media and Entertainment International
- PSI—Public Services International
- UADW—Universal Alliance of Diamond Workers.[44]

Of these, FIET, ICEM, IMF, and IUF have begun to play significant roles in corporate campaigns and related activities in the United States, and to engage in such campaigns internationally on their own.

As our discussion of the Steelworkers might suggest, one of the most active of these organizations has been the ICEM, which has coordinated two major corporate campaigns as well as a number of lesser efforts. ICEM includes member unions representing workers in such industries as energy, mining, chemicals and biological sciences, pulp and paper, rubber, glass, ceramics, cement, and environmental services. The organization sees as a key element of its mission coordinating labor's dealings with multinational employers in these industries. As of 1996, it had 404 member unions representing approximately 20 million workers in 113 countries.[45]

ICEM's role in the Continental Tire campaign provides an illustration of the organization's philosophy in practice. Continental is a global corporation based in Germany. When workers at its Charlotte, North Carolina, plant in the United States struck and the company hired permanent replacement workers, the USWA and ICEM launched their campaign. While the Steelworkers focused on U.S.-based activities, ICEM carried the fight elsewhere. South African workers struck the company in support of their American counterparts, and Scottish workers threatened to do the same. Australians picketed a German consulate in that country, and a meeting of trade unionists in Moscow also expressed support. ICEM also conducted what it termed a *cybercampaign* by providing a web site through which supporters could send e-mail messages to Continental's management in Charlotte and at the company's Hanover, Germany, headquarters, to German government officials, and to the German embassy in Washington.[46]

More substantial still has been the ICEM's own campaign against Rio Tinto, the world's largest privately owned mining company. The campaign began in 1998 when ICEM called a meeting in Johannesburg, South Africa, of unions with members employed by the company. The objectives of the meeting were to (a) develop a global profile of the company, (b) establish an international framework for unions dealing with it, and (c) devise a strategy for pressuring Rio Tinto. In a report on this meeting, the ICEM characterized Rio Tinto as follows:

> It has been identified by trade unionists, local communities, environmental activists, indigenous people and certain investors as one of the most ruthless mining companies in the world. The company's record of human and trade union rights violation, community destruction, environmental damage and disregard for indigenous people is very extensive.

> The company has been associated with military dictatorships (in Spain and Chile), the apartheid regime in South Africa and Namibia and more recently with repression by military and state police in Indonesia....

> Concern over environmental control at Rio Tinto operations has led to protests in many countries....[47]

In this statement, we find the full range of themes that characterized the subsequent campaign—themes that were restated in two ICEM white papers: *Rio Tinto—Tainted Titan*, and *Rio Tinto—Behind the Façade*, which were released to coincide with the company's 1998 and 1999 annual meetings, respectively. The campaign also included a video, "Naked Into the Jungle," a complaint to the Organization for Economic Cooperation and Development (OECD) and other elements typical of the corporate campaign. Indeed, the ICEM's Rio Tinto campaign could be considered the prototype for the transposition of the corporate campaign from the domestic U.S. arena into the international economic system.

In another forward-looking move, as we noted earlier, the USWA has also joined with a coalition of other domestic American unions that have in common their representation of workers at General Electric. Although multi-union cooperation was not a new phenomenon, the scale of this particular aggregation, the Coordinated Bargaining Committee (CBC), formed in 1998 in anticipation of company-wide bargaining set to begin the following year, was noteworthy on its own. Here, too, there was from the outset a plan for global outreach. This included coordination with the IMF, the metal trades ITS, which contributed a database of GE operations and labor relations worldwide.

Included in the CBC were such unions as the CWA, IAM, IBEW, PACE (the then-newly formed combination of the paper workers and the oil and chemical workers), SEIU, Teamsters, UAW, and the USWA, *all* of which had substantial corporate campaign expertise. The CBC Web site was maintained by the International Union of Electronic Workers (IUE). The roots of this effort probably lay in the previous round of negotiations, in 1995, when GE's outspoken CEO, Jack Welch, essentially dared the unions to take him on. Although they demurred at that time, by forming the CBC the unions signaled early on their intentions for the subsequent round. Initial actions included a worldwide "day of action" in June 1999 to protest the closing of a light bulb factory in Memphis, Tennessee, and the shifting of its production to Hungary and Mexico, and the introduction of two shareholder resolutions at the company's 1999 annual meeting.[48]

OTHER COALITIONS AND SURROGATES

In a number of corporate campaigns, much of the offensive rests not with the campaigning unions per se, but with other groups that they have created or with which they closely cooperate precisely for that purpose. There are many such groups, and they vary considerably in their composition and function depending on the requirements of the particular unions or campaigns at issue. Typically they operate as loose confederations or shell organizations rather than as centralized decision takers, and in the process they provide a form of symbolic cover for the unions. In this section, we discuss two of the more important of these organizations: Jobs with Justice and the Campaign for Labor Rights.

Jobs with Justice

Founded by Larry Cohen in 1987, at the time director of organizing of the CWA, Jobs with Justice is at once a national coalition of unions and labor-friendly organizations as well as an umbrella group composed of local coalitions of labor, community, religious, and other organizations mobilized in support of union organizing and worker justice campaigns. Planning and decision making in Jobs with Justice takes place at the national level, whereas the group's actions are organized locally. Among the members of the coalition at the national level are the AFL–CIO, its Industrial Unions Department, and the affiliated Coalition of Labor Union Women; more than a dozen unions, among them the CWA, IAM, PACE, SEIU, Teamsters, UNITE, UAW, UFCW, UMWA, the National Education Association, and USWA; the Gray Panthers; the United Church of Christ; and the United States Student Association.[49] Jobs with Justice has played a supporting role in many corporate campaigns, among them those at Overnite Transportation, K-Mart, Tyson's Foods, Ryder, and Crown Central Petroleum. The group's principal function is to generate moral pressure in support of one or another of the member unions and against management by mobilizing local religious, civil, and human rights activists and others.

To accomplish this, Jobs with Justice has developed a unique mechanism, the Workers' Rights Board. These boards are committees comprising local labor, religious, political, and community leaders who take the central role in direct action, media attacks, and "other highly visible and aggressive tactics"—in essence, substituting themselves for the union as the front line in the corporate campaign. This positions the company as opposing not the self-interest of a union, but the common interests of the community, and this is an essential tactic for gaining the moral high ground in many campaigns. In the words of Monica Russo, Florida president of UNITE, the objective of such boards is to "make union busting the equivalent of domestic violence or armed robbery."[50] Of particular importance to this enterprise is the recruitment of local religious leaders and the mobilization of support among their respective congregations. To facilitate this, Jobs with Justice has developed a "Religious Action Kit" that presents faith-based perspectives on workplace issues, worship and study materials, and guides to advocacy and action.[51]

When general moral suasion, demonstrations, and media events fail, the Workers' Rights Board often conducts a public hearing to review workers' complaints, inviting management to participate. Because these are hardly neutral forums, the public hearings are best understood as high-profile events designed to lend an aura of judiciousness and legitimacy to the campaign. Their function is put best by the group itself, which states in its literature that:

> It takes more than a quasi-judicial inquiry to stop [employers from engaging in anti-union or anti-worker behaviors]. WRB proceedings are part of a one-two counterpunch that includes direct action by labor, community and faith-based activists.[52]

In addition to its role in supporting employer-specific campaigns, but very much in keeping with its focus on local-level outreach and coalition building, Jobs with Justice is also an important component of the AFL–CIO's Union City program, which we described earlier.

Campaign for Labor Rights

A second union-based organization, the Campaign for Labor Rights (CLR), is a loose coalition of 14 unions and other organizations that served as the initial organizing locus for much of the activity associated with the campaign against sweatshops. The three unions in the coalition—UNITE, the United Farm Workers (UFW), and the United Electrical, Radio, and Machine Workers of America (UE)—are joined by several groups with interests in Latin America, most notably the US/Labor Education and Action Project (US/LEAP; known until 1999 as the US/Guatemala Labor Education Project [US/GLEP]), itself a coalition of some 20 labor, human rights, and religious groups including UNITE; the National Labor Committee (NLC), a labor-based group established in 1981 to oppose American policy in Central America; and the Committee in Solidarity with the People of El Salvador (CISPES), which was initially formed to support leftist revolutionary movements in Central America during the 1980s. Among the other CLR members are the International Labor Rights Fund (ILRF), Press for Change, and the National Interfaith Committee for Worker Justice (NICWJ). ILRF serves as a mechanism for linking trade policies such as those embodied in NAFTA or WTO to workers' rights and other elements of organized labor's agenda. Press for Change is an organization established and staffed by Jeff Ballinger, a one-time AFL–CIO representative in Indonesia who initiated the campaign against Nike. We discuss NICWJ in more detail in the next chapter. Besides Nike, other corporate campaign targets of the CLR and its members have included Disney and Wal-Mart (NLC), Guess! (UNITE), Han Young/Hyundai (UE), Phillips Van Heusen and Starbucks (US/GLEP), and campaigns against manufacturers and marketers of soccer balls and handmade rugs that are allegedly manufactured using child labor.[53]

The theme that unifies many of the CLR campaigns is the emphasis on child labor, exploitation of women, and the inhuman conditions in sweatshops, all set against the unwillingness of prominent companies to accept responsibility for the working conditions imposed by their suppliers. From a strategic perspective, this thematic clearly establishes CLR campaigns on the moral high ground, links them together into a seemingly unified whole, and points directly to a solution—the adoption of codes of conduct through which the Disneys and Nikes of the world can be leveraged to force improvements in wages and working conditions in Haiti, Central America, Indonesia, China, and elsewhere. In many instances, that is a legitimate exercise. However, the reliance on this theme also masks other, less altruistic interests, some economic and others political. It is clear, for example, that UNITE has a vested interest in raising the cost of production in low-wage markets to render domestic American production more competitive; it also has an interest in punishing companies that move jobs overseas. In the case of the NLC, CISPES, and the UE, which is widely regarded as a politically radical union by American standards, there is as well an ideological agenda being served. Indeed, the Latin American focus of some of these organizations comes very close to returning the corporate campaign to its political and intellectual roots in the North American Congress for Latin America (NACLA), where, we have argued, the entire phenomenon began.

A CONCLUDING THOUGHT

In this chapter, we examined a few of the unions and other labor-based organizations that have been especially active in conducting corporate campaigns. As we noted, the selection of these particular groups should not be taken to indicate that they are the only active participants. The full list is actually quite a bit longer.

And it is not the only list. There are also a large number of organizations that are not based in organized labor, but that, for their own reasons, participate in labor-based corporate campaigns as either allies of, or surrogates for, one or more unions. In addition, there is a limited but growing number of organizations that operate quite independently of organized labor and engage in corporate or anticorporate campaigns at their own initiative. In chapter 7, we examine some organizations of both types.

ENDNOTES

1.   For a retrospective on this transition, see William Serrin's obituary for Sweeney's successor, "Lane Kirkland, Former AFL-CIO Head, Dies at 77," *The New York Times*, August 15, 1999.

2. Quoted in James L. Tyson, "As Strikes Lose Potency, Unions Turn to Tactics Outside the Workplace," *Christian Science Monitor*, February 16, 1996, p. 1.
3. "Statement by the AFL–CIO Executive Council on Full Participation in the Labor Movement," Washington, DC, September 21, 1995.
4. Information on the AFL–CIO Organizing Institute was found at www.aflcio.org/orginst.
5. The program is described in detail at www.aflcio.org/unioncity/8stepsto/htm.
6. These were among the courses listed by the Meany Center during 1998, as posted at www.georgemeany.org.
7. Posted at ntserver.cands.com/georgemeany…fmuser/gm_listviewdetail.cfm?CRAID=92.
8. Posted at www.georgemeany.org/gm_htmlcode/gm_noncredit/class/gm_comm.html.
9. Frank Swoboda, "AFL-CIO Earmarks $15 Million For Midterm Election Activity; Final Budget Could Reach $35 Million or More," *Washington Post*, January 31, 1998, p. A6; and "The Union Plus Card Gets Promoted to Gold Status," *Credit Card News*, September 15, 1997, np.
10. Diane E. Lewis, "AFL-CIO ends pact with Ansara's firm; Group fears taint of Teamsters scandal," *Boston Globe*, January 24, 1998, p. E1.
11. Diane E. Lewis, "Union says firm threatened to move," *Boston Globe*, January 30, 1998, p. D3.
12. From the profile of the union found at www.cwa-union.org/aboutcwa, June 14, 1999.
13. See, for example, Anne Gonzalez, "Communication workers dial into better contracts," *Sacramento Business Journal*, February 8, 1999.
14. From the biography found at www.cwa-union.org/aboutcwa/bahr.htm, July 2, 1999.
15. Data provided by the Center for Responsive Politics at www.opensecrets.org, August 18, 1999.
16. Jon Jeter, "Democrats Shun Detroit Papers," *Washington Post*, August 31, 1998, p. A6; and "Democrats Desert ABC-TV in Droves," CWA news release, November 8, 1998.
17. "Virtual Employees: Hard Times at Microsoft," *The Guild Reporter*, October 9, 1998, p. 1.
18. Kate DeSmet, "Lessons of Detroit apply to San Jose," *The Guild Reporter*, October 9, 1998, p. 1.
19. "Unions rally for Avondale," *The Guild Reporter*, October 9, 1998, p. 3.
20. This section is drawn from Jarol B. Manheim, *Labor Pains: The Corporate Campaign Against the Healthcare Industry* (St. Michael's, MD: Tred Avon Institute Press, 1999), pp. 37–39.
21. Steven Greenhouse, "The Labor Movement's Eager Risk-Taker Hits Another Jackpot," *The New York Times*, February 27, 1999, p. A10.
22. Aaron Bernstein, "Andy Stern's Mission Impossible," *Business Week*, June 10, 1996, p. 73.

23. "SEIU Organizes More Than 60,000 Members; Adds Another 121,000 Through Affiliations," *Daily Labor Report*, December 30, 1998, p. A3.
24. Arthur B. Shostak, *CyberUnion: Empowering Labor Through Computer Technology* (Armonk, NY: M.E. Sharpe, 1999), p. 125.
25. SEIU news release, October 22, 1996.
26. SEIU Web site, January 26, 1999.
27. Ibid.
28. Greenhouse, op. cit.
29. SEIU, *Contract Campaign Manual*, 1988, p. i.
30. David Bacon, "Four Years of Class War End in a Union Contract," distributed online at www.igc.org/d-bacon/unions/19sacjan.html.
31. "Union Secures Textile Victory," Associated Press, November 11, 1999.
32. "Sidney Hillman Foundation Announces Annual Awards for Journalists Reporting on Social Justice Issues," UNITE news release, April 30, 1999.
33. Data provided by the Center for Responsive Politics at www.opensecrets.org, August 18, 1999.
34. "Forging Ahead: UFCW Leaders Set Priorities for 1996," *UFCW Action*, March-April 1996, pp. 16–18.
35. See, for example, Tom Alkie, "UFCW Files National Class Action Suit on Albertson's Pay Practices," *Daily Labor Report*, April 23, 1997, pp. A7–A8; Worth Wren, Jr., "Ex-workers' suit accuses Food Lion of unfair practices," *Fort Worth Star-Telegram*, September 9, 1991; "Florida's Largest Private Employer to Face New Discrimination Charges: Class Action Lawsuit to be Filed April 3 Against Publix Alleging Race Discrimination in Florida, Alabama, Georgia and South Carolina," UFCW news release, April 2, 1997; and "Service With a Grimace: Nordstrom's Two Faces," *UFCW Action*, May-June 1990, p. 13. Sometimes such litigation is merely waved as a threat in the course of a campaign. See "Perdue and Labor Policy Association Put on Notice: Anti-Union Slander Could Bring Lawsuit," UFCW news release, September 17, 1996.
36. "Wal-Mart Wolf Stalks the Grocery Industry," *UFCW Action*, January–February 1992, p. 18; and "Wal-Mart Juggernaut Reels Toward the UFCW," *UFCW Action*, November–December 1992, p. 5.
37. "The Gathering Storm: Expanding Mega-Discount Industry Threatens Jobs, Communities," *UFCW Action*, March–April 1993, pp. 10–12.
38. "Working Women 'Blow the Whistle' on Wal-Mart and K-Mart in Nationwide protest on May 8," UFCW news release, May 6, 1995; and Muriel H. Cooper, "Unions: Add justice to shopping list; Harry Woo helps kick off UFCW Wal-Mart drive," *AFL-CIO News*, December 1, 1995, p. 3.
39. Constance E. Beaumont, *How Superstore Sprawl Can Harm Communities And what citizens can do about it* (Washington: National Trust for Historic Preservation, 1994).
40. This summary draws on the history of the union found at www.uswa.org/history.html, June 14, 1999.

41. "USWA Leadership Team," *Steelabor*, March–April 1998, p. 10; and Steven Greenhouse, "Three Unions Say Conflicts Will Delay Merger," *The New York Times*, June 25, 1999.
42. Heather Landy, "Union seeks more members: Steelworkers boost organizing budget to rebuild roster," *Detroit News*, August 13, 1998; see also an untitled USWA news release dated August 13, 1998.
43. From the profile at www.icftu.org/english/icftu/whatitis.html, August 19, 1999.
44. Listed at www.icftu.org/itsWeb.html, August 19, 1999.
45. "ICEM: Defending the World's Workers," www.icem.org/abt_icem.html, August 19, 1999.
46. "ICEM/USWA Continental Tire Campaign Now Online," ICEM news release, June 8, 1999.
47. "Welcome to the ICEM Rio Tinto Campaign," www.icem.org/campaigns/rio_tinto/about_us.html, August 19, 1999.
48. "Welcome to the Coordinated Bargaining Committee," www.cbcunions.org, August 17, 1999.
49. "Members & Allies," www.igc.apc.org/jwj/AboutJWJ/MembAlly.htm, October 11, 1998.
50. Presentation at the annual meeting of the American Political Science Association, Atlanta, GA, September 3, 1999.
51. See www.jwj.org/OrgTools/RAK.htm.
52. "What Are WRBs?" found at www.jwj.org/WRBs/Whatis.htm, August 19, 1999.
53. "Campaign for Labor Rights: Partner Organizations," and "Campaign for Labor Rights: Document Library," found at www.compugraph.com/clr, February 7, 1998.

7

ATTACK OF THE "TREE-HUGGERS"

Two factors have helped to move the use of corporate campaigns well beyond the labor movement proper. The first is the origin of the campaign, which, as we have seen, owes much to social, religious, and other progressive activists with diverse agendas of their own. Through the Midwest Academy, through the National Council of Churches, and through a host of other organizations, the campaign has emerged as an accepted form of essentially political leverage—using the pressure generated against individual corporations or industries not only as a means to impose the campaigning group's agenda on the target, but often as a means to highlight perceived deficiencies and force changes in public policy. The logic of this approach is that, by demanding change on the part of influential corporations, the antagonists can leverage the target's discomfiture into support for their desired policy changes. The policies in question can range from affirmative action and civil rights to environmental protection, international trade, and human rights, or even to the domestic politics of other countries. Such a game was played, for example, with respect to the political situations in Burma and Indonesia in the 1980s and 1990s, in which attacks on such diverse companies as Freeport McMoRan, Nike, Pepsico, and Unocal were used to bring economic pressure and political embarrassment to bear on regimes that were anathema to the international human rights community.

The second factor contributing to the increasing reliance on corporate campaigns is the nature of the campaigns as developed by the AFL–CIO and the unions. Recall that a principal reason the labor movement turned to corporate campaigns as a means to pressure employers was that the unions' appeal and legitimacy were in decline. The campaign addressed this through its emphasis on carrying the message forward through a network of allies and surrogates, including churches and other religious organizations, civil rights groups, environmentalists, consumer advocates, and the like. Although a number of these labor-friendly groups were willing from the outset to cooperate with organized labor, most did not possess any corporate campaign expertise per se, nor did they necessarily even understand the overall nature of the enterprise. Rather, they were simply motivated by what they believed to be a good cause. But over the course of a quarter century of partnering with labor in these ventures, some groups began to develop their own appreciation of campaign techniques, their own expertise, and their own agendas.

To date, these politically motivated *anti*-corporate campaigns are far outnumbered by their labor-based counterparts, but they are capable of inflicting considerable pain on their corporate targets and they are increasing in number, duration, and sophistication. In this chapter, we examine a few of the groups that engage in such campaigns, beginning with those most closely allied with labor and concluding with those that appear to be operating with the greatest measure of independence from the unions. As elsewhere, our purpose here is not to identify and illuminate every such group, but merely to provide an overview of some of the more prominent campaign practitioners.

ONE DEGREE OF SEPARATION: THE NATIONAL INTERFAITH COMMITTEE ON WORKER JUSTICE

In September 1996, just a few months after John Sweeney assumed the presidency of the AFL–CIO, 40 religious leaders representing 18 denominations came together to form the National Interfaith Committee for Worker Justice (NICWJ). Sweeney, a prominent Catholic lay leader in his own right, had called for a closer alliance between labor and the churches; NICWJ was the response. As the president of the new organization, retired United Methodist minister and former auto worker Reverend Jesse DeWitt, stated at the time, "Providing shelter and food for the unemployed is not enough. We must protect their rights as workers as well."[1]

From its inception, day-to-day management of the NICWJ has been in the hands of executive director Kim Bobo, a Chicago-based activist with close ties to the Midwest Academy, the training school for activists established by former SDSer Heather Booth. Indeed, as we see in a later chapter, Bobo was the senior author of an extensive manual for activists published by the Academy. The NICWJ has been active in a number of corporate campaigns—from its first efforts working with the UFCW to help organize poultry workers at Case Farms in North Carolina to its more recent role supporting the SEIU by pressuring the religious orders that operate Catholic Healthcare West to revise their understanding of the Church's teachings on workplace justice. What these campaigns tend to have in common is that they focus on either religious employers per se or employers and industries that recruit low-wage workers with strong religious ties. The role of the NICWJ is to add an explicit moral and religious dimension to the campaign and, in the process, to provide it with an aura of legitimacy.

The National Interfaith Committee works through a network of more than 40 local interfaith committees in 24 states.[2] These committees, in turn, organize local congregations to support both labor actions in their respective communities and the broader objective of building a base in the religious community for appeals grounded in worker–justice issues. Central to this effort, and among the group's most prominent activities, has been the *labor in the pulpit* initiative—a drive to build labor-friendly messages into sermons during the Labor Day weekend each year. To this end, the NICWJ has distributed a "Litany for Workers"[3] as well as a listing of more than two dozen biblical passages that can be employed by the clergy in framing proworker messages.[4] By 1999, churches in more than 50 cities were participating in the program.[5]

The Labor Day initiative is but one dimension of a broader effort to support labor's organizing campaigns. Indeed, the NICWJ offers a 10-point plan for aiding workers, including, among other points:

- Pray for all workers, especially those who work in sweatshops, are on strike, downsized or locked out....
- Invite a union leader to speak to the congregation at an appropriate time....
- Encourage parishioners to advocate for public policies that seek justice for all workers, including decent wages and health care benefits....
- Boycott products produced by companies where workers are organizing to improve conditions and where boycotts are viewed as an effective means for encouraging a just resolution to the workers' problems....[6]

This broader agenda is advanced through a variety of means. For example, the NICWJ publishes a newsletter, *Faith Works*, that features religious groups' participation in organizing campaigns, frames codes of conduct for industries targeted by its own campaigns, and conducts conferences that bring together leaders of the religious and labor communities. In 1999, the group published a 56-page guide to workplace rights addressing such issues as compensation, health and safety standards, discrimination, and the right to organize and bargain collectively. In addition to English, the manual was published in Spanish, Polish, Chinese, and Korean editions. It was distributed at workshops and training sessions conducted in churches and homeless shelters.[7]

In October 1999, the NICWJ sponsored a conference, "Forging Partnerships for a New Millenium," timed to coincide with the AFL–CIO's "Working Families Convention" meeting in Los Angeles. Among the topics of workshops and discussions were media training and strategizing, grassroots fundraising, an overview of religion–labor work, new opportunities for the religious community, and a strategic planning session. Featured speakers included John Sweeney, several prominent religious leaders, and Jesse DeWitt and Kim Bobo of the NICWJ. In addition to the public sessions, the conference included a special "seminary track" for students enrolled in the training programs of the various denominations. This track added workshops on the history of the partnership between religion and labor, as well as opportunities to observe the contemporaneous AFL–CIO sessions.[8] In writing to urge the AFL–CIO's member international unions to participate in the conference, John Sweeney observed that, "I believe this is a defining moment historically in our relationship with the religious community."[9] Indeed, the 1999 conference, and especially the extra sessions for seminarians, were but one piece of the larger AFL–CIO strategy of reestablishing a relationship with the clergy. Other aspects of this strategy included the encouragement of teaching more labor-related courses at the seminaries as well as a planned program, modeled after Union Summer, in which dozens of seminary students were to spend their summers working with various unions.[10]

As should be evident from this discussion, although the NICWJ has been organized outside of the labor movement, it exists primarily to support not only the objectives of the movement, but its specific programs and campaigns as well, among them the campaigns against Case Farms, Catholic Healthcare West, Crown Central Petroleum, and Tyson's Foods. We can think of this as constituting one degree of separation from organized labor. Among the other groups that are similarly situated are Citizen Action, which served as a conduit for funds in the 1998 Teamsters election scandal and which also has close historical ties to the Midwest Academy; the Economic Policy Institute, a labor-friendly Washington think tank; and the Preamble Center for Public Policy, a research center established by prolabor interests in 1996 (the same year as the NICWJ) and devoted to "fighting the pro-market, anti-people conventional wisdom that has come to dominate our national economic debate and developing and promoting ideas for restricting the overwhelming power corporate and financial giants wield over virtually every aspect of American life."[11]

TWO DEGREES OF SEPARATION: ACORN

In chapter 1, we noted that one of the SDS experimental projects—the Economic Research and Action Project—had provided a model for community organizing that was soon adopted by the National Welfare Rights Organization (NWRO), which emerged in the late 1960s as a voice for the needs and rights of low-income people. The Association of Community Organizations for Reform Now (ACORN) was formed in 1970 when George Wiley, who headed the NWRO, dispatched Wade Rathke to Little Rock, Arkansas, to begin organizing poor people in the South. Arkansas was selected for this exercise because the state had a median income below $6,000, a large welfare-eligible population that was 35% African-American, and a capital city that was centrally located in the state. Rathke formed ACORN (the "A" originally stood for Arkansas), which established itself over the 1970s as a national grassroots organization, forged alliances with the International Ladies Garment Workers Union (now merged into UNITE) and other labor organizations and community groups, and began to involve itself in Democratic Party politics.[12] In the words of Gary Delgado, one of ACORN's founding members,

> In building ACORN, Rathke hoped to keep what he perceived to be good in his welfare rights experience (the membership base, the use of a replicable model, and the strategic manipulation of the press), while incorporating some parts of the old Alinsky model (strong ties to such existing organizations as unions and churches) and experimenting with electoral politics as a way to consolidate organizational victories.[13]

In 1979, the organization adopted what it labeled a *People's Platform*—a comprehensive statement of the ACORN agenda that was updated in 1990. The preamble to this document stated, in part,

> In our freedom, only the people shall rule. Corporations shall have their role: producing jobs, providing products, paying taxes. No more, no less. They shall obey our wishes, respond to our needs, serve our communities....

> Government shall have its role: public servant to our good, fast follower to our sure steps. No more, no less. Our government shall shout with the public voice and no longer to a private whisper. In our government, the common concerns shall be the collective cause.[14]

The centrality of the group's interest in labor-related issues is made explicit in a lengthy section of the platform headed "Work and Workers' Rights." One portion of this section defined the "fundamental rights of workers" as follows:

- The right to a job which does not endanger health or safety.
- The right to a job which is accessible from home.

- The right to a job which does not require overtime work as a condition of employment.
- The right to company or government financed child care for the workers' children.
- The right to a fair grievance procedure.
- Most fundamentally, the right to organize, which is promoted by:
  a) Extending the National Labor Relations Act coverage to all workers.
  b) Streamlining the union election and certification process.
  c) Restricting the use of anti-strike injunctions by courts.
  d) Providing stiff penalties—back wages times five—for employers who fire or demote workers for their organizing activities.
- The right to company or government financed health insurance.[15]

From these and other elements of the ACORN platform, we can see that the group's agenda meshes closely at some points with that of organized labor, even as it differs at others (e.g., as in ACORN's support for and organized labor's opposition to programs through which private employers are encouraged to hire workers from the welfare roles—so-called *workfare* programs). In most instances, ACORN and labor have found themselves on the same side and working as allies. Indeed, by 1986, ACORN had forged institutional ties with AFL–CIO Central Labor Councils in at least 30 cities.[16]

Emblematic of this cooperation is ACORN's joint leadership, with labor, of the Living Wage Campaign, an effort to replace the standard of the minimum wage with what amounts to a minimum standard of living—a standard that would require wages to be raised substantially across the economy.[17] As part of this campaign, ACORN, the Massachusetts AFL–CIO, and the Boston Central Labor Council co-hosted a 1998 National Living Wage Campaign Training Conference that brought together organizers from labor, community, and church organizations in 35 cities across the country. Organizers from the SEIU and HERE, as well as from ACORN, discussed the strategic use of living wage campaigns to promote union and community organizing.[18] In the words of one ACORN spokesperson, "The big picture isn't the individual workers being covered by living-wage laws. It's the organizing; ... it's the new coalitions being built."[19]

ACORN, then, independently traces its origins to the SDS—in this instance, to ERAP rather than to NACLA—with a bow, too, toward Saul Alinsky, and the group has its own agenda and independent leadership.[20] At the same time, labor issues represent an essential component of the ACORN agenda. As part of its own strategy for advancing its interests, the group has formed long-term alliances with organized labor to advance those issues. On this basis, we can conclude that ACORN operates at two degrees of separation from organized labor. Another similarly situated organization is the Interfaith Center for Corporate Responsibility (ICCR), which, as noted in chapter 3, was spun off from the National Council of Churches to provide research and legitimacy for religious organizations that have sought to impose progressive social and labor policies on corporations through their investment policies.

THREE DEGREES OF SEPARATION:
THE NATIONAL ORGANIZATION FOR WOMEN

At three degrees of separation—independent origin, independent leadership, independent agenda, but with a history of participation in labor-initiated campaigns—we find such traditional interest groups as the Sierra Club, the Nader-related U.S. Public Interest Research Group (USPIRG), and the NAACP. In South Florida, for example, the Miami–Dade chapter of the NAACP and the AFL–CIO have developed a common agenda on such issues as wages and working conditions, workers' rights, and voting rights, and the civil rights group has supported organizing campaigns like that at Goya Foods.[21] The Sierra Club has been the scene of a battle for control of the organization between mainstream environmentalists and more radical activists interested in moving its profile more toward that of Greenpeace.[22] A recent issue of the Sierra Club's magazine, *The Planet*, carried a series of articles on the use of boycotts and shareholder actions to hold corporations accountable to environmentalists.[23] But in the context of the corporate campaign per se, the most interesting of these third-degree groups may well be the National Organization for Women (NOW).

Although many campaign-active organizations evolved affirmatively from the early SDS experience, the women's rights movement of the 1960s and 1970s arguably traces its origins to the *negative* experiences of women who participated in SDS's ERAP experiment, where, even as they were made newly aware of their capabilities as organizers and leaders, they found themselves relegated to secondary roles supporting the activities of their male counterparts and subjected to what they came to regard as sexual exploitation.[24] From its very inception in 1966, NOW has served as the most prominent advocate of women's rights. Today the organization claims half a million members and 550 local chapters.

NOW has a wide-ranging agenda, incorporating such diverse issues as the Equal Rights Amendment, violence against women, affirmative action, abortion rights, gay and lesbian rights, and electing feminists to public office. Labor-related issues are not in and of themselves central to the NOW program except to the extent that they relate in some way to the rights of women in the workplace (e.g., advancement, equal pay, sexual harassment, etc). These tend to be issues to which organized labor attends, but only secondarily. Nevertheless, NOW has played a supporting role in several corporate campaigns dating back to the early 1980s, including those targeted at General Dynamics, Nike, Fionor A/S, and Consolidated Foods. Of greater interest, however, is the extent to which NOW appears to have applied the lessons learned from observing these labor-based efforts to campaigns of its own.

This is most evident in NOW's "Merchants of Shame" campaign—a component of its larger drive to promote a "women-friendly workplace." Together, the two represent a combination of threat and reinforcement, sharing in common the objective of ending discrimination and harassment in the workplace. Merchants of Shame is a collection of company-specific campaigns designed to pressure targeted employers to end practices that NOW finds unacceptable. At this writing, targets have included Smith Barney, Mitsubishi, and Detroit Edison. We have already detailed in chapter 5 the NOW campaign against Mitsubishi. At Smith Barney, female employees reported a number of offensive practices, the most egregious of which appears to have been the operation of a "Boom Boom Room" in the basement of one branch of the brokerage where male employees drank Bloody Mary's and joked about sexual harassment complaints. At Detroit Edison, similar claims of harassment were accompanied by allegations of gender and racial discrimination. In all three cases, the campaigns were centered on class action litigation.

The carrot that ostensibly accompanies this stick is a so-called *Employer's Pledge* to create a women-friendly workplace. NOW has asked all of the Fortune 500 companies to sign this pledge, which centers on the adoption and enforcement of strong antidiscrimination policies and zero tolerance for harassment.[25]

In NOW, then, we find a group that is independent of organized labor in every significant way, but has allied with labor in some of its corporate campaigns over more than 15 years and has applied the lessons of that experience to advancing the group's own agenda. Labor has not always reciprocated. As noted earlier, for example, just when a settlement was being reached in the Smith Barney campaign, a HERE Local objected because the investment firm had been identified as a secondary target in the union's campaign to organize food service employees at Aramark, which operated the cafeteria at Smith Barney's headquarters.

FOUR DEGREES OF SEPARATION: THE RAINFOREST ACTION NETWORK AND THE RUCKUS SOCIETY

In addition to the types of nonlabor-based groups already identified, we have begun to see an increase in corporate campaign-type activity by a fourth set of organizations that are independent not only with respect to their origins, leadership, and interests, but also to the objectives of their campaigns and the alliances they form. In campaigns initiated by these groups, workplace issues are seldom if ever targeted, and unions are only rarely involved. Rather, these campaigns center around human rights, environmentalism, and other progressive issues, and they tend to have a strong political component. It is here that we find the best contemporary examples of the anticorporate campaign envisioned by Michael Locker in the 1970 NACLA *Research Methodology Guide*. This represents what we can think of as a *fourth degree of separation*. Some of the groups that fall within this classification include Greenpeace, Project Underground, the Natural Resources Defense Council, INFACT, and Human Rights Watch. Greenpeace, for example, has pressured companies like Baxter International to end their use of vinyl packaging materials and has attacked Monsanto for its production of genetically modified seeds.[26] Project Underground describes itself as having "filled a niche for supporting ... focused corporate campaigns [that] work to inform people of corporate environmental and human rights abuses through innovative communication strategies...."[27] INFACT has led the attack against Philip Morris and other tobacco companies.

Among the most active of these organizations is the Rainforest Action Network (RAN). Founded in 1985, RAN is a grassroots organization claiming some 30,000 members. Its stated objectives are to protect the world's rainforests and old growth forests and the rights of the indigenous peoples who live in the forests. The group's first effort was a 1987 boycott of Burger King restaurants intended to force the company to stop importing beef from tropical countries where forests were being cleared to provide pasture land for cattle. The boycott was conducted in part through a network of local Rainforest Action Groups (RAGs) that staged demonstrations at Burger King restaurants in several U.S. cities. When the company announced that it would no longer import beef from the countries in question, RAN claimed credit for the policy change.[28] In the years since, RAN has directed a series of ever more sophisticated "corporate responsibility" campaigns against such targets as Mitsubishi, Home Depot, Freeport-McMoRan, Occidental Petroleum, MacMillan Bloedel, Georgia Pacific, Kimberley Clark, Texaco, and Conoco. We have already detailed the most elaborate of these efforts—the Mitsubishi campaign—in chapter 5. The unifying element of RAN campaigns is their focus on companies the group judges to be depleting the world's resources. As a result, RAN's targets tend to be multinational companies with extensive interests in the extraction and logging industries. RAN employs a wide range of tactics in these attacks, including corporate research of the type that is by now familiar, demonstrations, letter writing and petition campaigns, coalition building, media initiatives, and direct action.

One issue on which RAN and organized labor did find themselves in agreement was their opposition, albeit for different reasons, to the Multilateral Agreement on Investment (MAI)—a proposed treaty that would have imposed a new international jurisdiction in a variety of regulatory venues. Labor, whose case was carried to the public principally through the Preamble Center on Public Policy, saw the MAI as a globalization of the principles embodied in the North American Free Trade Agreement (NAFTA), which the unions regard as an endorsement of the right of American corporations to export jobs and production. For RAN and other environmental groups, MAI was seen as providing an alternative to the relatively strong environmental protections incorporated under U.S. law.

Closely allied with RAN is a second, much smaller group with a rather different style—the aptly named Ruckus Society—which focuses on supporting the initiatives of RAN and other groups. The Ruckus Society was founded in October 1995 by two long-time environmental activists, Howard Cannon of Greenpeace and Mike Roselle of RAN. Its objective is to "encourage the proliferation of skilled, non-violent, direct-action activists worldwide."[29] In other words, Ruckus exists to train activists in the techniques of direct action. Roselle, a cofounder and board member of RAN, was joined on the small paid Ruckus staff by Donna Parker—another RAN alumna who oversaw the RAN campaign against Mitsubishi.[30] Although no formal relationship appears to exist, the close ties between RAN and Ruckus are evident both in the interlocking of leaders and training staff—some of whom also have ties to Greenpeace—and in the frequency with which Ruckus training supports RAN actions. Most, if not all, of the RAN activists who have scaled trees, bridges, and buildings to hang banners attacking Mitsubishi and other targets have been trained by Ruckus, and even the banners have often been created by Ruckus associates.[31] Ruckus also trains antilogging activists in ways to disrupt logging operations in the nation's forests (e.g., by climbing trees that are about to be felled).

Some of this work is actually supported by corporations that regard themselves as politically progressive. For example, clothing-maker Patagonia, which tithes 10% of its profits to environmental activism, offers its employees civil disobedience training provided by the Ruckus Society. The company's literature proclaims: "It may sound as if we are training and subsidizing a bunch of tree huggers, hell raisers and brassbound ecologists. We are."[32]

One of the more extensive collaborative efforts between the two organizations came in the preparations for the extensive direct action targeted at the November 1999 meeting of the World Trade Organization (WTO) in Seattle, Washington, and the follow-up demonstrations at the World Bank and International Monetary Fund in Washington, DC, in April 2000. Environmentalists (and organized labor) see the WTO as a rationalizing umbrella under which are advanced trends in globalization of the economy that they oppose. At a meeting in June 1999, RAN, the Sierra Club, Friends of the Earth, and a number of other groups issued a statement on the forthcoming WTO session, which stated in part,

> The WTO is bad for forests. Measures to expedite trade in forest products will increase consumption without concurrently implementing conservation measures. In the WTO, trade provisions are supreme over the laws of nations, taking power away from local communities and governments and giving it to corporations. This makes it a direct threat not only to the world's remaining forests, but also to basic individual and states' rights.[33]

In preparation for the Seattle protest, in September 1999, RAN and Ruckus cosponsored a 6-day "Globalize This! Action Camp" for 150 experienced activists to plan and train for a series of protests, blockades, lockdowns, climbing actions, banner hangings, and other acts of civil disobedience to demonstrate opposition to the meeting.[34] This workshop on how best to disrupt the WTO meeting resembled other *camps* the Ruckus Society runs, albeit on a larger scale. A contemporaneous news article described the training:

> They have been conducting training sessions in rock climbing (the better to scale buildings in downtown Seattle), rappelling (the better to hang anti-WTO banners from the city's many bridges) and "direct action techniques" (for disrupting the meeting).
>
> They've been poring over Seattle street maps to plot strategy. They've staged elaborate role-playing exercises, to learn maneuvers designed to outsmart the city's police. And they've been brainstorming, refining and rejecting ideas for their planned civil protest. Filling cars with cement?... Chaining themselves to various buildings?... An aerial assault, possibly some parachutes?... Billboard liberation?[35]

A similar "Alternative Spring Break Action Camp" held in Arcadia, Florida, in March 2000 helped prepare student activists for the IMF and World Bank protests.[36]

In line with its self-proclaimed mission as a training center, the Ruckus Society has published a series of manuals for direct action, including one on scouting, one on planning, and one on using the media. The scouting manual emphasizes the importance of site selection if a direct-action event is to be both safe and successful. Much of this brief manual is a lengthy list headed, "What Should I Bring?" Included are such diverse items as aerial photos of the site (and suggestions on where to obtain them), baby wipes, bear mace (to protect oneself from bears), carpeting to throw over barbed wire (to facilitate climbing over it), doggie treats (to assuage an interested guard dog), a foam pad to sit on while waiting, a GPS receiver, and the like. Much of the manual is directed at scouting transportation routes and facilities, particularly those used in transporting forest products, but there are also references to infiltrating industrial facilities.[37]

The planning manual emphasizes the symbolic nature of direct action and the need to design such events for maximum impact. Included are considerations in defining and clarifying the issue, selecting the target audience for the message, and choosing a context that creates the proper frame for the desired message.[38]

The media manual—the third of the series—opens with a survey of how decisions are made in each of the several newsroom types (e.g., wire services, newspapers, radio, local television, and network television). This is followed by a checklist for most effectively exploiting the media, including a countdown of preparations from 1 month before a scheduled event until 1 day after its completion. Steps in the early planning include selecting a media strategist, settling on a single simple message, choosing a strong central graphic image, preparing effective sound bites, and scheduling the action for a day and time that will maximize coverage. Subsequent details include a variety of means for gaining maximum attention, including the use of cellular telephones by participants to answer reporters' questions during the event.[39]

All of these techniques were in evidence, for example, in the 1996 RAN demonstrations at key Bank of California locations in the course of the group's Mitsubishi campaign, as detailed in chapter 5, and at the 1999 WTO action in Seattle as well.

RAN, Greenpeace, and other similar groups that operate at the fourth degree of separation approach their relationship with corporations from a different starting point than does organized labor. Their objectives are generally defined in terms of broad public and corporate policies rather than in terms of specific economic demands. If successful, it is likely that their association with a given company will cease rather than intensify. In a sense, this frees them to be more creative in some of their attacks than a union seeking to organize workers can be, although it also relieves them of some of the direct pressure that unions confront in attempting to preserve their shrinking share of the workforce. The Ruckus Society is, in a sense, an expression of that freedom of expression, but it is also a marker of the greater degree of radicalism that characterizes some of the politically motivated anticorporate campaigns.

The anticorporate political agenda of some of the players operating at the fourth degree of separation is perhaps most evident in *Focus on the Corporation*, a series of online commentaries written by Russell Mokhiber and Robert Weissman beginning in 1999. At this writing, Weissman was the editor of *Multinational Monitor*, a magazine published by Ralph Nader's home-base organization, Essential Information, that has often published articles that were highly critical of companies being targeted in union corporate campaigns. Mokhiber was editor of a newsletter, *Corporate Crime Reporter*, that focuses on cases of corporate malfeasance.[40] The commentaries emphasize such topics as globalization and corporate power, corporate political influence, opposition to regulation, corporatization of the American culture, and "specific, extreme examples of corporate abuses."[41] The gist of their critique and the essence of their position were perhaps best captured in a commentary distributed in September of that year:

> The criminal element has seeped deep into every nook and cranny of American society.

> Forget about the underworld—these crooks dominate every aspect of our market, culture and politics.

> They cast a deep shadow over life in turn of the century America.

> We buy gas from them (Exxon, Chevron, Unocal).

> We take pictures with their cameras and film (Eastman Kodak).

> We drink their beer (Coors).

> We buy insurance from them to guard against financial catastrophe if we get sick (Blue Cross Blue Shield).

> And then when we get sick, we buy pharmaceuticals from them (Pfizer, Warner Lambert, Ortho Pharmaceuticals).

> We do our laundry in washers and dryers from them (General Electric).

> We vacation with them (Royal Caribbean Cruise Lines).

> We buy our food from them (Archer Daniels Midland, Southland, Tyson Foods, U.S. Sugar).

> We drive with them (Hyundai) and fly with them (Korean Air Lines).

> All of these companies and more turned up on *Corporate Crime Reporter*'s list of the top 100 Corporate Criminals of the 1990s....[42]

Even among those groups that are the most politically motivated, then, there are differences of emphasis and degree and a range of styles and objectives, with some pragmatic and some fundamentally radical.

FIVE DEGREES OF SEPARATION: NEW MODELS OF CORPORATE COMPETITION

At five degrees of separation from organized labor, we find a rather different class of antagonists—one whose corporate campaign-type actions are far more difficult to discern and document. This class includes competitors of a targeted company who employ strategic communication and other campaign devices to attack that company's stakeholder relationships in hopes of advancing their own competitive positions. Although their interests and actions may well bring them to form direct or de facto alliances with unions and other groups, these companies are invariably acting to serve their own, narrowly defined objectives, which are often directly antithetical to those of organized labor. It is for this reason that we have characterized them as campaigning at five degrees of separation.

Unlike labor unions and advocacy groups, competing companies are generally committed to masking their role in any attack. This makes reliable information about such activities difficult to obtain and renders any conclusions one might draw from the limited information available necessarily tenuous. Moreover, efforts to manipulate legislation, regulatory agencies and actions, media coverage, and the like to advantage have always been a component of business competition in the United States, and the boundary between such efforts in isolation and their incorporation in a systematic corporate campaign is ambiguous at best. Accordingly, we must regard the analysis of such cases as speculative in character.

That said, there is at least circumstantial evidence to suggest that such campaigns do occur, perhaps with regularity. One example might be the campaign against Nike, which was described in chapter 4. In that earlier discussion, we noted the role of the AFL–CIO and Press for Change (a group affiliated with the Campaign for Labor Rights) in singling out Nike for poster-child status in the attack on sweatshops. But there is another part of the story. In addition to Nike, the company's principal competitor, Reebok, was also purchasing shoes from suppliers in Indonesia and was also visited by Jeff Ballinger, at the time the AFL–CIO's organizer on the scene. But whereas Nike obviously balked at Ballinger's demands, it appears that Reebok had a rather different reaction. That, at least, is a conclusion one might draw from the company's subsequent actions, which included the establishment of the Reebok Foundation, whose executive director, Sharon Cohen, was also the company's vice president for public affairs and, through that foundation, the establishment of an annual award to recognize the achievements of human rights activists. Ms. Cohen also joined the Boards of Directors of Business for Social Responsibility, a group that presses companies to adhere to a defined agenda of "responsible" corporate behaviors, and the Social Venture Network, a group of large investors dedicated to supporting companies with what they regard as progressive policies on the workplace, the environment, and the like.[43] In April 1999, Reebok even invited the American Center for International Labor Solidarity, an arm of the AFL–CIO, to provide training on trade unionism and negotiations to workers in five Indonesian factories where its goods were manufactured.[44] It should be noted, however, that even the Campaign for Labor Rights viewed these actions with some distrust. In the words of one CLR missive, "Although some individuals within Reebok may honestly be supportive of worker rights, experience says that we have to assume cynicism at the corporate headquarters. Reebok's motivation is to one-up Nike on human rights issues while maximizing profits."[45]

That comment may be particularly telling in the present context in light of another action taken by Reebok's Ms. Cohen. The Reebok vice president participated in a March 1997 meeting of the Global Partners Working Group, an international network then being established by the Council on Economic Priorities—a frequent critic of companies targeted in corporate campaigns about which we say more in chapter 9. Among the other organizations represented at that meeting were the Interfaith Center for Corporate Responsibility, Progressive Asset Management (a social-responsibility investment firm), and the United Methodist Church.[46] What these groups have in common is that all were, at the time, members of the "Working Group on Nike"—a coalition that sponsored a boycott of Nike and, once the company agreed to follow the code of conduct adopted by the Apparel Industry Partnership, undertook to monitor Nike's compliance with that code.[47] Ms. Cohen's participation in the meeting thus placed her in the room with three leading antagonists of her company's principal rival at a meeting devoted to sharing information for use in anticorporate campaigns.

Even if they did not constitute participation in the campaign against Nike, such actions may well have insulated Reebok from attack. A September 1997 report prepared by two labor monitoring groups and distributed by the Campaign for Labor Rights found that practices in factories producing shoes for Nike *and* Reebok were in violation of the companies' own codes of conduct and the code of the Apparel Industry Partnership to which both subscribed.[48] Yet to date, the antisweatshop movement and other antagonists have concentrated their attentions almost exclusively on Nike.

A more complex, but in some ways potentially more telling, campaign at the fifth degree of separation is that apparently waged against Microsoft by several of its leading rivals and competitors, including AOL, Corel, IBM, Netscape, Novell, Oracle, and Sun Microsystems, a grouping colloquially known as NOISE (an acronym for Netscape, Oracle, IBM, Sun, and Everybody Else).[49] This campaign, in combination with the contemporaneous efforts of two other clusters of interests—consumer rights advocates and a union—at least arguably led to the Justice Department's antitrust action against the company, and promises additional challenges in the future.[50]

Figure 7.1 illustrates these three seemingly independent campaigns. The first, by groups claiming to represent consumer interests, was led at least spiritually by Ralph Nader, who sponsored a November 1997 conference, "Appraising Microsoft," at which many of the company's harshest critics attacked the company's business practices. Nader was an early critic of Microsoft on issues ranging from privacy to monopolistic practices. Two years before the conference, the magazine *Multinational Monitor*, published by his company, Essential Information, Inc., had accused Microsoft of antitrust violations. As the nation's premier icon of consumerism, Nader's involvement has afforded the anti-Microsoft campaign a strong presumption of protecting the rights of consumers. Except for the conference and a follow-up focusing on proposed remedies, however, Nader's interest in Microsoft has been advanced less directly, primarily through the Consumer Project on Technology, which he helped found.

In 1999, another group long associated with consumer protection, the Consumer Federation of America (CFA), entered the fray when it issued a series of reports attacking Microsoft as being anticonsumer and engaging in predatory pricing practices. CFA claims to be a coalition of consumer rights groups, but declined repeated requests to provide a list of its member groups. Such a list would be of interest because, during the course of the 1999 Microsoft antitrust trial, the CFA, together with two organizations with ties to Nader (the Media Access Project and US Public Interest Research Group), threatened to sue the company in behalf of consumers for $10 billion allegedly gained through illegal pricing schemes. At this writing, that litigation had yet to be filed.

Even as the consumer clouds were darkening, Microsoft was confronted by yet another campaign, this one being waged by the AFL–CIO and the Communications Workers of America (CWA) to win the hearts and minds of the thousands of workers that staffed Microsoft on a temporary basis through a network of contract employers. This organizing effort was first made public by Larry Cohen of the CWA in September 1998 and was subsequently featured in the October 8, 1998, issue of *The Guild Reporter*, the official newspaper of the Newspaper Guild, a component of the CWA.[51] Since that time, the organizing drive has become quite prominent.

Finally, we have the efforts of the competitors, which have taken two prominent forms. First, several of these companies—Corel, Netscape, Oracle, and Sun—joined together in 1998 to form ProComp, the Project to Promote Competition and Innovation in the Digital Age. ProComp's first project was to attack Microsoft for its alleged monopolistic practices. The group

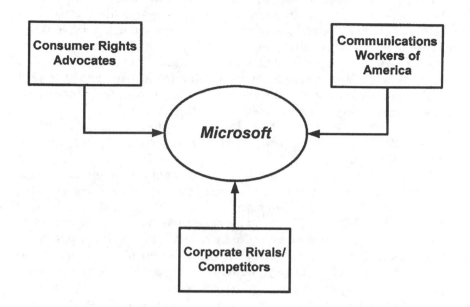

FIG. 7.1. Contemporaneous campaigns against Microsoft.

hired two prominent lobbyists, Robert Dole and Robert Bork, to advance its cause.[52] In addition, Novell, Oracle, and Sun, through their respective political action committees or their senior management, made contributions in 1997–1998 to the campaign of Senator Orin Hatch, the leading congressional critic of Microsoft. (Novell and a second software firm, Caldera, which filed suit against Microsoft alleging that it was the victim of monopolistic practices, are both based in Hatch's home state of Utah.) They were joined in those contributions during the course of the Microsoft trial by AOL, which shortly afterward acquired another of their number, Netscape.[53] After the trial, senior executives of several of these companies sponsored a fundraiser in support of Senator Hatch's presidential campaign, and the Senator asked AOL to fly him around on its corporate jet.[54]

As Chairman of the Senate Judiciary Committee, Senator Hatch held a number of hearings about Microsoft's business practices, most notably a March 1998 session in which James McNealy, CEO of Sun Microsystems, and James Barksdale, CEO of Netscape, were given an opportunity to skewer Bill Gates and Microsoft, and Gates was subjected to intense questioning by the committee. Afterward, Senator Hatch characterized the company as a monopoly.[55] A few weeks after this hearing, the Justice Department, joined by 20 states, filed its antitrust suit.[56]

Thus far, we have identified three separate lines of attack against Microsoft coming from three separate quarters. But is there any reason to believe that these attacks may have been coordinated, at least loosely, or that they may have contributed to the Justice Department's decision—exceptional at the time—to prosecute Microsoft under the Sherman Act, a Progressive Era antitrust statute that had been little used for decades? To answer that question, we must look for connections among the key players and connections to the Justice Department. Such connections will not constitute definitive proof of a coordinated and effective Anti-Microsoft Network, but their absence would surely rule out such a collaboration.

As it turns out, there are, in fact, a good number of connections among the participants in these attacks. For example, the keynote address at Ralph Nader's 1997 "Appraising Microsoft" conference was delivered by Sun Microsystems CEO James McNealy, and the session was also addressed by Netscape's General Counsel, as well as by Nader and James Love, director of the Consumer Project on Technology (CPT), a Nader-related group.[57] Similarly, during the same general time frame, CPT and the Communications Workers jointly sponsored a similar conference designed to attack the then-pending merger of WorldCom and MCI, an indicator of cooperation and common purpose between these two key players.[58] Kevin McGuiness, formerly Senator Hatch's chief of staff, played a leading role in the operations of ProComp, the anti-Microsoft lobby. After the trial was concluded, he moved on to direct the senator's presidential effort.[59] There are more such connections. Of all the interlocks, however, the most interesting appears to center on an online advocacy group, Net Action, that has taken a leading role in denigrating Microsoft through what it terms a *Consumer Choice Campaign*.

Founded in 1996, Net Action is a project of the Tides Foundation, which finances many progressive advocacy organizations and causes. On the advisory board of Net Action during the period leading up to the Microsoft trial were, among others, three persons of particular interest: Audrie Krause (the group's founder and executive director), Larkie Gildersleeve, and Glen Manishin. Ms. Krause also serves on the advisory board of Corporate Watch, an online center of anticorporate activity that is also sponsored by the Tides Foundation and active in the anti-Microsoft campaign, which we discuss in more detail in chapter 14.

Of particular note in the present context is an extended, public correspondence in which she engaged through a listserv on antitrust sponsored by Essential Information with James Love, director of Nader's Consumer Project on Technology. The exchange began in 1997, the year before the Justice Department filed its lawsuit. The subject of this correspondence was how to shape antitrust allegations against Microsoft. Ms. Krause opened the discussion on March 22 of that year when she wrote:

I'm hoping someone on this list can help point me to some online sources of information about anti-trust issues involving Microsoft. Any and all help is appreciated. Thanks![60]

The subsequent archive of the listserv is replete with Microsoft-related correspondence, most of it from Ms. Krause and Mr. Love, including regular postings of the NetAction online newsletter, *Microsoft Monitor*.[61]

For her part, while she was advising Net Action, Ms. Gildersleeve was serving as Director of Research, Information, & Technology for the Newspaper Guild of the CWA. Her participation on the Net Action advisory board began a full 2 years before the union publicly announced its organizing campaign at Microsoft. She was also a member of the Coalition of Labor Union Women and the Research Directors Committee of the AFL–CIO, both of which would have provided venues for gaining experience and building expertise in corporate campaigns.[62]

More interesting still is Mr. Manishin, a member of the Democratic National Committee (along with CWA President Morton Bahr) and an attorney with the law firm of Blumenfeld & Cohen. Among the clients served at various times by Mr. Manishin and his firm were Netscape, Oracle, Sun Microsystems, Computer Professionals for Social Responsibility (of which Ms. Krause was formerly executive director, one of four current or past directors of that group to serve on the Net Action board), and the Consumer Federation of America. Before joining the firm, Mr. Manishin was a trial attorney with the Antitrust Division of the Justice Department.[63] Nor was he alone in that connection. Indeed, both named partners in the firm also had antitrust experience, Gary Cohen as a Senior Trial Attorney with the Antitrust Division and Jeffrey Blumenfeld as the former head of the *US v. AT&T* section of the Antitrust Division and as a consultant to the Antitrust Division during an earlier investigation of the Microsoft Network.[64]

In point of fact, the group of Microsoft antagonists comprising NOISE had long maintained even more direct back-channel contacts with the Justice Department. Netscape and Sun provided a steady stream of complaints to government lawyers, and Netscape's Mr. Barksdale actually hosted a breakfast at his home for Assistant Attorney General Joel Klein, who headed the antitrust initiative. In the words of a contemporaneous assessment in *The Wall Street Journal*, "NOISE members ... collaborated to foment the government's antitrust investigation." As Oracle CEO Lawrence Ellison put it, "The whole Internet is part of the conspiracy to get Microsoft."[65]

Let us return to Mr. Manishin for a moment. In addition to his other roles, he served during the period of the trial as counsel to the Software & Information Industry Association (SIIA), whose membership included Corel, IBM, Netscape, Novell, Oracle, and Sun Microsystems, as well as

Microsoft, among others. It was Mr. Manishin who drafted the list of remedies the association was to propose for redressing Microsoft's monopolistic
practices should liability be found, which was not yet determined at that
time. This document, *Addressing the "Microsoft Challenge"—Restoring
Competition to the Software Industry*, was considered during a February
conference call among members of the group's Government Affairs Council. Over Microsoft's objections, on a motion from Sun Microsystems the
document was endorsed in a subsequent e-mail ballot.[66] Later, during the
penalty phase of the trial, the judge pressed the Justice Department to support a 3-way breakup of Microsoft rather than a 2-way breakup. The more
drastic remedy was presented to the court in a brief submitted by Mr.
Manishin's client, the SIIA.[67]

These interlocks among the seemingly disparate array of enemies confronting Microsoft during the late 1990s and beyond (illustrated in Fig. 7.2)

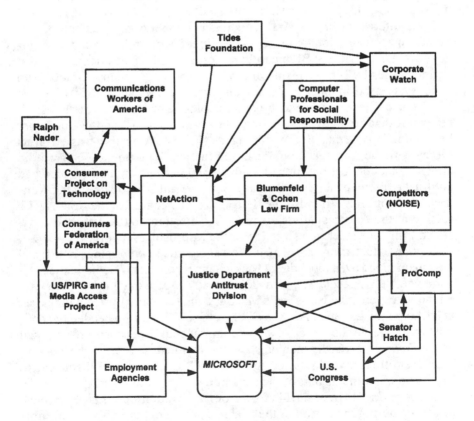

FIG. 7.2.   The Anti-Microsoft network.

would at the very least lend credence to an interpretation of events in which three sets of interests—each acting for its own purposes—came together, if not purposefully at least not entirely through inadvertence, to pressure Microsoft through some of its key stakeholder relationships—those with employees, customers, legislators, and regulators. They might suggest a good deal more. Although we have not explored it here, the campaign has also targeted media portrayals and public perceptions more generally in an apparent attempt to undermine Microsoft's reputation and standing,[68] especially through a series of highly personalized attacks on the company's founder and CEO, Bill Gates—including, among many elements, a satirical Bill Gates paper doll book and a real-time online "Bill Gates Personal Wealth Clock."[69] At one point, when it appeared that Microsoft was winning the public relations battle surrounding the trial, NOISE member Oracle Corporation went so far as to hire a private detective to sift through the trash of Microsoft's allies for a year and leak documents found there to the media. News reports suggested that the effort might have included stealing laptop computers to access documents on their hard drives. Oracle CEO Lawrence Ellison described his company's activity as fulfilling a "civic duty."[70] In the aggregate, then, this effort, like so many others, meets our definition of a corporate campaign.

A MATTER OF DEGREE

We have suggested here that nonlabor organizations that participate in corporate (or anticorporate) campaigns are best understood in terms of the degree of their respective separation from organized labor. This is a useful construct, and one that can help interpret the role being played by any particular group in a given campaign or in the attack on the corporation more generally. However, an emphasis on degrees of separation also carries a danger because it may lead us to conclude that campaigns waged or supported by groups at the farthest end of the spectrum from the unions are distinct in character or effect from those waged by labor and its closest allies. Although such campaigns have certainly been far less numerous to date, that conclusion is not necessarily warranted. To the contrary, we have already presented considerable evidence to suggest that nonlabor campaigns are far more similar to union-based efforts than they are different from them. This argument is enhanced substantially in chapter 8 when we review the historical development of campaign techniques. Moreover, because both labor-based and nonlabor-based campaigns have in common their focus on the failings of the corporation as a social, political, and economic form, in the aggregate they present and continually reinforce that negative image. As a result, even the most disparate of attacks contribute to one another's net long-term impact on the public consciousness.

ENDNOTES

1. Diego Ribadeneira, "Religious groups to back workers; coalition set to address labor issues," *The Boston Globe*, September 9, 1996, p. A3.
2. A list of these committees was posted at www.nicwj.org/page17.htm, September 26, 1999.
3. Malcolm Boyd, "Litany for Workers," www.nicwj.org/laborday/labor_in_the_ pulpits, September 26, 1999.
4. "Selected Biblical Passages on Justice for Workers," www.nicwj.org/laborday/ labor_in_the_pulpits.
5. Steven Greenhouse, "Clergy and Unions Teaming Up Again as Roots of Labor Day Are Recalled," *The New York Times*, September 6, 1999.
6. "10 Things You Can Do to Help Workers," www.nicwj.org/laborday, September 26, 1999.
7. William Bole, "Interfaith Group Backs Workers' Rights," *Cleveland Plain Dealer*, September 11, 1999, p. 3F.
8. The program for the conference was found at www.nicwj.org/conf_inf.htm, September 26, 1999.
9. Quoted in *Work in Progress*, AFL–CIO weekly newsletter, September 13, 1999.
10. Greenhouse, op. cit. See also, "Labor leaders seek unity with churches," *San Jose Mercury News*, October 9, 1999; and for a profile of a related group, Clergy and Laity United for Economic Justice (CLUE), described by one staff member as a "timely melding of 'spirit and socialism,' " see Erin Aubry, "With Blessings: Religion on the (picket) line," *LA Weekly*, October 8–14, 1999.
11. Found at www.igc.apc.org/preamble/backgrnd.html, February 1, 1998. The center's mission statement has since been modified as follows: "Preamble's mission is to promote vigorous public dialogue about the economic problems confronting America's working families and encourage the development of serious, workable solutions. Through research, analysis and the dissemination of information to the public, we seek to challenge outdated and unproductive ideas and assumptions and develop new analytical and policy approaches for the long term." www.preamble.org, September 26, 1999.
12. Gary Delgado, *Organizing the Movement: The Roots and Growth of ACORN* (Philadelphia: Temple University Press, 1986), p. 43; and "ACORN's 25 Year History," found at www.igc.org/community/ACORN_25_history.html, October 8, 1998.
13. Delgado, op. cit., p. 46.
14. From the ACORN People's Platform, www.igc.org/community/people's_platform.html, October 8, 1998.
15. Ibid.

16. Delgado, op. cit., pp. 26–27. These pages contain an especially valuable chart that compares four community organizing networks—ACORN, Citizen Action, National People's Action, and the Industrial Areas Foundation—on a number of structural, programmatic, and procedural dimensions.

17. For a table of living wage rates adopted by cities across the country as of late 1998, see Todd Henneman, "Living-Wage Policy in San Jose May Spur Activists Around Bay," *San Francisco Chronicle*, November 28, 1998, p. A17. San Jose, California, led the nation with a wage rate of $9.50 per hour with benefits, $10.75 without.

18. Found at www.igc.org/community/reports/acornrep06.1998.content.html, October 8, 1998. Interestingly, ACORN has been joined in this effort by a coalition of church-based groups affiliated with the Industrial Areas Foundation (IAF). Recall that IAF is a precursor of the corporate campaign founded by Saul Alinsky. See Michael A. Fletcher, "Religious Leaders Push 'Living Wage' as Issue in Election," *Washington Post*, October 31, 1999.

19. Statement by Jen Kern of ACORN, quoted in Peter Waldman, "Prosperity Is Good for Living-Wage Drive," *The Wall Street Journal*, December 20, 1999, p. A1.

20. ACORN shares the stage with other urban grassroots organizations that are even more directly tied to Alinsky in that they are affiliated with the Industrial Areas Foundation that he founded. An example is the Greater Boston Interfaith Organization, a church-based group with a similar agenda. See Ben Geman, "Faith in Numbers," *Boston Phoenix*, February 24–March 2, 2000.

21. Andrea Robinson, "Rights groups seeking more worker respect," *Miami Herald*, September 7, 1999.

22. Jim Carlton, "Sierra Club Faces Revolt From Radicals," *The Wall Street Journal*, March 15, 2000.

23. See Vol. 5, No. 6 (July/August 1998), and especially the lead article, John Byrne Barry, "Making Corporations Accountable."

24. Delgado, op. cit., p. 20; and James Miller, *Democracy Is in the Streets* (New York: Simon & Schuster, 1987), p. 257.

25. The full language of the pledge was found at www.now.org/nnt/spring-99/wfw.html, September 27, 1999.

26. See, for example, "Greenpeace and the Vinyl Industry: Same Science, Different Policy," Greenpeace news release, December 10, 1999; and David Barboza, "Monsanto Sued Over Use of Bio-technology in Developing Seeds," *The New York Times*, December 15, 1999. The latter case is discussed in more detail in chapter 11.

27. From the group's mission statement, found December 1, 1999, at www.moles.org/ProjectUnderground/info.html.

28. Bill Shireman, "Talking brings eco-radicals, CEOs together," *Sacramento Business Journal*, March 30, 1998; and information found at www.ran.org/about_ran/ran_info/html, June 29, 1998.

29. Nick Davis, "Raising a Ruckus: Learning How to Monkey-Wrench at Direct Action Camp," *E/The Environmental Magazine*, November-December 1997.

30. Biographical information was found at www.ruckus.org/about.html, June 29, 1998.
31. Ibid.
32. Philip Bourjaily, "Patagonia: Green Business Practices," Environmental News Network, November 30, 1999.
33. "Worldwide Campaign Launched to Combat WTO Assault on Last Remaining Forests," RAN news release, June 28, 1999.
34. Details were found at www.ruckus.org/wto.html, September 27, 1999.
35. Helene Cooper, "Activists' Boot Camp Teaches How to Confront Trade Leaders," Wall Street Journal, September 20, 1999, p. A1.
36. Announcement of the camp found at www.ruckus.org/spring-break.html, February 20, 2000.
37. Found at www.ruckus.org/man/scouting_manual.html, June 29, 1998.
38. Found at www.ruckus.org/man/planning_manual.html, June 29, 1998.
39. Found at www.ruckus.org/man/media_manual.html, June 29, 1998.
40. For a profile of Mokhiber, see Diana B. Henriques, "Crime dog on trail of corporate citizens," San Jose Mercury News, September 27, 1999.
41. Robert Weissman, "Corp-Focus Listserve Announcement," distributed online, September 6, 1999.
42. Russell Mokhiber and Robert Weissman, "The Criminal Element," Focus on the Corporation, online newsletter, September 6, 1999.
43. Ms. Cohen's affiliations were found in her biography at www.bsr.org/bsrboard.htm, April 6, 1997.
44. "Reebok and American Center for International Labor Solidarity Partner in Labor Rights Training for Workers in Indonesia," company news release, April 6, 1999.
45. "Union Training in Reebok Shoe Factories," Labor Rights: Nike Campaign Update, distributed online by the Campaign for Labor Rights, May 24, 1999.
46. Jordana Friedman and Colin Chellman, "Corporate Social Responsibility Movement Goes Worldwide: Global Partners Working Group," found on the CEP Web site at www.accesspt.com/cep/news996.htm, April 6, 1997.
47. Interhemispheric Resource Center, "Blood, Sweat & Shears: Corporate Codes of Conduct," found online at www.igc.org/trac/feature/sweatshops/codes.html, October 15, 1999. Other members included Amnesty International/USA, Campaign for Labor Rights, Coalition of Labor Union Women, Development and Peace, Global Exchange, Informed Investors, Justice Do It Nike, National Organization for Women, Press for Change, Research and Reports Service, US/GLEP and Vietnam Labor Watch. These groups are listed in an online mailing from the Campaign for Labor Rights, May 30, 1997.
48. Asia Monitor Resource Centre and Hong Kong Christian Industrial Committee, "Working Conditions in Sports Shoe Factories in China Making Shoes for Nike and Reebok," September 1997, distributed by the Campaign for Labor Rights. The company released its own report in October 1999. See "Reebok Releases In-Depth Report on Conditions in Indonesian Factories," Reebok news release, October 18, 1999.
49. This summary of the campaign against Microsoft is derived from a more comprehensive analysis that I have undertaken in collaboration with W. Lance Bennett.

50. In the latter regard, in June 1999, the Securities and Exchange Commission initiated an investigation of the company's accounting practices. See John Markoff, "SEC Is Investigating Microsoft's Accounting Practices," *The New York Times*, July 1, 1999.

51. "Virtual Employees: Hard Times at Microsoft," *The Guild Reporter*, October 8, 1998, pp. 1, 8.

52. "What Is ProComp?," found at www.procompetition.org/procomp/index.html, August 24, 1999; and Jon Swartz, "Dole, Bork Denounce Microsoft," *San Francisco Chronicle*, April 21, 1998, p. C1.

53. These contributions are included in reports available from the Center For Responsive Politics.

54. John Mintz, "Microsoft Foes Team Up for Hatch Fund-Raiser," *Washington Post*, December 9, 1999, p. A26.

55. Rajiv Chandrasekaran, "Competitors, Senators Assail Gates," *Washington Post*, March 4, 1998, p. A1.

56. "Justice Department, 20 States File Suits Against Microsoft," *Wall Street Journal Interactive Edition*, May 18, 1998.

57. Jeri Clausing, "Nader Conference Levels Sights in Microsoft," *The New York Times*, November 14, 1997; and "Partial List of Speakers," listing found on the conference's Web site at www.appraising-microsoft.org/speakers.html, September 18, 1998.

58. "Nader and Bahr: Proposed WorldCom/MCI Merger Would Hurt Consumers, Create Internet Monopoly," CWA news release, March 13, 1998.

59. Mintz, op. cit.

60. See www.essential.org/listproc/antitrust/msg00229.html.

61. See, for example, www.essential.org/listproc/antitrust/thrd6.html. See also "CPT's Microsoft Antitrust Page" found at www.essential.org/antitrust/microsoft, September 18, 1998.

62. From the biographical summary found at www.netaction.org/board.html, May 29, 1998.

63. From the biographical summary on the Blumenfeld and Cohen Web site found at www.technologylaw.com/manishin.html, November 6, 1998.

64. From the biographical summaries on the Blumenfeld and Cohen Web site found at www.technologylaw.com/blumenfeld.html and www.technologylaw.com/cohen.html, November 6, 1998.

65. *The Wall Street Journal*, November 19, 1998.

66. As recorded in the minutes of the meeting.

67. James Grimaldi, "Judge Signals He'll Split Microsoft, *Washington Post*, May 25, 2000, p. A1

68. One of the many indicators of the elements and success of this personalization campaign appeared on the cover of the September 1998 issue of *Brill's Content* in the form of a police mug shot of Gates taken when he was arrested in Albuquerque, New Mexico, on a traffic charge.

69. Chris Alpine, *Bill Gates 99 Paper Doll Book* (New York: St. Martin's Griffin, 1999). The clock was found at www.Webho.com/WealthClock, June 15, 1998.

70. Ted Bridis, Glenn Simpson and Mylene Mangalindan, "When Microsoft's Spin Got Too Good, Oracle Hired Private Investigators," *The Wall Street Journal*, June 29, 2000, p. 1; and John Markoff, "Oracle Leader Calls Spying Against Microsoft a 'Civic Duty,'" *The New York Times,* June 29, 2000.

8

Campaigning By the Book

In his important 1987 book, *Union Corporate Campaigns*, Charles Perry suggests that these campaigns are best understood in terms of several games in which the campaigners engage, including what he termed the games of *principle, politics, protest, pressure,* and *principal.* Each of these games, in turn, had key components. The Game of Principle, for example, was composed of conflict escalation and coalition formation, while the Game of Protest focused on the corporation, its directors, and shareholders. In each instance, Professor Perry found regularities in the pattern of campaigning that he saw as defining the game in question. In these pages, too, we have often resorted to game-related terms—players, rosters, strategy, and the like.

The game analogy is a useful one in this context, but the game has continued to evolve in the years since Perry wrote, particularly with respect to the sophistication with which it is played. In this chapter, we begin to explore the contemporary version of the corporate campaign by examining the intellectual infrastructure that has been developed to guide and support it. The maturation of that infrastructure has been captured, fossillike, in a library of campaign how-to manuals through which labor and other advocacy group theorists and planners have set out to train a cadre of knowledgeable campaign activists.

THE COMPLEAT CORPORATE CAMPAIGNER

As noted in chapter 1, the earliest how-to manual on anticorporate campaigning was produced by NACLA in 1970 in the form of the *Research Methodology Guide*. It was followed shortly afterward by Saul Alinsky's more spirited, but far less detailed, parting words to the new generation of activists, *Rules for Radicals*. Within a few years, particularly through the efforts of Ray Rogers and Michael Locker, the center of gravity for these campaigns shifted into the labor movement, where it became something of a catalyst for the generational change in leadership and perspective that culminated in the election of John Sweeney to the presidency of the AFL–CIO in 1995.

For all of their respective strengths, the NACLA and Alinsky volumes were not adequate in themselves, either to ground so complex an array of activities as the fully matured corporate campaign or to instruct neophytes in its conduct. Once the campaign moved into so highly structured a set of organizations as the labor unions, then, and once there was an opportunity to apply and test its components, it was both necessary and inevitable that these works would come to be supplemented by others. That is precisely what happened. Let us consider some of the more noteworthy markers of this emerging instructional literature.

Manual of Corporate Investigation

The first labor-based corporate campaign manual, the *Manual of Corporate Investigation*, was published by what is now the Food and Allied Service Trades Department (FAST) of the AFL–CIO in 1978; it was revised in 1981.[1] In the broadest sense, the FAST manual closely resembled the earlier NACLA volume in that it focused exclusively on the research process—how and where to learn as much as possible about a given corporate target. This book of some 70 pages, however, is far more detailed than its predecessor, providing the reader with an annotated listing of such sources as company publications and SEC filings, real estate records, court records, banking information, data on corporate directorships, labor relations sources, pensions and benefit plans, computer databases (including the Corporate Data Exchange), and a variety of information available from the federal, state, and local governments. As stated in the introduction to the *Manual*,

> This manual ... explains how to gather the information necessary to successfully organize and bargain with employers ... how to frame a complete picture of the

company structure, its finances, management, strengths and weaknesses....
Much of the information uncovered can suggest new pressure points, new strategies to win a contract. For example, one can uncover the financial ties between a
bank and an employer, and expose unethical or possibly illegal activity on the
bank's part. Such actions create economic pressure to supplement the traditional
strike weapon, or perhaps avoid a strike.[2]

Even from this brief passage, we can see both the intellectual debt the authors of this volume owed to the NACLA guide and the far more conservative objectives these early labor campaigners had in mind in comparison
with the New Left activists of the 1960s. However, the real lesson of the
FAST manual was the substantial detail of the guidance it provided to the
would-be campaigner—far more information than was provided in Michael Locker's 1970 chapter. In effect, Locker provided the outline and, 8
years later, FAST wrote the text.

The *Manual* recommended that corporate researchers organize their in-
quiries and findings under five general headings: administrative, financial,
products and services, corporate environment, and labor relations. The first
task was to prepare what essentially constituted a still photo of the company—its history, management structure, executive compensation practices, operating structure and location of facilities, and assessment of the
personalities of top managers and directors. The second task—financial
analysis—included such items as sales, profits, debt structure, liquidity, assets, and liabilities. Third, the researchers were to examine the range of the
company's products in relation to competitors—essentially to paint a picture of the marketplace in which the company functioned. Fourth—and
here is where we see most clearly the sort of power analysis that derived directly from the NACLA research guide, but also reflected the principles
that Ray Rogers was aggressively espousing at the time this book was being
written—researchers were to investigate such environmental factors as the
company's interlocking directorships, institutional and other major shareholders, pending litigation, banking relationships, public relations practices and positioning, and the influence on its operations of government
regulations and contracts. The final task was to understand the company's
relations with labor—everything from its corporate culture in relationship
to unions to its pension structure and its NLRB record.[3] The main body of
the volume provides a series of starting points and suggestions for completing this analysis.

In these categories, we can see both the inherent limitations of the FAST
Manual and the future development of the corporate campaign. It would be
fair to categorize this work as a critical point (in the mathematical sense), a
point at which the corporate campaign learning curve of organized labor
turned sharply upward. The *Manual of Corporate Investigation* not only
provided a solid basis for researching prospective targets, but, because it issued forth from within the AFL–CIO, served to legitimize these efforts at a

time when they were not widely accepted. More than that, it undoubtedly stirred the imaginations of many who read it and contributed significantly to the growing momentum of the campaign phenomenon.

Developing New Tactics: Winning
With Coordinated Corporate Campaigns

For all of its evident strengths, however, the FAST volume had an evident limitation: It defined the starting point for a corporate campaign—thorough research on the target—and offered the means to reach it, but it did not outline the nature of the campaign. For that, the unions turned to yet another AFL–CIO department, the Industrial Unions Department (IUD). In 1985, IUD published organized labor's first internal guide to actually conducting a campaign under the title, *Developing New Tactics: Winning With Coordinated Corporate Campaigns.*[4] Included in this volume was the following definition:

> A coordinated corporate campaign applies pressure to many points of vulnerability to convince the company to deal fairly and equitably with the union.
>
> In such a campaign, the strategy includes workplace actions, but also extends beyond the workplace to other areas where pressure can be brought to bear on the company. It means seeking vulnerabilities in all of the company's political and economic relationships—with other unions, shareholders, customers, creditors, and government agencies—to achieve union goals. It will also often mean marshaling support from other groups in the community to supplement union efforts.[5]

The IUD campaign guide provided much the same listing of research tasks suggested by FAST and suggested some additional sources. However, two other components of this particular volume are of more interest in the context of our present discussion. The first is a relatively brief, but nevertheless significant, discussion of tactics to be employed in pressuring companies. Among the topics discussed here were coalition building, media relations, public relations, legislative and regulatory initiatives, consumer actions, pressuring lenders, using pension fund assets, and inplant tactics.[6] In these passages, the IUD guide set forth the principal lines of attack on a target company—a delineation that stands to this day. The second is an extended discussion of the use of shareholder actions as a component of the campaign. Various sections of this discussion focus on workers as shareholders, strategies for scoring points at annual meetings, and a primer on the use of shareholder resolutions that included instruction in obtaining shareholder lists, soliciting proxies, and running candidates for a corporate board of directors.[7] The booklet also offered four brief examples of campaign tactics at work, not on a massive scale as in the J.P. Stevens or Beverly Enterprises campaigns, but on a small scale where limited pressure was sufficient to achieve limited objectives.[8] In this regard, too, the IUD guide pointed forward.

The Inside Game: Winning with Workplace Strategies

The following year, in 1986, the IUD published a companion volume focused on what had come to be called the inside game. This was a series of techniques developed largely by Jerry Tucker of the United Auto Workers during a job action at an auto parts supply firm, Moog Automotive, in 1981 and 1982.[9] Its attraction was that, like the external elements of the corporate campaign that were delineated in the 1985 IUD booklet, the inside game was an alternative to a strike, and therefore a less costly form of union action. However, unlike the external campaign, which depended on stimulating action by various of the target company's stakeholders for its impact, the inside game was completely controlled by the union. It was also a terrific morale builder.

In fact, much of the focus in *The Inside Game* is on team-building and finding devices that generate membership solidarity while undermining the self-confidence of management. Examples included intermittent informational picketing at some symbolic location, especially by family members and supporters from the community; daily prework rallies followed by *en masse* marching into the workplace; and wearing union attire, buttons, armbands, or the like.[10] In addition, the manual describes a variety of work-to-rule tactics such as working to the exact job description, refusing overtime work, working at a normal rate of speed, resisting call-ins, coordinating legally due sick days and personal leave days so masses of workers take them together, taking personal tools home so the company must replace them, and refusing to work under adverse health and safety conditions. Then essentially to show management what it was missing, the manual called for staging an occasional *union day*—a day on which workers would produce at peak speed and efficiency, ostensibly illustrating the benefits of a satisfied workforce.[11]

Although, many of these tactics had become staples of the expression of labor's dissatisfaction with management, the objective of this manual was to weave them into a coherent strategy and build an interface between the inplant strategy and more externally oriented aspects of the corporate campaign. A prime example of this dual functionality at work is the section on regulation, which points out that every workplace is subject to regulation from a multiplicity of government agencies and that workers are especially

well situated to recognize violations of these regulations. In the words of
the manual,

> With proper training and coordination ... workers can spot violations and bring
> about investigations that pressure employers and make a real contribution to their
> own health and safety.[12]

In effect, the workers become an intelligence-gathering arm of the government, which, in turn, becomes a source of external pressure on the employer. Because no large-scale workplace is ever truly free of violations, the
decision by the workers to turn from co-conspirators to whistleblowers represents a significant threat and a potent component of the inside game.

The last half of *The Inside Game* is devoted to a series of detailed guidelines on developing and communicating issues by conducting membership
surveys and one-on-one visits, focus groups, and editorial board visits; and
to legal discourses on the protection afforded to "concerted activity" such
as that advocated earlier in the volume and the requirement that the union
bargain in good faith.[13] Both of these sections are carefully delineated and
highly detailed. The legal memoranda, in particular, are unique to this volume among all of the corporate campaign manuals no doubt because the actions advocated here come the closest to testing the limits of the form of
labor–management relations that had actually been anticipated in the nation's labor laws. Other aspects of the corporate campaign, of course, were
being designed precisely to circumvent those limits.

Numbers That Count: A Manual on Internal Organizing

In 1988, the Department of Organization and Field Services, AFL-CIO,
published a short manual on workplace organizing, *Numbers That Count*.[14]
In general, organizing per se lies beyond the scope of our present analysis,
and we will not attend to many of the details of this particular publication.
That said, given the expanding interest in the corporate campaign by 1988,
it would be reasonable to expect that even such a routine and traditional subject would be presented with a sensitivity to the changing context of labor–management relations. *Numbers That Count*, although basic and not
especially sophisticated, especially in comparison with the closely related
The Inside Game, would not disappoint because the treatment emphasized a
blending of direct actions that involved union members with community
outreach that drew in legislators, the clergy, and the local media, as well as
civil rights, women's rights, and senior citizens.[15] The central argument of
the booklet is that effective organizing is best accomplished when centered
on issues and when the issues themselves meet three criteria: They are popular among the members (thereby contributing to unity), they are winnable

(adding to the union's appearance of power), and they "have an underlying moral dimension that may attract public as well as membership support."[16]

Contract Campaign Manual and Mobilizing for the '90s

Around 1990, some of the individual unions took over the task of creating textbooks for the corporate campaign. This was a logical next step, in part, because the sources and techniques that are most likely to prove effective will vary across industries and, additionally, because, as the principal protagonists in the field, by the end of the 1980s a number of unions had their own direct experience on which to draw. Two of these union-specific texts—one published by the Communications Workers of America (CWA) and the other by the Service Employees International Union (SEIU)—are particularly noteworthy.

Mobilizing for the 90s was first published by the CWA in 1990; a revised edition appeared in 1993. This is easily the most sophisticated of the labor-generated campaign manuals to date. What set this volume apart was the degree to which the presentation incorporated and, in the process explained to the members, the rationale underlying corporate campaign actions and their interconnectivity. As its title indicates, this book centered on *mobilization*, which it defined as "a continuous process of (1) organization,... (2) education, (3) collective action." Organization, according to the CWA, refers to establishing an effective communication network among the workers, education to becoming informed about the issues the workers face, and collective action to effecting change.[17] Not surprisingly, much of the volume emphasized organizing within the workplace, which the union presents as a scale of actions that continually increase the pressure on the employer. Points along the scale of collective action include, among others, wearing union T-shirts, displaying buttons or balloons, 1-minute stand-ups on the job, marching in to work together, picketing the homes of company executives, product boycotts, sick-outs, work-to-rule, and strikes.[18]

Having set out the strategy of escalation, the book then presented a litany of inplant tactics that more or less mirrored those set forth in IUD's *The Inside Game*. Among the suggestions not found in that earlier volume were tapping (e.g., with pencils on desks at a given time), a children's march for the union, candlelight vigils and mock funerals, and car caravans passing vendors or other employer-related businesses. In addition, the book recommended encouraging friendly legislators to hold hearings at which the union could air its positions as a way of pressuring the employer.[19] Echoing the oft-quoted advice of the Chinese general, Sun Tzu, the CWA manual advised members to develop a wide range of options but to use them imaginatively. "Predictable players," it says, "are the easiest to beat."[20]

Finally, *Mobilizing for the 90s* presented a Venn diagram showing the various overlaps among internal education, collective action, inside tactics, and the corporate campaign, which it defined to include customer-related actions, informational picketing and other company-centered events, Wall Street initiatives, board of directors actions, legislative and political pressure, and generating support from international unions. The twin objectives were to empower the union's members and wear down the target company.[21] This could be accomplished in part, the volume argued, by mobilizing support within the broader community, specifically among the following groups: other unions, religious organizations, women's groups, civil rights groups, issue-advocacy groups, senior citizens, elected officials, groups affected economically by a given issue, civic groups, and public figures.[22] This precise configuration is typical of corporate campaigns to this day.

As we noted, the CWA was not the only union to produce its own how-to manual for corporate campaigning. A second such book, *Contract Campaign Manual*, was issued by the SEIU at about the same time.[23] Although substantial in its own right, this volume is significant as well because its preparation was guided by then-SEIU President John Sweeney, whose personal commitment to the corporate campaign approach to labor–management relations would later set the direction for the entire labor movement. Built around four major topics—research and goal setting, organizing the campaign, pressuring the employer, and bargaining—this manual made particularly extensive use of examples and specific applications, as opposed to theory as in the CWA book, to make its points. Although written as a guide to bargaining, it is best understood in the present context as a manual for organizing because that has been one of its principal applications by the union in the years since its publication.

With that in mind, it is the third section of the document—that dealing with pressuring the employer—that is most worthy of our attention here. In the words of the manual,

> Outside pressure can involve jeopardizing relationships between the employer and lenders, investors, stockholders, customers, clients, patients, tenants, politicians or others on whom the employer depends for funds.

> Legal and regulatory pressure can threaten the employer with costly action by government agencies or the courts.

> Community action and use of the news media can damage an employer's public image and ties with community leaders and organizations.[24]

The manual then went into considerable detail about how to generate these various forms of pressure. According to the SEIU, the strategic keys included the selection of tactics that were designed to exploit to best advantage the particular weaknesses of the target company, advanced planning so that no time would be lost if such tactics were called for, and flexibility in choosing and then sticking with tactics depending on their demonstrated effectiveness.[25] Then echoing the words of Saul Alinsky, the manual advised that "the threat of action often has more psychological effect on management officials than the action itself because they don't know exactly what the impact will be."[26] The choice of tactics, the SEIU stated, should be based on seven considerations, including, among others, the purpose to be served, whether union members or supporters will enjoy carrying it out, how long it will take for the tactic to have an impact, and how much it will cost to implement. Among the possible objectives to be served are increasing costs or reducing productivity as a way of costing the employer money, directly affecting the lives or careers of the individual executives or managers who are targeted, raising the visibility of the campaign or the morale of the campaigners, building alliances within the community, distracting management from doing its job, or embarrassing the company's executives or managers among their friends, neighbors, and families.[27] It is the degree of this personalization of the conflict inherent in a corporate campaign that comes through most clearly in the *Contract Campaign Manual*, and that has greatly typified campaigns conducted by the SEIU.

This volume is also noteworthy for the degree to which it set forth specific areas in which pressure might be brought through government regulatory agencies. Among those mentioned were:

- Safety and health hazards on the job
- Discrimination on the basis of race, gender, age, ethnic origin, or sexual preference
- Failure to pay overtime or minimum wage as required by federal, state or local fair labor standards laws
- Subcontracting of public employees' work in violation of state or local charters, codes or constitutions ...
- Failure to provide enough staffing or cutting corners in other ways that threaten public safety
- Evasion of taxes on property or income
- Failure to live up to commitments made when obtaining low-interest public financing such as industrial revenue bonds ...
- Environmental hazards such as toxic waste dumping ...
- Failure to disclose information to the public as required by laws or regulations.[28]

The book also provided a guide to filing charges of unfair labor practices and included a sample federal form for doing so.[29] Although only a partial selection of these regulatory tactics is employed in the typical corporate campaign, the list is indicative of the level of pressure that can be generated. In at least one instance, the SEIU's campaign against Sutter Health, the union appears literally to have thrown the book—the whole book—at the company.

The balance of the section on pressuring the employer focused on identifying specific groups within the community—students, renters, patients' rights groups, consumers' rights and environmental groups, as well as the more generic categories that are commonly listed in these various manuals—that could be mobilized to support the union, and it also provided an extensive treatment of developing themes for and sympathy within the media. Most significant here was a discussion of ways to *create* news—a subject to which we return in a subsequent chapter.[30] As a reality check, the section also included a discussion of how to work with lawyers, particularly to identify ways to design campaign activities so as to minimize the associated legal risks.[31]

A Troublemaker's Handbook

Unions are not the only labor organizations that have produced corporate campaign manuals. One of the more influential of these books was published in 1991 by the widely read pro-union newsletter, *Labor Notes*, a publication of the Labor Education and Research Project. Assigned the revealing title, *A Troublemaker's Handbook: How to Fight Back Where You Work and Win*, in appearance this book by labor activist Dan LaBotz is a relatively more formal textbook on organizing than the others we have reviewed.[32] The book addressed many of the same topics as its predecessors, albeit in a rather more anecdotal and narrative fashion and, more than the other efforts, set the corporate campaign and a host of associated strategies and tactics into the context of the changing environment faced by organized labor. Although replete with ideas and suggestions for strategies and tactics, this book is considerably less taxonomic and detail-oriented than, for example, either the CWA or SEIU volumes. Rather, its principal contribution to the literature was the breadth of its coverage and its extensive use of examples to educate, including summaries of key events in a number of corporate campaigns.

Although many of the approaches discussed in this book have appeared as components of corporate campaigns, the chapter devoted explicitly to these campaigns centered on two case studies—Hormel and BASF—and added little to the already extant knowledge base. Set against that, however, was an extraordinarily detailed outline of the information to be sought in preparing for a campaign based on the experience of Richard Leonard, at the time Special Projects Director (a title commonly associated with the senior-most union official in charge of corporate campaigns) for the Oil,

Chemical and Atomic Workers (OCAW) union. Recommended to be included in the intelligence-gathering exercise were such items as:

- A history and overview of the company or plant that will be subjected to the campaign, including photos, news clippings, financial statements, litigation, and the company philosophy on such issues as ethics, human relations, and the environment;

- A profile of the neighborhood(s) surrounding company facilities, including demographics, the proximity of schools or other sensitive buildings, perceptions of potential risks associated with the facilities, and community groups with grievances against the company;

- An environmental assessment including a documented history of accidents and violations, the role and functioning of safety committees, possible OSHA violations, safety problems associated with the company's contractors, and potential issues associated with the nearby air, groundwater, or soil;

- A listing of banks the company does business with and a review of how it financed any recent expansions;

- An identification of any friendly contacts the union members have with reporters or others working for the local media, and of potentially supportive professors at local universities;

- A comprehensive outline of the company's or plant's production process, including flow charts and maintenance practices, an analysis of product quality, and an overview of its competitive situation;

- A profile of the company's customers, including such items as their relative importance, their individual preferences, and its suppliers and outside contractors; and

- A study of management personnel, even including their personal real estate holdings, friends and associates, home addresses and spouses' names, driving records, personal financial situations, and penchants for gambling, drinking, or other vices.[33]

Even this seemingly extensive summary does not do justice to the breadth and thoroughness of the OCAW list. If the numerous earlier efforts to delineate a strategy for researching the corporation and its relationships with stakeholders were more thorough than this one with respect to how to approach the problem and where to find the requisite information, this appendix in *A Troublemaker's Handbook* provides far and away the most comprehensive answer to the "what" question: What is the information being sought?

Into the Wired World

One of the dominant technological trends of the latter half of the 1990s was the growth in accessibility and influence of that portion of the Internet known as the World Wide Web or, simply, the Web. The Web is a natural venue for organizing, recruiting, and educating—all essential functions of the corporate campaign. By the end of the decade, it was a staple of journalistic and other research efforts as well. Among the attractions of the Web is its interactivity—the ability it provides to move rapidly from one *page* or document to another, even one provided by a different organization. These so-called *links* are facilitated by the language of the Web, *html*, which stands for hypertext mark-up language. Because of this capability, a user viewing one document can click the mouse on a highlighted reference and move to a source that is physically located thousands of miles away—literally around the world in many instances—at the speed of light (adjusted for a few electronic twists and turns).

Not surprisingly, a number of unions have begun to take advantage of this capability in developing their corporate campaign efforts. For example, the research department of the United Mine Workers union has for several years posted to its Web site links to a number of private and governmental data sources,[34] a service duplicated with annotations by the American Federation of State, County, and Municipal Employees.[35] Older materials are also being updated and distributed on the Internet. For example, a much revised version of FAST's *Manual of Corporate Investigations* is now available online.[36]

There is, in fact, nothing novel about the content of these listings. They have been available in more or less the same form since the publication of the NACLA *Research Methodology Guide* in 1970. However, with the assistance of the Web, research tasks that took weeks or months to complete in 1970, or even as recently as the early 1990s *if* they could be completed at all, and that were potentially expensive and logistically difficult, can now be accomplished quickly, inexpensively, and easily. As a result, the unions are positioned to research, evaluate, and plan more corporate campaigns than ever before and look to a future that will further expand their capabilities.

THE COMPLETE *ANTI*CORPORATE CAMPAIGNER

We can see from our review of these manuals that, over the past quarter century or so, the labor movement has made substantial progress in developing a broad array of strategies and tactics for attacking corporations as a means of pressuring them either to or at the bargaining table. However, just as organized labor was not alone in its growing devotion to the corporate campaign, it was not alone in developing a literature to reflect and support these efforts. That task was joined by a number of other activists as well. In the balance of this chapter, we examine a selection of these nonlabor-based campaign texts.

There are, in fact, quite a number of manuals designed to instruct political activists in proselytizing, organizing, and bringing pressure to achieve their objectives. A relatively recent example is Randy Shaw's book, *The Activist's Handbook: A Primer for the 1990s and Beyond*, which includes chapters on coalitions, the media, lawyers, and direct action, among others.[37] These guides to action draw on the same traditions as the others we have examined, they cover many of the same classes of strategy and tactics, and they have, in all likelihood, been read by and influenced anticorporate activists. For our present purpose, however, we focus on a much narrower segment of the genre—those manuals that specifically address the ways and means of attacking corporations per se. Of these, four examples are especially worthy of attention. As one might expect, each draws even more directly than do the labor books on the ideological traditions of the SDS and NACLA.

Meeting the Corporate Challenge: A Handbook on Corporate Campaigns

The first of our ideologically driven guidebooks to attacking the corporation was published in 1985 by the Transnationals Information Exchange (TIE) under the title, *Meeting the Corporate Challenge.*[38] To help place the book in both historical and intellectual context, it will be useful to summarize briefly the history of this organization.

In 1977, the World Council of Churches, of which the National Council of Churches is the U.S. affiliate, held a major international consultation in Nairobi to discuss the issues associated with multinational corporations. Recall that this was about a decade after the National Council of Churches had helped establish NACLA, and shortly after it had spun off the Interfaith Center for Corporate Responsibility. The conference included representatives from trade union, research, and activist groups as well as from the Church and a few corporations. The activists attending this meeting decided to establish an organization through which they could institutionalize the analysis of the "problem" of multinationals and formulate a strategic response. TIE, established in 1978, was the product of that decision, which was endorsed and supported by the Commission on Transnational Corporations of the World Council. Over the next several years, interest and membership in TIE expanded, eventually including links to some of the international trade federations—most notably, the IUF.

In the mid-1980s, TIE began to develop a particular approach to confronting multinational corporations, one based in an analysis of the chain of production. It has applied this approach to such industries as automobiles, rubber, steel, textiles and garments—industries that have all seen active corporate campaigns. TIE's American representative has worked closely with the staff of *Labor Notes* and has been active in the opposition to NAFTA—a central element of organized labor's policy agenda.[39]

One of the editors of *Meeting the Corporate Challenge* was John Cavanaugh, then a Fellow and more recently Director of the Institute for Policy Studies (IPS), a Washington think tank that serves as a central node—and, according to some critics, the mother ship—of a network of progressive organizations with an aggressively anticorporate agenda. The volume was an outgrowth of a 1984 Washington conference of the same name that was sponsored by IPS and its European affiliate, the Transnational Institute.[40]

The difference between these ideological texts and those produced by labor is immediately evident in the TIE report, which begins with a discussion of such macroeconomic constructs as oligopoly, the growth of conglomerates, mergers and acquisitions, and cross-subsidization (i.e., the transfer of corporate profits from one product line or production center to another). This is followed by an analysis of the impact of new technologies on the international economy.[41]

When the report turns to what it terms *counterstrategies*, it provides a brief survey of a now-predictable roster of topics, which are generally categorized as either research- or action-oriented. Still the discussion of research makes an important distinction and one that had not previously appeared in the literature under review. There are, suggests TIE, three temporally separate classes of research: initial research, the function of which is to contribute to the design of the campaign strategy; ongoing research, which can be used to evaluate the campaign and note any changes in the environment that occur while it is in progress; and monitoring research that is conducted after the conclusion of the campaign to ensure that the target company is in compliance with any agreements into which it entered.[42] This discussion of monitoring is noteworthy because it helped provide the underpinning for a more recent development associated with corporate campaigns and the anticorporate movement more generally, the growing pressure for codes of conduct to be adopted by target companies. In their earliest incarnations, these codes provided for incompany monitoring of the sort described in the TIE report; later this was extended to efforts to enforce compliance with a company's code on the part of all of its vendors and other business partners—a sort of snowball effect.

The action strategies discussed in *Meeting the Corporate Challenge* are by now familiar: publicity, coalition building, boycotts, legislative and regulatory pressure, shareholders actions, and corporate campaigns. Of these, the most extensive treatment is afforded to corporate campaigns, with a focus on the generating of pressure through banks and insurance companies, retailers, and companies with board-of-directors interlocks.[43] The balance of the book is devoted to a series of corporate campaign case studies, including some, like those against Nestle, Browne and Sharpe, and Coca Cola, that are not extensively treated elsewhere in the literature.

Organizing for Social Change: A Manual for Activists in the 1990s

The Midwest Academy, founded (as noted in chapter 1) by SDS alumna Heather Booth to carry forward community organizing within the Alinsky tradition, began producing guides to organizing in its early years; it first published its own comprehensive textbook on the subject in 1991. Written by former SDSer Steve Max, Kim Bobo of the National Interfaith Committee for Worker Justice, and Jackie Kendall, who succeeded Ms. Booth as Executive Director of the Academy, this book, *Organizing for Social Change: A Manual for Activists in the 1990s,* focuses primarily on direct action.[44] Although this volume does not target corporations per se, it does provide several pages of highly detailed information on how to research corporations—a function the manual describes as intelligence gathering rather than research to emphasize its connection to action planning. It also includes a chapter on how to coordinate actions with local unions and central labor councils.[45]

Of greater interest, however, are the detailed instructions presented elsewhere in the book on such topics as how to build coalitions, use the media, and work with religious organizations. These, of course, are central elements of corporate campaign strategy. In the Midwest Academy's text, however, they are presented in a way that helps us understand this process from a different perspective—that of community activists who may participate in corporate campaigns as partners of labor, but who have their own needs and interests. In the discussion of coalition formation, for example, the authors advise that, before joining in a coalition, a group should ask several questions, among them who is behind the coalition, whether it is a functioning entity or a shell, and how joining serves the group's own self-interest.[46]

Organizing for Social Change does an especially good job of setting forth the rationale (as well as some notes of caution) for incorporating religious organizations in a campaign coalition. Among these are that:

> Religious institutions have lots of material resources in addition to their human ones. They have money, buildings, buses, office equipment and many other in-kind and financial resources that are needed in organizing work....

> Few institutions bring as much respect and credibility as religious groups. Many organizing campaigns need respect and credibility....

> Religious institutions provide leadership on issues of moral concern....[47]

The authors go on to suggest the primary reason that such groups would be inclined to participate in community organizing or, by extension, in the kinds of campaigns that are of particular interest to us—those targeted at corporations.

> Most religious denominations believe that part of their ministry is to be a witness in the world. Justice is a fundamental theme for most denominations. And yet ... congregations are confused about how to act effectively on their concerns and

values.... [S]ocial action groups can provide concrete strategies for putting their faith into action.[48]

It is this precise rationale—set forth more clearly here than in any other volume we have reviewed—that powers the substantial involvement of religious organizations in the corporate campaign. They were present at the point of origin of the campaign in the form of the National Council of Churches. As a review of the campaigns listed in Appendix A makes clear, they are active today in many community-centered corporate campaigns, providing psychological support for workers who are members of their congregations, resources, legitimacy, and the aura of a moral crusade. These efforts are complemented by national-level religious activists such as the Reverend Jesse Jackson and Ms. Bobo's own organization, the NICWJ.

An Activists' Guide to Research and Campaign on Transnational Corporations

Like unions, politically motivated corporate antagonists have turned to the Internet to energize their various movements. Indeed, as we will detail briefly in chapter 15, the use of the Web by political activists has emerged as a highly significant phenomenon over the past few years. Anticorporate crusaders of various stripes and interests have been very much at the forefront of that development. Without doubt, the best and most comprehensive example of this is provided in *TNCs and India: An Activists' Guide to Research and Campaign on Transnational Corporations*, which was published in 1995 by the Indian affiliate of the Public Interest Research Group (PIRG), one of the multitude of organizations nurtured by Ralph Nader, and available in electronic form on the Web site of Corporate Watch, a project of the Transnational Resource and Action Center (TRAC).[49]

Despite its main-title reference to India, this handbook is widely applicable to anticorporate campaigning in the United States and elsewhere. Although the work originated with an affiliate of PIRG, it is undoubtedly its electronic distribution by TRAC that has contributed to its influence. Therefore, it is worth taking a brief moment to consider this organization, which we have not previously encountered. TRAC is connected in several ways to the historical development and current institutional structure of the anticorporate movement. For example, John Cavanaugh, Director of the Institute for Policy Studies and lead editor of the TIE handbook, *Meeting the Corporate Challenge*, serves on the group's advisory board. The Data Center, an SDS spin-off, is listed as a Corporate Watch affiliate, as is *Multinational Monitor*, a publication of Ralph Nader's Essential Information, Inc., that often takes the lead in attacking companies targeted in labor's corporate campaigns. Other campaign-active groups, including Project Underground, the Rainforest Action Network, Sweatshop Watch, and the Sierra Club, also have ties to TRAC or Corporate Watch. All of that is simply to indicate that there is a substantial, motivated readership for this particular handbook.

The text is divided into various chapters on research, labor actions, legal actions, environmental actions, shareholder actions, and government resources, each of which is more or less interactive. The general format is to provide a body of prescriptive text in each chapter followed by a listing of related resources. There is little in the substance of the document that is new or unique. However, because it is so readily available to would-be activists who might well not have been exposed to much of the other literature we have described here, which tends to receive rather limited distribution, it is nonetheless significant. In fact, it tends to move some of the more compelling elements of the earlier manuals into a more public sphere. For example, the discussion of research related to labor actions replicates in substantial detail Richard Leonard's and OCAW's listing of the types of information to be sought, which were first published in *A Troublemaker's Handbook*.

Leverage for the Environment

Our final entry in the how-to sweepstakes, *Leverage for the Environment: A Guide to the Private Financial Services Industry*, published by the World Resources Institute—an environmental research and advocacy center founded in 1982—is quite limited in scope. It focuses only on one industry cluster, but it is nevertheless the most intellectually sophisticated of all the materials under review here.[50] Moreover, by elucidating in depth the pressure points available in the financial services sector, this volume explicitly takes the campaign back to its roots in power analysis.

The authors of this book have developed a generic model for the analysis of financial service providers. Components of the model include the decision-making relationships, sources and applications of capital, information flows, external relationships, and client relationships for such companies. These are evaluated using the model for the purpose of identifying prospective points of leverage. Having set out this analytical model, the authors then proceed to illustrate its application to eight distinct segments of the industry, including commercial banks, investment banks, mutual funds, pension funds, property and casualty insurers, life insurers, venture capital firms, and foundations. Each segment is evaluated strategically with respect to such characteristics as its time horizon, its degree of risk aversion, its susceptibility to regulatory pressures, and the availability of information about its operations. In the words of the authors:

> For each industry segment, we have identified a preliminary list of potential "leverage points" for influencing various actors to integrate environmental considerations into decisionmaking. The identified leverage points are intended to serve

as a starting point for discussion by the public interest community in the context of strategic planning....[51]

Focusing on applications relating to the environment, but setting forth general principles likely to be used by activists in support of other causes as well as by organized labor, they next identify four classes of leverage:

- *Bottom-line leverage*—appealing to the desire to avoid the costs associated with risk,
- *Policy leverage*—exploiting "the sensitivity of financial decisionmakers to changes in regulations or to taxation consequences" of their actions relating to the environment,
- *Reputational leverage*—demonstrating to companies that noncompliance with the activists' objectives can damage their public images, and
- *Values-based leverage*—exploiting the willingness of certain investors to promote an environmental (or other) agenda even if doing so is contrary to their financial interests.[52]

The balance of the book uses segment analyses and case studies to illustrate the application of these principles.

From the outset, the aspect that has set the corporate campaign apart from other attacks on the corporation has been its grounding in an assessment of the stakeholder relationships on which every company depends to survive and prosper. As Michael Locker, Ray Rogers, and others realized early on in their secondary targeting of banks and insurers, business is dependent on finance above all else. *Leverage for the Environment* provides a comprehensive blueprint for identifying the vulnerabilities in any company's financial relationships and for exploiting them. In the years ahead, this is likely to be an especially influential analysis.

LIVE AND LEARN

In this chapter, we have reviewed nearly a dozen corporate and anticorporate campaign handbooks that have been developed within two interrelated, but nevertheless distinctive, activist traditions. To help put these reviews and, more important, the intellectual development of the campaign in context, we would do well to summarize the chronology of development in a timeline. That is accomplished in Fig. 8.1. In the figure, the small arrows indicate some of the specific directions of developmental flow we have identified in this discussion.

Based on this review, we can say with some assurance that corporate campaigns do not occur by accident, and they are not driven by happenstance. To the contrary, they are, at least when developed to their fullest potential, carefully planned, meticulously crafted and executed packages of actions and messages that are increasingly grounded in both theory and experience. The motivations of the corporate antagonists can vary quite widely, from gaining the advantage in a contract negotiation to using a cascade of such campaigns to alter the economic system itself. Because of the importance of coalition building and outreach in such efforts, a wide range of such motives can be at work even in a single campaign (e.g., Nike) although one or another motive may predominate depending on the origins of the attack.

It is one thing to document the existence of manuals such as those we have described here and another to demonstrate the dynamics of their con-

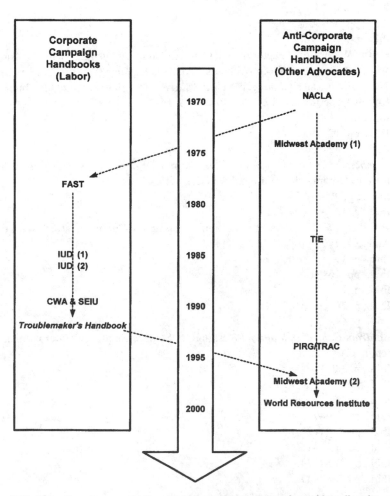

FIG. 8.1.   Developmental timeline of campaign manuals and handbooks.

tent as they play out in the strategies and tactics that together comprise the corporate campaign. The chapters that follow turn to that task.

ENDNOTES

1. *Manual of Corporate Investigation* (Washington: Food and Beverage Trades Department, AFL–CIO, 1978, 1981).
2. Ibid., p. 1.
3. Ibid., p. 4.
4. *Developing New Tactics: Winning With Coordinated Corporate Campaigns* (Washington: Industrial Unions Department, AFL–CIO, 1985).
5. Ibid., p. 1.
6. Ibid., pp. 4–10.
7. Ibid., pp. 25–30.
8. Ibid., pp. 11–12.
9. Henry Weinstein, "Factor in McDonnell Douglas Dispute: Unions Turn to 'In-Plant' Tactics to Avoid Walkouts," *Los Angeles Times*, April 7, 1987, p. 1:1.
10. *The Inside Game: Winning With Workplace Strategies* (Washington: Industrial Unions Department, AFL-CIO, 1986), pp. 14–15.
11. Ibid., pp. 16–18.
12. Ibid., pp. 18–19.
13. Ibid., pp. 42–83.
14. *Numbers That Count: A Manual on Internal Organizing* (Washington: Department of Organization and Field Services, AFL–CIO, 1988).
15. Ibid., pp. 30–31.
16. Ibid., p. 18.
17. *Mobilizing for the 90s*, second edition (Washington: Communications Workers of America, 1993), p. 2.
18. Ibid., p. 15.
19. Ibid., pp. 16–21.
20. Ibid., p. 22.
21. Ibid., p. 24.
22. Ibid., p. 49.
23. *Contract Campaign Manual* (Washington: Service Employees International Union, n. d.)
24. Ibid., p. 3:2.
25. Ibid.
26. Ibid., p. 3:3.
27. Ibid., pp. 3:6–7.
28. Ibid., pp. 3:21–22.
29. Ibid., pp. 4:10–11.
30. Ibid., pp. 3:50–73.
31. Ibid., pp. 3:47–49.

32. *A Troublemaker's Handbook: How to Fight Back Where You Work and Win* (Detroit: Labor Notes, 1991).
33. Ibid., pp. 239–242.
34. The can be found at www.access.digex.net/~miner/rd1.html.
35. See www.afscme.org/afscme/wrkplace/corprsch.htm.
36. This access-limited document can be found at www.fastaflcio.org/manual.htm.
37. Randy Shaw, *The Activist's Handbook: A Primer for the 1990s and Beyond* (Berkeley: University of California Press, 1996).
38. John Cavanaugh, Martha McDevitt, Jeroen Peijnenburg, and Deborah Smith, editors, *Meeting the Corporate Challenge: A Handbook on Corporate Campaigns* (Amsterdam: Transnationals Information Exchange, 1985).
39. "General Description of TIE," in document labeled "Appendix," (Amsterdam: Transnational Data Exchange, circa 1993), pp. I–VI.
40. Cavanaugh et al., op. cit., p. 6.
41. Ibid., pp. 11–23.
42. Ibid., pp. 27–28.
43. Ibid., pp. 28–35.
44. Kim Bobo, Jackie Kendall, and Steve Max, *Organizing for Social Change: A Manual for Activists in the 1990s*, second edition (Santa Ana, CA: Seven Locks Press, 1996).
45. Ibid., pp. 150–161, 173–181.
46. Ibid., pp. 74–75.
47. Ibid., p. 141.
48. Ibid.
49. Jed Greer and Kavaljit Singh, *TNCs and India: An Activists' Guide to Research and Campaign on Transnational Corporations* (New Delhi: Public Interest Research Group, 1995), available online at www.corpwatch.org/trac/resrch/resrch.html.
50. John Ganzi, Frances Seymour, and Sandy Buffett, *Leverage for the Environment: A Guide to the Private Financial Services Industry* (Washington: World Resources Institute, 1998).
51. Ibid., p. 6.
52. Ibid.

In recent years, corporate campaigns have become collaborative affairs, especially as unions have begun to take unified approaches to dealing with multi-national, multi-union employers. This poster was produced by the Combined Bargaining Committee, a group of fourteen unions in the U.S. and around the world, as part of a campaign designed to pressure General Electric during the 2000 round of contract negotiations. Courtesy of the Coordinated Bargaining Committee of GE Unions/IUE.

These two charts, produced by Ray Rogers and Corporate Campaigns, Inc., illustrate the strategic perspective on campaign research and action known as "power structure analysis." Both charts copyright 1995 by Corporate Campaigns, Inc. (Ray Rogers). Courtesy of Corporate Campaigns, Inc.

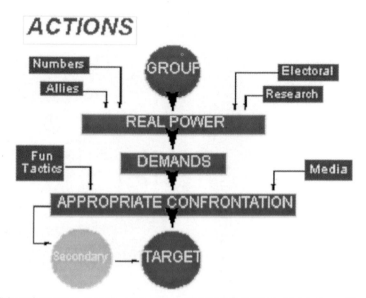

This rather more generic approach to campaign strategy is employed by the Midwest Academy, a training center for community organizers with a curriculum grounded in the teachings of Saul Alinsky. Courtesy of Midwest Academy and its Web site at www.midwestacademy.com

Corporate campaign art often plays on the slogans or logos of target companies. In this example, the Nike swoosh becomes the central symbol of the boycott message. Reprinted with the permission of Tin Le (tin@le.org). Courtesy of Vietnam Labor Watch.

Corporate greed is a common campaign theme, as exemplified in this sign from a Jobs with Justice demonstration. Photo by Jerry Atkins, Jobs with Justice. Courtesy of Jobs with Justice.

Another common theme is respect for the rights and dignity of workers. Here we see this theme as a component of the logo for an organizing campaign at Los Angeles International Airport. Courtesy of Respect at LAX Campaign.

Many corporate campaigns employ humor and graphic imagery in developing their themes. Here, for example, are two cartoons from the UAW's campaign against Caterpillar, one employing the corporate greed theme and the other workers' rights. Reprinted with the permission of Rick Flores, Labor Cartoonist, Workers' Communications Press, PO Box 1044, Marion, IN 46952.

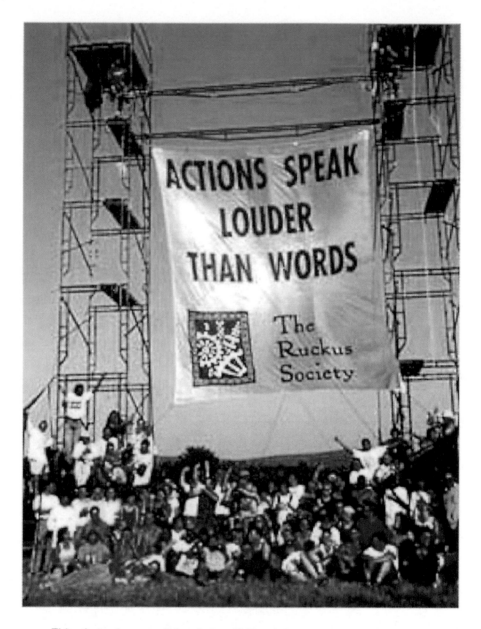

This photo shows participants in a 1998 training camp run by the Ruckus Society. At these camps, environmental and other activists are taught such skills as climbing the sides of buildings and other structures to hang banners calling attention to their causes. Many of the participants in the 1999 anti-WTO demonstrations in Seattle were alumni of Ruckus Society camps. Photo courtesy of the Ruckus Society.

The "Battle in Seattle" — a 1999 protest over the policies of the World Trade Organization — brought the unions together with environmentalists, human rights activists and others and became the symbol of an emerging new coalition. This photo captured some of the action. Photo courtesy of Neil Lahaie, www.labornet.org.

The collaboration of Ray Rogers (top and left) and Michael Locker (right) produced success in the J.P. Stevens campaign and set the direction for corporate campaign development and organized labor's new approach to organizing and negotiating with employers. Today, Rogers heads a company, Corporate Campaigns, Inc., that wages campaigns in behalf of private and public sector workers and other causes. Locker heads a consulting firm, Locker Associates, Inc., that is a highly regarded source of financial information in the steel industry and advises such unions as the Steelworkers and the Teamsters. Rogers news conference photo by Lauren Draper. Rogers portrait photo by Tim Lally. Rogers photos courtesy of Corporate Campaigns, Inc. Locker photo courtesy of Locker Associates, Inc.

9

THE CODES OF THE WEST

What sets the corporate (or anticorporate) campaign apart from other public relations campaigns, lobbying campaigns, or organizing campaigns is the central role played in these efforts by research and strategy. Corporate campaigns simply operate on a higher plane of sophistication. Rather than arising from a particular grievance against a specific company or industry, corporate campaigns have evolved from a philosophical orientation through a stage of basic conceptualization to a combination of tactics driven by theory and observation.

It is the role of strategy to weave all of these elements into a unified and dynamic whole—to apply the theory, shape the research, and, guided by the results, frame the attack on the target company. In effect, strategy is the glue that binds the disparate elements of the corporate campaign together, and it is that coming together in a comprehensive and organized manner that distinguishes the corporate campaign from its lesser cousins. In this chapter, we examine some of the principal elements of campaign strategy and see how they have shaped the challenge that confronts the business community today.

TO CAMPAIGN OR NOT TO CAMPAIGN:
THAT IS THE (FIRST) QUESTION

Every corporate campaign shares common elements with every other corporate campaign, and yet each is unique. This observation suggests that, although there may exist no hard and fast laws of campaign behavior, there
are discoverable continuities that can help us understand and predict the
scope and form that any particular campaign is likely to assume. At the most
fundamental level, these continuities—let us call them *rules*—can suggest,
for example, the likelihood that a campaign will be launched and its likely
intensity. Given the paucity of data available on corporate campaigns at this
time, these rules are at best subjective, but they can nevertheless offer considerable insight. Based on a review of the campaigns included in the present study, we can identify at least the following three such rules.[1]

The Rule of Scale

Not all corporate campaigns employ the full range of attack weapons available in the campaign arsenal. Some—like those against Beverly Enterprises,
Food Lion, Hormel, International Paper, or Oregon Steel—incorporate most
or all of the available lines of attack, whereas others—ENI, Marriott International, Sprint—are more selective in their tactics. An early decision that must
be made by a would-be campaigner—subject to change as circumstances
warrant—is the determination of the scale of the attack.

Although less costly than strikes, full-scale corporate campaigns are
nevertheless big-ticket items for a union. They require research, legal analysis and action, government and public relations activities, and the like, all
of which carry costs in time, money, attention, and other resources. At the
same time, less-than-full-scale corporate campaigns—which is to say the
selective use of campaign-type tactics absent a unifying framework—are
now fairly commonplace in small-scale labor disputes. This suggests that
union leaders have in mind a threshold level, and that disputes that exceed
the threshold will receive more comprehensive treatment than will those of
lesser magnitude. Put another way, the bigger the stakes, the more comprehensive the campaign. This is the *rule of scale*.

Arguably, the same logic applies to other, nonunion campaigners. In
most instances, however, the advocacy groups in question simply do not
possess the resources to conduct an all-out campaign. There are exceptions,
as, for example, in the hybrid campaign against Microsoft, where a patch-
work of unions, self-styled consumer groups, and electronic ideologues
have carried the campaign with the support and encouragement of the company's principal competitors. But by and large, these essentially political,
or anticorporate, campaigns gravitate toward the lower end of the range of
magnitudes.

The Rule of Motivation

In general, unions employ corporate campaigns to obtain one or another of the following objectives:

- to influence a contract negotiation or bring a unionized employer to the bargaining table,
- to pressure nonunion or double-breasted employers into either facilitating union organizing (as through card check) or, at least, not impeding it (as through neutrality agreements),
- to protect market share in areas where existing union strength is threatened by the expansion of nonunion companies, and
- to punish an aggressively anti-union employer, including companies that hire permanent replacement workers or encourage decertification of existing union representation, even to the point of driving it out of business.

The key dimension of variation here is the extent to which the union has a vested interest in preserving or damaging the target company. The greater the long-term commonality of interest between company and union, the more restraint the union will show. The less the commonality of interest, the less restrained the attack will be. This is the *rule of motivation*.

This is one key point at which union campaigns and those conducted by other kinds of groups diverge. In many circumstances, a union will, in fact, have some degree of common interest with a company that it seeks to pressure. The same cannot be said of the environmentalists, human rights activists, or others who might choose to launch an attack. For them, it is a matter not of self-interest, but of principle. Their only stake is in the aggregate policy outcome of their campaign, not in the financial well-being or survival of the target company. As a result, their attacks are likely to demonstrate a measure of zeal that is often lacking in union-based campaigns. Although lacking the resources to attack across the full range of available tactics, these groups typically operate toward the upper end of the range of motivation. This adds a measure of both intensity and unpredictability to the campaigns that they wage: They just keep coming, sometimes doing things—like climbing the sides of buildings to hang banners—that seemingly rational people would not be expected to do.

The Rule of Opportunity

Even in a conflict that should be muted according to the rule of motivation, unions are sometimes tempted to ratchet up the level of campaign rhetoric simply because they can. In some industries, or with respect to some companies, the availability of potentially effective lines of attack is so compelling that the union is unable to resist using them. Particularly vulnerable in this way are industries such as supermarkets, pharmacies, nursing homes, and airlines that deal directly with the public and directly with the public safety—industries where any performance failure can be dramatized and magnified in importance and where victims of failure can be given names and faces. In other circumstances, as we have seen, certain unions or union locals may have one or more relatively aggressive leaders, a culture or history of confrontational behavior, important community or political allies, or control over pension or other resources that give them an unusual measure of influence. Or they may simply have an established infrastructure of corporate campaign activists eager to employ their skills. The more attractive the themes or the more eager the organization, the more aggressive the tactics a union will employ in a campaign. This is the *rule of opportunity*.

In this regard, unions and other organizations are likely to operate in relatively similar fashion. Anticorporate activists will be presented with the same structural and thematic opportunities as will their labor counterparts, and their campaigns are restricted or enhanced by the same mix of infrastructure and capabilities. We would then expect the rule of opportunity to apply to them much as it does to the unions.

To the extent that these three rules point in the same direction, we can expect that the resulting campaign will be relatively stable and predictable. To the extent that they conflict, the resulting campaign will be less stable and less predictable. The balance that will be struck among the three is one of the first decisions union or activist leaders must make before undertaking a campaign. The continuing tension among these forces will determine in large measure the unity and effectiveness of the campaign as it goes forward.[2]

TURNING STAKEHOLDERS INTO BREATH-HOLDERS

Although these general rules can help us develop broad-scale expectations about the likely shape and intensity of a given corporate campaign, they do not offer much in the way of specific guidance as to how such a campaign is likely to develop—what particular form the attack will take. And the selection and application of campaign tactics is highly idiosyncratic. But by understanding the conceptual foundations and the body of information from which the selection of tactics derives, we can actually predict with some confidence the shape that a given campaign is likely to assume. The best place to begin such an exercise is at the very point where the campaigners start their work, the analysis of what they commonly term the corporate *power structure*—the set of stakeholder relationships on which the target company depends for its well-being.

Recall William Serrin's summary of Ray Rogers' account of how he prepared the ground for the first full-scale corporate campaign, the attack on

J.P. Stevens. "For six weeks," Rogers tells us through Serrin, "he studied his target, drawing a circle to represent Stevens and arrows pointing toward the center to represent every conceivable way to apply pressure."[3]

In effect, what Rogers did was to identify each of the key stakeholders or points of leverage that supported Stevens, and research each relationship to identify any associated strengths and vulnerabilities. He then set about developing a strategy designed to exploit the areas of greatest vulnerability.

Joseph Uehlein, Director of Special Projects for the AFL–CIO's Industrial Unions Department (IUD), not only provided a succinct statement of the importance of such analysis, but also pointed the way to future developments, when he observed in 1992 that:

> Power structure analysis, identification of vulnerabilities, developing aggressive strategies and creative tactics, participation in coalitions, organizing at the worksite, operating on an international basis, and more, need to evolve from their current application in crisis situations to application in every day trade union endeavors.[4]

An early example of this power structure analysis appears in the IUD's own corporate campaign manual, *Developing New Tactics: Winning with Coordinated Corporate Campaigns*. Included are such stakeholders as the company's shareholders, customers, and creditors.[5] In employing this power analysis—and drawing directly from the first and ninth of Alinsky's rules for radicals—the manual advises prospective campaigners that "power is not only what the union has, but what the company thinks it has. Sometimes the threat exerts more pressure than the action itself."[6]

What might such an analysis look like? Taking a cue from Mr. Rogers and the IUD, as well as from such other sources as the CWA's *Mobilizing for the 90s*, we can easily develop a generic representation of a company's stakeholder relationships and from it begin to see the essential character of the corporate campaign. Figure 9.1 illustrates this analysis.

The application of this chart is quite straightforward. A researcher employing the sources and methods first identified by NACLA and later more fully developed by FAST, the Midwest Academy, and others gathers all available information that relates to each of the identified relationships, including the names and vital statistics of each specific entity (e.g., the lead banks on corporate bond issues, the particular analysts who follow a given company, the reporters who cover it most frequently, the principal regulatory authorities that oversee the company, specific pension funds and other institutions that hold large blocks of the company's shares, and so forth) and the nature of its relationships with the company. These are then prioritized and examined with an eye toward finding the areas of greatest leverage. For a company that is heavily dependent on one or two banks to sustain its operations, those banks would be key points of leverage. For a company

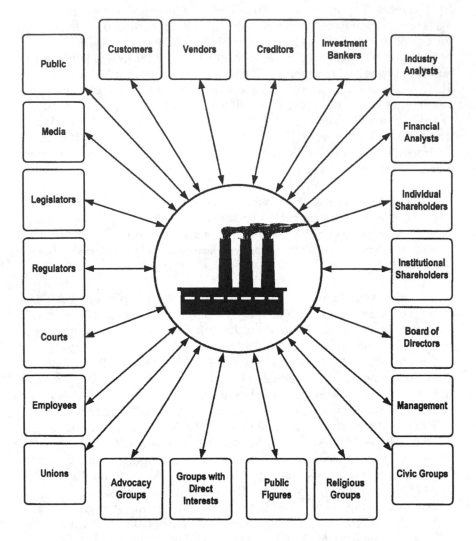

FIG. 9.1. Power structure analysis of stakeholder relationships.

that is heavily regulated, some combination of state and federal agencies might be used instead. The specific selection of leverage points will vary, but the logic is always the same: Find the most cost-effective means of using its dependency on various stakeholders to threaten or do actual harm to the target company. Increase the pressure until management yields to the demands of the union or activists.

Unions may engage in power structure analysis on their own or they may draw on a supportive infrastructure of researchers and consultants. Corporate Campaigns Inc., Ray Rogers' firm, is one such service provider. Another is the Labor Research Association (LRA), which advertises itself as "the leading independent one-stop shop for strategic campaign research and communications expertise for unions.... "[7] LRA's promotional materials urge unions to

> Contact LRA for a full analysis of the ways in which you can raise the costs to the employer of fighting the union sufficiently to produce a victory. LRA's staff will provide your union with a comprehensive "power analysis" and "work up" on every aspect of the employer's business, political, corporate and other connections that can be used to reduce employer resistance.[8]

The focus on stakeholder and power structure analysis unites labor and other anticorporate activists—indeed, many of these interests have now come together in a grouping called The Stakeholder Alliance. The stated purpose of the alliance—which includes, among others, several unions and labor groups (the Machinists, UAW, UNITE, FAST, IUD, the Coalition of Labor Union Women, and the International Labor Rights Fund) and such other now-familiar groups as Citizen Action, the Council on Economic Priorities, Feminist Majority Foundation, and the Government Accountability Project—is to press for greater corporate accountability. Even taking that at face value, however, its agenda, summarized in a document entitled *The Sunshine Standards for Corporate Reporting to Stakeholders*, includes the public release of virtually all of the strategically sensitive information about the policies and operations of companies that has been identified in the various corporate campaign research manuals as useful for assessing corporate vulnerabilities.[9]

In subsequent chapters, we examine in some detail a number of the specific stakeholder relationships identified in this generic model and the ways in which they have been exploited in corporate campaigns. For the balance of the present discussion, however, let us aim a bit higher by looking first at the larger ways in which this strategic perspective plays out. To accomplish that, we focus our attention on four factors: overarching campaign themes, coalition building, metacampaigns, and the framing of codes of conduct. Our discussion here will help put in context all that follows.

THE HOLE-IN-THE-WALL GANG

In his book *Union Corporate Campaigns*, Charles Perry identified three themes that recurred in virtually all campaigns, at least those conducted by labor unions. These three overarching themes were corporate greed and outlawry, exploitation of human misery, and unfairness or injustice to labor.[10] In the years since, this tripartite thematic alliance has remained in place even as it has developed in new ways. Indeed, the longevity of these themes over many years and across many campaigns is now one of their greatest strengths. Through repetition the media and the public have become somewhat conditioned to accept them—a fact that lowers the barrier to persuasion based on these themes in contemporary and future campaigns.

An example of this theme structure can be found in the industry-wide campaign to organize health care workers, which was spearheaded in the 1990s and into the new century by the SEIU and was joined by a sizable number of other unions. The central element of that campaign was a fear appeal built around the concept of victimization. This is a variant of the corporate outlaw theme, but in a form specifically tailored to an industry—hospitals and nursing homes—to which people fear losing their independence at the very time when decisions are made that fundamentally affect their lives and well-being. In the underlying narrative of the health care campaign, corporations acting in their own economic self-interest were portrayed as deciding the fate of weak and helpless individuals, acting through work rules and remote, bureaucratic decision makers. These rules and decisions were being imposed, according to the thematic, not only on hapless hospital patients or nursing home residents and their families, but on the very people who were trying to care for them—the doctors, nurses, other trained professionals, and support staff of the nation's health care facilities who were victims of the same remorseless forces. The union was portrayed as the only thing standing between the public interest and that of health care workers, on the one hand, and total medical repression, on the other. It was a compelling thematic partly because it derived so clearly from real systemic pressures and trends, but not least because it lent itself especially well to personalization—to singling out specific, individual victims of the system whose stories and pictures could be used to symbolize and add emotional content to the core narrative.[11]

As these themes, in their various iterations, come to be woven into the fabric of a campaign, they lead quite naturally to one of the principal campaign objectives—to define the moral high ground in such a way as to ensure that the union (or activist group) holds it and that the company cannot. Corporate campaigns are built on the assumption that reality is socially constructed. Sociologists Peter L. Berger and Thomas Luckman encapsulated this notion of the social construction of reality in their landmark 1966 book, *The Social Construction of Reality*, which concludes with these words:

> Man is biologically predestined to construct and to inhabit a world with others.
> This world becomes for him the dominant and definitive reality. Its limits are set
> by nature, but once constructed, this world acts back upon nature. In the dialectic between nature and the socially constructed world the human organism itself
> is transformed. In this same dialectic *man produces reality* and thereby produces himself.[12]

Berger and Luckman's essential and, in its day, highly innovative argument is that people live in a world of institutions, roles, and relationships that they define for themselves, whether through education and learning, mediated communication, or interpretation of their direct experience. This notion is now sufficiently well established to be considered a part of the so-called conventional wisdom, but that does not diminish its significance. Indeed, the whole of strategic communication is grounded in this observation and in its fulfillment through carefully shaped and targeted messages designed to create and interpret reality in some particularized sphere.

So, too, is the corporate campaign. The real issues in a labor dispute might be, for example, the common organizing troika of card check, neutrality, and master agreements. However, the fact is that these issues will not garner, let alone mobilize, support among the public. They are too narrow, technical, and reflective of labor's well-understood self-interest, and the unions know it. But experienced corporate campaigners understand that the themes of the campaign serve a different purpose than the union's objectives at the bargaining table, and that they can be generated and managed more or less independently of any specific demands the union may present to the company. The goal in bargaining is to achieve particular objective outcomes; the goal in campaigning is to pressure the union's bargaining adversary to maximize the likelihood that these outcomes will be achieved.

In the health care campaign, for example, the unions' real objective has been to organize workers. In 1999, the health care industry was estimated to contain a reservoir of between 6 and 7 million nonunion workers who might be brought under organized labor's umbrella. They represented a potential source of political power for the labor movement, not to mention literally billions of dollars in annual dues that would be added to union coffers.[13] The unions' goal was to be achieved following precisely the type of wholesale organizing strategy detailed in chapter 2 of this book. But recall the themes of that campaign—victimization and corporate greed. If one were to examine both the bargaining objectives and the public face of the campaign, one might well perceive a disconnect. But the public never does that; it sees only the simplified representation of the issues presented in the media or by other means of communication. For the public—and for any stakeholder group called on to understand aspects of a company that go beyond its direct experience—that simplified representation is the only context they have in which to understand the company's behavior and the union's or activists' allegations about that behavior. For them, the *image* of the corporate campaign *is reality*.

The theme structure of the corporate campaign is designed to draw on the underlying distrust that many Americans harbor about major corporations, and to evoke strong feelings about social problems that can then be blamed on those same, untrustworthy (greedy, self-interested, profiteering, uncaring, etc.) corporations. That is where the moral high ground in the corporate campaign is to be found. Once claimed, it is then exploited systematically in ways that we explore in more detail in a later treatment of the role of media in the corporate campaign.

No company—no institution—is immune from this strategy. The best evidence of that can be found in the campaign waged by Local 250 of the SEIU against a hospital operator, Catholic Healthcare West. Recall that in that campaign, the union went so far as to suggest that the Catholic religious orders that owned the company were not living up to the moral teachings of their own Church, which the union and the National Interfaith Committee for Worker Justice argued required that workers be unionized.

The issue here is legitimacy—the question of which side can claim to be aligned with the dominant values of the society. The selection of themes for a campaign is driven by the desire to paint the company into a moral corner from which it can escape only by doing its antagonists' bidding. In effect, management is portrayed as a band of societal outlaws—a sort of commercial version of Butch Cassidy's Hole-in-the-Wall Gang, stealing from or, in some other way, violating the public interest to serve its own greedy purposes and then hiding in its corporate towers.

KNOWN BY THE COMPANY THEY KEEP

Legitimacy. Morality. These are great issues on paper. However, the problem the unions face—as documented quite thoroughly in chapter 2—is that they have no more credibility or moral standing among the public than do the corporations with which they do battle. It is not just issues or positions that can be lacking in legitimacy, but institutions as well. In that sense, labor operates in a campaign setting from a position of substantial weakness. It is for that reason that corporate campaigns—especially those initiated by organized labor—rely heavily on coalitions of nonlabor groups to carry the attack on the target company.

The rationale is simple. If the unions carry their own message, the impact of the message is mitigated to the extent that the audience—often the general public—distrusts the source or its motives. However, if the same message is carried by groups widely considered to be public-regarding—environmentalists, women's rights and civil rights groups, human rights advocates, patients' rights advocates, consumer groups, and the like—not only is the adverse interpretation eliminated, but it may well be replaced by favorable cause-related perceptions that actually enhance its credibility. Where this occurs—and it is common in corporate campaigns—the target company ends up confronting not the union, which is its true core adversary, but the public-regarding cause groups that are carrying the attack. To the extent that its coalition-building is successful, then, labor can use this device to stake its claim to the moral high ground.

The single most common cluster of allies on whom labor has called in its corporate campaigns are found in the religious community. This is not surprising when viewed through an historical lens when we recall, for example, that the National Council of Churches was literally, in Dean Acheson's marvelous phrase, "present at the creation" of the corporate campaign. It is less surprising still when one realizes that alliances with religious interests serve directly the principal objective of building coalitions in the first place because these groups almost invariably define their own objectives in moralistic terms.

Members of local religious communities—most notably groups of local ministers—are among the most frequent secondary participants in corporate campaigns. However, national organizations like the Interfaith Center for Corporate Responsibility or the National Interfaith Center for Worker Justice are frequently involved. Several arms of the United Methodist Church—ranging from those with an interest in social justice to the Church's pension board—have actively supported corporate campaigns, as have a number of Catholic ministerial and lay groups. Several orders of Catholic nuns are regular participants in these campaigns, particularly through shareholder initiatives. The National Baptist Convention—the organization representing the nation's African-American Baptist churches—has become increasingly active, especially in campaigns where many of the affected workers are African Americans. The Reverend Jesse Jackson alone has been visible in at least a dozen campaigns. The strategy here is one of displacement—positioning the target company in opposition not to a union, but to religious values personified. In the words of labor activist Charles Kernaghan, "The companies really, really hate it when the nuns get involved and start writing letters. I mean, what are they going to say against nuns, right?"[14]

Not all of these partnerships between labor and its allies are grounded in philosophical agreement alone. For example, the long-time head of one consumer rights group, the National Consumers League, was married to an organizing director for the AFL–CIO. In addition, the spouse of a UFCW vice president chaired the Safe Food Coalition, a group that counts the UFCW among its members and helped legitimize that union's campaigns in the meat and poultry industries, and later assumed the leadership of the Consumer Federation of America, an umbrella group representing unions and other organizations, shortly after that group announced plans to file a $10 *billion* lawsuit against Microsoft, which was the target of a CWA organizing campaign. Similarly, the five-member Board of Advisors of Children Against Underage Servitude and Employment (CAUSE), an arm of the Made in the USA Foundation that organizes children in the United States to oppose child labor elsewhere, includes Charlie Mercer, secretary treasurer of the AFL–CIO's Union Label Division, and Jack Sheinkman, president of the Amalgamated Bank.[15] The bank was a creation of the Amalgamated Clothing and Textile Workers Union, which Mr. Sheinkman also headed for many years. He served as secretary treasurer of the union during its path-breaking J.P. Stevens campaign, in which he worked closely with Ray Rogers.[16] Through these associations and others like them, labor is able to generate pressure on target companies, or entire industries, without flaunting its own involvement.

We do not argue here that groups partnering with labor—with the possible exception of some that have explicit ties to the labor movement—are acting as either dupes or shills for the unions. Quite the contrary, these groups have their own, legitimate concerns and their own agendas, and they typically act at their own initiative to advance them. That is precisely the point. In shaping a corporate campaign, one of the tasks of the initial research is to identify groups that might be mobilized to confront a target company with their own internally defined concerns and that might, in the process of doing their own business, support the union's objectives and add to the pressure on the company. Corporate campaigns do not generally push rocks up hill; they identify the ones that are poised on the down-slope and give them a shove.

An increasingly important variant of the use of coalitions in corporate campaigns is the participation of the international labor federations. As we noted in chapter 6, in campaigns against companies that have critical international interests—either facilities or markets—the American unions have begun to join more and more frequently with their European and international counterparts to generate added pressure. Although this would seem, at first glance, to run contrary to our assertion that coalitions are required to mask labor's role or interest in a campaign, that is actually not the case.

The involvement of the international unions and labor federations receives little notice in the American media or among the public, which would assign it little significance in any event. In contrast, in European and other countries around the world, organized labor is afforded far greater legitimacy in its own right than is the case in the United States. By allying themselves with these international unions and federations, then, U.S. unions are able to take advantage of this credibility in generating public and political pressure against the international operations of companies targeted in campaigns without drawing unfavorable attention to themselves in the domestic arena.

The American unions, although not awash in money, have been far stronger financially than most of their counterparts around the world, and have developed a high degree of expertise in corporate campaigns, but they lack legitimacy and public support. The international federations have long enjoyed public esteem around the world, but have lacked both resources and the knowledge base to conduct effective corporate campaigns. Now that the two sets of organizations have extended their institutional ties and begun to cooperate on particular projects, one likely trend for the future is that toward the internationalization of the corporate campaign to a far greater extent than is currently the case.

For political activists engaged in anticorporate campaigns, such coalition-building is often far less necessary. Some of these groups, like the National Organization for Women, are well established and well known, with an agenda that is perceived by large segments of the public as serving the interests of a defined class, but not the economic self-interest of the organization per se. The media are generally willing to take the pronouncements of such an organization at face value and accept in some measure the validity of its positions. In other words, these groups have a degree of inherent credibility. They may choose to join with other groups in a coalition to increase their influence, but that is quite different from using the coalition to mask their involvement and carry their message. NOW's participation in the Rainbow Coalition's campaign against Texaco is a case in point. Other groups, like the Rainforest Action Network, are less well known and, if captured face-on in the klieg lights, might be rather more controversial among media and public alike. However, these groups typically have public-regarding names and espouse causes that attract public and journalistic sympathy—who could be against saving the rainforests, for example?—both of which make it less likely that they will attract such scrutiny. As a result, coalitions are employed to different ends and are, in some ways, less central in campaigns by these nonunion activists.

THE METACAMPAIGNS

From the standpoint of communication strategy, one of the principal benefits of building diverse campaigns around a series of recurrent themes—like Perry's trio of corporate greed and outlawry, the exploitation of human misery, and unfairness or injustice to labor—is that over time the public becomes conditioned to hearing them and may, by virtue of their repetition, incorporate them into its already critical view of big business. Similarly, as more and more campaigns transpire in which labor is seen, even behind a veil, to be allied with the true forces of all that is good and righteous—with religious leaders, civil rights leaders, consumer advocates, and environmentalists—labor itself may assume something of the aura of public-regardingness that attaches to these relatively popular causes. What, we might ask ourselves, would happen if both of these factors—a potent thematic and a visible cleansing of base motives—could be institutionalized by labor in some form? Might that provide the impetus for a successful march out of the wilderness after 40 (or more) years?

This is not a hypothetical question. To the contrary, it is precisely the point of several overarching campaigns launched (or joined) by organized labor in recent years— among them the campaigns for a living wage (typically as much as twice the national minimum wage), which labor has been working to implement through friendly local legislatures,[17] and against NAFTA and other free-trade agreements, which the unions see as further internationalizing the labor market and driving wages down; the Burma campaign and its lesser known counterpart in Nigeria, which were initiated by political activists but, with the participation of OCAW (now PACE), have focused extensively on forcing several international oil companies to cease operations in these countries; and the anti-sweatshop movement. In each instance, labor has created or associated itself with a moral-high-ground thematic—family values, saving jobs, ending political oppression, and ending economic exploitation (especially of children). It has developed or participated in a relatively broad coalition that enhances its own standing. In each instance, the campaign is waged not against a single company, but against an industry or an entire commercial regime.

A similar phenomenon occurs within specific industries. In health care, for example, the rubric of patients' rights is employed in campaigns against numerous companies. Indeed, it is the glue that holds the thematic structure of that particular campaign in place. It is the appeal to patients' rights that provides the logical and emotional link between the positions of the workers and the public, and that is used by the unions to justify their demands for higher staffing levels, different work rules, more employee independence, and greater compensation. Absent the rubric of patients' rights, these demands would appear to the public as the usual, self-interested demands of organized labor. With that rubric, they are demands being made in the interest of the public itself.[18] The same role is played by food-safety campaigns in the supermarket and meat-packing industries, passenger-safety campaigns in the airline industry, environmental-protection campaigns in the chemical industry, and so forth.

Let us term these overarching campaigns, with their respective enduring central themes and cast of coalition partners, *metacampaigns*. These campaigns appear to transcend company-specific labor–management disagreements even as they are often used by the unions to frame them. They also appear to transcend the narrow self-interests of a union or the labor movement even as they advance them.

The point is not that these metacampaigns are based on untruths. Every corporate campaign is based on some form of truth; in the present instance, there undoubtedly are genuine instances of oppression, exploitation, and other evils that should be addressed. Even a socially constructed reality must pass the occasional reality check, and any campaign that fails such a check will not succeed.[19] Rather, the point is that labor's use of, and association with, these campaigns is driven in significant measure by its own economic and political motives and organizational needs. The metacampaigns are a means toward those ends.

A case in point is the anti-sweatshop campaign, which began in earnest in the mid-1990s and within 5 years had grown into something approaching a full-fledged social movement. Sweatshops and child labor offer a particularly attractive thematic for labor, harking back as they do to the days of Samuel Gompers and the Triangle Shirt fire, a time when the unions were gaining in legitimacy and influence, placing the unions on unassailable moral ground, and creating a natural avenue for outreach to college students, human rights activists, the religious community, and a host of other self-motivated allies.[20] They also have three added virtues. First, Third World sweatshop labor provides a useful stalking horse for labor's agenda regarding international trade, illustrating as graphically as any campaigner could desire the wages and working conditions against which American workers must compete. Second, the sweatshop theme can be employed to support organizing efforts in diverse industries—everything from shoe manufacturing and the garment industry to the chip-makers of Silicon Valley, with its "hi-tech sweatshops"—and to attack companies ranging from Nike to Intel. Finally, no matter what American companies, unions, or consumers may do, sweatshops will not disappear anytime soon. The economics of world trade render that a virtual certainty. As a result, the unions' investment in the stop-sweatshop thematic can be expected to yield returns for many years.

According to the Campaign for Labor Rights (CLR), a group examined in detail in chapter 7, the anti-sweatshop campaign originated with one of its members, UNITE, the union that resulted from the merger of the ACTWU and the International Ladies Garment Workers Union, which employed the theme in its campaign against the May Company, a subsidiary of Federated Department Stores.[21] It was a theme that clearly resonated with a wide-ranging audience. As recently as January 1998, CLR was still, in its own words, "looking for an effective way to support this campaign."[22]

By May 1999, the group was hiring regional organizers to build local coalitions, promote anti-sweatshop activism, and organize speaking tours for sweatshop workers to call attention to their plight. In the meantime, the campaign had expanded to Canada, produced a curriculum package for schools, targeted not only American retailers but contract producers in a number of countries, swept up in its attacks companies like Nike and Disney and Guess?, been featured on the television program *Hard Copy*, and had even come to incorporate the agenda of other CLR members like CISPES and US/GLEP for economic and political reform in Central America. The National Labor Committee had produced a video—*Mickey Mouse Goes to Haiti*—contrasting the affluence of American consumers with the poverty of the Haitian workers who stitched garments for Disney, while Phillip Knight, CEO of Nike, had issued his famous *mea culpa* at the National Press Club and pledged to exploit foreign workers no more.

The so-called Apparel Industry Partnership (AIP), which included the prolabor National Consumers League, the International Labor Rights Federation, and UNITE, as well as a small number of manufacturing firms, was formed with the encouragement of the Clinton administration. It was intended to create a set of labor standards that outlawed sweatshop and child labor and provided for compliance to be monitored by unions, human rights groups, and other third parties. However, by 1999, when the standards were issued, UNITE and the Interfaith Center for Corporate Responsibility decried them and began to attack the AIP.[23] By then, a new labor-supported group, United Students Against Sweatshops (USAS), had helped organize chapters and demonstrations on campuses across the country, and an increasing number of colleges and universities, led by Duke University, had adopted codes of conduct under which they pledged that goods made under license and featuring their official logos would not be assembled by sweatshop labor. In short order, however, USAS also began to disparage monitoring by the AIP-based Fair Labor Association and insist instead on review by a Workers' Rights Consortium of its own design.[24] Central to this effort was an insistence on disclosure by retailers of all the factory names, locations, and wage rates of their suppliers. The National Labor Committee, for example, distributed a prototype disclosure policy for students to present to their universities, and disclosure emerged as a central demand of many campus USAS groups.[25]

THE CODE(S) OF THE WEST

In some of these latter developments of the anti-sweatshop campaign, we can see the emerging face of the next generation of corporate campaigns, which are likely to be built around the insistence that target companies adopt codes of conduct and agree to external monitoring by groups that have traditionally been their adversaries, or at the very least have not shared with them a substantial commonality of interest.

A code of conduct is an agreement by a company to adopt business practices and policies that are consistent with some set of social objectives, and to be held accountable for behaving in a manner consistent with its commitments. At one level, this is a natural outgrowth of the social responsibility movement—ably chronicled in its early years by Vogel[26]—that traces back to the promulgation of the Sullivan principles for companies doing business in South Africa in the 1970s and to the activist agenda of the National Council of Churches and NACLA. As matters have developed in the years since, the movement toward codes has risen as well in the priorities of organized labor, for which they offer a means of both codifying the achievement of its objectives and wrapping its pursuit of those objectives in a banner of quasilegalities.

Codes of conduct may include a variety of emphases—attending to the needs of communities where a company has facilities, being sensitive to the environmental impact of corporate activities, pursuing diversity in a company's employee population or in its contracting practices, and so forth. Usually union-friendly labor practices are included. However, what is most interesting about many of these codes is what we might think of as their *snowball* clauses. Companies are asked to agree to standards for their own workers and facilities and to agree to impose those same standards on all of their business partners. So, for example, if a manufacturing company signs a code under which it agrees to cover all cement floors in its plants with rubber tiles, under a snowball clause it might also be agreeing to require that every supplier from which it purchases parts and every distributor to which it ships finished goods must also install rubber tiles over their respective cement floors or risk losing the company's business.

In their content, then, codes of conduct encapsulate the core themes that are commonplace in corporate campaigns. In their provisions for independent third-party monitoring, they place the company that agrees to a code at the effective mercy of its greatest critics, leaving it to defend any specific action that offends the monitors against a moral standard to which the company has visibly acquiesced.[27] In their snowball clauses, they convert companies that had been targeted in campaigns into *de facto* allies in subsequent campaign iterations. On the whole, it is a potent strategy.

We can see the logic of this code-based campaigning carried to its extreme in what is known as "SA8000"—portrayed as an international standard for corporate accountability. SA8000 has been advanced by a group of 19 organizations, including such companies as Reebok and the Body Shop, the Amalgamated Bank (whose pedigree we have already examined), Franklin Research and Development (a family of mutual funds that invests in companies it regards as socially responsible), and Amnesty International. The lead organization in the group, and the "Accreditation Agency" for SA8000, is the Council on Economic Priorities (CEP).[28] Founded by Alice Tepper Marlin in 1969, CEP publishes reports on corporate social performance, makes annual awards for corporate social responsibility, and provides research on these topics for investors. The group maintains a database on more than 700 companies. It also has published from time to time a listing of "America's Least Wanted"—companies that it regards as acting irresponsibly. It is worth noting that a significant proportion of these companies—some examples include Albertson's, ConAgra, Food Lion, International Paper, Maxxam, Texaco, Tyson's Foods, and Wheeling-Pittsburgh—have also been targets of corporate campaigns. CEP was singled out as a resource by Michael Locker in his chapter on corporate research in the NACLA *Research Methodology Guide*, where he wrote in 1970:

> For information on business firms relevant to anti-corporate campaigns (around such issues as pollution, Vietnam, militarism, racism, etc.) see ECONOMIC PRIORITIES REPORT, published monthly by the Council on Economic Priorities....[29]

In many ways, SA8000 is the culmination of decades of work by the CEP because it incorporates in distilled form a set of standards and practices the organization has long promulgated and places CEP in the position of certifying compliance. Grounded in a variety of positions that have been adopted over the years by the International Labor Organization (ILO) and in the *Universal Declaration on Human Rights* and the United Nations *Convention on the Rights of the Child*, this document sets forth a host of labor standards to which signatory companies are expected to adhere. These include among others:

- a minimum working age of 15 years and mandatory school attendance for young workers
- provision of a safe and healthy working environment
- the right to form and join trade unions and free access for union representatives to their members while in the workplace
- a commitment to the nondiscriminatory hiring, compensation, access to training, promotion, termination, and retirement of workers without regard to their race, caste, national origin, religion, disability, gender, sexual orientation, union membership, or political affiliation
- no tolerance for sexual harassment
- no corporal punishment, coercion, or verbal abuse
- a maximum work week of 48 hours, a limit on overtime, and 1 day in 7 off
- no labor-only contracting
- wages to be paid at not less than the legal minimum or the industry standard.[30]

The Code provides that, to achieve a certificate of compliance, companies must submit to an external audit of their practices and, once certified, must submit to annual follow-up audits.

The power and appeal of SA8000 derive from its elegance and simplicity, and from the evident reasonableness of its requirements. But from a business perspective—and especially that of an embattled company that is under pressure to adopt this code or one like it—it is a potential Trojan Horse. For example, what does it mean to provide a safe and healthy working environment? Is it sufficient to comply with applicable regulations in a company's home country, or must the company meet some alternative international standard? Is the right of employees to form trade unions to be interpreted to mean that those workers have the right to participate in NLRB-administered representation elections, or does it require acceptance of a card check procedure? Given the practice in some European countries, it may not even require that unionization is the choice of a majority of workers. What is the industry standard wage—the wage paid in advanced industrialized countries or that paid in lesser developed countries? Precisely what constitutes verbal abuse? From a corporate perspective, these are but a few of the many legitimate questions associated with SA8000. The threat to the companies is that the answers to these questions will come from CEP and its international board of standard-setters, whose interests do not necessarily accommodate concerns that a company might regard as essential.

From the unions' perspective and that of some anticorporate activists, this is precisely the point. Not only do these codes carry the potential to alter the behaviors of corporations on a large-scale and self-sustaining basis, but they have the further advantage, if fully implemented, of sustaining labor's position on a wide range of issues, not least of which is its opposition to free trade. That is the case because full implementation of SA8000 or its equivalent would, under some interpretations, minimize or eliminate the wage differentials and other economic incentives for American companies to export their operations—all of this to be accomplished in the name of social accountability.

It is for that reason we can regard SA8000 and the class of documents it represents as the ultimate refinement to date of the corporate campaign as a strategic exercise. Behind such documents lie the full weight of the history and theory of the campaign as waged by unions and other activists alike. And if the sponsors of H.R. 4596, a bill introduced in Congress in June 2000, have their way, added to that will be the full weight of the federal government. This legislation, termed the "Corporate Code of Conduct Act," would, if passed, incorporate the principal elements of SA8000 into law and require that all U.S. companies with more than 20 overseas employees abide by them—and impose them on their business partners. In this case, however, it would not be the CEP that was authorized to monitor implementation, but rather the Secretaries of Commerce, Labor and State and the Administrator of the Environmental Protection Agency.[31]

ENDNOTES

1. From a social scientific perspective, these rules are actually no more than hypotheses that predict particular relationships between the characteristics and needs of the campaigners—the independent variables—and the attributes of the campaigns—the dependent variables. Their presentation in the text is intended only to suggest the relationships that seem to be supported in the present, exploratory examination of the topic.

2. Portions of the discussion in this section are drawn from Jarol B. Manheim, *Labor Pains: The Corporate Campaign Against the Healthcare Industry* (St. Michael's, MD: Tred Avon Institute Press, 1999), pp. 23–24.

3. William Serrin, "Organized Labor is Increasingly Less So," *The New York Times*, November 18, 1984, p. 4:3.

4. Joseph Uehlein, "Confront Corporate Power," in *The Future of Labor* (New York: Labor Research Association, 1992), p. 73.

5. *Developing New Tactics: Winning with Coordinated Corporate Campaigns* (Washington: Industrial Unions Department, AFL-CIO, 1985), p. 2.

6. Ibid., p. 3.

7. Found at www.lra-ny.com, February 16, 1999.

8. Found at www.lra-ny.com/lra/corppower.html, February 16, 1999.

9. The report, and information about the Alliance itself, are available through the Center for the Advancement of Public Policy at www.essential.org/capp.

10. Charles R. Perry, *Union Corporate Campaigns* (Philadelphia: Industrial Relations Unit, The Wharton School, University of Pennsylvania, 1987), pp. 20–31.

11. Adapted from Manheim, op. cit., pp. 31–32.

12. Peter L. Berger and Thomas Luckman, *The Social Construction of Reality: A Treatise in the Sociology of Knowledge* (New York: Doubleday, 1966), p. 183.

13. Manheim, op. cit., p. 7.

14. Randy Kennedy, "After Life of Wandering, Labor Advocate makes the Sweatshop Wars His Calling," *The New York Times*, December 9, 1999.

15. The board's members are listed on the Foundation's Web site at www.madeusa.org/cause.htm. The board of the Made in the USA Foundation itself is not listed. For information on the Amalgamated Bank, see Frank Swoboda, "A Union Bank Tries to Build Its Membership," *Washington Post*, February 1, 1999, p. F16.

16. "A Boycott Battle to Win the South," *Business Week*, December 6, 1976, p. 80.

17. According to an analysis by LPA, Inc., as of July 1999, more than two dozen communities had adopted such provisions in one form or another, among them Baltimore, Boston, Chicago, Detroit, Los Angeles, Milwaukee, Minneapolis, New York City, Oakland, San Antonio, and San Jose. *LPA Memorandum 99-124* (Washington: 1999). Advocate Lawrence Glickman puts the number of such communities at more than 200. Quoted in "Movement growing to replace minimum wage with 'living wage,' " *CNN Interactive*, June 4, 1999.

18. Manheim, op. cit., p. 33.

19. A case in point is the attack on Food Lion by a group known as Consumers United with Employees, which seemed to be quite effective until it was revealed that the group's "office suite" was actually a box at a commercial mail drop and that its telephone rang at UFCW headquarters.

20. A Marymount University survey in 1999 showed, for example, that three in four consumers would avoid shopping at a retailer they knew to sell garments manufactured in sweatshops, and 86% of respondents indicated a willingness to pay an extra dollar on a $20 garment to ensure that it was not made in a sweatshop. Mirroring the claims of the anti-sweatshop campaign, twice as many respondents indicated in 1999 that retailers as well as manufacturers should be held responsible for ending sweatshops as had so indicated in a 1995 survey. "Marymount Survey: Consumers Don't Want Sweatshops," news release from Marymount University, December 6, 1999.

21. This information was posted at one time on the CLR Web site at www.compugraph.com/clr/clrwho.html.

22. Statement posted on the CLR Web site at www.compugraph.com/clr/partner.html.

23. Maria Stephens, "Code Name: Cover Up," *UNITE Magazine*, Winter 1999.

24. See, for example, Jennifer B. Wang, "Champion factory disclosure not enough to satisfy Students Against Sweatshops," *Yale Daily News* (Yale University), November 18, 1999; Ryan Gabrielson, "U. Arizona anti-sweatshop group supports alternative factory monitoring," *Arizona Daily Wildcat* (University of Arizona), November 16, 1999; and James Thompson, "Columbia U. student activists protest sweatshop labor," *Columbia Daily Spectator* (Columbia University), November 18, 1999.

25. "The People's Right to Know: A Model Procurement Policy Calling for Full Public Disclosure of All Factory Names, Locations and Wage Rates," distributed by the National Labor Committee through the Campaign for Labor Rights, November 1999. For examples of the implementation of this demand, see Robert K. Silverman, "Harvard's largest apparel manufacturer to disclose sites," *Harvard Crimson* (Harvard University), November 16, 1999; and Joseph S. Pete, "Indiana U. defines sweatshop policy," *Indiana Daily Student* (Indiana University), November 16, 1999. Note, too, that the articles in this and the preceding footnote were published at essentially the same time. They were, in fact, among a large number of such articles in campus newspapers, each independently and locally authored—an observation that is itself indicative of an orchestrated publicity effort.

26. David Vogel, *Lobbying the Corporation: Citizen Challenges to Business Authority* (New York: Basic Books, 1978), passim.

27. Some code advocates, like United Students Against Sweatshops, have most recently claimed that the "independence" of these third-party monitors may not be sufficient to achieve their goals. They have argued for their replacement with monitors based among workers and local, proworker NGOs. See, for example, Mike Gonzales, "Global solidarity needed instead of corporate cover-ups," *Badger Herald* (University of Wisconsin), December 7, 1999; and Tim Sullivan, "Georgetown Stays in Fair Labor Association," *The Hoya* (Georgetown University), December 7, 1999.

28. See www.sa8000.com/pages/overview/organizations.html.

29. Michael Locker, "Corporations," in *Research Methodology Guide* (New York: North American Congress on Latin America, 1970), p. 19.

30. These are selectively but closely paraphrased from a listing that can be found on the Web at www.sa8000.com/pages/requirements/requirements_operat_crit.html.

31. H.R. 4596, 106th Congress, Second Session.

10

MONEY TALKS ...

We have devoted a great deal of space and thought to the philosophical underpinnings of the corporate campaign, its development as a manifestation of the art and science of strategic political communication, the strategic assumptions on which it is based, and the likely future directions of its evolution. The time has now come to slice into the belly of the beast—to illuminate some of the many tactics through which these campaigns are implemented.

There are many ways we might accomplish this task. We could, for example, focus our attention on each stakeholder relationship, in turn using these multiple corporate constituencies to cast light on the campaign tool chest. We do some of that. Or we could employ case studies to provide anecdotal evidence of campaign tactics, drawing some more general lessons as we go. We do some of that as well. However, the most productive avenue for the moment is probably to begin where the campaigners typically begin—with the inherent *corporateness* of the corporation. In the words of Watergate's hidden hero, Deep Throat, let us simply "follow the money."

Why start with the money? Calvin Coolidge once observed that "the chief business of the American people is business."[1] Without wanting to be taken too literally, we might add that the chief currency of business is just that—currency—money. Favorable public opinion is important. Friendly regulators are important. Satisfied customers are important. But in the end, all of these stakeholder relationships and a host of others are measured in only one place where it counts—on the bottom line of the corporate profit-and-loss statement. Michael Locker, Ray Rogers, and the other pro- genitors of the corporate campaign realized this from the outset, and they placed the inevitable financial dependencies of a target company squarely in the bulls' eyes of their campaign dart boards. More recently, and as fur- ther evidence of the strategic centrality of capital to capitalism, the authors of the World Resources Institute's attack manual, *Leverage for the Envi- ronment*, have offered sophisticated guidance for identifying and exploit- ing vulnerabilities in these financial relationships. Bruce Raynor, International Secretary-Treasurer of UNITE, has put it more bluntly.

> Employers think we're out of our minds, and the result is we win ... because we're willing to do what's necessary....
>
> We're not businessmen, and at the end of the day they are. If we're willing to cost them enough, they'll give in.[2]

For the same reason, it would seem to serve our own present purposes by starting here in the world of corporate finance.

Among the primary targets of the finance dimension of the corporate campaign are the target company's investment and commercial bankers (often including insurance companies, which are major lenders), its indi- vidual and institutional shareholders, and the financial and industry ana- lysts who most closely follow its fortunes. Let us look at some of the tactics directed at each of these groups in turn.

YOU CAN BANK ON IT ... OR NOT

From the beginning, the corporate campaign has included efforts to mobi- lize a target company's banking relationships as a source of pressure against it. In the J.P. Stevens campaign, for example, one of Ray Rogers' major targets was Metropolitan Life, one of the company's principal lend- ers. Other examples through the years include the targeting of Manufac- turers Hanover in the 1982 OCAW campaign against Texaco, Crestar Bank in the 1988–1989 UMWA campaign against Pittston, NationsBank by the Teamsters in their 1994–1995 Pony Express campaign, Mellon Bank by the USWA in its 1996–1997 campaign against Wheeling-Pittsburgh, and Wells Fargo Bank in the USWA's late-1990s campaign against Kaiser Aluminum.

In their 1996 Rogers-aided campaign against Washington Gas Light, the International Union of Gas Workers launched a boycott of Crestar Bank, a major financial backer of the company that also had important interlocks with its directors. With the support of the AFL–CIO, the UE, and other un- ions, the Gas Workers threatened to withdraw $114 million in pension and other funds from the bank. Meanwhile, in 1991, the Association of Community Organizations for Reform Now (ACORN), a national community-based organization that often supports union campaigns, had named Crestar its "Redliner of the Year." Redlining is the practice of routinely discriminating in lending, hiring, and other decisions on the basis of race. These charges were renewed during the corporate campaign by the A. Philip Randolph Institute, a black trade-unionist group affiliated with the AFL–CIO. The bank, based in Richmond, Virginia, was also attacked for promoting a plan to celebrate Robert E. Lee's birthday together with that of Martin Luther King, Jr. As usual, Rogers was very open about the strategy. "We're using Crestar as leverage," he stated at the time. "The unions have money in that bank and therefore have more power in money than they do as labor. Our strategy is to fight Crestar."[3]

More recently, the Steelworkers pursued a similar plan by pressuring Wells Fargo Bank to gain leverage in their campaign against Oregon Steel. The union staged demonstrations at the bank's headquarters in San Francisco as well as its office in Portland, Oregon, where the company is based. At a December 1997 rally in Pueblo, Colorado, where a strike at one of the company's facilities had sparked the campaign, John Sweeney pledged the support of the AFL–CIO for the strikers and the campaign. At that point, several unions began withdrawing funds, led by an alliance of Carpenters' locals that withdrew a reported $5 million in Colorado, and by a USWA local and its employer, Northwest Aluminum, who withdrew a $20 million retirement fund.[4] George Becker, president of the USWA, said of the move, "The corporate campaign will not fail. If it's not working we escalate it. We don't give a damn what it costs."[5]

Early in 1999, two Oregon Steel lenders, Union Bank of California and its parent Bank of Tokyo–Mitsubishi, both of which were being pressured separately in the Rainforest Action Network's campaign against Mitsubishi, withdrew from the lending syndicate. In the spring, a union representative and two of labor's political friends in California—Scott Wildman, chair of the General Assembly's Joint Legislative Audit Committee, and Los Angeles city controller Rick Tuttle—met with Paul Watson, who was in charge of Wells Fargo's corporate banking, to suggest that lending to a company like Oregon Steel that was employing replacement workers "wasn't a good business practice." The politicians denied making any threats, such as the withdrawal of public pension funds from the bank, whereas those on Wells Fargo's side of the table indicated that they had been reminded by the intervention of these political leaders of the pro-union climate in the state. By June 1999, the union claimed that its boycott had led to the withdrawal of $1.2 billion from Wells Fargo, although the bank set the figure considerably lower. Whatever the amount and whatever the pressure, in July of that year, Wells Fargo withdrew as lead bank in the consortium of Oregon Steel lenders, although it continued to provide credit to the company.[6]

Companies targeted in corporate campaigns are potentially vulnerable to these attacks on their banking and other financial relationships for two interlocking sets of reasons: one having to do with banking and the other with corporate finance. In the first instance, banks are extremely risk-averse institutions. Their income, in the form of interest and other returns on investment, is based on successfully pricing the level of risk associated with a company or project (e.g., the higher the risk, the higher the interest rate or expected return must be if the bank is to participate, and vice versa) and on managing a portfolio of variably risky investments to maintain profitability, which is achieved by borrowing money at low rates in the form of deposits and lending it safely at higher rates. Because the costs of obtaining deposits serve to reduce their profits, banks greatly prefer to attract large corporate or institutional depositors rather than small individual ones. Pension funds and other major accounts, then, are both large and stable sources of funds and hence of profitability. That establishes leverage for the holders of such accounts, and it makes the banks sensitive to their interests.

This potential leverage is augmented by the fact that virtually no large-scale corporate enterprise in the United States today is self-financing. To the contrary, companies routinely finance their growth, and even their day-to-day activities, using lines of credit, bonds and debentures, and even mortgages provided by banks and such other risk-averse institutions as insurance companies and investment funds. The corporate economy literally runs on credit. Taking these two observations together, we can see that, in threatening to disrupt the flow of such credit, the unions have a potentially viable source of pressure, the effectiveness of which will be determined by the extent of discomfort they are able to produce among the lenders, who will, in the end, act in their own self-interest.

This discomfort can arise from at least two rather different forms of pressure. The first is public embarrassment. When the RAN activists attacking Mitsubishi climbed 80-foot palms in Beverly Hills or rappelled from the roof of a 15-story bank tower to hang banners attacking Union Bank or chained themselves to cement blocks outside the bank's San Francisco office to form a barricade, that was embarrassment at work. Although the unions tend to be rather less dramatic, they, too, employ adverse publicity in an effort to influence the banks. The attacks on Crestar as a redliner and the demonstrations at Wells Fargo's headquarters in the Oregon Steel campaign are cases in point.

Attacking banks through claims and antics such as these are a commonplace of the corporate campaign, and banks, as one might expect, do not like the publicity that often results. Yet in general, they appear to withstand such pressures, often appealing to the public with the claim that they are being singled out unfairly in a (labor) dispute to which they are not a party. But if street talk—the language of banners and demonstrations—does little more than get a bank's attention, there is another form of expression that

has the potential to do far more. It is the sound of money talking and especially of money walking ... out the door of the bank.

PENSION POWER

A 1997 *Business Week* estimate placed the sum total of money in union pension holdings at $1.4 trillion—an amount that has only continued to grow in
the years since. With that in mind, the AFL–CIO, under John Sweeney, has
established an Office of Investment and a Center for Working Capital, both
mechanisms to "coordinate the holdings of all unions and union members
and turn billions of pension assets into a new weapon for labor." A part of
this strategy is to play a more aggressive role in determining where labor's
funds are invested.[7]

Despite the magnitude of these pension funds, however, labor does not
actually control the ways in which they are invested, having to share that
power with employers, state officials, and others on the various pension
fund boards. In addition, moving this money around to serve the purposes
of a corporate campaign can be quite complicated, and it can even be contrary to the pension managers' fiduciary obligations to the funds' beneficiaries. For these reasons, only a part of the unions' pension-based
strategy—at least in the context of the corporate campaign—focuses on
such movements. Another element—often far more important—is directed
at influencing corporate policies through shareholder actions, which is to
say not moving capital around so much as voting with it.

In a publicly held corporation, every share of stock is a vote, and every
shareholder is a voter imbued by law and the Securities and Exchange Commission with certain (albeit very limited) inalienable rights. This is "economic democracy" at work—one share, one vote. Although management is
shielded in some measure from the intervention of its voter shareholders in
daily decision making, if they are ever able to coordinate their votes in sufficient numbers, these absentee owners do, in fact, exercise some leverage
in the setting of corporate policy. That is a rare event, but one that labor,
working closely with some of its allies—actively encourages. Here the unions employ a three-pronged strategy focused on maximizing the influence
of their own holdings, forging coalitions with major institutional shareholders, and exercising, directly or through surrogates, the rights of individual shareholders.

At the forefront of the movement to mobilize labor's pension power is
the AFL–CIO, which has published a set of guidelines that it hopes will be
used by trustees in exercising their ownership rights. In the words of this
document,

> During this decade, multiemployer and public employee funds have changed the
> contours of corporate governance in this country. They have helped achieve

greater accountability of corporate management to shareholders, instituted reforms to ensure more board independence, developed such innovations as binding by-law amendments and increased management awareness that workplace and human rights issues are important to long-term corporate competitiveness and fund performance.[8]

To understand the meaning of these words and the function of this document, one must consider the nature of trusteeship in a pension fund or other, similar institution. The first objective of such a trustee is to vote in a manner consistent with the economic best interests of the plan's participants and beneficiaries. Historically, that has been interpreted to mean that trustees were obligated to support management policies and initiatives that maximized profits by whatever legitimate means. Usually this meant holding costs down, often at the expense of organized workers. As already noted, however, over the last three decades, there has been a significant movement to espouse an alternative model of fiduciary responsibility—one in which *socially responsible* business practices (which is to say those that are sensitive to environmental, human rights, and other concerns) are adjudged the most consistent with the long-term well-being of the corporation and therefore the most worthy of trustees' support. In the words of Tim Smith, executive director of the Interfaith Center for Corporate Responsibility, "What we're trying to do is press corporations to pay attention to the double bottom line of both financial performance and corporate citizenship."[9]

Organized labor has worked closely with the advocates of this position to ensure that an expansion of labor rights, along with principles of corporate governance that serve labor's interests, are included on any list of socially responsible practices. The function of the AFL–CIO guidelines is to codify—and, in the process, legitimize and advance—that position. Indeed, recalling that ICCR and labor's corporate campaigns both trace to a common origin in the National Council of Churches, this focus on labor issues in the context of social-policy resolutions marks an important trend—initiatives that once moved apart from one another now appear to be merging, and the AFL–CIO guidelines provide something of a bridge between the two.

The document begins this task by identifying six issue areas where participants and beneficiaries may have a long-term interest. Only two of these—the value of shares and the dividend yield, and company policies that directly affect the job security or wages of participants—fall within the traditional model. The remaining four—company policies affecting local economic development and stability, those that affect the growth and stability of the national economy, the responsibility of the company to its employees and their communities, and workplace and environmental safety and health—go far beyond it.[10] In their content, they embody the thrust of the movement for socially responsible investment. In their ambiguity, they carry the potential for the support of extraordinarily wide-ranging changes in the ways corporations operate.

From that point forward, the AFL–CIO guidelines set forth at considerable length a series of preferred voting positions on issues that may come before shareholders, and hence pension fund trustees, for a vote. Among these are the following:

- support efforts to ensure that a majority of board members in any company must be "independent," which is to say that their only material connection to the company is their service on its board;
- support efforts to eliminate staggered-term elections and establish the practice of electing all directors to concurrent terms;
- generally oppose efforts to limit the personal liability of board members and support those to make them personally accountable for meeting their own fiduciary responsibilities to the company;
- generally oppose dual-class voting, in which certain shares have more rights than others;
- generally support cumulative voting, a practice that allows shareholders to cast all of their votes for a single board member;
- support proposals calling for the adoption of principles or codes of conduct relating to a company's business practices in other countries, to the environment, and to employee health and safety;
- support resolutions calling for compliance with, and public reporting on, government policies on discrimination and affirmative action, workplace safety and health, the environment, the quality of health care, labor protections, and the like; and
- support for resolutions calling on management to avoid doing business with foreign firms that employ child labor or that fail to meet applicable standards with regard to the wages and working conditions of their employees.[11]

Each of these positions can be seen as either enhancing the power of organized labor or advancing its policy agenda. For example, if a majority of a company's directors are outsiders, if all of its directors are elected to coterminous positions, and if cumulative voting is employed, a minority of shareholders—such as a union engaged in a corporate campaign together with its allies—might be in a greatly enhanced position to influence the policies of this company. And any shareholder resolutions proposing reforms along the lines indicated would be given substantial support from at least one set of institutional investors—the pension funds.

In truth, the prospect of a union pension fund redirecting by its own votes the policies of a major corporation is remote, not least because other institutional investors might well see the self-interested behavior of the unionists as contrary to the interests of the company and might be obligated to oppose them. That is where the second component of labor's pension-fund strategy comes into play.

Recall that the key to understanding coalition formation in the corporate campaign is the realization that every participating organization is acting in its own, self-defined interests. The strategy of coalition formation, then, is one of identifying those groups whose interests coincide with labor's and mobilizing them. The same strategy applies to the world of institutional investing. Here the unions seek to find a commonality of interest with other major shareholders such that these potentially union-averse investors will support union-initiated proposals. Because many such institutions share labor's views on corporate governance, if not on substantive policies, it is in this area that such alliances are most often forged.

Perhaps the clearest example of this gathering of strange economic bedfellows is provided by a proxy fight involving Marriott International, the hotel chain, in 1998. At the time, Marriott was facing a campaign by Local 2 of the Hotel Employees and Restaurant Employees International Union (HERE) centered at its downtown San Francisco hotel, where a majority of workers had signed union cards in 1996, but where a first contract was still pending. To pressure the company, which is widely regarded by labor as unfriendly to unions, HERE launched a nationwide corporate campaign. The *San Francisco Chronicle* described this campaign as a clash of workplace rules and cultures:

> Marriott is a quintessential 1990s nonunion firm: It preaches teamwork and empowerment of its employees, whom it calls "associates." It has a 401(k) plan rather than a traditional pension plan. And it rejects ideas such as a seniority system and fixed job descriptions—both longtime practices of unionized hotels.

> Local 2, meanwhile, insists that traditional practices like seniority in assigning shifts are essential to a fair and dignified workplace. And it says the standard contract in place at 52 other unionized San Francisco hotels should apply to the Marriott, too.[12]

The Marriott family owns approximately 20% of the company's stock and individual shareholders another 30%, leaving half the stock in the hands of institutional shareholders. A vote was scheduled at a special meeting of shareholders in March 1998—called primarily to spin off the company's food service business into a new company called Sodexho Marriott, Inc.—that would establish two classes of stock in Marriott International, one of which was a so-called *super-voting* class. Those super shares, mostly held by members of the Marriott family, would carry 10 votes each rather than just 1. The company said the dual-stock structure would better enable it to expand through acquisitions; critics claimed it was an effort to ensure that the Marriott family retained control of the company.[13]

At that point, HERE launched a campaign to line up votes against the dual-stock proposal. Through a Web site called "Unbundle.com," which carried the slogan "protecting our rights as Marriott International share-holders," the union posted news items critical of the company and proxy materials for a countersolicitation and asked shareholders to oppose the management plan.[14] The countersolicitation drew on several of the corporate governance positions in the AFL–CIO guidelines, most notably those relating to coterminous terms for directors, limitations on by-law amendments, and, of course, dual-class stock.[15] In effect, this document focused on the issues most likely to establish a common interest with nonunion institutional investors.

The proposed change was approved at the March meeting, but the company immediately came under considerable pressure from its institutional investors to reconsider and agreed to resubmit the issue to shareholders at the annual meeting the following May.[16] At this point, Institutional Shareholder Services (ISS), an influential firm that provides proxy research, advisory, and voting services to more than 400 institutional investors—including, among others, public employee and union pension funds—assumed the lead. After meeting three times with Marriott officials, ISS came out in opposition to the dual-stock plan.[17] The firm formed a *de facto* alliance with HERE, as each worked for its own purposes to defeat the proposal. In the end, that is precisely what happened. With support from the California Public Employees' Retirement System (CalPERS), the nation's biggest public pension fund and a frequent institutional activist, as well as similar pension funds from New York City, New York State, and elsewhere, opponents garnered 53% of the votes cast—an extraordinary outcome in the world of shareholder resolutions, where votes customarily line up with management by overwhelming margins.[18] Matthew Walker, the union's research director who ran the campaign for HERE, gave voice to labor's strategy of reaching out to prospective institutional allies and others when he observed that:

> [p]eople assume that there is a division between labor and capital. The fact is that we demonstrated an ability to identify with our fellow shareholders in Marriott and to build an alliance with shareholders that many people didn't think was possible.[19]

In April 2000, ISS and other public–employee pension funds provided a similar endorsement for a shareholder resolution on pensions at IBM that was backed by the CWA.[20]

The role of CalPERS and the New York Common Fund in the Marriott campaign was not unique. Indeed, the greatest proportion of labor's pension money—$948 billion at the time of the *Business Week* survey cited earlier—is held in public–employee pension funds, most of which have one or more union trustees. These funds, and especially CalPERS, play a substantial role in advancing the agenda for labor-friendly corporate reform. As of March 2000, CalPERS controlled an estimated $170 billion in retirement funds.[21] Each year the fund lists approximately 10 companies that it regards as underperforming their respective industries because of poor management, and it targets these companies for corporate-governance resolutions.[22] It is not unusual to find companies on this list—like Tyson Foods in 1999—that are also the targets of union corporate campaigns.[23] This is not surprising when one realizes that the CalPERS Board of Administration recently included—in addition to the Mayor of San Francisco—the chair of the California Faculty Association's Political Action/Legislative Committee, a member of the International Executive Board of the SEIU, and a vice president of the Laborers' International Union who also serves on the executive board of the Labor Council for Latin American Advancement, an AFL–CIO affiliate.[24] It seems likely that the AFL–CIO pension fund guidelines have been designed to afford both guidance and a legally defensible rationale for labor's representatives on the boards of CalPERS and other funds better to enable them to advance the movement's agenda.

However, the federation has not stopped at providing such guidance and legitimacy. To make sure the point is not lost on pension managers, the recently established Center for Working Capital has begun rating the voting performance of fund managers on shareholder resolutions of interest to labor. In 1999, for example, it rated the votes of 106 funds on 40 such resolutions.

Taking a slightly different tack, in 1994, MFS Investment Management created the Union Standard Equity Fund, which employs a series of labor-friendly standards for determining where to invest:

> At least 5 percent of the company's employees must be unionized; the company cannot be involved in a strike or lockout; it cannot make products that are on the boycott list of the AFL-CIO; it must meet certain health, safety and labor laws, and it must not show a pattern of outsourcing—the transfer of work to other companies. The fund only buys American companies.[25]

An advisory board composed of senior labor officials, academics, and others rates companies on a Labor Sensitivity Index that, in 1998, included 540 stocks, of which the fund actually invested in approximately 70. Although this fund is open to the public, 90% of the money invested is from unions.[26]

One union—the International Association of Machinists—has gone further still, having set up its own mutual fund—investing in companies with which the IAM has labor agreements—as a 401(k) option. One objective is to use the investment power of the union's 730,000 members to force the management of these companies to be more sensitive to IAM positions on such issues as tying executive compensation to employee satisfaction.[27] Institutional investors that managed IAM pension funds committed about $60 million to the new fund at its initiation.[28]

THEREFORE BE IT RESOLVED

Under the nation's securities laws, as we noted, a company's shareholders have certain rights, one of which is to propose resolutions for consideration and vote at the company's annual meeting. Specifically, what is known as Rule 14a-8 allows shareholders who meet certain minimal criteria to include a proposal and a 500-word supporting statement in a company's proxy materials, subject to certain constraints. Historically, the Securities and Exchange Commission (SEC), which administers the rule, had held that companies could exclude from these solicitations resolutions regarding workplace-related social issues under what is termed the *ordinary business exclusion*. In May 1998, after receiving more than 2,000 letters from activists, the SEC revised Rule 14a-8 to permit some of these social-policy resolutions to proceed, even over management's objections.[29] It is these shareholder resolutions that are anticipated in the AFL–CIO proxy voting guidelines.

That document treats such resolutions as if they simply drop from the sky, advising trustees that if a proposal of one kind or another should somehow be brought before the company's shareholders, they should vote their shares as indicated. However, the guidelines are silent as to just how such a thing would happen, and they do not suggest that the trustees themselves should initiate it. That does not mean, however, that the unions are prepared to leave such an important matter to chance.

In fact, one of the earliest corporate campaign handbooks, the IUD's *Developing New Tactics*, offers an extensive discussion of the why and how of submitting shareholder resolutions. In the words of the manual,

> With careful planning and preparation, the annual stockholder meeting can be transformed from what is normally a showcase for corporate self-glorification into a forum for important union and social issues....

> Often the press covers these resolutions, especially if they have a unique angle, and thus the general public is exposed to the issue as well.[30]

Of course, as this manual anticipated, annual meetings do more than provide a venue for voting on issues of governance and social policy. They also provide a highly public forum for demonstrations of dissatisfaction with the company and its management, which can occur either within or outside the meeting. Many of the corporate and anticorporate campaigns listed in Appendixes A and B, for example, included some form of demonstration at an annual meeting of shareholders.

At this writing, the most comprehensive analysis of the sources and disposition of shareholder resolutions is one based on those introduced in 1997, the year before the SEC broadened the rules for submission and before the AFL–CIO institutionalized its Office of Investment and Center for Working Capital. Nevertheless, the data from that year are quite informative. They show that 869 shareholder resolutions were submitted to companies during the year, of which 582 pertained to issues of corporate governance and 287 to issues of social policy. Of these 869 resolutions, 376 were actually put to a vote (the balance having been withdrawn or omitted under an SEC ruling). Fully 49% of the governance resolutions were subject to a vote, compared with only 31% of their social policy counterparts—a result that is not surprising in light of the extant interpretation of Rule 14a-8 at the time.

Of the 90 social-policy resolutions that came to a vote, 50 were submitted by religious organizations (most notably the Interfaith Center for Corporate Responsibility), 6 by union funds, and 5 by other pension funds. The remainder were submitted primarily by individuals, many of whom may well have represented labor or activist groups, but whose status was classified on the basis of their personal ownership of the shares in question. The unions also submitted 41 corporate governance proposals. Of those social-policy resolutions that were omitted from proxy solicitations, 17% were excluded on procedural grounds and 50% under the ordinary-business exclusion. (The comparable rates of omission for corporate governance resolutions were 39% and 25%, respectively.) Because the latter rule has now been reinterpreted, we can expect that more and more social-policy resolutions will, in fact, reach shareholders for a vote.

Among the issues addressed in both corporate governance and social policy resolutions in 1997 were many that resonate with the AFL–CIO's agenda as detailed in its guidelines. On the governance front, these included, among others, items relating to the independence, diversity, tenure, or compensation of corporate boards and their members; repeal of staggered terms for board members; executive compensation; and the repeal of so-called *golden parachutes* and *poison pills*—devices aimed to reward management in the event of a friendly takeover and to defend a company against a hostile one. On the social-policy front, the issues of interest included such items as compliance with CERES Principles and other environmental initiatives, equal opportunity, human rights, and *maquiladoras*.[31]

These shareholder resolutions are not always embraced and endorsed by management. In fact, quite the opposite is the case. If management had wanted to introduce the policies put forward in these resolutions, it would have done so without such prompting. The significance of the SEC's change of heart on Rule 14a-8, then, means that an increasing number of issues hostile to management's wishes will be on the agendas of annual meetings across the country. In fact, sometimes the proponents of these reforms may not wait for the meeting at all. To get a sense of how this dynamic can play out in the course of a corporate campaign, let us turn again to the case of Oregon Steel.

In the summer of 1998, the AFL–CIO's Office of Investment, together with a fund operated by the union-based Amalgamated Bank and Crabb Huson, a money management firm, claiming that Oregon Steel was in financial difficulty, aimed a series of four nonbinding shareholder resolutions at the company on what are now familiar grounds—making directors' terms coterminous, moving to the annual rather than triennial election of directors, requiring shareholder approval of any poison pills, and making shareholder voting confidential. In an unusual move, the proponents then solicited shareholder approval of the resolutions without a shareholders' meeting—a procedure that is termed *consent solicitation*. Management objected to both the resolutions and the procedure. In the end, all of the resolutions failed, after which the proponents sent letters to all of the company's directors asking them to reconsider and support the changes.[32]

AIMING AT ANALYSTS

Although pension fund trustees and other shareholders share a common interest in preserving the value of the shares of companies in which they invest, the same cannot necessarily be said of unions. To the contrary, in some instances, a union may see a great advantage in pressuring a company by undermining confidence in its stock. This would be the case, for example, in a corporate campaign targeting a nonunion company like a Food Lion or a Microsoft, where stock ownership is both an important employee benefit and a source of loyalty to the company, or in one against a company that depends for its growth on ensuring that its shares are highly regarded in the financial markets. It can also be an attractive option in attacking a prominent CEO whose compensation or net worth is judged to be highly dependent on the price of the company's stock.

In some instances, it is enough for investors to learn that a union is engaged in a major dispute with a given company—the perceived risk associated with the company's shares will rise and the share price will fall. Investors have traditionally been advised not to sell on news of a strike because strikes tend to be resolved. However, selling on news of a corporate campaign that has the potential to last for many years and to drag a target company's reputation through the muck is an altogether different prospect. If the industry and financial analysts who most closely follow a given company and whose advice is most influential in valuing its shares and predicting their direction of movement can be convinced that the company is in for a protracted period of difficulty—for whatever reason—the image of the company and the value of its stock will be in play and at risk.

To achieve that objective in the course of a corporate campaign, unions may pursue a variety of tactics, such as dispatching representatives to meet personally with analysts to convey their doubts or concerns about the company, distributing anticompany materials at the show-and-tell sessions that companies routinely schedule to update analysts on their performance (e.g., a common action is to leave critical handbills in the restrooms outside of such meetings), or scheduling their own conference calls and briefings in which interested analysts are invited to participate. In one such instance, at a planned 1998 initial public offering (IPO) of stock by Overnite Transportation, the Teamsters sponsored a briefing for analysts by Michael Locker at which were addressed a series of financial, labor, and managerial concerns. Locker was joined at the briefing by union representatives and workers from Overnite terminals around the country.[33] The IPO was cancelled.

Perhaps the most elaborate of the devices employed by the unions is the issuance of highly detailed reports, or white papers, that attack the management practices, regulatory record, and/or financial condition of a target company. These reports, which are quite common, are directed at a number of different stakeholder groups, including the media, the public, and the regulatory community. They are usually also distributed on Wall Street, where their purpose is to generate visibility for the campaign and uncertainty about the target company.

The titles of these reports typically incorporate some form of play on words involving either the name of the company, its logo, or its advertising slogans. The reports generally mix statistical analysis with anecdotes to suggest that the company is being mismanaged at the expense of the public, which may be defined in terms of consumers, shareholders, patients, or some other role. Some of these reports employ extremely pejorative language in an effort to stir the emotions of the reader, whereas others employ language best characterized as sterile in an apparent attempt to assume an aura of authority. All are uniformly critical of the company at which they are directed. Examples abound, among them:

- *Ripe for Fairness*—from the Teamsters campaign against Stemilt Growers and other Washington State apple growers;
- *Rio Tinto: Behind the Façade* and *Rio Tinto: Tainted Titan*—from the ICEM campaign against the mining company;
- *Running Over the American Dream*—from the USWA campaign against Bridgestone/Firestone;
- *System Breakdown*; *Bad Care in Beverly's Back Yard*; and *The Care Gap: A Report on Patient Care and Profits at Beverly Enterprises*—from the UFCW and SEIU campaign against Beverly Enterprises;
- *Rolling the Dice*, *House of Cards* and *Bad Deal*—from the SEIU campaign against Genesis Healthcare Ventures;

- *The Investor's Right to Know Less: A Case Study of Environmental Disclosures to Shareholders by Phelps Dodge*—produced by the USWA;
- *Half a Job Is Not Enough*—from the Teamsters campaign against UPS;
- *Wal-Mart's Buy America Program: Using Patriotism to Deceive the American People*—from the FAST/UFCW campaign against Wal-Mart;
- *Formula for Disaster*—an attack on the sale of allegedly outdated infant formula published by a union surrogate group in the UFCW campaign against Food Lion;
- *Bad for Business*—from the USWA campaign against Titan International; and
- *False Profits*—produced by the Campaign for Labor Rights for the campaign against the WTO, IMF, and World Bank.

As part of its corporate campaign against AK Steel, in March 2000, the Steelworkers union dispatched a lengthy letter to shareholders, which it simultaneously released to the media, setting forth the union's views on the dispute and pointing out that the value of the company's stock had declined by some 60% during the course of the campaign and the lockout that gave rise to it. In an evident appeal to analysts, the letter opined that

> What really caught many investors and analysts by surprise ... was the Company's belated revelation that the outlook for 2000 would be far worse than they had previously been led to believe.... Clearly stunned by management's failure to disclose [certain costs], JP Morgan warned clients that "AK's reputation as providing consistent accurate guidance makes this sudden downward adjustment even more striking."[34]

We cannot know what effect, if any, these initiatives have on the perceptions and recommendations of the analysts at whom they are directed. The salient point in context, however, is that they are routinely included as part of a far larger strategy aimed at using the instruments of corporate governance and finance as components of corporate campaigns—a strategy that lies at the heart of such undertakings.

CONCLUSION

If we regard the effort to revoke the corporate charter of Unocal, which was described in chapter 5, as the business equivalent of thermonuclear war, it is clear that most of the activities discussed in the present chapter fall far short of that mark. Rather than doing away with the company, these latter initiatives aim at making it more responsive to the goals of labor unions and their allies. This is true at the procedural level, as reflected in the active labor agenda of corporate governance reforms and at the social-policy level as well. In this light, then, we might see these as relatively modest efforts at encouraging change.

However, if we view the aggressive stewardship of union pension funds and other initiatives directed at the financial community and at shareholders in the context of our analysis of the movement to establish codes of conduct in chapter 9, we can see the current cluster of tactics as part of a much larger and systematic attempt to restructure the nation's fundamental economic priorities in a manner consistent with both the self-defined economic interests of labor and the self-defined political interests of other, more ideologically driven corporate critics. In this alternative light, the determination of labor to wield its capital as a weapon presents corporate America with a far greater challenge.

Whichever view one takes, it was inevitable—and it is clear—that pressuring a company's financial stakeholders lies at the heart—is the very essence—of the corporate and the anticorporate campaign. It is this element—and the insight from which it derived—that separates these efforts from routine strikes, routine negotiations, routine public relations, and the routine experience of most corporations.

ENDNOTES

1. Coolidge reportedly made this statement in a speech to the American Society of Newspaper Editors, January 17, 1925.
2. Presentation at the annual meeting of the American Political Science Association, Atlanta, GA, September 3, 1999.
3. "Crestar is Boycotted for Backing Gas Co.," *The Regulatory Compliance Watch*, Vol. 7, No. 18 (May 6, 1996), p. 2.
4. Tripp Baltz, "Unions Support Strikers, Close Accounts At Bank Giving Credit to Colorado Steel Mill," *Daily Labor Report*, December 16, 1997, p. A-9; and John Norton, "Steel union head vows to keep heat on Oregon Steel," *Pueblo Chieftain*, January 30, 1998, p. 1. The USWA posted a list on its Web site of numerous unions and other organizations that had withdrawn funds from the bank in support of the boycott, including $11 million by a sheet metal workers local in Phoenix, Arizona. Found at www.uswa.org/cfi/wells1.html, December 9, 1999.
5. Quoted in Norton, op. cit.
6. Sam Zuckerman, "Wells Distances Itself From Steel Company," *San Francisco Chronicle*, July 2, 1999, p. B1.
7. Aaron Bernstein, "'Working Capital': Labor's New Weapon?" *Business Week*, on-line edition, September 18, 1997.
8. *Investing in Our Future: AFL-CIO Proxy Voting Guidelines* (Washington: AFL–CIO, n.d.), Foreword.

9. William Bole, "Shareholders work to improve corporate responsibility," *Albany (NY) Times Union*, April 18, 1999, p. A21.

10. Ibid., p. 2.

11. Ibid., pp. 4–12.

12. Ilana DeBare, "S.F. Marriott, Hotel Union Clash," *San Francisco Chronicle*, February 19, 1999, p. B1.

13. Judith Evans, "Small Investors May Hold Key Votes in Marriott Fight," *Washington Post*, May 15, 1998, p. F1.

14. Located at www.unbundle.com.

15. *Counter-Solicitation for Marriott International Special Meeting*, distributed to shareholders by the Hotel Employees and Restaurant Employees International Union.

16. "Marriott International Changes Record Date for Spinoff to March 27, 1998," Marriott International news release, March 17, 1998. Although not mentioned in the title, the release announced the company's intention of including a separate ballot proposal on the dual-class stock in its proxy statement for the annual meeting.

17. Evans, op. cit.

18. Timothy Burn, "Stock class warfare ends at Marriott," *Washington Times*, May 21, 1998; and Christina Binckley, "Marriott Shareholders Vote Down Plan to Create Two Stock Classes," *Wall Street Journal*, May 21, 1998.

19. Quoted in Binckley, op. cit.

20. "ISS backs employee shareholder resolution to restore pension, retiree medical benefits at IBM," CWA news release, April 13, 2000.

21. Andrew LePage, "Brown gets ball rolling at CalPERS: Two nominees quickly approved," *Sacramento Bee*, March 14, 2000.

22. This and other CalPERS corporate governance activities are posted at a special Web site, www.calpers-governance.com, which the system maintains as part of its reform drive. "CalPERS Launches New Corporate Governance Web Site," CalPERS news release, February 17, 1999.

23. Margaret Price, "No Way, Jose," *Treasury and Risk Management*, Vol. 9, No. 4 (May 1999), pp. 51–52, 54.

24. The full listing of Board members is available on the CalPERS Web site at www.calpers.ca.gov/about/board/structure/bios/bios.htm.

25. Kenneth N. Gilpin, "A Labor-Friendly Fund Helps to Channel the Power of Unions," *The New York Times*, September 6, 1998.

26. Ibid.

27. Bruce Shutan, "Concerns over fiduciary mission take control," *Employee Benefit News*, May 1, 1999.

28. Laurence Zuckerman, "Finding the Union Label in a Fund," *The New York Times*, May 16, 1999.

29. Cynthia J. Campbell, Stuart L. Gillan, and Cathy M. Niden, "Current perspectives on shareholder proposals: lessons from the 1997 proxy season," *Financial Management*, Vol. 28, No. 1 (March 22, 1999), pp. 89ff.

30. *Developing New Tactics: Winning With Coordinated Corporate Campaigns* (Washington: Industrial Unions Department, AFL–CIO, 1985), pp. 25, 27.
31. Campbell, et al., op. cit. Shareholder proposals are almost never successful, although governance resolutions generally fair better than those on social issues. The average vote in support of union-submitted governance resolutions, for example, was 31.9%, whereas that in support of the union's social policy initiatives was a mere 6.6%.
32. Price, op. cit.
33. Invitation letter found at www.teamster.org/overnite/invltr07.html, February 18, 2000.
34. "USWA letter to AK Shareholders Details Costs of Company's 'Union-Busting,'" USWA news release, March 8, 2000.

11

... AND THE CUSTOMERS WALK

The corporate campaign, at least as practiced by organized labor, was nearly stillborn: At the heart of the campaign is the effort to use one or another stakeholder group as a leverage point against the target company—a task that is often achieved by bringing pressure against this secondary target, be it a bank, vendor, retailer, or some other entity, through the simple expedient of a real or threatened boycott. If the stakeholder did not lend its support to the union, or at least cease its support for the company, the union would seek to drive its own customers away or deprive it of some other asset of value. The tactic was employed by the ACWU against Farah Manufacturing in the first prototype campaign and by the successor ACTWU in its landmark campaign against J.P. Stevens, and it has been a central feature of the majority of corporate campaigns since.

The problem for the unions, as distinct in this instance from other prospective campaigners, was that such efforts might have been interpreted by the courts as constituting what are termed *secondary boycotts*—a term of art applied to just such an instance of pressuring one actor to influence another. This was a problem because, in passing the Taft–Hartley Act of 1947, which was designed to reign in what were viewed by the Republican

Congress of the era as the excesses of organized labor, Congress had explicitly forbidden the unions to engage in secondary boycotts. In its narrowest interpretation, this legislation prohibited calling the workers of a neutral employer out on strike, but broader interpretations were possible. Yet the Ray Rogers model of the corporate campaign was heavily dependent on generating secondary pressure on otherwise neutral parties—one of the factors that undoubtedly contributed to the discomfort he generated among mainstream labor leaders in the 1970s and 1980s. Even Rogers himself had to be careful of the legalities here. So, for example, when the Paperworkers published leaflets emphasizing another company's relationship to International Paper—say Avon Products or the Bank of Boston, which Rogers attacked for their interlocks with IP—every handbill carried a disclaimer noting that it "is not a call for a consumer boycott of anybody's products."[1]

That cause for concern was eliminated in 1988, when the Supreme Court issued its decision in *Edward J. DeBartolo Corp. v. Florida Gulf Coast Building & Construction Trades Council.*[2] This case had arisen almost a decade earlier, in December 1979, at the East Lake Square Mall in Tampa, Florida, which was owned by DeBartolo. Members of the union had distributed handbills at all of the mall's entrances asking the public to boycott the mall and all of the businesses located there because a construction company building a new department store at the mall allegedly paid substandard wages. After failing to convince the union to change the language of the handbills, DeBartolo filed an unfair labor practice charge with the National Labor Relations Board, which eventually led to the Supreme Court opinion. Writing for the Court, Justice Byron White said that, in the absence of picketing or any form of coercion, workers did have the right under the First Amendment to attempt to persuade consumers to engage in a boycott.[3] This decision had an immediate effect on corporate campaigns. As Rogers put it in the course of broadening the then-ongoing campaign against International Paper, "This is a decisive action that will give us the opportunity to highlight the power of money in labor disputes."[4]

THE USE OF BOYCOTTS IN CORPORATE AND ANTICORPORATE CAMPAIGNS

The term *boycott* has deep Irish roots. During the 19th century, Irish peasants were routinely mistreated by the British landlord class. Their land was confiscated, their homes were destroyed, and their wages were reduced to the point where starvation was a real threat. Among the most notorious of the landlords' agents who imposed these conditions was one Charles Cunningham Boycott, a retired captain in the British Army. In the summer of 1880, Boycott dispatched his tenant farmers into the fields to harvest crops at minuscule wages, which they refused to do. After Boycott and his family then attempted unsuccessfully to do the work themselves, the agent's wife convinced the tenants to return to work and the harvest was completed. On the next rent day, however, when they had not earned enough to cover their obligations, Boycott dispatched constables to evict them from their homes, whereon the tenants held a meeting at which they convinced Boycott's servants and other employees to desert him. Thus was launched the first *boycott*.[5]

The objective of a boycott is to politicize consumer behavior—to add moral or political considerations to the list of criteria that consumers employ when making their purchasing decisions—and to do so in sufficiently large numbers to influence the behavior of the target company with whom they do business. This is one of the key places, then, where holding the moral high ground has direct and measurable potential benefits. It is a practice with a long history in the United States, but one that seems to have been reinvigorated in the middle of the last century. In David Vogel's words, written in 1978,

> Allowing one's political or moral preferences to influence one's purchase of products is not, of course, an idea that was invented in the sixties. Consumer boycotts played an important role in the American colonists' prerevolutionary struggle against England and have been used periodically both by and against various economic and ethnic groups throughout American history. And the American trade union movement has frequently encouraged the boycott of various products as a way to apply pressure on recalcitrant employers. But over the last fifteen years, such consumer boycotts have become more frequent, better organized, and identified with a much broader range of issues.[6]

Indeed, during the years when the (anti-)corporate campaign was being developed by the New Left, the effectiveness of the boycott was being demonstrated daily by the civil rights movement—prime examples being the Montgomery, Alabama, bus boycott and the sit-ins at Woolworth lunch counters—and by environmentalists and consumer rights advocates alike. As we saw in chapter 1, the effort to boycott commerce of any kind with South Africa was much on the minds of those early activists, especially those associated with NACLA.

As a tactic for pressuring companies, then, the boycott long precedes the corporate campaign, and the presence of a boycott, even with labor participation, is not itself indicative of a corporate campaign. That said, however, the two often go hand in hand. Of the 162 union-initiated corporate campaigns listed in Appendix A of this volume, for example, more than two dozen involved some form of boycott, either of a target company's banks, its business partners or its products. An early example came in 1984 as a component of the United Brotherhood of Carpenters' campaign against lumber producer Louisiana-Pacific. The union organized regular boycott activities at more than 400 retail lumber yards across the country.[7] A more recent example would be the Teamsters' boycott of the linen retailer Bed, Bath & Beyond, which offended the union by doing business with Overnite Transportation, the object of a Teamsters' corporate campaign in which union President James Hoffa, Jr., had invested much of his personal capital.[8] Similarly, the Teamsters would follow Overnite trucks to various other destinations, typically warehouses; then, before a truck could unload, they would establish a picket line to disrupt the process.[9] Hoffa, together with AFL–CIO President John Sweeney, traveled to the Bed, Bath & Beyond flagship store in Manhattan to declare the boycott. In his announcement Hoffa stated,

> Overnite's customers keep this union-busting anti-worker company in business. Let Bed, Bath & Beyond and every other one of Overnite's customers understand that the Teamsters are in this for the long haul. If they want to keep Overnite in business, then their business might suffer as well.[10]

One good indicator of the importance of boycotts in the corporate campaign is found on the national boycott list maintained by the Union Label and Service Trades Department of the AFL–CIO. At least 8 of the 19 boycotts listed there as of December 1999 arose directly from corporate campaigns, most of them ongoing.[11] These included among others:

- Brown & Sharpe Manufacturing. This company, which manufactures measuring, cutting and machine tools, and pumps, was targeted by the Machinists union for a corporate campaign in 1982 after a bitter strike and has remained on the boycott list ever since.[12]
- Diamond Walnut. The Teamsters launched a corporate campaign against this company in 1992, following a strike in which the company hired permanent replacement workers. The boycott has been in place ever since.[13]
- Mount Olive Pickle Company. Similar in many ways to the Campbell's Soup campaign of an earlier era, the organizing drive that spawned this boycott, begun in 1997, was directed by the Farm Labor Organizing Committee at organizing workers on the farms that supply the company with cucumbers.[14]
- Crown Central Petroleum. Initiated by PACE in October 1996, this boycott, and the broader corporate campaign of which it is a component, arose from a lockout of workers at the company's Pasadena, Texas, refinery after they were accused of sabotaging the facility.[15]
- New Otani Hotel & Garden. Here the boycott and corporate campaign began in 1997 when the hotel declined to participate in a city-wide master contract covering hotels in downtown Los Angeles.[16]

Of particular interest on this list, because it illustrates that boycotts are not limited to retailers and consumer products manufacturers, is the boycott against Oregon Steel. We already discussed the related secondary boycott against Wells Fargo Bank, which led a consortium of Oregon Steel lenders, and which even included driving a genuine Wells Fargo stagecoach, through the streets of San Francisco to the bank's main downtown branch.[17] But the Steelworkers' boycott activity was not limited to the bank. Noting that a principal product of the company's Pueblo, Colorado, mill, where the dispute was centered, was steel rail for use in railroad and mass transit systems, the union began contacting Oregon Steel's customers, who turned out to be railroads and local government agencies. The message was safety or, more specifically, a claim that the rail being manufactured by the company's replacement workers was substandard and unsafe. This message was carried, for example, in a brief "research alert" that called for establishment of a national commission to ensure that Oregon Steel rail was not endangering the public.[18] The union also wrote to customers such as San Francisco's BART system, alleging that the company's rail "poses potential safety dangers" and asking the system to cease doing business with a "lawbreaking" company like Oregon Steel.[19]

California municipalities seemed particularly responsive to this initiative. In June 1999, for example, the mayor of San Jose, a Santa Clara County supervisor, and the Chair of the Santa Clara Valley Transportation Authority all expressed their concern about the quality of the company's rail.[20] In August of that year, the San Francisco Board of Supervisors adopted a resolution calling on BART to refrain from buying rail from the company.[21] By September 1999, the initiative had moved eastward as the Hennepin County Regional Railroad Authority passed a similar resolution calling on the Minnesota Department of Transportation to stop doing business with Oregon Steel.[22] In December, BART adopted a binding resolution not to do business with Oregon Steel, whereon the company filed suit against the authority to prevent it from turning to alternate rail suppliers.[23]

The boycott effort reached a crescendo of sorts in Sacramento, California, where the union pressed a claim that the company failed to meet state requirements as a responsible bidder for a light-rail extension project and provided substandard rail. The company countered that its rail had been found satisfactory in the local transit authority's own tests and that the union sought only to delay the project and raise its cost by hundreds of thousands of dollars. In the end, the transit authority staff recommended the continued use of the company's product, and the authority's board voted—by a narrow 4 to 3 margin—to do so.[24]

Nonlabor corporate campaigners are similarly enamored of the boycott. According to one listing, as of December 1999, boycotts were being conducted by groups as diverse as:

- Animal Emancipation, Inc.
- Earth Island Institute
- Family Farm Defenders
- Free Burma Coalition
- Friends of the Earth
- Friends of the Wolf
- INFACT
- Justice! Do It Nike!
- Natural Resources Defense Council
- PETA
- Rainforest Action Network
- Tibetan Rights Coalition

In all, 44 different, mostly nonlabor groups were identified in this listing as maintaining boycotts.[25] Their targets were similarly wide-ranging, including, among others,

- American Express—targeted by PETA for selling fur in its catalog;
- American Home Products—targeted by PETA for treating pregnant mares inhumanely while harvesting their urine to manufacture Premarin;
- Amoco—charged by the San Juan Citizens Alliance for polluting the groundwater in southwestern Colorado;
- Clorox—singled out by the Committee for Universal Security for producing chlorine compounds that threaten the environment;
- The Gap—boycotted by Save the Redwoods because the family that owns the company is clear-cutting California redwoods;
- Monsanto—targeted by several groups for producing genetically engineered foods and for encouraging corporate rather than family farms;
- Nestle—charged by INFACT with using unethical marketing practices to sell infant formula in developing countries; and
- PepsiCo—targeted by Showing Animals Respect and Kindness for supporting bullfighting through its advertising and licensing.

Again, the list is considerably longer.[26] Although some of these causes and targets are unrelated to corporate campaigns, and although some may strike any one reader as more serious or genuine than others, all testify to the appeal of the boycott as an anticorporate strategy. One group, Coop America, even publishes an electronic boycott newsletter, *Boycott Action News*, to allow aficionados to stay abreast of the latest developments.[27]

BOYCOTTS IN THEORY AND PRACTICE

In his unique book, *Consumer Boycotts: Effecting Change Through the Marketplace and the Media*, Monroe Friedman provides important insights into the factors that make these efforts more or less effective. Several of these take the form of what amount to hypotheses predictive of success. They include, among others:

1. The more widespread and prominent the news media coverage, the more likely the target will yield to the demands of the boycotters....
2. The more image-conscious the target, the more likely it will yield to the demands of the boycotters....
3. The higher the likelihood that the target perceives the news coverage of the media-oriented boycott as leading to a marketplace-oriented boycott, the greater the chances that it will yield to the boycotters' demands....
4. The more inflexible and non-adaptive the target's policies regarding reactions to outside organizational pressures, the more likely it will refuse to yield to the demands of the boycotters....
5. The more realistic the boycotters' demands, the more likely they will be met....
6. The more capable the target is of launching a successful counteraction to the boycott, the less likely it will yield to the boycotters' demands.[28]

Friedman sees several specific factors that mark a target company as potentially vulnerable to a boycott. In his view, the most vulnerable companies are those that (a) are highly visible, either themselves or through one or more prominent brands; (b) are seen as sufficiently socially responsible that they can be expected to care about their reputations; (c) have suffered some recent setback in the marketplace that is likely to sensitize them to a prospective loss of sales; and (d) are owned by interests in the country where the boycott is to be conducted.[29] What is the best way to carry this attack? Although the ultimate objective may be defined in the marketplace—more jobs, higher wages, union recognition, or some other change of corporate policy—the objectives of the boycott per se are achieved by creating a negative image of the target company in the media. This can be accomplished through such devices as using creative parodies based on corporate names or slogans, staging a national or international day of protest, involving children as activists, using graphic pictures to convey the boycott message, or engaging in acts of civil disobedience. All of these are commonplace devices to attract and frame news coverage of target companies.[30]

In Friedman's view, then, boycotts are effective to the extent that they rely on the basic tenets of strategic communication and symbolic political action—crisp and richly symbolic messages carefully targeted at susceptible and influential audiences and designed to have a high likelihood of demonstrable results. These, of course, are some of the same factors that lead to success in the corporate campaign more generally. There is an evident natural fit between the tactics of the boycott and the objectives of the corporate campaign.

However, in the context of the corporate campaign, boycotts have one more characteristic of particular significance: It is often through a boycott or the threat of a boycott that third-party allies (e.g., religious groups, community leaders, civil rights activists, etc.) are able to express their support for the campaign. Boycotts provide such groups with a focal point around which to organize their activities and mobilize their members or sympathizers. There is, in fact, an interesting circularity at work here. Corporate campaigns are typically cast in terms of such high-ground thematics as social and economic justice, public safety and security, or protecting the national interest precisely to draw these parallel activists into coalitions, and campaign surrogates around which they may be invited to coalesce are similarly named for the same purpose. However, once such coalitions are formed and begin to confront the target company, their participation enhances the legitimacy of the campaign and helps shield the initiating union from any appearance of acting in a self-interested manner. Put another way, the campaign is framed on the moral high ground to attract coalition partners whose subsequent participation further enhances that frame, often through their sponsorship of a campaign-related boycott. In the same way, boycotts occasionally have the potential to engage the general public as well, with the effect that the campaign becomes a true community effort to oppose the evil deeds of a corporate malefactor.

AN INTEGRATIVE TACTIC

In this light, we can see that, in the context of the corporate campaign, boycotts may not be intended to stand on their own or even to succeed in any direct sense. Rather, they function as a component of the campaign's communication strategy with the objective of building and exploiting surrogates and coalition partnerships to bring pressure in the media against the target company. In contrast, in the context of an anticorporate campaign, such as that waged by the Rainforest Action Network against Home Depot, the boycott may actually be intended to exert direct pressure because such groups have less cause to be concerned about masking the interests with which they are identified. In either situation, however, the boycott is a common device for attempting to draw consumers and the general public into the extant dispute and to add their not inconsiderable weight to the pressure being generated against the target company.

ENDNOTES

1. Jonathan Tasini, "For the Unions, A New Weapon," *The New York Times*, June 12, 1988, p. 6:24.
2. 485 U.S. 568; 108 S. Ct. 1392; decided April 20, 1988.
3. Ibid.
4. Quoted in a news release from the UPIU and Corporate Campaign, Inc., June 8, 1988.
5. Monroe Friedman, *Consumer Boycotts: Effecting Change Through the Marketplace and the Media* (New York: Routledge, 1999), pp. 5–7.
6. David Vogel, *Lobbying the Corporation: Citizen Challenges to Business Authority* (New York: Basic Books, 1978), pp. 4–5.
7. Charles R. Perry, *Union Corporate Campaigns* (Philadelphia: Industrial Research Unit, The Wharton School, University of Pennsylvania, 1987), pp. 187–188.
8. Steven Greenhouse, "Freight Strike a Test of Hoffa's Mettle," *The New York Times*, November 5, 1999.
9. Frank Swoboda, "Traveling Picketers Aim to Bring Hauler to Table," *Washington Post*, January 7, 2000, p. E1.
10. "Hoffa and Teamsters to Launch Boycott of Bed, Bath & Beyond," News release from the International Brotherhood of Teamsters, December 9, 1999.
11. Found at www.unionlabel.org/donotbuy/main.htm, December 13, 1999.
12. Found at www.unionlabel.org/donotbuy/brown.htm.
13. Found at www.unionlabel.org/donotbuy/diamond.htm.
14. Found at www.unionlabel.org/donotbuy/mtpickle.htm.
15. Found at www.unionlabel.org/donotbuy/crown.htm.
16. Found at www.unionlabel.org/donotbuy/newotani.htm.
17. Michael Maloney, "Steel Workers Stage Unique Protest Against Wells Fargo," *San Francisco Chronicle*, April 28, 1998.
18. "Falling Apart: A Research Report on Quality Concerns at CF&I/Oregon Steel," report published by the United Steelworkers of America, nd.
19. Letter from Eric Lerner of the USWA to Dan Richard, president of the BART Board of Directors.
20. As evidenced in letters from these officials to the company.
21. "San Francisco Board of Supervisors Pass Groundbreaking Resolution," USWA news release, August 3, 1999.
22. "Hennepin County Regional Railroad Authority Calls on MnDOT to Sever Ties with Oregon Steel, Based on USWA Struggle," USWA news release, September 29, 1999.
23. "Oregon Steel Subsidiary Sues Customer," USWA news release, February 16, 2000.

24. "Rocky Mountain Steel Not 'Responsible' Under California Law," USWA news release, March 9, 2000; "Recent Union Activities Threaten Integrity of Sacramento Transit Board's Public Bidding Process," Oregon Steel Mills news release, March 9, 2000; "Time Runs Out on Community Effort to Hold Oregon Steel 'Responsible," USWA news release, March 15, 2000.

25. "Boycott Organizers," found at www.coopamerica.org/boycotts/bandirectory.htm.

26. "Boycotts in Action," found at www.coopamerica.org/boycotts/bantargetchart.htm.

27. Found at www.coopamerica.org/mban.htm, June 29, 1998.

28. Friedman, op. cit., pp. 25–26.

29. Ibid., p. 220.

30. Ibid., p. 221.

12

THE TOOLS OF CAPITALISM

Although most of the strategies and tactics of the corporate campaign are outward looking in the sense that they target the external constituencies on whose good will and custom a corporation's well-being depends, there is one set of activities employed by labor that focuses on the company itself—its internal practices and procedures, its culture, its workers, its leadership, and its management minions. These activities are known collectively as *inplant strategies* or the *inside game*. They are designed to disrupt the workplace rhythms of the target company and to reduce its ability to do business as usual. In effect—and sometimes quite literally—they turn the tools of capital against the company that owns them.

SOLIDARITY FOREVER

Typically, playing an inside game requires that the union in question is, in fact, inside. At one level, of course, that is obvious on its face: Workers cannot disrupt a company from the inside if they are on the outside. However, it is also true because the key to success in the inside game often lies in using the company's own, union-negotiated rules and practices against it. If there is no preexisting contract or rule book, there is far less legal and logistical support for such activities. Accordingly, inside strategies are most often found in campaigns whose purpose is to influence a pending or ongoing contract negotiation, rather than in campaigns employed to help organize new workers or for other purposes.

Essentially, inside games are a form of civil disobedience in which the union seeks to build morale among its members even as it undermines the morale of middle and low-level managers. For the workers, inside games, when effectively implemented, provide a means to participate in a corporate campaign that might otherwise be waged without their direct involvement. In that sense, they serve much the same psychological purpose as a strike—building solidarity and buy-in. For those who must manage these workers, the effect can be just the opposite—a sense of being alone on the front lines of an increasingly personalized dispute in which they must work daily in a hostile environment. To the extent that they succeed, then, inside tactics can contribute to a primary objective of the corporate campaign—the disorientation or demoralization of management. This is precisely what Ray Rogers had in mind when he spoke of "organizing workers [and] disorganizing companies."[1]

However, there is more to the strategy of the inside game than merely increasing management's discomfiture. These efforts fit squarely with a much larger objective of organized labor. Recall that one reason the unions have eschewed the formal strike and adopted in its place the tactics of the corporate campaign is that strikes are expensive. At one and the same time, they cut off the flow of union dues and open the tap for an outflow of funds to conduct the strike and support the strikers and their families. As Herbert Northrup put it,

> The basic contrast between a traditional strike and a combination corporate campaign and inside game, if successful, is that in the latter case, workers continue to receive paychecks and unions are not called on to pay strike benefits, unless employees are discharged. Thus, one object of the corporate campaign-inside game combination is to force the company to subsidize a strike against itself.[2]

As noted in earlier chapters, Jerry Tucker, at the time on the staff of the United Auto Workers, is widely credited with creating the inplant strategy, although his actual contribution appears to be less one of designing tactics, many of which had been around for some time, than of unifying a range of tactics into a coordinated, goal-directed strategy. In this chapter, we will look more closely at such efforts.

RANCOR ON THE DISORIENT EXPRESS

The inside game is based on the assumption that companies require a smooth, orderly, and predictable workplace to achieve their economic objectives. At a formal level, this is achieved by specifying policies and practices that workers are to implement to the best of their abilities. At an informal level, it is achieved by those same workers bending the rules to make their work more efficient. In this model, the company provides a framework for the completion of the tasks at hand while the workers add a measure of initiative and good will to smooth the rough edges of the extant formal guidelines. Union contracts often focus on the formalities while stewards selectively enforce contract language and counsel with workers and management to accomplish the requisite informal interpretations.

The inside game turns this model on its head. When such a game is afoot, the formalities rule, but in their narrowest possible interpretation, and informalities are manipulated to demonstrate to management just how dependent it is on the workers' good will. The idea here is to raise the level of workplace stress, at least for managers, and generate a sense on the part of the workers that their supervisors are their enemies. This is an intensely personal enterprise that is designed, among other things, to force managers into overreactions that constitute unfair labor practices.

In one of the more comprehensive studies of inside tactics, Northrup has identified several tactical components. These include staging symbolic demonstrations to build solidarity, overloading the established grievance machinery, developing warlike language and imagery, employing ridicule, working to rule and refusing to work overtime, sabotage, and feeding complaints into the regulatory strategy that often accompanies these initiatives—allegations filed with the Occupational Safety and Health Administration (OSHA) and the Environmental Protection Agency (EPA), for example, as well as with the National Labor Relations Board or the Department of Labor.[3]

Solidarity

The building of worker solidarity is a central focus of a manual of inside game strategies published by the Industrial Unions Department of the AFL–CIO in 1986, which suggests, for example, that union members stage rallies each day before going in to work, gathering at some symbolic location to sing a union song and listen to a speaker. Similarly, the manual recommends "showings of hats, buttons, armbands, stickers, bumper stickers and T-shirts, with everyone wearing or displaying the same symbol on the same day."[4] The manual also suggests complementing the stick with a carrot, for instance, a day on which union members work at top speed and efficiency to show the company what it is missing.[5]

These exercises are designed to generate group identity and peer pressure, both of which are essential as the level of conflict is systematically escalated. As one observer of the process, an attorney who has represented management in confronting such efforts, has characterized it, over time the tone and conduct of these message-events:

> become increasingly negative, hostile, anti-management, and personally anti-supervisor.... The average employee will be reluctant to wear, display, distribute, or chant overtly hostile, rude, disrespectful, abusive messages. They were raised better. But, over time, they can be moved gradually in that direction as the activities become more overt and the confrontation more personalized on the shop floor. What results over time is an insidious denigration of, and challenge to, authority and a disrespect for the institutions and ordering principles without which no organization can survive.[6]

Grievances

Labor contracts typically provide some process through which workers can file grievances when they believe their rights under the contract have been violated. These filings are reviewed by some combination of union and management representatives, with the particular players and procedures being governed by the contract and/or the stated policies of the company in question. Typically, issues that eventually come to be filed with the NLRB as unfair labor practices must first traverse the grievance process to demonstrate that the available lesser remedies have failed to resolve them. This is one of the critical points at which the union and management can cooperate to calm troubled seas or at which the union can exert pressure on management through its unwillingness to cooperate.

One pamphlet advocating inside strategies asserts that "grievances are the cholesterol of production."[7] The idea here is that, by grieving every single departure from past practice or the employer's contractual obligations, workers can overwhelm management, reduce predictability on the shop floor, and slow production all under the legalistic cover of implementing an established policy.[8] Where possible, advocates argue, entire groups of workers should file a collective grievance; when the grievance is heard, all of them should attend the proceeding. Because grievances must be heard during working hours, this can amount to a legally protected work stoppage—in effect, a mini-strike.[9]

Warlike Language and Imagery

The perceptions held by the parties to a conflict are largely the product of the way in which the conflict is framed—the words and images through which it is communicated and understood. With respect to the inside game, the union's idea is to maximize the intensity of feeling, both among the workers to motivate them and build morale and among management to force mistakes and undermine morale. This is accomplished through the use of highly pejorative words and symbols. A clear example of these tactics at work occurred in the UAW's campaign against Caterpillar. As summarized by Gangemi,

> Contract Action Teams promoted their "war zone" mentality by encouraging employees to report for work arrayed in helmets, camouflage fatigues, and other military paraphernalia. The union rented billboards to declare Caterpillar facilities "War Zones." Such slogans as "In Your Plant and In Your Face," "No Contract, No Peace," "Are You Pissed Off Yet?," "You Are Entering A War Zone," "Nothing Runs Like a Deere Except a Scared CAT," and "CAT Busters," were promulgated.... On "Red T-shirt Days" members were encouraged to wear red apparel, not only because it showed support for the UAW, but also because it represented the "blood" shed for the union movement.[10]

Ridicule

The resort to ridicule is but one manifestation of a larger communication strategy—the personalization of the dispute. Workers are more likely to be energized, and management more likely to overreact, when the attacks move from abstract issues and principles to personal actions and relationships. At Caterpillar, for example, handbills distributed inside the company's plants carried pictures of the CEO inside urinals and on pistol targets. The union distributed the names and addresses of managers to its members, whom it encouraged to mail campaign materials to their homes or even stage "drive-bys" for the purpose of embarrassing or intimidating them.[11] At Ravenswood Aluminum, Marc Rich, determined by the Steelworkers to be the hidden power behind the company, was branded an international outlaw and literally hounded into supporting a settlement of the dispute.[12] At Eastern Air Lines, CEO Frank Lorenzo was systematically demonized by the unions to the extent that he was prevented from ever engaging in the air transportation industry again.[13] At Titan International, CEO Morry Taylor was branded a liar in Steelworker news releases, and a white paper issued by the union—*Bad for Business*—was built around a claim that Taylor's ego was driving the company into ruin.[14]

More recently, such efforts have gone high-tech. In the Steelworkers campaign against Oregon Steel, for instance, locked-out workers began flooding a Yahoo electronic bulletin board devoted to the company with offensive characterizations of senior management. One such message, for example, referred to CEO Joseph Corvin and Senior Vice President Thomas Boklund as "The bald headed queer NO GO MOE JOE CORVIN and his girlfriend Tammy Boklund."[15] Yet another message was directed at the company's replacement workers. It read:

> How does it feel to know that the rest of your life you are marked as a scab? No matter where you go, you are a scab. There are always scab hunters out there. Your family are all scabs, your children, wifes [sic], husbands, mothers, fathers, sons, daughters, everyone. And no matter how this ends you will still be a scab. When you die, your family will still be a scab family.... Every time something happens to you or your family, no matter what the reason, your [sic] going to wonder if it was because I was a scab. You will always wonder who was in that car that slowly drove past my house at 3 in the morning.[16]

Work to Rule

Working to the contract or the company's rule book is the very essence of the inplant strategy. In the words of the IUD manual, "The central idea of a 'work-to-rule' campaign is ... do only what you were hired to do, what you are absolutely required to do, nothing more, nothing less."[17] Subject to terms of the contract and various legal considerations, which come into play in this instance, the manual advises workers to:

- work precisely to their job descriptions,
- refuse or resist overtime,
- "work to the clock," which is to say, leave work as is when the shift ends and do not rush to finish a task,
- work at a normal rate of speed, and no faster,
- arrange with other workers to take personal leave or sick days on the same days,
- take personal tools home and leave them there, making the company provide whatever is needed to get the job done, and

- refuse to work under conditions that threaten health or safety.[18]

The SEIU's *Contract Campaign Manual* carries the tactics even further, advising members to follow supervisors' instructions to the letter, avoid making any suggestions or solving any problems on their own, report every equipment problem and insist that it be addressed before work continues, stop talking to supervisors except when that would clearly be insubordinate, and even decline to participate in company-sponsored social events or charity fundraisers. The SEIU places great emphasis on training and preparation, much of which focuses on the line between legal and illegal activity.[19]

Sabotage

The destruction of equipment or vandalizing of the workplace would clearly fall into the latter category of activity, and under normal circumstances most workers would never consider doing such things. However, the level of anger generated during an inplant campaign is such that vandalism is relatively commonplace, and overt acts of sabotage do occur from time to time. In the campaign by the Allied Industrial Workers against A.E. Staley, for example, the manufacturer of corn sweeteners alleged that its workers had sabotaged the company's effluent discharge system, which could lead to a shut-down order by the local sanitary district. The company also accused its workers of "altering tank identification labels, contaminating products, tampering with locks, and closing certain valves which then shut down equipment."[20]

However, sabotage need not be so overt to be effective. To the contrary, more subtle forms of disruption can be even more effective in no small measure because of their very subtlety. We might think of these as a form of de facto sabotage—disrupting production (or other types of business activity) by inaction or altering human behavior rather than property. We can get a sense of how such tactics might play out by considering two of the nine sets of action questions for planning an inside game found in one of the more widely available anticorporate manuals, *A Troublemakers Handbook*.

5. What is the production process in your plant? (You might want to make a map.) What are the most crucial operations? What are the key departments in the plant? What are the key machines in those departments? What would it take to stop those machines? Who fixes them? What are the key links between departments? Where are the potential bottlenecks? Which workers have jobs which allow them to travel around from one department to another? Is there one group of workers that is particularly powerful if they impede production?....

6. Do you have ties to unions at your company's supplier plants? At customers? Would they be willing to raise their quality standards for your company's product? Do you have ties to the unions of the truck drivers, railroad workers or others who move your parts or finished products? Can you establish ties with those workers that can make life more difficult for your company? How does it affect production if raw materials or parts arrive late? How do your customers react if your production schedules arc not met?[21]

Regulatory Complaints

We defer to the next chapter much of our discussion of regulatory strategies in the corporate campaign. In the present context, it is important to note the degree to which such strategies are grounded in the inside game. Complaints of unfair labor practices are an obvious case in point, but they come nowhere near capturing the full range of possibilities. Environmental regulations, trade practices, advertising claims—these and many other aspects of daily business can be challenged as part of the corporate campaign. To the extent that any allegations—whether by a union, one or more individual whistleblowers, or a third party—are based in or supported by anecdotes or data drawn by employees from the company's own records and information systems, these regulatory initiatives are a form of outreach from the inside game.

One of the most common sets of regulatory complaints that get aired in a corporate campaign is that relating to health and safety, either of employees or the general public. We have already seen one manifestation of this phenomenon in the campaign against the health care industry, where doctors, nurses, and other workers are portrayed as acting to protect the public. Other campaigns focusing on the ostensible protection of the public are found in the supermarket and airline industries, among others. In most cases, however, the emphasis is more directly on the health and safety of the workers. That is especially the case in organizing campaigns, where workers' concerns about such issues can be used to generate support for the union. As one analysis put it,

> The organizer's job is to awaken interest in health and safety, make connections between hazard and health, and show workers that the union can be a vehicle to improve workplace conditions.[22]

However, the authors clarified that even these internally directed efforts are enhanced when framed by a broader thematic:

A union pressure campaign also has a better chance of being portrayed positively in the press if the issues are defined broadly to reflect environmental concerns that impact the community. Local politicians, district attorneys, religious and community leaders are more likely to play a role in an effort that is defined as involving health, safety and the environment. The portrayal of workers as only being interested in their jobs is recast as workers exercising their right to healthy conditions and using their knowledge to prevent unsafe practices by the company. Workplace hazards and injured workers can present powerful testimony to the community and help rally important external support.[23]

As one example, this precisely characterized the strategy employed by the UFCW in its drive to organize poultry workers.

The United Auto Workers union has distributed a comprehensive manual for using health and safety as components of an inplant strategy. This document explains to workers the role of OSHA in protecting workers, arguing that the agency has been of limited value except where workers have been proactive in initiating complaints and demanding investigations of employers. To this end, it recommends that the union local at a given facility copy all of the entries from the company's "OSHA 200" log—a mandatory record of all workplace-related deaths, illnesses, and injuries—and then initiate its own incident log and use a reconciliation of the two as the basis for a complaint to OSHA if any discrepancies are found. Another proposed tactic is to identify 10 unlabeled containers in a given work area, report them to the company, and record the response, again with an eye toward establishing a record of discrepancies.[24]

Perhaps the most telling page of the UAW manual, and the one that links it clearly to the strategy of personalizing the inside game, is a brief form provided for photocopying (see Fig. 12.1).[25] What supervisor would sign such a document, which, in the process of relieving the employee of liability for performing a task, also acknowledges the task to be unsafe? What supervisor would not react negatively to being asked to sign such a form perhaps even to overreact? That, of course, is precisely the point.

PLEASE PASS THE SALT

The inside game has obvious limitations when directed against nonunion employers as part of an organizing effort. In such cases, the union may not be inside at all or in any significant numbers. How, then, does one generate internal pressures? At least part of the answer is found in the technique known as *salting*.

Authorization to Perform Unsafe Work

I,_____authorize_____ to perform the following unsafe work tasks:_____. It is understood
that the performer of said unsafe tasks is not responsible for any
accidents that may occur. It is also understood that the above
named will not be charged or penalized with warnings,
counselings, or days off for performance of above said unsafe
tasks.

Signature of Supervisor_____

Date_____

FIG. 12.1. **"Authorization to Perform Unsafe Work" form from the UAW
manual.**

Salting is the practice by unions of placing paid organizers inside the
workforce of a targeted company for the express purpose of organizing
other workers. In effect, a *salt*, as such inplant plants are termed, is working
for two employers who are at evident cross-purposes—the union and the
company. On its face, this might appear to constitute a breach of the employee's duty of loyalty to the employer—a long standing element of both
commercial and common law without which companies could not function.
Under the National Labor Relations Act, however, an employer cannot refuse to hire an employee it suspects of being a union organizer—a position
that has been sustained by the NLRB and even the Supreme Court.[26]

One of the unions that most actively engages in this practice is the International Brotherhood of Electrical Workers (IBEW), which has aggressively employed salts in its efforts to organize the construction industry.
The union's Special Projects Department has produced a legal analysis that
cites a number of relevant precedents and suggests a strategy for deriving
maximum benefit from salting. This document states in part:

> The employer should be watched closely for the commission of even minor ULPs
> and evidence, including affidavits, should be carefully accumulated. A time may
> come when the Local will want to pull its salts and supporters out on a minority
> ULP strike to encourage the hiring of temporary replacements, set the stage for an
> unconditional offer to return, and for further actions.[27]

In other words, the union's strategy is to infiltrate the workplace, generate
unfair labor practice allegations, use these as an excuse to walk off the job,
and then, when the employer hires replacement workers to maintain production, use that as a focal point for further organizing efforts. In the construction trades, where staying on schedule can mean the difference

between profit and bankruptcy, the pressure generated on management by such tactics can be immense.

Perhaps not coincidentally, the primary test case on salting—the one that produced the Supreme Court's refusal to review the NLRB's pro-salting position—involved Willmar Electric Service, a Minnesota-based electrical contractor headed by John Chapin, who was also at the time the national president of the Associated Builders and Contractors, a strongly anti-union trade association. In this instance, a journeyman electrician, Michael Hendrix, a full-time field organizer for the IBEW, applied for a job with Willmar and disclosed his intention to organize workers during the lunch hour. The project foreman, charged with hiring, declined to hire Hendrix, allegedly telling him, "Well, it's kind of hard to hire you when you're out there on the other side, picketing." The NLRB's Administrative Law Judge concluded that Hendrix had been improperly denied a job based on activity that was protected by law.[28] In effect, this set up a pure test of the practice of salting, and the Court's refusal to review the decision on appeal greatly strengthened the legal support accorded the practice. Then, in a 1995 case, *Town & Country Electric v. NLRB*, the Court affirmed the right of unions to salt.[29]

Although salting is often undertaken surreptitiously, the IBEW report makes clear that this need not be the case:

> If the employer is large or is in a hiring mode ... a time may come when the Local will want to openly send salts to make application, or to submit job applications by cover letter, or even to have applications delivered by a union official.[30]

That measure of directness may be commonplace in the construction industry, but elsewhere the subtle application of salts is still the general rule. Still, in the wake of the *Willmar* decision, the unions clearly have, and take advantage of, a greater sense of freedom of action in this area. One good indicator of this might be the following help-wanted advertisement that appeared on a union-sponsored electronic job listing in May 1998:

> Training and Salting Coordinator, Seattle Organizing Center. The SOC will link unions and their campaigns in coordinated, large-scale drives aimed at organizing King County workers into unions. The Training and Salting Coordinator will [work] with SOC unions to create salting and organizer training programs ... [and] create a multi-union salting program that includes systems to recruit, train, place and support large numbers of salts.[31]

Shortly after this advertisement was placed, the CWA began large-scale organizing campaigns at such Seattle-area employers as Microsoft and Amazon.com.

PAYING RIGHT INTO THE UNION'S HANDS

One aspect of the inside game that has seen new emphasis in recent years is the comparison—inevitably invidious—between the paycheck of the average worker and the compensation packages of corporate CEOs. A direct play on the theme of corporate greed, such comparisons have long been part of the game, typically in the form of flyers or handbills distributed in the plant. In the Caterpillar campaign, for example, the UAW produced a handbill showing a fat cat—a standard image that in this case provided a particularly appropriate play on words—with a sack of money in one hand and a bulldozer in the other. The text attacked company CEO Don Fites for accepting a 74% increase in salary and bonuses (for a total of $3,143,833) as well as more than $1.5 million in stock options even as he sought to impose a three-tier wage system with a starting rate of $8 per hour for new hires.

More recently, such comparisons have gone high-tech. In 1997, the AFL–CIO established Executive Pay Watch, a Web site that allows workers at hundreds of companies to compare their salary or wages against the compensation of the company's CEO. The site provides both individual ratio calculations (i.e., your CEO earns 126 times what you earn) and a variety of more general comparisons. For example, visitors to the site are told that the CEO of a particular health care company earned as much as three U.S. presidents, three AFL–CIO presidents (whom, one is assured, have not had a pay increase since 1992), five chairmen of the Joint Chiefs of Staff, 25 average workers, or 59 minimum-wage workers. Putting the same comparison another way, the site advises that an average worker would need to work 25 years to receive as much pay as this CEO received in just 1.[32]

More pointed still is the "Bill Gates Personal Wealth Clock," a real-time Web site that updates the Microsoft founder's personal wealth second by second based on his holdings of Microsoft stock. The site also divides Gates' net worth by the population of the United States—also updated in real time—to determine the "personal contribution" of the average visitor to his wealth.[33]

CONCLUSION

The inside game is essentially a form of psychological warfare with two interrelated objectives: to build up the morale of the union's forces while undermining that on the other side. Indeed, one of its key functions is to generate among workers the feeling that there are, in fact, two opposing sides—a perception that, once established, it exploits aggressively. It is as part of the inside game that the vilification of management and the personalization of the dispute come to the fore, although these frames may well play out in more public venues as well. It is the inside game that often sparks the legal and regulatory attacks on target companies, which we discuss in more detail in the next chapter. Where it is employed, then, we can see the inside game as pivotal in the creation and communication of a unified front against the company and as a significant component of the corporate campaign.

ENDNOTES

1. William Serrin, "Organized Labor is Increasingly Less So," *The New York Times*, November 18, 1984, p. 4:3.
2. Herbert Northrup, "Union Corporate Campaigns and Inside Games as a Strike Form," *Employee Relations Law Journal* 19 (Spring 1994), p. 537.
3. Northrup, op. cit., pp. 516–535.
4. *The Inside Game: Winning with Workplace Strategies* (Washington: Industrial Unions Department of the AFL–CIO, 1986), pp. 15–16.
5. Ibid., p. 18.
6. Columbus R. Gangemi, Jr., *Inside Game Tactics: Understanding Work-to-Rule and Other In-Plant Campaign Strategies* (Washington: Labor Policy Association, 1997), p. 14.
7. Michael Eisencher, *Creative Persistent Resistance (CPR): A Primer for Unions Taking the Strike Inside*, Revision 1.2 (San Francisco, NP, September 1990), p. 6.
8. Or as the SEIU puts it, "A contract campaign can be a good time for members to file grievances over every possible contract violation." *Contract Campaign Manual* (Washington: Service Employees International Union, 1985), p. 3–9.
9. Eisencher, loc. cit.
10. Gangemi, op. cit., p. 12.
11. Ibid., pp. 12–13.
12. The pursuit of Rich is detailed at length in Tom Juravich and Kate Bronfenbrenner, *Ravenswood: The Steelworkers' Victory and the Revival of American Labor* (Ithaca: Cornell University Press, 1999).
13. For an insider's view of this attack, see Richard K. Danforth, "Lorenzo's Wings Were Clipped Unjustly," *PR Central: Reputation Management*, circa 1996, found at http://prcentral.com/rmndlorenzo.htm, December 6, 1999.
14. See, for example, "Titan Releases Disastrous 1999 Financial Results: The Numbers Don't Lie—Does Taylor (Again)?" USWA news release, February 23, 2000; and *Bad for Business: Titan CEO Morry Taylor Sets a Course for Disaster*, found at www.uswa.org/news/titanbad.html, March 1, 2000.
15. Dumbermeister, "He's not fooling anybody," Yahoo! Finance, "OS," message number 2285, posted August 30, 1999.
16. Dingmaster, "Question, Question, Question?," Yahoo! Finance, "OS," message number 924, posted March 20, 1999.
17. *The Inside Game*, op. cit., pp. 16–17.
18. Ibid., pp. 17–18.
19. *Contract Campaign Manual*, op. cit., pp. 3-11–3-12.

20. Based on news accounts quoted in Northrup, op. cit., pp. 526–527.

21. Dan La Botz, *A Troublemakers Handbook: How to Fight Back Where You Work—And Win!* (Detroit: Labor Notes, 1991), p. 126.

22. Diane Factor and Joe Uehlein, "Organizing for Safe Work in a Safe World," *Labor Research Review* 16 (Fall 1990), p. 3.

23. Ibid., p. 11.

24. *Health and Safety for Inside Strategies* (NP: United Auto Workers, nd). Pages in this document are unnumbered, and various versions contain different combinations of pages.

25. Ibid.

26. In February 1993, the Supreme Court denied a petition from the company to hear and reverse the decision of an NLRB Administrative Law Judge in *Willmar Electric Service, Inc., Cases 10-CA-20137 and 20138* (September 1, 1989), which tested this issue. The case is summarized later.

27. Michael D. Lucas, *Salting as Protected Activity Under the National Labor Relations Act* (Washington: International Brotherhood of Electrical Workers, March 1993), p. 14.

28. *Willmar Electric Service, Inc., Cases 10-CA-20137 and 20138* (September 1, 1989).

29. *Town & Country Electric v. NLRB*, 116 S. Ct. 450 (1995).

30. Lucas, op. cit., p. 13.

31. Distributed by e-mail.

32. The gateway to these comparisons was found at www.aflcio.org/paywatch/index.htm, November 22, 1999.

33. Found at www.Webho.com/WealthClock, June 15, 1998.

13

The Campaign Branches Out

From the beginning and in its very essence, the corporate campaign has depended not solely on the resources of the union or other group waging it, which are likely to be quite limited in comparison with those of the target company or industry, but on mobilizing the resources of others who are either sympathetic to the advocates' cause or can be pressed into service through secondary pressure tactics. With the exception of the media, whose role, as we shall see later, is ubiquitous, no set of institutions has been more consistently or effectively employed for these purposes than the three branches of government—executive, legislative, and judicial. Through the federal regulatory agencies, the Congress and the federal courts, as well, at times, as through their state and local counterparts, campaigns have relied on the government for information, legitimization, and pure, unadulterated pressure of a kind they are themselves incapable of generating. Willing or not and knowing or not, the government has served for many years as the partner of unions and other advocates bent on changing corporate behaviors or, in some instances, attacking the corporation per se. In this chapter, we outline the role played by government institutions in corporate campaign strategy.

REGULATE THIS!

Charles Perry noted in his initial treatise on corporate campaigns—and it is still generally the case today—that most of the efforts to employ the executive branch of government on behalf of the unions center not on mobilizing elected officials—although that does occur—but on exploiting the powers of the departments and agencies that carry out the executive function.[1] In that regard, the corporate campaign manual of the AFL–CIO's Industrial Union Department offers this particularly telling strategic insight:

> Businesses are regulated by a virtual alphabet soup of federal, state and local agencies, which monitor nearly every aspect of corporate behavior. Although these watchdog agencies employ inspectors to monitor compliance by companies, most also rely on employees and other individuals to file complaints about violations. Once the regulators are alerted to violations by a company, they sometimes assume an adversarial relationship toward the offender.
>
> Regulatory agencies exist to protect citizens, and unions can use the regulators to their advantage. An intransigent employer may find that in addition to labor troubles, there are suddenly government problems as well.[2]

Dan LaBotz, writing in *A Troublemaker's Handbook*, was more pointed still:

> Every law or regulation is a potential net in which management can be snared and entangled. A complaint to a regulatory agency can cause [*sic*] the company managerial time, public embarrassment, potential fines, and the costs of compliance. One well-placed phone call can do a lot of damage.[3]

In its own how-to manual, the SEIU makes the point yet again, but in considerably more detail. Noting that most employers are not only required to obey laws and regulations that may be enforced by government agencies, but also depend on permits, licenses, low-interest public financing, and other government actions to conduct their affairs profitably, the union identifies a number of ways to exploit this key stakeholder relationship. These are divided into two general categories: those pertaining to workers and the workplace, and those pertaining to customers, stockholders, or the health and safety of the general public. The first category includes:

- Safety and health hazards on the job.

- Discrimination on the basis of race, gender, age, ethnic origin or sexual preference.
- Failure to pay overtime or minimum wage as required by federal, state or local fair labor standards laws.
- Subcontracting of public employees work in violation of state or local charters, codes or constitutions.[4]

Included in the second category are:
- Failure to provide enough staffing or cutting corners in other ways that threaten public safety.
- Evasion of taxes on property or income.
- Failure to live up to commitments made when obtaining low-interest public financing such as industrial revenue bonds.
- Failure of hospitals to meet obligations ... to provide care to patients who cannot afford it.
- Failure of nursing homes to meet patient care standards or to make changes in their facilities to accommodate handicapped patients as required under federal anti-discrimination regulations.
- Environmental hazards such as toxic waste dumping or exposed asbestos in office buildings.
- Failure to disclose information to the public as required by laws or regulations.[5]

The manual goes on to outline suggested techniques for investigating potential violations in any of these regulatory areas; for building coalitions with other groups, particularly those that have already sued the company over related matters; and for using the threat of regulatory intervention as leverage in bargaining or organizing. As the SEIU rightly recognizes, however, there is a fine line to be walked here.

> Be sure that you offer only to give the employer a chance to eliminate legal and regulatory violations without charges having to be filed or without publicity—as opposed to offering to ignore the violations entirely. For the union to know about violations and not insist that they be corrected is not only a violation of our moral obligations to members and the community, but may in some cases make the union liable to legal charges itself.[6]

In chapter 4, we saw what may well be the ultimate expression of this strategy to date in the SEIU's campaign against Sutter Health, where a broad panoply of federal and state regulatory agencies, ranging from the California Department of Corporations to the United States Department of Defense, were recruited to the union's cause. The same regulatory strategy is evident in the SEIU's broader campaign against the health care industry. In its attack on Beverly Enterprises, for example, the union claims to have prevented the company's expansion through acquiring existing nursing homes in Michigan and Georgia, and defeated Beverly's proposals for public financing through Industrial Development Revenue Bonds in Massachusetts and Ohio.[7]

Variations on this strategy are commonplace across the full spectrum of corporate campaigns. In the USWA's Oregon Steel campaign, for example, the union filed charges in July 1998 with the National Labor Relations Board alleging that the company had failed to bargain in good faith, had refused to reinstate striking workers after they had offered to return to work (recall that Oregon Steel had hired 600 replacement workers), and had made a "regressive" contract proposal.[8] A month later, the Steelworkers filed a report with federal bank regulators calling on them to examine the community lending practices of Wells Fargo Bank, targeted as the lead lender in the company's financing consortium, before approving its merger with Norwest Bank. The union's report claimed that Wells Fargo was in violation of the Community Reinvestment Act.[9] By June 1999, the Occupational Safety and Health Administration (OSHA) was in the game, citing the company's Pueblo facility for six "serious" workplace violations.[10] When Colorado's State Air Quality Control Division, which had been encouraged by the union to hold public hearings on alleged clean-air violations before issuing certain environmental permits to the company, instead moved toward a private settlement with the company, the union issued a news release accusing the state of colluding with the company to harm the public.[11] The union even wrote to the state Commissioner of Education, asking that he vote to deny the company an extension of a property tax incentive it had been granted by the local school district in Pueblo, Colorado, where the dispute centered. In the words of Ernest Hernandez, the president of the striking local,

> I ask you to send a message to CF&I/Oregon Steel. Your denial of the property tax credit extension will put CF&I on notice that the state of Colorado is well aware that the company has failed miserably at promoting economic development opportunities in Pueblo County School District 60. You will be telling the company that it is time to honor its tax responsibilities and to promote economic development by negotiating a fair and decent contract with our workers....[12]

Sometimes the regulatory component of a campaign relies on the sheer numbers of complaints rather than on the merits of any particular one. In the Teamsters campaign against Overnite Transportation, for example, the union filed more than 1,000 charges of unfair labor practices against the company with the NLRB. The allegations included intimidation, harassment, and unlawful discharge.[13]

The bounds of an acronymic strategy of regulatory mobilization are determined more by the limits of the campaigners' imaginations than by any limits on the number of local, state, and federal entities that might become engaged. Among those federal agencies that have played roles in various corporate campaigns are the following, each with an indication of the type of regulatory authority it exercises and an example of one or more campaigns where it has been active:

- DOJ—Department of Justice—fraud in government contracts, partial jurisdiction over antitrust enforcement—General Dynamics, Microsoft
- DOL—Department of Labor—especially through the Wage and Hour Division, which investigates allegations of child labor and overtime violations—Albertson's, Food Lion, Guess?, Publix
- DOS—Department of State—represents the United States in its dealings with such international agencies as the Organization for Economic Cooperation and Development (OECD), which are sometimes used as leverage points in campaigns against multinational companies—BASF
- EEOC—Equal Employment Opportunity Commission—enforces laws against employment discrimination and sexual harassment—Mitsubishi, Publix
- EPA—Environmental Protection Agency—primary federal agency responsible for environmental regulation—Bayou Steel, International Paper, Louisiana-Pacific
- FAA—Federal Aviation Administration—regulates safety of airlines and the air transportation system—Eastern Air Lines
- FDA—Food and Drug Administration—enforces the nation's food safety laws—Food Lion
- FTC—Federal Trade Commission—truth in advertising, partial jurisdiction over antitrust enforcement—may have been involved in the Microsoft campaign by bringing antitrust action against Intel, which then became a government witness against Microsoft
- HCFA—Health Care Finance Administration—enforces Medicare regulations, investigates related allegations of fraud—Sutter Health
- HHS—Department of Health and Human Services—regulates provision of health care services—Sutter Health
- IRS—Internal Revenue Service—enforces tax laws and investigates allegations of fraud or evasion—Sutter Health
- NLRB—National Labor Relations Board—technically part of the DOL, administers union-recognition and decertification elections and rules on allegations of unfair labor practices by both unions and companies—involved in virtually every corporate campaign, notably Caterpillar, Overnite Transportation

- OSHA—Occupational Safety and Health Administration—technically part of the DOL, sets and enforces standards for workplace safety and health, including ergonomic standards—Bayou Steel, BE&K, Bridgestone/Firestone, nursing home industry campaigns, UPS
- SEC—Securities and Exchange Commission—regulates the securities industry, including the rules on corporate disclosure and those regarding the placement of shareholder resolutions on ballots for annual meetings—involved in many corporate campaigns

The point, of course, is that this list, as extensive as it is, does not capture the full range of federal agency participation in the corporate campaign. It does not even begin to capture the involvement of local zoning authorities, state and local taxing and finance authorities, state and local regulatory agencies, and the like that are also subject to recruitment.[14] But in each instance, the key to this regulatory strategy is the same: By stimulating a government agency to focus on a particular company, the union or other campaigner can, in effect, wield the powers of government to get the target company's attention and alter its behavior.

In pursuing this strategy, the unions are aided by the fact that public records are just that—public. The federal government and every state have some form of Freedom of Information Act (FOIA) under which any citizen can request copies of agency records or other public filings relating to a company's regulatory performance or any other activity. Because companies in most industries are heavily regulated and regulators compile detailed inspection records and maintain files on every company they oversee, such FOIA requests are likely to turn up information useful to the campaign either in the form of data critical of the company in some area of performance or, in the alternative, anecdotes and incidents relating to violations. Absent that, there may at least be files of allegations of wrongdoing that can be exploited. In chapter 10, we noted the propensity of campaigning unions and others to prepare white papers detailing the shortcomings of their respective target companies. Much of the data for those reports is gathered through the FOIA process.

THERE OUGHT TO BE A LAW

As one might expect, regulatory strategies are often accompanied by political strategies that tend to center in various legislative bodies, most often, but not exclusively, in the U.S. Congress. Typically we think of the primary function of Congress as the passing of laws. To be sure, it does pass labor-related laws from time to time, some of which—the Wagner Act, the Taft–Hartley Act—have had a significant direct impact on labor–management relations, and others of which—the Clean Air Act—have simply broadened or restricted the range of arenas available for pressuring employers.

These legislative initiatives are relatively rare, however, and they seldom deal directly with the issues in a given corporate campaign. Far more important in the present context than these legislative products is the legislative process. For in addition to passing laws, members of Congress hold hearings, write letters to regulatory agencies, meet with company officials, and generally involve themselves in the business affairs of the nation. It is no secret that, in general, Republican members are relatively friendlier to the interests of the business community and Democratic members to those of labor. Indeed, organized labor works rather systematically to exploit this difference of preferences by demonstrating its importance to congressional Democrats by the simple device of showering them with money. According to the Center for Responsive Politics, for example, in the 1997–1998 election cycle, labor unions contributed $45.5 million to congressional candidates, of which $41.1 million (90%) went to Democrats.[15] For the 1999–2000 cycle, the AFL-CIO committed $46 million for a voter mobilization and issue advertising campaign targeting 35 congressional districts in 15 states—that in addition to any direct contributions labor might provide to individual candidates or parties.[16]

This strategic approach to political contributions can be expected to pay off especially well when the Democrats control the Congress, and there is good reason to think that the legislative product and process alike are most effective in that circumstance. The fact is, members of Congress can find ways to conduct hearings or otherwise express their views from the minority side of the aisle as well, especially when their party controls the White House and, as a consequence, the regulatory powers of the executive branch. Such companies as Diamond Walnut, IBP, and Food Lion, for example, have found themselves the subjects of hearings and letter-writing campaigns to regulatory agencies conducted by labor-friendly members of Congress. Even the Republicans get into the act from time to time. For example, it was Senator Orin Hatch, the Republican of Utah, who called Microsoft's Bill Gates on the carpet and pressured the Department of Justice to bring its antitrust action.

Here, too, the SEIU has pointed the way in its campaign manual:

Political pressure may be used in two ways.

First, you may be able to draw politicians into the debate on negotiating issues.

Second, you can show management officials that, if they don't bargain fairly, union members will be inclined to push for legislative action on other issues that would affect management ... in the way employers are taxed, awarded public funds, or required to provide service.[17]

Of course, the SEIU deals in many instances with public employers, but the strategy it propounds—which includes generating political pressure through demonstrations, petitions, and the news media—is far more broadly applicable.

Legislative strategy is often implemented at the state and local level as well. In the Louisiana-Pacific campaign, for example, the United Brotherhood of Carpenters linked a rally against the company on Wall Street to hearings held by the Labor Committee of the New York State Assembly on "The Plight of the Collective Bargaining System." It got city councils in two cities where the company had manufacturing facilities to pass resolutions supporting the strike.[18] The Speaker of the California State Assembly formed a committee to monitor the balloting in an SEIU representation election at Mercy Healthcare Sacramento, a key strategic target in the union's drive to organize workers at Catholic Healthcare West—this despite the fact that the NLRB—a federal agency—conducts all such elections.[19]

In the Oregon Steel campaign, 29 members of the Colorado legislature wrote an open letter accusing the company of "show[ing] its utter disrespect for the town of Pueblo and its citizens, as well as for our federal labor laws...."[20] Similarly, a group of California legislators attended a rally and march in support of the union's boycott of Wells Fargo Bank,[21] and the chairman of the Joint Legislative Audit Committee of the California State Assembly visited the company's president to press the union's case. When that committee scheduled hearings in Sacramento where the union was invited to air its grievances, workers in Boulder held a protest "news conference" where they wore gags to symbolize their claim that the company would retaliate against any worker who spoke out.[22] Even the Governor of Colorado got into the act, urging the company "to bring this damaging situation to a speedy conclusion by returning to the bargaining table and remaining there until you reach a settlement with the Steelworkers Union."[23]

The unions are not alone in directing their attention to the legislative process. In one study of Capitol Hill lobbying activity, for example, political scientist Jeffrey M. Berry found that, where economic issues were the central focus of legislation during the 1960s, by 1991 fully 71% of congressional hearings dealt with legislation on quality of life issues and the most active lobby was the Natural Resources Defense Council. The Sierra Club, the Consumer Federation of America, and the Ralph Nader organizations were also especially active.[24]

A FULL COURT PRESS

The third branch of government has its role to play in the corporate campaign as well. Litigation is commonplace in these campaigns and sometimes, as in the case of NOW's effort against Mitsubishi, can even provide the stimulus for them. These efforts are often accompanied by what is known as *litigation journalism*—using news management and other tactics to establish a favorable setting for one's side in a pending lawsuit.

The mother of all lawsuits relating to a corporate campaign is probably that brought by the Justice Department against Microsoft in 1998, where the government took as its objective the breakup, or at least the substantial weakening, of the company. As soon as the judge's initial findings of fact were released, a wave of secondary litigation broke over the company, with still more in prospect. This served the interests of the Microsoft competitors who had, as we saw in chapter 7, encouraged the Justice Department to act, some of whom were litigants in related private lawsuits against Microsoft as well. It also served the interests of consumer advocates who planned their own follow-up litigation and of the CWA, which stood to gain from any resultant undermining of employee morale and from the general distraction of the company's management.

A similarly wide-ranging lawsuit, this one a private antitrust class action, was filed against Monsanto late in 1999 by a group of farmers in the United States and France encouraged by environmental activists.[25] Recall that Monsanto was the target at the time of a campaign initiated by Greenpeace to force the company out of the business of producing genetically modified plants and foods. Indeed, Greenpeace was among several environmental groups serving as advisers on the case.[26] In brief, the lawsuit alleged that:

- In 1996, Monsanto "devised an anti-competitive scheme to control prices and restrain trade in the GM [genetically modified] corn and soybean seed markets."
- Since that time, Monsanto and several co-conspirators had imposed excessive fees and unfair restrictions on farmers using this seed.
- Monsanto did not adequately test these seeds for human and environmental safety. (The lawsuit did not allege that they are unsafe, only that they were not properly tested.)
- Monsanto's failure to test GM seeds properly "has caused the rejection of GM crops at market, and has thus ... threatened the economic vitality of farmers' businesses, especially those of the American family farmer and small farmers in developing countries."[27]

The bottom line? According to the plaintiffs,

Monsanto's unlawful conduct in aggregating the power to control all aspects of the production of corn and soy appear to be motivated by its desire to control the basic means of production of the global food supply.[28]

We can see even in this abbreviated summary of the complaint several distinctive elements. First, consistent with our arguments about anticorporate campaigns like those waged by Greenpeace, this is an inherently political claim as opposed to an economic one. That is apparent, for example, in the bullet-four reference to family farms and developing nations, as well as in the rhetorical flourish in the preceding paragraph. Second, the argument is more than a tad disingenuous. Even as the farmers were complaining that the market has rejected their crops because of Monsanto's failings, the environmentalists who encouraged them, including Greenpeace, had been leading a campaign in Europe and the United States whose objective was precisely that—rejection in the marketplace. Finally, we can see here an evident effort to position Monsanto in the moral lowlands and the litigants on the bluffs above. Indeed, as a report in *The Wall Street Journal* at the time of filing summed up their objectives:

> Activists hope the lawsuit gives them a high-profile stage to air their complaints against bio-engineered foods, arguments that U.S. regulators from the Food and Drug Administration to the Justice Department have largely rejected.[29]

Monsanto's response to the ongoing campaign came barely a week later, when the company announced plans to merge with Pharmacia & Upjohn, Inc., to form one of the world's largest pharmaceutical and biotechnology companies. The plan included a spin-off of Monsanto's agriculture division—the target of the environmental activists.[30]

Both the Microsoft and Monsanto cases were expansive legal assaults on their respective targets that addressed core business practices. To be sure, there are other examples of large-scale litigation. In the case of corporate-campaign target Wal-Mart, for example, attorney Lewis Laska went so far as to create the "Wal-Mart Litigation Project," an online database established

> to assist lawyers who sue Wal-Mart to force the company to act properly toward its customers and employees. The project's goal is to "level the playing field" so plaintiffs have a better chance of winning suits where Wal-Mart has done wrong … by facilitating communication between plaintiffs' lawyers on issues of law, discovery and litigation tactics.[31]

The site maintains a referral database of attorneys around the country who have been active in suing Wal-Mart. It claims to have identified more than 100 different types of lawsuit that have been filed against the company.[32]

In the grand scheme of things, such broad-scale attacks are unusual. Far more common is litigation grounded in charges of sexual harassment, discrimination in employment, wage and hour violations, and other equally mundane allegations that relate to the narrower themes of a particular corporate campaign. A typical example is that of Albertson's, the target of a corporate campaign by the UFCW, which found itself on the receiving end of a wage-and-hour lawsuit charging that the company forced employees to work overtime without pay—a so-called *off-the-clock violation*. In all, eight such lawsuits were filed by and on behalf of the union, all of which were eventually consolidated for hearing in Boise, Idaho, where the company is headquartered. In December 1999, the parties reached an agreement under which the company denied the allegations, but agreed to set aside $37 million for payouts, including $17.5 million for the attorneys who brought the cases.[33]

In using the courts, the unions are afforded some important protections that are unavailable to their corporate targets. Not least, they can lose in civil litigation without fear of retribution. In contrast, should a company, as part of its response to a corporate campaign, bring suit against a union and lose, the NLRB may determine that in the act of filing the company has committed a retaliatory act against the union, which is forbidden, and may require the company to reimburse the union for the legal expenses it incurred in defending itself. This so-called *Bill Johnson's rule*—named for the Supreme Court decision in which it was established—was applied, for example, in a case involving BE&K Construction, which was targeted in a corporate campaign by building trades unions in California.[34]

A PROCESS APPROACH: THE A–M–L–R CYCLE

Although regulatory, legislative, and legal initiatives serve as direct and often significant pressure points on a target company in their own right, their overall role as components of corporate campaign strategy may be best understood in the context of their use as instruments of public humiliation, which is to say as part of the campaign's communication strategy. One useful way to think of this—admittedly oversimplified—is in terms of what I have elsewhere termed the *A–M–L–R Cycle—Accentuate, Mediate, Legislate (or Litigate), Regulate*.[35] This cycle is illustrated in Fig. 13.1.

In this view, a union or other antagonist identifies a theme that it plans to utilize against a target company. Through a series of direct actions, it first accentuates this theme by bringing it to public attention, placing it on the public agenda. Next it mediates the theme by orchestrating media coverage of the target company in the context of the theme. This has the dual effect of reinforcing the association in the public mind between the company and the theme and legitimizing the theme by filtering it through the media—a process we discuss in more detail in the following chapter. Third, it legislates the theme, which is to say it recruits supporters on Capitol Hill or in the states to channel the theme and target company through the legislative process in the manner described above. Alternatively, it uses private or class action litigation, with its attendant filings and proceedings, to the same end. Finally, it regulates the theme by orchestrating the filing of numerous individual and class-action complaints with the various relevant agencies, soliciting information through FOIA requests, publishing quasi-regulatory

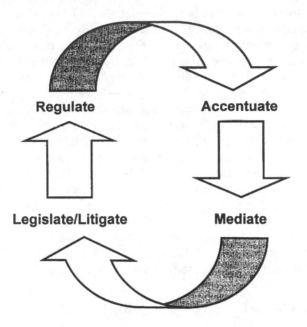

FIG. 13.1.   The A–M–L–R cycle.

white-paper reports, and the like. All of this legislative, judicial, and regulatory activity, in turn, reifies the issue, provides events and news pegs for
further accentuation, and renders it worthy of further media attention as the
cycle repeats itself.

Depending on the issue and the nature of the corporate response, the
half-life of these cycles can range from days to years. Although the order of
operations and the particulars of this process vary from instance to instance, the presence of such a cycle is apparent in such campaigns as those
against Caterpillar, Food Lion, Microsoft, Oregon Steel, Ravenswood Aluminum, Publix, and many others. The Monsanto litigation offers a particularly good example. In that case, recall that the issue was first aired before
the Justice Department and the FDA, where it made news but no waves.
Then the day before the lawsuit was filed, the Center for Media and Democracy, an anticorporate think tank based in Madison, Wisconsin, published a
collection of articles in its newsletter, *PR Watch*, attacking genetically engineered foods in general and Monsanto in particular.[36] The same day, *The
Nation*, another publication with close ties to the progressive community,
published a feature story on what it termed *Frankenfoods*; it opened by singling out Monsanto for ridicule and closed by echoing the sentiments in the
litigation.[37] This was followed by the filing of the lawsuit, which in turn

produced a wave of coverage in all of the major media.[38] The media coverage drew specific connections between the theory of this case and that of the
recently tried Justice Department action against Microsoft.[39] That, in turn,
pointed toward further pressure on the regulatory process.

CONCLUSION

Although political and governmental actors are not customarily thought of
as corporate stakeholders, the fact is that companies are at least as dependent on maintaining a relatively benign political and regulatory environment
as they are on raising capital on Wall Street or satisfying their customers. A
failure to accomplish this objective can reduce profits, damage reputations,
or quite literally make it impossible to do business.

From the outset of the corporate campaign phenomenon, the unions have
recognized the strategic importance of these public institutions and the substantial leverage they can provide. Moreover, to the extent that they are
amenable to influence, regulatory agencies and public officials play to one
of labor's enduring strengths—its ability to mobilize large numbers of volunteers and a significant pool of funds in support of friendly candidates and
causes. To the extent that these agencies and officials—and the
courts—lend their collective weight in validation of the allegations and
themes that are floated during the course of a corporate campaign, they not
only help legitimize the campaign, but they help lift it to that chosen firma-
ment—the moral high ground. In this way, these hands-on legal and political activities contribute directly to the communication strategy that drives
the campaign. In the following chapter, we turn our attention more directly
to this broader area of strategy.

ENDNOTES

1. Charles R. Perry, *Union Corporate Campaigns* (Philadelphia: Industrial Research
   Unit, The Wharton School, University of Pennsylvania, 1987), pp. 39–40.
2. *Developing New Tactics: Winning With Coordinated Corporate Campaigns*
   (Washington: Industrial Union Department, AFL–CIO, 1985), p. 6.
3. Dan LaBotz, *A Troublemaker's Handbook: How to Fight Back Where You
   Work—and Win!* (Detroit: Labor Notes, 1991), p. 127.
4. *Contract Campaign Manual* (Washington: Service Employees International Union, ND), p. 3:21.
5. Ibid., pp. 3:21–22.
6. Ibid., p. 3:23.
7. Ibid.
8. "Oregon Steel is hit with new charges," *The (Portland) Oregonian*, July 9, 1998.

9. Greg Chang, "Steelworkers urge bank regulators to delay OK of Wells Fargo merger," *Pueblo (Colorado) Chieftain*, August 20, 1998.

10. Karen Vigil, "OSHA hits steel mill for safety violations," *Pueblo (Colorado) Chieftain*, June 11, 1999, p. 8A.

11. "Steelworkers Call for Reinstatement of Public Hearings on Environmental Permits for Oregon Steel/CF&I Pueblo Mill," USWA news release, September 17, 1999.

12. Letter from Ernest Hernandez to William J. Moloney, Colorado Commissioner of Education, February 19, 1998.

13. "Somerville, Mass., Native Helps Build Teamsters' Strategy against Trucker," *Boston Globe*, October 30, 1999.

14. Zoning boards, in particular, play a surprisingly important role in some campaigns, most notably that of the UFCW against Wal-Mart. In this campaign, which centers on a claim that the company's growth threatens traditional communities and local merchants, the union challenges many of the company's planned new locations before local zoning bodies. See, for example, Kathy Mulady, "Council to Review Wal-Mart Deal," *Spokane XXX*, December 6, 1999; and "UFCW Ups the Ante In Las Vegas With the Wal-Mart War," UFCW news release, December 7, 1999.

15. These data, based on reports to the Federal Election Commission, were found at www.opensecrets.org/pubs/bigpicture2000/bli/bli_all.ihtml, December 13, 1999. Businesses gave considerably more money through their political action committees during the same cycle—$387.6 million—but divided this amount more equally between the parties, with Republicans receiving 59% and Democrats 41%. Nonlabor groups have been less committed to electoral initiatives. One exception, however, was the Sierra Club, which, in late 1999 during the presidential primary campaign, blanketed New Hampshire radio and television stations with advertisements attacking the environmental record of Texas Governor and Republican front-runner George W. Bush. "Sierra Club Takes Aim at Bush," Associated Press, November 30, 1999.

16. Frank Swoboda, "AFL–CIO Pledges to Win Back a Democratic House," *Washington Post*, October 12, 1999, p. A2.

17. *Contract Campaign Manual*, op. cit., p. 3:25.

18. Perry, op. cit., p. 190.

19. Jean P. Fisher, "Workers at Mercy seek union election: Speaker to monitor Sacramento labor effort," *Sacramento Bee*, November 16, 1999.

20. "An Open Letter to CF&I Chief Operating Officer Joe Corvin From Colorado Elected Officials," USWA handbill.

21. "Officials protest bank aid to Oregon Steel," *Pueblo (Colorado) Chieftain*, May 22, 1999.

22. "Workers Call on Oregon Steel to Remove Gag Order; Allow Workers to Testify Without Retaliation; Public Has Right to Know of Air Pollution, Safety Problems," USWA news release, December 17, 1999.

23. Letter from Governor Roy Romer to Joe Corvin, President of Oregon Steel, November 14, 1997.

24. Jeffrey M. Berry, "A Look At Liberalism's Transformation," *Washington Post*, July 11, 1999, p. B3.

25. John Schwartz, "6 Farmers in Class Action vs. Monsanto," *Washington Post*, December 15, 1999, p. E1.

26. David Barboza, "Monsanto Sued Over Use of Biotechnology in Developing Seeds," *The New York Times*, December 15, 1999.

27. *Bruce Pickett et al. V. Monsanto Company*, complaint filed December 14, 1999, U.S. District Court for the District of Columbia, passim.

28. Ibid., p. 4.

29. Scott Kilman, "Monsanto Faces Class-Action Suit Over Genetically Altered Crops," *The Wall Street Journal*, December 15, 1999.

30. David Barboza, "Monsanto and Pharmacia to Join, Creating a Pharmaceutical Giant," *The New York Times*, December 20, 1999.

31. Found at www.wal-martlitigation.com/front.html, March 1, 2000.

32. Ibid.

33. Arthur C. Gorlick, "Albertson's will settle overtime lawsuits," *Seattle Post-Intelligencer*, December 1, 1999.

34. The Supreme Court case in question was *Bill Johnson's Restaurants v. NLRB, 461 U.S. 731 (1983)*. The NLRB case was *BE&K Construction Co., 329 NLRB No. 68 (1999)*.

35. Jarol B. Manheim, *Corporate Campaign Communications: Union Attack Strategies* (Washington: Labor Policy Association, 1998), pp. 16–17.

36. Karen Charman, "Force Feeding Genetically Engineered Foods"; "Monsanto and Burson-Marsteller Hire a Consumer Organization"; and Karen Charman, "'Biotechnology Will Feed the World' and Other Myths"; all found online at www.prwatch.org/99-Q4 on December 14, 1999.

37. Maria Margaronis, "The Politics of Food: As Biotech Frankenfoods Are Stuffed Down Their Throats, Consumers Rebel," *The Nation*, December 27, 1999, found online at www.thenation.com/issue/991227/margonis.shtml, December 13, 1999.

38. See, for example, Schwartz, op. cit.; Barboza, op. cit.; and Kilman, op. cit.

39. Barboza, "Monsanto Sued ...," op. cit.

14

Telling the Public What It Thinks

Whether it is waged by organized labor or some other advocacy group, the most vital component of any corporate campaign is the planning and implementation of an effective communication strategy. The legal, legislative, regulatory, and other aspects of the campaign are important, but it is the communication strategy that binds these various constituent elements into a unified whole, drives their development, and ultimately carries the campaign to its target audiences, where it will either succeed or fail.

As noted in Chapter 1, the communication strategies employed in corporate campaigns are direct descendants of the techniques developed over the last half century by political marketers—those who manage campaigns for political candidates and issues. The appeal to emotion rather than reason, the reliance on graphic visual imagery, the intense and unyielding negativity of the attack—these and other far more subtle aspects of the typical corporate campaign have all been developed, tested, and refined in the electoral and policy arenas. But when these techniques migrated to the realm of labor–management relations, they landed on especially fertile ground. For here were found virtually none of the constraints that had long held campaign strategists in check—the limits on resources and time with which to operate, the reporting requirements and generally high level of media and public scrutiny, the prohibition on masking one's true identity through surrogates, and the *de facto* boundary between the communication campaign and other dimensions of advocacy. In the land of the corporate campaign, strategy was truly king—free to take the unions and other advocates wherever it might lead. From the perspective of communication strategy, then, much of the history of the corporate campaign has revolved around the optimization of the tools and techniques of persuasion.

THE STRATEGIC OBJECTIVE OF CORPORATE CAMPAIGN COMMUNICATION

Virtually all campaign events—boycotts, demonstrations, letter-writing or telephone campaigns, legal filings, regulatory initiatives, scheduling of legislative hearings, staged crises, and the like—are designed and implemented in large measure because of their expected communication effects. Where actions or events occur for other reasons, they are invariably packaged and manipulated insofar as possible for their maximum communication value. It is the natural interplay between events and communication that literally defines the public face of the corporate campaign.

Although the particular tactics employed by the campaigners are varied and unpredictable, from a communication perspective, the underlying strategic objective of the corporate campaign is consistent and predictable—undermine the image of the target company among key audiences using the media as primary agents of change. One way to conceptualize this objective is summarized in Fig. 14.1, which is drawn from a more elaborate model of strategic communication developed elsewhere.[2] Using the amount of media visibility and the balance between favorable and unfavorable coverage as its key dimensions, the figure identifies four distinct configurations of a target company's media image, any one of which might be in place at a given point in time. Each configuration represents a more or less different situation with respect to what a corporate campaign can and should seek to accomplish to weaken its target, and each is accompanied by a more or less unique set of tactics for achieving this. But, as the arrows in the figure indicate, in each instance, the ultimate communication objective is to raise both the visibility and negativity of the company's image.

Indeed, it is the guiding principle of many corporate campaigns that the image of the target company should be systematically moved—either by blunt force or by more subtle, long-term persuasion—from wherever it resides at a given moment to a point as far north and west in the diagram as possible. There it should be held captive, whatever the cost. Food Lion comes to

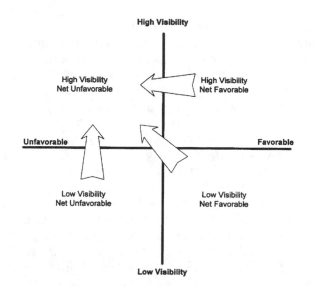

FIG. 14.1. Image-management objective of the corporate campaign.

be associated in the media and the public mind with rotten meat, Mitsubishi with sexual harassment, Nike with sweatshops, Wal-Mart with urban sprawl and the destruction of historic and small-town America, the California strawberry growers with unsanitary working conditions, the health care industry with profiteering at the expense of patient care, and so forth. Under the pressure of a massive, consistent, and intense communication campaign, such images come literally to define a given company in the public mind: They become the socially constructed corporate reality to which we alluded earlier in this volume. This is a reality without nuance or direct experiential referents, and it may be a reality that is grounded in some base of fair and objective truth only at the margins if at all. It is immensely difficult for companies to persevere under the type of pressure that such an effort, if successful, can generate. Yielding to the demands of the union or other antagonist emerges as a relatively more attractive option.

In chapter 9, we examined the power structure analysis employed by campaign protagonists, the essence of which is to identify the relative vulnerabilities of each key stakeholder relationship on which the success of a target company depends. Although it has other purposes, the primary objective of this research is to support the communication strategy that underlies the campaign. In essence, each stakeholder group is a prospective audience, and each audience is more or less susceptible to persuasion (to the view that the company must change its behavior in some way) and mobilization (to act in a manner designed to force or facilitate change). The assessment of that differential susceptibility—and of the themes, messages, and media that can best exploit it—is the heart and soul of power structure analysis. Part of the attack on a company's power is real and direct (e.g., unions removing their funds from banks that lend to the company). But, because the unions lack the strength to confront companies effectively one on one, much more of the attack is directed at changing the *perceptions* of reality held by the key stakeholders so that they are motivated to pressure the company while acting in what they believe to be their own best interests. This is accomplished by manipulating the image of the company in the media that reach the various stakeholder groups.

Not all of these stakeholder groups, of course, will hold the same initial image of a given company. Customers may be more or less favorably inclined than investors, employees more or less supportive than the public, bankers more or less satisfied with the company's performance than shareholders, environmentalists more or less satisfied than regulators, and so forth. These differentials may be attributable to differing information about the company, differing criteria on which judgments are based, differing expectations regarding performance or appropriate behaviors, or a host of other factors. From the perspective of the company's antagonists, each of these groups can be targeted more or less independently based on its own profile of needs and perceptions as they relate to the company. This is particularly true where the means exist to *narrowcast* (target) the campaign messages—to deliver them in such a way that what is said to one audience is not overheard by the others. At the extremes, this is the difference between conveying a message on the CBS Evening News where everyone will have at least the potential to receive it (literally broadcasting), on the one hand, or delivering it through targeted direct mail, on the other. One of the ways in which corporate campaigns have become more sophisticated over the years is in their increasing use of narrowly targeted media for specialized communication. In particular, the expanding use of the Internet and the World Wide Web, which we treat in more detail in the next chapter, is emblematic of this trend.

Figure 14.2 illustrates the diversity of prospective campaign audiences. The point here is that the same dynamic we described in analyzing Fig. 14.1 operates more or less independently for each separate constituency. Because of the differing interests of these respective audiences, the same message can have different effects as it lands among varied stakeholder groups. For example, the news that a company is engaging in cost-cutting or downsizing might appeal strongly and positively to the financial community, yet generate a sense among the general public that the company is callous and uncaring, producing a negative image shift there. The same information might infuriate the company's employees, yet have no influence at all on yet another constituency, such as regulators.

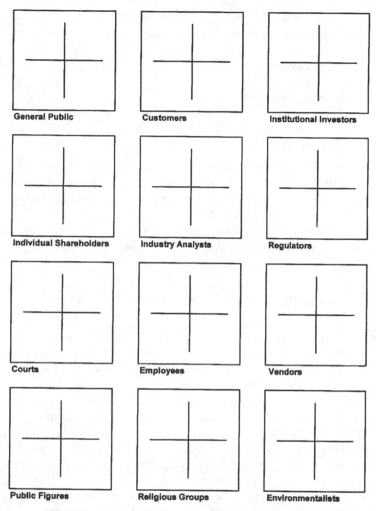

FIG. 14.2. Audiences for corporate campaign messages.

Effective campaign communication strategy, then, takes the diversity of audiences into account in two ways. First, it shapes messages that are likely to reach a number of different audiences to be broadly compatible with the general objectives of influence across as many of these groupings as possible. Second, it shapes messages that are likely to reach narrower, selected audiences to appeal to the unique perspective or interests of each. These latter messages are then delivered not through the mass media, but through other channels, such as industry newsletters or direct mail, that are likely to reach their intended constituencies with minimal spillover to other groups. In the words of one union corporate campaign manual:

There are three things to consider when framing an issue:

1. The audience

2. The audience, and

3. The audience.

You should frame your issue in a way that appeals specifically to the person or organization whose support you are seeking. This means that you may present or frame the issue differently for different people or groups. For example, if the issue is the closing of a billing office in a small town, the issue for the membership is job security. But if you are seeking the support of the American Association of Retired Persons, perhaps you might additionally frame the issue as one of access....[3]

FROM THEORY TO THEMATIC

The first of these objectives, appealing to a significant cross-section of stakeholder groups, is typically accomplished through the use of broad themes that are subject to multiple interpretation. Perhaps the best example of this is found in the health care industry campaign, where, for example, the corporate greed theme appeals to patients and their families at one level and to the employees the unions are trying to organize at quite another. However, this same theme illustrates the limitations that are imposed on broadcast, or multi-audience, messages. Profit-driven behaviors that may not play well on Main Street, for example, may play exceptionally well on Wall Street.

As this example suggests, it is generally easier to broadcast messages than to narrowcast them, and there is always a risk that a message intended for one audience will leak over to another perhaps with adverse consequences for the campaign. Partly for this reason, the unions and other corporate antagonists have adopted the practice of framing the corporate campaign in terms of a small number of broadly appealing themes and using their more targeted communications, such as white papers distributed to shareholders or analysts, to illustrate or develop these same themes. The importance of continuity and simplicity is suggested in this advice proffered by the SEIU through its campaign manual:

To support other pressure tactics and counteract management's propaganda, your media efforts must get across three basic messages:

1. What we are asking for is fair.

2. Management can afford what we are asking.

3. What we want is also good for the community.[4]

Central to this effort is one overarching objective of the communications campaign discussed earlier—to define and then claim the moral high ground, in effect, to define the "truth" about the campaign as it is to be understood by the target audiences. The essential idea here is to set the terms of the public debate that is about to ensue over the motives, actions, and even the fundamental legitimacy of the target company. Once an antagonist has successfully convinced members of one or more audiences as to what criteria they must employ to render judgment about the company—and, more specifically, has convinced those audiences that the criteria in question are precisely those on which the company's position is least defensible—the outcome of the battle for hearts and minds has largely been settled. Absent a major tactical blunder—and those do occur—everything else is mere detail.

This task is accomplished through the construction of a simple morality play in which the evil company is confronted by its good-hearted but weaker adversary. Health care professionals are standing up for the rights of patients, who are defenseless against an uncaring industry. That they should also be campaigning for more power in the workplace, higher levels of staffing and higher rates of compensation is incidental. The UFCW is protecting the public against unsanitary practices and discrimination in the supermarket industry. That these practices seem to be commonplace only at the nonunion companies in this industry—Albertson's, Food Lion, Publix—is merely incidental. In these and many other instances, the objective of the campaign is to construct and promulgate a narrative that so embarrasses the targeted stakeholder groups about being associated with an evil company that they—its best and greatest friends—pressure it to change its ways. Shareholders ask embarrassing questions at the annual meeting, banks withdraw from important lending consortia, analysts turn bearish on the company's stock, and the company starts its slide down the slippery slope.

In pursuing this strategy, the campaign protagonists are able to exploit two basic advantages. First, as we noted, corporations in the United States and elsewhere do not enjoy a high level of public trust and respect—a fact that helps make them vulnerable to corporate campaigns in the first place. One consequence of this low public standing is that it creates an opportunity for the campaign to go negative even as it is defining the high ground.

In particular, two of the audiences that play essential roles in almost every campaign—journalists and the general public (cum customers, cum shareholders, cum employees)—are predisposed from the outset to accept and respond to negative messages about any given company. This makes the task of attacking a target company much easier. The antagonist need only attach specific corporate names and images to preexisting negative feelings, rather than having to begin undermining a target company's image from scratch.

Second, corporate campaign strategists are further aided by the growing inventory of current and past corporate campaigns. That is the case because, for all their differences, virtually all corporate campaigns share a common theme—an emphasis on the evils of large, impersonal corporations. Whether it is through their wanton disregard for the rights or safety of workers at home or abroad, for consumers, for the environment, or for any other victim, corporations are universally portrayed in corporate campaigns as entirely self-interested. This unifying theme finds its most comprehensive embodiment in the notion, often made explicit in precisely these terms, that corporations are outlaws that need to be brought to social, economic, and political justice.

One need not take such a broad view to find other cross-target effects that are routinely exploited by the campaigners. Fill in the blanks. As the public becomes convinced that one (a) supermarket chain, restaurant chain, nursing home chain, trucking company, retailer, chemical manufacturer, tire company, telephone company, or steel mill tries to (b) gouge excessive profits, disregard public safety, ignore fundamental human rights, exploit its workers, engage in racist practices, or act contrary to the interests of the nation and its people by (c) selling outdated products, preparing food in unsanitary conditions, allowing bedsores to fester, operating unsafe equipment, forcing employees to work overtime without pay, or destroying the environment ... is it not reasonable for that same public to believe that others in the same industry are equally guilty? Prior repetition of the same themes across corporate campaigns in a single industry, or in thematically related industries, also provides campaigners with a pre-existing base of media and public perception that they routinely exploit.

COMMUNICATION AS A COMPONENT OF OVERALL CAMPAIGN STRATEGY

To understand the function of communication strategy in the corporate campaign, it is useful to return once again to the power structure analysis employed by campaigners since the earliest days, but this time with a twist. For, even if they are of equivalent interest to the campaigners in some ways, various stakeholders typically play specialized and unique roles in the corporate campaign—roles that derive from their potential contribution to the underlying communication strategy. The most important of these roles are illustrated in Fig. 14.3.

The key to the figure lies in understanding that a corporate campaign is composed of various bands of activities and objectives, all of them grounded in the core strategies described in detail throughout this book. At the center of the campaign (lower left in the figure) is the union or other advocacy group that has initiated the attack. At the extreme is the target company or, more precisely, the particular policies or actions of that company that the initiator is attempting to change—organizing the workforce, limiting the outsourcing of jobs, imposing "green" practices, or the like. In between lie a series of bands that denote specific roles to be played in the influence process.

The first of these consists of various surrogates, allies, and insiders whose function is to legitimize the campaign, and especially any allegations of immoral behavior on the part of the target company. The need for this function arises, as we have noted, from the fact that unions, in particular, are not widely popular or respected among the public (in its various manifestations), and from the related but independent fact that the evident self-interest of a union in certain outcomes can, in and of itself, undermine a campaign's appeal to widely held public values. That need is met in different ways by these various legitimizing agents.

Religious leaders and groups, for example, simply by virtue of their participation, symbolize the campaign's holding of the moral high ground, while support from environmentalists, civil or human rights activists, consumer groups, and the like conveys similar, but more specialized messages. We discussed this process at some length earlier in this book. Pro-union insiders, either current or former, are useful as activists (e.g., in conducting inside games), but also to affix to campaign allegations the aura of apparent authority that comes with their position. In the Teamsters campaign against Overnite Transportation, for example, much was made of a former manager for the company who "confirmed" the union's allegations of unfair labor practices.[5] More generally, so-called *whistleblowers* are routinely employed to validate the antagonists' claims. Surrogates, such as Consumers United with Employees, the group created by the UFCW in the course of its campaign against Food Lion, are the least useful of these legitimizing agents because they have no independent existence of their own and are solely dependent on the public-regarding impression created by their names for their impact. Even these "groups" can be effective until their origins are revealed, although at that point they can become sources of embarrassment—precisely the sort of tactical blunder that can set back a campaign.

In the second band out from the center are found the mediating agents of the campaign, those whose function is to *launder* the campaign (in the sense

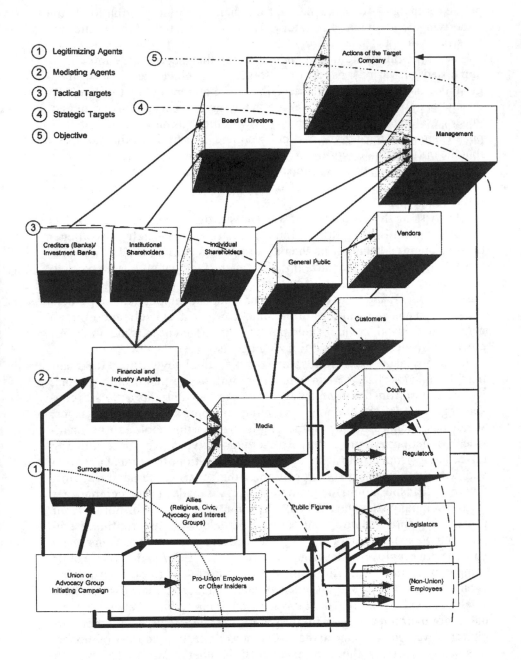

1. Legitimizing Agents
2. Mediating Agents
3. Tactical Targets
4. Strategic Targets
5. Objective

Actions of the Target Company

Board of Directors

Management

Creditors (Banks)/ Investment Banks

Institutional Shareholders

Individual Shareholders

General Public

Vendors

Customers

Financial and Industry Analysts

Courts

Media

Regulators

Surrogates

Allies (Religious, Civic, Advocacy and Interest Groups)

Public Figures

Legislators

Union or Advocacy Group Initiating Campaign

Pro-Union Employees or Other Insiders

(Non-Union) Employees

FIG. 14.3.   Communication in the context of campaign strategy.

that these agents are not working in the interests of the union or other advocacy group per se, but that they nevertheless convey its messages) and broaden their distribution. With the exception of those engaged in social-responsibility investing, for example, financial analysts could hardly be said to favor the kinds of actions that unions or activists typically attempt to impose on corporations if only because these actions tend to raise costs and lower profits. Yet acting in their own interests and those of their clients, these same analysts will feel obligated to pass along any concerns they may have about the financial stability and business prospects of companies that they follow. In doing so, of course, they increase the pressure on the company—pressure that can be stepped up still further if the campaign chooses to publicize the analysts' reservations. In the Titan International campaign, for example, after Moody's Investors Service, which publishes widely respected ratings of corporate debt instruments, lowered its rating of Titan's notes and lines of credit, the Steelworkers trumpeted the reduction under the banner, "Moody's Slashes Titan Ratings."[6]

Similarly, as we have argued, journalists may have somewhat greater sympathy for the architects of a given campaign, but their professional function is to detect, define, and convey the news. Because most of the events associated with a corporate campaign are *designed* to be news, they, too, while pursuing their own independent objectives, serve the interests of the campaigners, and their reach is especially substantial.

Finally, public figures also play a mediating role in some corporate campaigns. This may generally take either of two forms. The first includes local or national politicians or other prominent figures, such as Jesse Jackson, who adopt the objectives of the corporate campaign for their own political purposes and add their personal prestige and influence to the effort. The second includes celebrity endorsers or others similarly associated with a target company—Candice Bergen with Sprint, Kathie Lee Gifford with Wal-Mart, and Michael Jordan with Nike—who are targeted in their own right in the hope that they will be sufficiently embarrassed by the unwanted publicity to turn on their corporate benefactors.

From the perspective of a corporate campaign strategist, three characteristics give the news media special importance as mediating agents. The first characteristic is credibility. Most audiences make a clear distinction between news and propaganda—perhaps a clearer distinction than is warranted. Journalists, and especially local journalists with visible ties to the community, are generally liked, trusted, and believed much more than are either corporations or unions and their allies. People actually seek out the journalists' words and pictures and pay, directly or indirectly, to receive them. The campaign that can harness the news as the vehicle for its themes and messages gains a share of the credibility of the news itself, and is advantaged.

Second, the corporate campaign has a story to tell, and the news media have an institutional interest in telling stories.[7] Indeed, they are organized for this very purpose—to spend money and devote staff time to research and writing. To the extent that they do this independently, they may uncover facts of value to the corporate campaigners. To the extent that they can be managed or encouraged to do it on stories that relate to campaign themes—such as the major series of articles on the plight of poultry workers and the environmental threat posed by the poultry industry published in *The Washington Post* in 1999 during the course of the UFCW's organizing campaign[8]—they add their resources and prestige, wittingly or unwittingly, to those of the corporate antagonists. The process was well described from labor's perspective in the IUD's campaign manual:

> The union should shape the message that it wants to convey, and work to see that it comes across....
>
> The [union] should initiate dialogue with reporters and make sure that they have a complete understanding of the issues involved and the union's position. It may require several "background" discussions with reporters before the union's position filters into news reports. It is in the union's best interests to keep the dispute in the news.[9]

Finally, most journalists are strongly skeptical of corporations and business in general, which they see as self-interested institutions inclined to work against the public interest. Indeed, such skepticism is actually embodied in the journalistic code of ethics, which calls on them to "give voice to the voiceless" and "be vigilant ... about holding those with power accountable."[10] The point is not that there is anything inherently wrong with such a perspective, but only that it is widely held and strongly reinforced. It is also a perspective that, in the context of a corporate campaign, can be readily exploited.

In the third band are the tactical targets of the campaign—those groups that are most noteworthy not for their ability to mobilize others, but for the pressure they can exert directly on the company through their respective general relationships with it. The idea here is to convince the targeted groups that the company has significant failings, and then energize them to take those up with the company's board or management by acting out their normal roles as shareholders, customers, regulators, and the like. The Steelworkers boycott of Wells Fargo Bank to pressure Oregon Steel, the SEIU's mobilization of numerous regulatory agencies to pressure Sutter Health, and HERE's recruitment of Investor Shareholder Services to lead the opposition to a Marriott stock plan are but a few cases in point.

The fourth band, which we have designated strategic targets, comprises the Board of Directors of the target company and its management—senior, mid-level, and operational alike. Collectively, these groups constitute the company, and it is they who will determine its policies and practices. The corporate campaign is designed to generate the maximum possible discomfort on these key corporate decision makers even to the point of picketing outside their homes to raise the temperature. Think of the classic child's experiment with sunlight, lens, and paper. If the union or other antagonist is the source of the heat and light and the key stakeholders the lens through which both are projected, then the directors and management of the company are the paper on which the light and heat are focused. The assumption is that they will cool the action before being consumed by flames.

Finally, the figure portrays the actions of the target company. These are the product of an interplay between the board and senior management—an interplay that can take such diverse forms as the resignation of board members (e.g., a common objective of campaigns run by Ray Rogers), replacement of the CEO or other top personnel, development of a determination to resist the pressure at almost any cost, or adoption of fundamental changes in corporate policy, to name but four possible outcomes.

CONCLUDING COMMENT

From this analysis, it should be clear not only that communication is an essential element of the corporate campaign, but that the overall strategy of the campaign is inextricably interwoven with the communication strategy in particular. In point of fact, this takes us back to our definition of the corporate campaign, which had two distinctive components: the selection of intermediate targets of influence based on an analysis of the power structure underlying the company against which the campaign was to be waged, and the strategic use of communication to implement the attack. At this point, and particularly in Fig. 14.3, we can see how these elements interact and reinforce one another to the detriment of the company in the crosshairs.

Communication is not always conducted through the mass media nor is it always focused on the "education" and mobilization of the general public alone. To the contrary, a significant proportion of campaign-related communication is directed at such infrastructure-building tasks as raising funds, communicating objectives or assignments to internal campaign audiences, or simply boosting morale, to name but three. More and more, this is accomplished through the so-called *new media*, those that rely on the Internet—and most often on the subset of the Internet known as the World Wide Web—to reach their intended audiences. The Internet and the Web provide opportunities for both the broadcasting and the narrowcasting, or targeting, of messages, and the transmission of data and multimedia materials, all with a measure of interactivity that is absent in more traditional media. In the following chapter, we explore in some detail the increasing, and increasingly sophisticated, use of these electronic media as a component of the corporate campaign.

ENDNOTES

1. Substantial portions of this chapter are based on or drawn from two earlier publications, Jarol B. Manheim, *Corporate Campaign Communication: Union Attack Strategies* (Washington: Labor Policy Association, 1998), and Jarol B. Manheim, *Corporate Campaign Communication: Strategic Response* (Washington: Labor Policy Association, 1998).
2. Jarol B. Manheim, "A Model of Agenda Dynamics," in Margaret L. McLaughlin, ed., *Communication Yearbook* 10 (Beverly Hills: Sage, 1987), pp. 499–516; and Jarol B. Manheim, *Strategic Public Diplomacy and American Foreign Policy: The Evolution of Influence* (New York: Oxford University Press, 1994), pp. 125–157.
3. *Mobilizing for the 90s*, second edition (Washington: Communications Workers of America, 1993), pp. 45–46.
4. *Contract Campaign Manual* (Washington: Service Employees International Union, ND), pp. 3:57-3:58.
5. Steven Greenhouse, "Manager Fired by Company Supports Teamsters on Strike," *The New York Times*, October 27, 1999; and "Teamsters Say: Overnite's Berlin Wall Cracks, Memphis Operations Manager Steps Forward, Offers 'Smoking Gun' Evidence of Overnite Conspiracy to Target Union Activists and Violate Workers' Rights," Teamsters news release, October 26, 1999.
6. "Moody's Slashes Titan Rations: Action Follows Release of Disastrous Financial Statement," *Solidarity News*, Number 72, USWA, March 1, 2000.
7. On this point see W. Lance Bennett, *News: The Politics of Illusion*, Third Edition (New York: Longman, 1996), pp. 157–159.
8. The centerpiece of the series with respect to labor issues *per se* was Lena H. Sun and Gabriel Escobar, "On Chicken's Front Line," *The Washington Post*, November 28, 1999, pp. A1, passim.
9. *Developing New Tactics: Winning with Coordinated Campaigns* (Washington, Industrial Union Department, AFL-CIO, 1985), p. 5.
10. *Code of Ethics*, Society of Professional Journalists.

15

WEAVING A WEB, WORLDWIDE

One of the main themes of this book has been the willingness of the labor movement to innovate or, perhaps more properly, the recognition among key labor leaders that, absent innovation, their movement would decay beyond salvation. For the most part, we have centered our discussion of that theme on the development and adoption of new social technologies—those of systematic social research, strategic communication, and the corporate campaign. However, we would be greatly remiss were we not to recognize as well the changes that have occurred in labor's use of new information technologies, most notably the personal computer and the Internet, both of which came into being during the same period. The AFL–CIO and the unions were relatively slow to recognize the potential impact on organizing and other activities of these lifestyle-changing technologies, slower in fact than some of the other advocacy groups whose activities we have discussed.

By the end of the 1990s, however, all of these groups had fully integrated the new technologies into their daily operations. More to the present point, all had begun to exploit the potential of these technologies—and especially the Internet—in carrying forward their corporate campaigns. By the end of 1999—a time point symbolized by the so-called Battle in Seattle, which is to say, the demonstrations called to protest the actions of the World Trade Organization (WTO)—this *cybercampaigning* had been refined to a fine art.

LABOR AND THE INTERNET

As Arthur Shostak, a labor educator who serves on the faculty of the Meany Center, has noted, it was not until 1996 that the AFL–CIO held its first meeting to discuss ways the Internet might be put to service in the labor movement. Over the next 2 years, the federation held two meetings of information technology officers and conducted a survey of the ways its affiliated unions employed these capabilities. Symbolic of this effort, the federation also invested $20 million in rewiring its own headquarters building with a fiber optic LAN system capable of handling streaming video and other advanced technologies.[1] Shostak advocates a system in which the unions employ information technologies to fulfill such functions as surveying members to ascertain their wants and needs, as well as their preferences among options that might be before the union; using a homepage to keep members informed about developments and using e-mail or interactivity to receive feedback from the rank and file; and making the union's officers and staff available to the members through e-mail.[2] A number of unions are moving toward this model.

However, there are other uses of the Internet that the unions are exploiting with increasing effectiveness as well. These include a number of functions associated with organizing in general, and more specifically with the corporate campaign. For example, the technology makes information gathering and planning faster and easier, and, in some cases, even permits unions to do things they could not previously undertake. Consider this hypothetical description of starting an organizing drive.

> Employees of Company XYZ have come to me ... for help in organizing their workplace. They even bring me a list of employee names to help me get started.

> The company is [publicly traded], so from Hoovers Online (www.hoovers.com), an Internet site with hundreds of companies listed, I find the names of the CEO, the board of directors, last year's gross sales numbers, employee growth figures, and even the company's Web site address. I visit the company's Web site and find more information....

> Since I already have the employee names, I again turn to my computer and go to People Search (www.cedar.buffalo.edu/AdServ/person-serach.html), an online people locator, to find and download the addresses and phone numbers of all plant employees. Next I access Mapquest (www.mapquest.com), an online map ser-

vice, to download maps of those addresses. Each map not only shows the street where my organizing target lives, but a star is placed where his house should be. I divide my organizing committee up and hand each of them a list of names, complete with phone numbers, addresses, and even maps for house calls. I do all this without leaving my office and at no cost.

Then, as the campaign progresses, my Web master is constantly updating our Web site.... Leaflets with our Web site address are passed out, and our Web page becomes the primary place for the passing of information.[3]

These precise skills are taught in seminars within individual unions, but also at the Meany Center. A week-long course on "Internet for Union Activists" at the Silver Spring campus in December 1999, for example, focused on using the Internet to raise visibility, stimulate activism, research employers and industries, and generally build an information infrastructure at the level of local unions and Central Labor Councils.[4] For those unable to attend such a session, the AFSCME has e-published a manual on its own Web site entitled *Putting Your Union on the Web: A "How To" Manual for Activists*. This is an exceptionally detailed guide to Web tools and skills that covers everything from finding an Internet service provider to practica in hypertext markup language (HTML—the programming language of the Web) and graphics design.[5]

In 1990 or 1991,[6] the AFL–CIO created an Internet service called LaborNet to facilitate the exchange of information among activists and affiliates. In 1992, the service moved to CompuServe and then later, with the advent of the World Wide Web, to a host site maintained by the Institute for Global Communications (IGC). This is a Tides Center project that provides infrastructure and other support for a variety of progressive organizations and causes. In November 1999, LaborNet moved to its own independent Web site, although IGC maintained a members-only discussion group on labor issues.[7]

LaborNet serves as a clearinghouse for electronic action alerts, which are calls to action dispatched by e-mail or other means to activists around the nation and, with the advent of the Web, literally around the world, and also for news and other articles from the media and other labor-based discussion groups and Internet sites. The network also offers features on events or campaigns of interest to the labor movement, as well as links to labor studies programs, lists of strikes, and a geographically indexed clearinghouse for jobs with labor organizations. Of most interest in the current context is a set of links to ongoing corporate campaigns and organizing drives.[8]

In addition to LaborNet and a growing host of other sites dedicated to serving the labor movement generally, almost every international union, and a rapidly increasing number of local unions, maintain a presence on the Web, and there are specialized sites that serve segments of workers such as one established for retail workers by several individuals who were involved in organizing drives at Borders Books and Barnes & Noble.[9] Unions are also employing e-mail as an organizing tool. In one instance, for example, a union organizer dispatched a series of messages to 2,000 Pratt & Whitney engineers using the company's internal e-mail addresses.[10] Regardless of whether the cyber *union* envisioned by Shostak is in place today, it is clear that the cyber *labor movement* is.[11]

UNIONS, THE INTERNET, AND THE CORPORATE CAMPAIGN

Although these general uses of the new information technologies are interesting, the application of these technologies to the conduct of the corporate campaign is more interesting still. It is increasingly the case that e-mails, Web sites (both public and restricted), public electronic forums, and other computer-based services are being fully integrated into campaign communication strategies and, in some instances, constitute perhaps the greatest part of the campaign. In effect, we are seeing the emergence of the virtual corporate campaign—one built on the fact that, as more and more corporate executives, board members, investors and members of other key stakeholder groups come to operate routinely in the virtual environment of the Internet, e-mails and Web sites come to define their respective realities much as did the traditional mass media in the past. Campaigns that are widely disseminated and demonstrate apparently broad support in this electronic world, then, will be capable of generating significant pressure on target companies. As these virtual attacks are blended with real-world demonstrations, boycotts, strikes, and other more traditional activities, their effect will be enhanced still further. What was once, for a brief period, a sort of underground venue for organizing scattered protests will emerge as an important source of leverage for the corporate campaign. The 1999 anti-WTO protest in Seattle is a case in point: The event was massively recruited and advertised on the Internet for months in advance of the meetings, with the size and vehemence of the crowds and the collapse of the talks serving to validate the effort.[12] In the period since, the organizers have acted aggressively, again in large measure through the Internet, to press what they perceive as their advantage, including mobilizing support for the follow-up demonstrations at the April 2000 Washington meetings of the International Monetary Fund and the World Bank. In this latter instance, two Web sites in particular served as loci for presenting a perspective on the issues and for planning and organizing events.[13]

In addition to the types of research and organizing capabilities we have already discussed, unions employ information technologies in corporate campaigns in several ways. For example, in its effort to organize hotel workers in California, the Hotel Employees and Restaurant Employees International Union (HERE) maintains a "Travel Advisory" Web page on which it posts the names of hotels where visitors can expect to encounter disruptions. The union warns that:

> A handful of California hotels are currently the sites of major labor disputes and frequent demonstrations. Whether you are a traveler, or a travel agent, a meeting or wedding planner, it's important for you to know the hotels where you or your clients will be faced with a noisy, uncomfortable situation.[14]

The site also provides a geographically indexed listing of hotels with unionized workforces where such discomfiture can be avoided.

Other largely informational sites are also commonplace. As noted in an earlier chapter, for example, in 1998, a consortium of 14 unions representing General Electric workers formed what they term the *Coordinated Bargaining Committee* to present the company with a unified front when contract bargaining took place in 2000. The consortium then established a Web site devoted to disseminating negative information about the company. A members-only section—an increasingly common component of such sites—was designed to keep members of the various unions apprised of both strategy and developments.[15]

In January 2000, the SEIU launched what may have been the first "virtual leaflet" to be employed in a corporate campaign in conjunction with its organizing drive against AHL Services/Argenbright Security. This interactive banner advertisement was displayed in three areas of the Yahoo! Web site. Whenever a user typed certain terms (e.g., *AHL Services* or *fulfillment* [one of the company's business specialties]) into the Yahoo! search engine, the banner would be displayed. Clicking on the banner took the user to a Web site—www.unfulfilled.com—that provided information critical of the company's business practices and outlined the ongoing labor dispute.[16] Once Yahoo! realized the nature of these advertisements, it canceled the campaign, setting off a dispute of its own with the union.[17]

As one might expect, Web-based attacks are especially common and sophisticated in the high-technology industries. Together with health care, which we have previously discussed, these industries and companies offer the largest and most concentrated pools of available, nonunion workers who might be targeted in organizing campaigns. Where health care organizing is dominated by the SEIU, the organizing of high-tech workers is dominated by the CWA. Two companies in particular—Microsoft and IBM—have attracted the union's attention, and both have seen similar Web-based activity as part of their respective organizing efforts.

At Microsoft, as noted in chapter 7, a number of relatively distinct campaigns have been underway, one of which is the work of the CWA through a local organization known as the Washington Alliance of Technology Workers (WashTech). Initially WashTech has set out to organize the several thousand temporary workers (e.g., programmers and product testers) on whom Microsoft has depended to staff such short-term projects as product updates. These workers are actually employed by staffing agencies who, in effect, lease them to Microsoft and other companies on a project-by-project basis. The union hopes to recruit what it calls these *permatemps* as a wedge to gain access to the company's permanent workforce.

Judging from the extensive resources that were clearly committed to it between 1998 and 1999, the WashTech Web site was a central component of this effort. This, of course, is easily understandable once one considers that all of the workers in question are highly computer literate. At this writing, the Web site had published a number of internal company documents, even including the results of employee surveys, as well as a wide variety of informational and educational items designed to mobilize the targeted population of workers. WashTech also offered updates on labor-related litigation involving Microsoft and appeared to be soliciting potential claims for additional future class action lawsuits. In addition, through its Web site, the group conducted its own large-scale survey of job satisfaction among temporary workers, the results of which were posted. In all, the site contained the equivalent of several hundred pages of information designed to state the union's case in a way that appealed to the workers it sought to organize.[18]

At IBM, where organizing efforts did not begin in earnest until the fall of 1999, the site was less fully developed by year's end, but was following a similar pattern. Here the CWA adopted the local name of Alliance@IBM, and the union assumed a rather higher profile. At IBM, the initial organizing issue was not temporary workers, but a proposed change in the pension program for mid-career full-time employees that stirred considerable resentment and may have broken a psychological bond of trust between the company and its employees. Both the theme of distrust and the target audience are evident in the opening words of the group's self-description.

> Alliance@IBM is made up of career-minded IBM employees who are concerned about our future. We are concerned about recent actions which undermined the retirement security of tens of thousands of IBM's most devoted employees.... We are committed to IBM's success, but we are also stakeholders in IBM and we deserve a voice in shaping policies that affect our pensions, healthcare benefits and livelihood.[19]

Indeed, where temporary workers are intended to provide the wedge at Microsoft, the union is apparently encountering some resistance to even including them in its efforts at IBM. Among a listing of a dozen "myths and realities" about the Alliance posted on its Web site, for example, is "Myth #5: We don't want 'temps' in our union." The answer, suggests the union, is that the positions of permanent workers will be threatened unless and until the lot of temporary workers is improved to the point where there is no incentive to bring them in.[20]

Finally, there is a group known as FACE Intel, an acronym for Former and Current Employees of Intel, the chip manufacturer. FACE Intel does not claim to be a union nor is there evidence that it is affiliated with a union or otherwise engaged in organizing. However, the group, which at year-end 1999 claimed approximately 350 members (a figure disputed by the company), has launched a vehement Web-based attack on Intel built in large measure around the case of its founder and spokesperson, Ken Hamidi.[21] Hamidi is a former Intel employee who was dismissed from his job in 1995 after a disability leave and who sent e-mail messages to more than 30,000 Intel employees at their company e-mail addresses in six waves between 1996 and 1998 detailing what he regarded as Intel's abusive and discriminatory employment practices. The company asked him to stop, but he refused; he also managed to continue his distributions despite Intel's efforts to block them. Intel sued Hamidi and, in April 1999, a California state judge granted the company summary judgment in the case.[22] Hamidi then resorted to an older technology, delivering 40,000 printed messages to the company's headquarters by horse and buggy.[23]

Although this particular endeavor does not meet our definition of a corporate campaign, the FACE Intel Web site, which is replete with news, photos, events, organizing messages, and the like, constitutes a primer for the use of the Web in such campaigns,. Of particular note is the compilation of more than 60 labor lawsuits that have been filed against the company in various state and federal courts.[24] When one realizes that one of the primary audiences for campaign-related Web sites is composed of journalists to whom campaign-related stories have been pitched or who are engaged in enterprise reporting of their own, the presence of such compilations, which can be easily verified, provides a form of external validation for the campaign and can be a source of campaign-related news.

Web sites have begun to demonstrate added value in more traditional labor settings as well, most notably during a strike. When members of an independent union of engineers at Boeing walked out in February and March 2000, for example, they established a network of unofficial Web sites to supplement their official union site. These included such materials as personal journals, cartoons, and satirical portrayals of top company managers, and one site even displayed the names of alleged "scabs" against a black background with a warning that their actions would be long remembered.[25]

Nor are unions and other adversarial employee groups limited to establishing and maintaining their own Web sites to carry forward a virtual campaign. The Web is replete with opportunities to employ Usenet (chat) groups and other public venues to spread the campaign message. One popular forum for such activity is the set of financial bulletin boards maintained by the Internet company Yahoo!. These postings are designed for shareholders or other stakeholders to exchange views on a given company's performance or prospects. On occasion, they have been taken over, or at least substantially exploited, by unions engaged in corporate campaigns.

A case in point is the Yahoo! bulletin board for Oregon Steel Mills. Since the Steelworkers launched their campaign against the company, this site has been inundated with messages from supporters of the union attacking both the Oregon Steel management and the permanent replacement workers ("scabs") the company hired to replace striking union members.[26] We detailed some of the more egregious of these messages in chapter 11 in our discussion of the use of ridicule as a component of the inside game. Here the point is that these same messages not only reach corporate insiders, where their aim is to intimidate and undermine morale, but also reach outside audiences—in this case, analysts and shareholders who may well take away a somewhat different message (e.g., that this or some other target is not a stable company). Such a message can easily undermine the price of the target company's stock, which can have substantial repercussions for its financial standing and performance. Indeed, in November 1999, Commissioner Laura S. Unger of the SEC issued a lengthy report calling for a study of the effects of such postings on corporate stock prices. The SEC was not thinking of unions engaged in corporate campaigns so much as it was individuals engaged in fraud to manipulate stock prices for profit. However, the core issue—the ability to influence stock prices through Internet postings—is essentially the same, and any subsequent SEC action is likely to impact on these union and union-inspired activities as well.[27]

THE VIRTUAL WORLD OF NONLABOR CAMPAIGNERS

Labor unions, as we have already observed, were not the first to discover the potential of the Internet as a campaign tool nor have they been the most innovative. That prize would surely go to some of the nonlabor groups that have engaged in anticorporate activities. Canadian environmentalists from the Forest Action Network, for example, tried to discourage clear-cutting by Western Forest Products by taking digital photos of the company's operations, loading them into a laptop, uploading them by satellite, and posting them on the group's Web site.[28] Further, ecopledge.com, created in October 1999 at a meeting of environmentalists at the University of Pennsylvania, has launched a campaign encouraging students to pledge that they will not accept employment with companies the group identifies as placing the environment or public health at risk. At this writing, Coca-Cola and BP Amoco were on the list, and the organizers claimed to have received between 10,000 and 15,000 signatories.[29]

As this latter example suggests, some of these "groups" literally *exist* solely or largely in cyberspace—they are not only engaged in virtual campaigns, but are, in effect, virtual *groups*. We have already seen the handiwork of one such group, the Free Burma Coalition, which has waged campaigns, some successful, against such corporate foes as PepsiCo and Unocal. The diversity of activities for which such groups employ information technologies, and especially the Web—organizing, fundraising, publicizing, mobilizing, and the like—more or less match those of organized labor.[30] However, the enthusiasm and thoroughness with which such players engage the Web is unrivaled in the labor movement. To make the point, let us examine two such organizations, both of which we mentioned earlier in this volume: Corporate Watch and NetAction.

A project of the Transnational Resource & Action Center (TRAC), Corporate Watch describes itself as

> An online magazine and resource center designed to provide you—every day Internet users—activists, journalists, students, teachers and policy makers—with an array of tools you can use to investigate and analyze corporate activity.
>
> We are committed to exposing corporate greed by documenting the social, political, economic and environmental impacts of these transnational giants....
>
> We also aim to take action!
>
> Corporate Watch works to support efforts to build a movement for democratic control over corporations, human rights and environmental justice.
>
> With this in mind, we are working to harness the Internet as a vehicle for activism.[31]

TRAC is a collaboration among such groups as the Institute for Policy Studies, the Tides Foundation, the Rainforest Action Network, and the Sierra Club, which are all active in, or actively supportive of, anticorporate campaigns and the more general attack on the legitimacy of the corporation as a social institution. Among its affiliates are the Multinationals Resource Center, a project of *Multinational Monitor* magazine, whose role in corporate and anticorporate campaigns we have already discussed; Project Underground, which has participated in campaigns against such companies as Shell and Freeport-McMoRan; and The Data Center, which, you may recall from chapter 1, was established by NACLA in 1977 to serve as a repository for research and data to support anticorporate attacks.[32] Corporate Watch, then, has deep and broad roots in the anticorporate progressive community, representing, in effect, one of that community's principal efforts at Web-based activism.

In chapter 8 we saw one form that activism has taken—the online distribution of an extensive manual for researching and attacking multinational corporations. Corporate Watch has also played a supporting role in the campaign against Nike and in the anti-sweatshop movement generally, the Microsoft campaign, and a campaign to force an end to the manufacture of the pesticide methyl bromide.[33] The Corporate Watch Web site includes a series of image galleries tied to its campaigns. In 1998, for example, one such gallery included a series of photographs of assembly workers in high-technology industries. This effort against "high-tech sweatshops" was designed around a theme of racial exploitation that included allegations of racial discrimination in hiring and compensation, lack of concern for the health of women and employees of color, and dumping environmental toxins into communities with large minority populations.[34] The photos were accompanied by graphics depicting computers, chips, circuit boards, and monitors, each described in terms of the gases and waste products associated with its manufacture. Singled out for particular attention in this on-line feature was Intel.[35]

One member of the Corporate Watch advisory board, Audrie Krause, also serves as executive director of NetAction, whose central role in the Microsoft campaign was described in chapter 5. A project of the Tides Foundation, NetAction, has positioned itself as a virtual voice of consumer advocacy. Of particular interest to us here is the group's interactive training course, entitled "The Virtual Activist" and available on its Web site.[36] Included is online instruction in the use of e-mail and Usenet (discussion) groups for organizing and advocacy, the shaping and use of web-site content, dos and don'ts of issuing electronic action alerts, fundraising on the Web, cookies and encryption, and even advice on proper *netiquette*.[37] The training course is supplemented by a number of articles on Internet activism published in the group's online newsletter, *NetAction Notes*, which are identified among a number of other related materials in a bibliography that accompanies the course.[38]

ENTANGLING THE WEB

Although the Internet has existed for many years now, the World Wide Web is a relatively new phenomenon, stimulated by the creation of Netscape's innovative browser software and developing for the most part since 1995. Union, anticorporate, and other activists are only now beginning to explore its potential as an instrument of political and economic influence. However, two things are already clear.

First, the Internet in its present and future iterations is destined to play an essential role in many pressure campaigns, perhaps supplanting the traditional mass media and traditional hands-on organizing in some key ways. For example, to the extent that Web-based information sources are judged to be credible, they can be employed effectively to generate campaign-supportive images that are far more subject to control by the campaigners than are image-management efforts that must be channeled through journalists and news organizations for their credibility. To the extent that workers, environmental activists, or others can be reached *en masse* or in targeted clusters through their computers rather than through direct personal contact or telephone trees, messages can be delivered, actions planned, and supporters mobilized with tremendous efficiency. As access to computers becomes more widespread, these efficiencies only grow. That is no doubt one of the principal reasons that in 1999 the AFL–CIO committed to a program designed to facilitate the purchase and online connection of personal computers by union members.[39] As CWA President Morton Bahr put it,

> Can you imagine being able to instantly ask millions of union members to refuse to buy a product or to bombard elected officials with e-mail in protest? This will be a revolutionary tool.[40]

The AFL–CIO program is complemented by a commercial venture, WebGalaxy, that provides online services to unions and sells low-cost computers to their members. As of its formation in 1999, the company's Advisory Board included representatives of four unions—the UFCW, BCT, HERE, and LIUNA.[41] A different model, and a potentially important precedent, was established the next year when Ford Motor Company, in cooperation with the UAW, announced that it would provide to every Ford worker a computer, color printer, unlimited Internet access, and an e-mail account for $5 per month.[42]

Second, although an American invention, the Internet is today inherently international, and its use as a campaign tool is reflective of this fact. We can see this in campaigns like that of the Free Burma Coalition against the SLORC regime, which is being waged almost entirely online and is centered, not in Burma/Myanmar itself, but in Madison, Wisconsin. The targets here are multinational corporations whose willingness to operate in Burma has brought them pressure in a number of other countries. The internationalism of the Internet is also evident in the labor movement and the anticorporate activist community—not only in the number of international sites that participate, but in the growing internationalism of the movements. It is probably not a coincidence, for example, that the outreach efforts of American unions to their European and Asian counterparts, and to the ICFTU, have corresponded in time with the growing reliance on electronic communication. The issues, needs, and capabilities of the respective parties to these emerging partnerships—the impetus to collaborate—have long existed. What is new is the ease of doing so that has come with e-mail and the Web. The coordinated internationalism of the opposition to the World Trade Organization that was manifest in Seattle, London, and elsewhere in late 1999 is but one of the more obvious cases in point.

Given this recent history, the rapid spread of access to the Internet, and the demonstrated efficiencies and effectiveness of the new information technologies as instruments of influence, it seems a safe bet that we will see these media come to be increasingly integrated into the activists' toolbox generally and into the corporate and anti-corporate campaign as well.

ENDNOTES

1. Arthur B. Shostak, *Cyber Union: Empowering Labor Through Computer Technology* (Armonk, NY: M.E. Sharpe, 1999), pp. 187–188.
2. Ibid., p. 113.
3. Carl D. Cantrell of the IBEW, quoted in Shostak, op. cit., p. 43.
4. "Internet for Union Activists," offered December 6–9, 1999, and found at ntserver.cands.com/georgemeany...fmuser/gm_listviewdetail.cfm?CRAID=81, August 17, 1999.
5. *Putting Your Union on the Web: A "How To" Manual for Activists*, published by the American Federation of State, County and Municipal Employees and found on the union's Web site at www.afscme.org/publications/puttc.htm, September 8, 1999.
6. Shostak, op. cit., p. 186 argues the former, whereas the LaborNet Web site puts the date of origin at the latter (see www.labornet.org/aboutus.html as of December 10, 1999).
7. Shostak, loc. cit.; LaborNet, loc. cit.; and an IGC posting announcing the 1999 move that was found at www.igc.org/igc/gateway/formernets.html on November 30, 1999.
8. This information was found at www.labornet.org as of December 10, 1999.
9. With some variations, the union sites are generally accessed in the form www.[acronym of union].org (e.g., www.cwa.org). The site targeting retail workers was found at www.retailworker.com as of July 12, 1999.
10. Harry Kelber, "Email for Organizing," *Labor Talk*, found on the Web at www.igc.org/igc/ln/hl/9908313535/hl5.html, September 8, 1999.
11. Many of these issues and initiatives were discussed at a January 1999 conference in New York, "Labor Online: Building Union Power Through Interactive Technology." A summary of the conference was found at www.igc.org/igc/ln/hg/lonrep.html as of February 1, 1999.
12. See, for example, Paul Nyhan, "Labor's claim of WTO victory is validated," *Seattle Post-Intelligencer*, December 8, 1999.
13. These included the sites of the U.S. Network for Global Economic Justice, found on February 20, 2000, at www.50years.org, a group dedicated to transforming the World Bank and IMF, and of the Mobilization for Global Justice, found on March 13, 2000, at www.a16.org. As its URL suggests, the latter site was entirely devoted to the April protest.
14. "Travel Advisory: Your On-Line Guide to California's Trouble Spots," found at www.scruznet.com/~herewest/welcome.htm, September 30, 1998.
15. Found at www.gecontract2000.com, December 9, 1999.

16. "Employer Wrongdoing Exposed Through Cyber-Leaflet," United Labor Online, January 21, 2000.

17. "LA Airport Security Workers Rally at Yahoo! Headquarters to Protest Cancellation of Internet Ad Campaign," SEIU Local 1877 news release, February 22, 2000. Oddly, despite its title, this release included no information about the rally itself, which may or may not have actually occurred.

18. The gateway to this site was found at www.washtech.org as of November 23, 1999.

19. "Why We Need Alliance@IBM," found at www.allianceibm.org/mission.asp, November 30, 1999.

20. Found at www.allianceibm.org/myths.asp, November 30, 1999.

21. The gateway to this effort was found at www.faceintel.com on November 30, 1999.

22. Carl S. Kaplan, "In Intel E-Mail Case, Property Rights vs. Free Speech," *The New York Times*, May 28, 1999. For a more general analysis of the emergence of e-mail as a union organizing tool, see Noam S. Cohen, "Corporations try to Bar Use of E-Mail by Unions," *The New York Times*, August 23, 1999.

23. Maria Alicia Gaura, "E-Mail Delivered by Horse-Mail: Intel gadfly carries on his vendetta the old-fashioned way," *San Francisco Chronicle*, September 29, 1999, p. B2.

24. Found at www.faceintel.com/lawsuits.htm, November 30, 1999.

25. Sascha Segan, "Striking Out Online: Boeing Workers Build Solidarity on the Web," ABCNews.com, March 10, 2000.

26. These can be found at www.yahoo.com under "OS" in the section of the site devoted to financial bulletin boards.

27. Neil Hare, "Internet Financial Chat Rooms Raise Concerns for Regulators, Companies," *Corporate Law Weekly*, December 1, 1999.

28. "Protestors set up virtual blockade," United Press International, July 21, 1998.

29. Daun Chung, "Campus environmentalists join Web-based campaign," *Harvard Crimson*, March 3, 2000. The site was found at www.ecopledge.com, March 6, 2000.

30. Of particular interest for the future because of the trend toward facilitating electronic commerce is the use of the Web for fundraising. This activity is still in its early stages, as suggested by the experience of the Rainforest Action Network, which in 1997 reported receiving approximately $400 weekly from online pledges. RAN's Web site received an average of 28,000 hits weekly at that time, about 5 of which produced a contribution. This rate of .00017% compared with a 2% success rate for the group's direct mail. However, the average online donation was $39 compared with $28 for direct-mail solicitations, and the group anticipated considerable growth in its online revenue stream as people became more accustomed to giving their credit card numbers on the Internet. Rachelle C. Marquez, "For raising funds, Internet gets mixed reviews," *Business Journal of San Jose and Silicon Valley*, October 13, 1997.

31. "About Corporate Watch," found at www.corpwatch.org/trac/about/about.html #partners, September 18, 1998.

32. Ibid. An earlier version of this listing, found on October 1, 1997, also listed the Institute for Global Communication, a project of the Tides Center, as a major partner in this enterprise.

33. Ibid.

34. Found at www.corpwatch.org/trac/gallery/sweat, June 15, 1998.

35. Found at www.corpwatch.org/trac/feature/hitech, June 15, 1998.

36. Found at www.netaction.org/training, on May 28, 1998.

37. Ibid.

38. Found at www.netaction.org/training/reader.html, May 28, 1998.

39. Steven Greenhouse, "AFL–CIO Members to Get Online Access and Discounts," *The New York Times*, October 11, 1999.

40. Sam McManis, "Unions Seek New Heights: AFL–CIO enters cyberspace age with Web site as it woos nontraditional workers," *San Francisco Chronicle*, November 19, 1999, p. B1.

41. "Two Major U.S. Unions Sign Letters of Intent with WebGalaxy," company news release, February 4, 1999; "Four Prominent Union Leaders Join WebGalaxy Advisory Board," company news release, February 16, 1999; and "WebGalaxy Inc. and Union Friendly Systems Inc. Sign Agreement to Sell Computers on United Labor Online Website," company news release, December 6, 1999.

42. Keith Bradsher, "Ford Offers Workers PC's and Internet Service for $5 a Month," *The New York Times*, February 4, 2000.

16

BACK TO THE FUTURE

The corporate campaign has always been a creature of its context. It was developed in the turbulent 1960s—first as an experiment, then as an institutionalized means of challenging a newly understood corporate establishment. After some early and controversial testing, it was ever more widely adopted in the 1980s by a labor movement cast adrift by the Reagan revolution. In the 1990s, it was a principal means of building bridges between labor and the "progressive" community and of reasserting the legitimacy of both as they struggled to overcome the political paralysis of two decades. In that history, we can also see the future, at least in the near term, of the corporate campaign.

The New Left of the early 1960s—the Tom Hayden–Michael Locker–Paul Booth–Heather Booth-Steve Max Left—distrusted labor as much as it distrusted corporations. The degree of this distrust is best illustrated by the NACLA *Research Methodology Guide*, which, we should recall, contained not only a chapter on using research to infiltrate the corporation, but a similar chapter on penetrating the unions as well. Labor, in the minds of these activists, suffered from two seemingly contradictory shortcomings. First, labor was the leading icon of Old Left radicalism—one could not be a true radical of the Old Left unless one were firmly rooted in the working class, if not by sociology, then at least by ideology. The needs of labor defined and drove the Old Left, including the League for Industrial Democracy, the old-line group that initially nourished the SDS. Second, labor was a creature of the establishment—a willing co-conspirator in the preservation of an economic system that had, albeit reluctantly, opened its arms and embraced the workers, or so their leaders had led them to believe. The New Left took root not among the workers, but among the young intelligentsia on the nation's campuses. It developed in its early years, before being consumed by ideological warfare with the Old, as an intellectual exercise and an incubator for new programs and ideas independent of both labor influences. The corporate campaign, in its earliest formulations, was a mechanism of rebellion against corporations and labor alike.

This inherent distrust between labor and the New Left, magnified as it was by the politics of the civil rights movement and the Vietnam Era, helps explain labor's reluctance to adopt this strategic view of the corporation and the package of tactics available to exploit it. The perspective of established labor leaders of the period may be best distilled in the comments of Tony Boyle, who was, in the early 1970s, the president of the United Mine Workers Union. Boyle was under attack for union corruption and was being challenged for control of the union by a group called Miners for Democracy. At a 1972 election rally in the coal fields near Grundy, Virginia, Boyle told his supporters that Miners for Democracy was supported by "a gang of outsiders with support from rich foundations,... Washington lawyers,... [and] hippie-looking people who passed out Communist literature at our meeting in New York."[1]

Ray Rogers was among those working with Miners for Democracy during this period. We have no way of knowing, of course, whether Boyle had Rogers in mind when he made his comment, but that is of no consequence. The point here is that Boyle's views of the union reformers more or less typified those of his fellow establishment labor leaders, and those views, writ large, framed the context into which Mr. Rogers and the corporate campaign more generally entered with Farah and J.P. Stevens. The old-line labor leaders were resistant to the corporate campaign because they did not trust Ray Rogers and the New Left wave of which he was, to them, the symbol. Rogers' flirtation with the Old Left of Communist and Socialist Workers parties at Hormel and elsewhere only exacerbated their anxieties.

By the 1980s, in the wake of the PATCO debacle, labor's desperation bred a new willingness to try anything and a deeply felt need to strike back at the hard-nosed business culture engendered by Reaganism. In effect, desperate times were seen as calling for desperate measures. From labor's perspective, the corporate campaign at Phelps Dodge came too late to stop the juggernaut of replacement workers, downsizing and the exporting of jobs to lower cost Third World economies. With planning and foresight, perhaps others could eventually succeed. Not coincidentally, it was in this period of intense fear and loathing that labor began in earnest to build its library of campaign manuals and its educational and financial infrastructure in support of the corporate campaign. It was in this period that labor began to view an assault on the reputations and support networks of management—especially of those companies that it regarded as most hard-nosed in their dealings with unions—as legitimate, appropriate, and perhaps even promising. It was in this period that there emerged within the labor movement a generation of leaders who came of age, at least figuratively, during this era of bitter confrontation and who took as their mantra a fundamental antagonism to the essential corporate nature of their adversaries.

John Sweeney's rise to power, first within the SEIU and later within the labor federation, personifies the interplay of these forces. His election as president of the AFL–CIO in 1995 marked the triumph of those international unions committed to new and more aggressive tactics over those still committed to following the old path; it marked the full legitimization of the corporate campaign as an instrument of the struggle. From that point forward, the federation and many of its member unions have devoted more and more resources and energy to such campaigns.

Figure 16.1, which is based on the data reported in Appendix A, reports the number of new, labor-based corporate campaigns started annually from 1974, when the Farah prototype effort ended, through 1999. We can draw three conclusions from this tally, all of which are consistent with our analysis to this point. First, corporate campaign activity increased markedly beginning in 1983, in the wake of the Reagan election and the firing of the PATCO strikers. This sharp up-tick shows that corporate campaigns gained momentum in direct response to the changing labor–management environment. Second, campaign activity took a second step-jump in the early 1990s, an indicator of the growing support within the labor movement for adopting these new, aggressive methods and, perhaps, reflecting the expectation that federal agencies in a Clinton administration would be more willing to support labor in these conflicts, whether directly through the NLRB or indirectly through the other regulatory agencies. Finally, we can see that in the years since the Sweeney election, campaign activity has continued to grow significantly.

Yet thus far organized labor has failed to reverse its declining share of the workforce. As we saw in chapter 2, fewer than 1 in 10 Americans working in the private sector is a member of a labor union, and fewer than 1 in 6 of all workers are unionized. A 1999 study commissioned by the AFL–CIO found that in the 30 fastest growing sectors of the economy between 1984 and 1997, with 26 million new jobs, only 1 worker in 20 joined unions. In contrast, in the eight sectors with the greatest job losses, four fifths of the 2 million lost jobs belonged to union members.[2] The hole in which labor finds itself is a deep one, and the need to fill it with 600,000 new workers a year to

Corporate Campaign Startups
Number, By Year, 1974-1999

— Number of Campaign Starts

Figure 16.1

reverse the trend is a daunting one. As a solution to this problem, and despite a gain of 112,000 in private-sector union membership in 1999, the corporate campaign has not proven to be the panacea that some had hoped.[3] But there are indications that labor's strategists have in mind a new and more sophisticated use for these campaigns—as central components in a drive to rebuild support for labor among college students in an effort to forge a pro-labor generation that will come to control the political system and the economy over the next decades.

One means to this end is through a nationwide series of labor teach-ins and a program of outreach to sociologists and other university faculties.[4] The twin centerpieces of this effort are the following: (a) the Stop Sweatshops movement, which has been designed to appeal to students on an emotional level—ending child labor, repression, and exploitation—in a way that allows them a sense of involvement through local direct action, such as pressing their schools to adopt codes of conduct for manufacturers of logo items; and (b) Union Summer, a program of month-long internship experiences in which college students work with union organizers to aid the workers at the bottom of the American economy. The sweatshop campaign provides motivation and legitimacy, the internships an opportunity to move from the campus to the real world. We have already discussed the sweatshop campaign in some detail in our examination of the moral-high-ground thematic, so let us focus briefly here on Union Summer.

Union Summer was initiated by the AFL–CIO in 1996, the first full year of the Sweeney administration; in that year, it placed more than 1,000 student interns with organizers from UNITE, the UFCW, and other unions in 22 cities around the country. More than half of the participants were women and more than half minorities. The students walked picket lines, visited nonunion workers in their homes, organized rallies, and participated in various forms of direct action. Along with their work came study—on labor history, organizing models and skills, power analysis, and political economy. The program continued in 1997, when students in Seattle gathered signatures supporting the Teamster's apple worker organizing campaign. Others in New York staged a demonstration against Disney that gained air on ABC's "Good Morning America" as the network's engineers—members of the Communications Workers of America—sought to bring pressure on management from ABC's parent company. In 1998, some Union Summer interns helped power a Justice for Janitors campaign in Seattle, while others lobbied on Capitol Hill in behalf of Avondale workers.[5] In its first 3 years, an estimated 2,000 students from 45 states had completed the program.[6]

Largely as a result of this initiative, students' interest in labor issues is now becoming institutionalized. As one Columbia University sociology graduate student put it, "One of the great untold stories of the '90s is that Union Summer has created from almost nothing activism on campus to a point where labor issues are among the leading issues among students today."[7] In April 1999, coordinated student conferences at Harvard, Yale, Kent State, and Stanford, with the active support of labor, formed the National Student Labor Action Movement (SLAM) with a plan to hire paid organizers to work in coordination with unions and the labor movement through a National Student Labor Solidarity Network.[8] About 3 weeks later, AFL–CIO President Sweeney said of the campus activism, "Students have created a passionate blaze for workers' rights across the country."[9] By early 2000, labor was taking an even more explicit stand in support of student activism. When police removed a group of anti-sweatshop activists staging a sit-in at the Chancellor's office at the University of Wisconsin, USWA President George Beckers pronounced himself "appalled." "Instead of violating these students' rights," he said, "the university should be applauding their moral fortitude."[10] Can one imagine such sentiments being expressed by the labor leaders of the 1960s?

A key element of the Union Summer program is its educational component, which, as noted, includes workshops on such topics as power analysis and political economy. One obvious function of this curriculum is to help recruit promising new organizers who have been exposed to the theory and philosophy of the corporate campaign. The program appears to be meeting that objective: A number of Union Summer alumni have already moved into the labor movement as researchers and organizers.[11] However, the emphasis on political economy suggests yet another objective—one that takes us back to our larger point.

Organized labor in the 1960s defined itself as separate from the Left—from the Old Left in reaction to the McCarthy period and the desire to distance the movement from its explicitly socialist and communist elements, and from the New Left in reaction to what Tony Boyle aptly termed "hippie-looking people" with whom the movement simply had little in common. As a result, labor found itself cut off from the progressive community. This division was not responsible for the decline in labor's fortunes in the workplace, but it surely contributed to the movement's inability to respond effectively.

Although perhaps not entirely in the manner that NACLA's young theorists anticipated, a new generation of leaders has now gained control of the labor movement, bringing with them new perspectives on strategy, tactics, and outcomes. The corporate campaign is a prominent symbol of that new thinking. Yet because of the recent history of the movement, these labor activists, although they may feel a strong kinship with their cousins on the contemporary political left, are not full partners in today's progressive, which is to say in the present context anticorporate, movement. They share a common methodology, and they have built organizational bridges through coalitions and common causes. However, they still lack the legitimacy of a human rights activist or an environmentalist, to pick just two. It was surely this concern that Sweeney had in mind when he stated in his inaugural address as AFL–CIO president:

"We will use old-fashioned mass demonstrations, as well as sophisticated corporate campaigns, to make worker rights the civil rights issue of the 1990s."[12]

It appears that Union Summer and the sweatshop campaign, together with outreach to the environmentalists and a host of other initiatives, are designed to redress this shortcoming and achieve Sweeney's stated objective—and, in the process, alter the political culture to labor's advantage at a fundamental level. This is the counterattack to the Reagan Revolution, and the corporate campaign is in the forefront. Just as the anticorporate activism embodied in the corporate campaign wrote labor out of the Left in the 1960s, labor hopes to employ the very same device to lead the way in *creating* the Left of the 21st century. Under such a definition, labor would resume its customary role at the front of the line.

This is a view on which both Left and Right seem to agree, although they certainly address it in different terms and view its consequences quite differently. Writing in *The Nation*, for example, Marc Cooper has drawn an explicit contrast between the simultaneous student meetings in April 1999 on the campuses of Harvard, Yale, Stanford, and Vietnam-era symbol Kent State for the purpose of firming up links with organized labor, on the one hand, and the 1962 SDS meeting at Port Huron, on the other. "No stirring Big Picture Statement of a generation's anguish came out of this particular conference," he observed. But "we just might be witnessing, finally, the birth of a new national student movement."[13] In the words of Amy Dean, executive officer of California's South Bay Labor Council,

> This is a strategic, deliberate move by Sweeney's AFL–CIO. The Vietnam War's been over for a long time now. It's time for us to get back together with students. We need the coalition that working with students brings us.[14]

But this is not your granddad's 1960s. In the words of one student activist from Johns Hopkins University,

> I see the sixties as very chaotic, as something that scared the establishment. We are more pointed, more focused. We don't believe things are going to change overnight. We believe that the chaos will come from within the system, not from without.[15]

Cooper sees the combination of Union Summer and the sweatshop movement as generating a new radicalism among students—a view reflected in the comments of a University of Wisconsin student who observed, "Anti-sweatshop work is *very* radicalizing. It doesn't take long before you begin to understand how capitalism works."[16] It would appear that the lessons in political economy have landed on fertile ground.

The language and the focus on the Right are a bit different, but the main point is the same: The labor movement has moved to the left even as it has become decidedly more political. In one 1996 Heritage Foundation report entitled *From Meany to Sweeney: Labor's Leftward Tilt*, for example, analysts Kenneth Weinstein and August Stofferahn asserted that:

> An activist labor movement may be the most significant new force in American politics, but the agenda of labor's new leaders is radically different from that of the traditional labor movement.

> While political parties have moved to the center and right, union activism has shifted decisively to the left.[17]

The Heritage analysis goes on to link Sweeney with the Democratic Socialists of America (DSA), which claimed the AFL–CIO president as a member. According to the report, the DSA was encouraging young activists to participate in the Union Summer experiment. To the extent *that* was the case, the seeds sown through Union Summer would have fallen not merely on fertile ground, but on *fertilized* ground.

For our part, we cannot specify with any certainty at this point in time either who has participated in these various union initiatives or, in the aggregate, what effect the experience has had on those who have. We cannot assess the impact that these programs have had or will have on either generating renewed support for organized labor or strengthening its bridges to left-leaning movements. However, our present purpose does not require a definitive statement of such effects. It only requires that we understand the role played by the corporate campaign in this outreach to the Left. On that point, the result seems clear.

The corporate campaign, understood in the largest sense, has served as a principal mechanism—perhaps as *the* principal mechanism—for shaping, framing, energizing, and mobilizing activists, and for building new points of contact between the labor movement and those concerned primarily with human rights, civil rights, consumer rights, progressive religious activism, and the environment. This is a function of establishing genuine connections. Where surrogates and virtual groups have been invented to mask the unions' activities and interests, it is also the product of a conscious effort by labor to construct a social reality in which such connections *appear* to exist. Both the real linkages and those that are merely apparent have been fostered in large measure through the 30-year development of the corporate campaign.

If there were any doubt of this, it must be dispelled when one considers the increasing importance of such hybrid coalitions as the Campaign for Labor Rights, which brings together unions with political activists, or the National Interfaith Committee for Worker Justice, which combines labor activists, religious activists, and community organizers. It must be dispelled when one reviews the developmental chronology of campaign manuals or the listing of anticorporate campaigns in Appendix B and recognizes the emergent interactivity between those whose motives are economic in a relatively narrow sense and those whose motives are driven by policy concerns or ideology. It must be dispelled when one considers the flow of people and ideas between labor and the community of activists. It must be dispelled when one considers the words of the labor leaders themselves, who are quite explicit in stating their objectives.

Just as the corporate campaign has matured and changed since its invention in the 1960s and 1970s, the role of the campaign is likely to mature and change in the years ahead. At the very least, as corporate and anticorporate initiatives merge, the individual companies that are targeted may recede in importance while the issues and political objectives that transcend the various campaigns become more important. That is an inevitable by-product of the reliance on unifying themes across multiple campaigns that we have documented, and of the socializing effect that so many years of such consistent messages on so great a scale must inevitably have. It is a macrolevel communication effect that is already evident in the metacampaigns discussed in chapter 8.[18] There is every reason to expect that we will see more. In the longer run, the boundaries that delineate the campaign as a phenomenon may fade from both view and significance as the techniques of persuasion and mobilization that have been developed in these laboratories of activism infuse themselves into the fabric of political and economic life in industrialized societies.

Indeed, in the penultimate month of the 20th century, we may well have seen the next step in this development with the so-called Battle of Seattle, the gathering of tens of thousands of protestors against the policies of the World Trade Organization (WTO). The preparations for this event were extensive, whether on the part of organized labor, which viewed it as an opportunity to press its objections to what it regarded as the failure of the WTO to take labor standards into account in its policies; environmentalists, who saw in the organization a shield for environmental exploitation by multinational corporations; or ideologues, who viewed the WTO as a government of corporations rather than of people.[19] As we have already seen, these are long-standing agenda items in each camp. The Seattle meeting of the WTO in November and December 1999 provided both an opportunity for them to join together in an expression of progressive outrage and a marker of the extent to which they have already found common ground. Michael Elliott of *Newsweek* offered one summary of events that resonates with our analysis here:

> There's something in the air; a new mood of radical activism of a kind and—perhaps—scale not seen for years. To be sure, there have always been those who raged against the machine, long before the favorite rock band of those on the streets in Seattle was ever heard from. In the history of American protest, the 70s and 80s are not lost decades, a long ellipses between (say) the Weather Underground and Earth First! The movement to disinvest in South Africa, ACT UP and all the other AIDS/HIV awareness groups—none of them depended on either the Port Huron generation or the body-pierced one. But there does seem to be a common sense of alienation among a surprising number of Americans....
>
> "We are people of this generation, bred in at least modest comfort ... looking uncomfortably to the world we inherit." Port Huron, 1961. But not a bad text for Seattle, 1999.[20]

But perhaps it is most fitting to leave the coda on this analysis to Tom Hayden, author of the *Port Huron Statement*, who decades later participated in the anti-WTO demonstrations in Seattle and then summarized his observations in an op-ed piece in the *Washington Post*:

> The 1968 protest in Chicago was the crest of a wave that had been rising for eight years, through thousands of protests from the civil rights movement to the

anti-war movement. The Seattle protest, rather than riding a wave, allowed a whole new generation of activists to surface....

Seattle will have greater consequences. In Chicago we were dealing with a single issue: the Vietnam War. The Seattle activists were confronting the very nature of the way economics, environmentalism and human rights are going to be shaped for the rest of our lives.[21]

Corporate campaigns are but one example of a more general phenomenon that has swept through the American political system over the last 30 to 40 years, the increasing reliance on the techniques of strategic communication to shape political discourse, and, through it, to shape the political system and the public policies that it produces.[22] In all such settings and outcomes, there are winners and losers. More and more, it is the ability to control information and its flow that determines who is which.

That is, in fact, precisely the game that organized labor is playing with its reliance on the corporate campaign and the game that other activists—on the Right as well as the Left—are playing as well. At stake is the character of the global, as well as the American, political economy—and the status and influence of the corporation as a fundamental form of economic organization—for many years to come.

ENDNOTES

1. Untitled, *The New York Times*, September 5, 1972, p. 12.
2. Steven Greenhouse, "Union Leaders See Grim News in Labor Study," *The New York Times*, October 13, 1999.
3. Steven Greenhouse, "Growth in Unions' Membership in 1999 Was the Best in Two Decades," *The New York Times*, January 20, 2000.
4. Steven Greenhouse, "Liberal Academics and Labor's New Leaders Pulling in Tandem Once More," *The New York Times*, September 22, 1996, p. 36.
5. "Union Summer in Review," a discussion of the program found on the AFL–CIO's Web site at www.aflcio.org/unionsummer/inreview.htm.
6. Francine Knowles, "Unions Take Aim at Generation X," *Chicago Sun-Times*, September 6, 1999.
7. Quoted in Steven Greenhouse, "Activism Surges at Campuses Nationwide, and Labor Is at Issue," *The New York Times*, March 29, 1999.
8. An overview of these organizing efforts and the objectives of the groups was found at www.stanford,edu/group/slac/slam.html.
9. Courtney Leatherman, "AFL–CIO President Sweeney Credits Campus Activism," *Chronicle of Higher Education*, May 5, 1999.
10. "USWA Denounces University of Wisconsin's Strong-Arm Oppression of Student's Rights," news release, United Steelworkers of America, February 21, 2000.

11. "Where are they now?", a sample listing of biographical sketches found on the AFL–CIO's Web site at www.aflcio.org/unionsummer/theynow.htm.

12. James L. Tyson, "As Strikes Lose Potency, Unions Turn to Tactics Outside the Workplace," *Christian Science Monitor*, February 16, 1996, p. 1.

13. Marc Cooper, "No Sweat: Uniting Workers and Students, a New Movement Is Born," *The Nation*, June 7, 1999.

14. Quoted in Cooper, op. cit.

15. Quoted in Cooper, op. cit.

16. Quoted in Cooper, op. cit.

17. Kenneth R. Weinstein and August Stofferahn, *From Meany to Sweeney: Labor's Leftward Tilt*, Backgrounder No. 1094 (Washington: Heritage Foundation, 1996), p. 1.

18. An example of this trend toward generalization, one based in the university community and arising from the anti-sweatshop metacampaign, is Matt McLaughlin, "Corporations operate based on wealth, not well-being," *Daily Collegian* (Pennsylvania State University), February 7, 2000. "But it is not only in sweatshops that humans are being ignored in the quest for profits," notes McLaughlin. "... Many large companies have actively worked to destroy the future environment for all of humanity."

19. On labor, see, for example, "Labor Groups Want Their Voices Heard at Trade Conference in Seattle," *Seattle Times*, November 7, 1999; "Labour body demands worker rights in trade talks," Reuters, November 19, 1999; and any of the host of news releases from the ICFTU and numerous U.S.-based international unions proclaiming their opposition to WTO policies. On the environmentalists' emerging collaboration with labor, see Todd Wilkinson, "Environmentalists discover a curious ally," *Christian Science Monitor*, December 13, 1999. For an overview of the elaborate preparations for the protests, see, for example, Luis Cabrera, "Activists mobilize for protest," *Akron Beacon Journal*, October 3, 1999; and "Globalize This! Action Camp 1999," invitation for 150 experienced activists to attend a special training camp operated by the Ruckus Society, found August 10, 1999, at www.igc.org/igc/ln/aa/990806-4054/aa1.html. ITN News reported on November 29, 1999, that Anita Roderick, CEO of the Body Shop chain, had contributed £200,000 to support groups travelling to Seattle for the festivities. On anticorporate ideologues and related activists, see Russell Mokhiber and Robert Weissman, "10 Reasons to Dismantle the WTO," *Focus on the Corporation*, November 23, 1999; Danielle Knight, "Big Business and Democracy on a Collision Course at WTO," InterPress Service, September 15, 1999; John Burgess, "Activist Group Public Citizen Joins Attack on WTO," *Washington Post*, October 14, 1999, p. E1; and Jerry Mander and John Cavanaugh, "WTO feeds corporate greed," *USA Today*, December 3, 1999, p. 14A. Corporate Watch even set up a daily radio program carrying news of the activity in Seattle. "Special Announcement—World Trade Watch Radio," Corporate Watch news release, September 27, 1999. Helene Cooper provides a more general overview of the confluence of forces in "Globalization Foes Plan to Protest WTO's Seattle Round Trade Talks," *The Wall Street Journal*, July 16, 1999, p. A1, in which she credits Mike Dolan of Global Trade

Watch, a spin-off of Nader's group, Public Citizen, as the coordinator of events. See also Steven Greenhouse, "Protestors Could Steal the Show at Seattle Trade Talks," *The New York Times*, November 29, 1999.

20. Michael Elliott, "The New Radicals," *Newsweek*, December 13, 1999.

21. Tom Hayden, "The Battle in Seattle: What Was That All About?," *Washington Post*, December 5, 1999, p. B1.

22. W. Lance Bennett and Jarol B. Manheim, "The Big Spin: Strategic Communication and the Transformation of Pluralist Democracy," in W. Lance Bennett and Robert M. Entman, eds., *Mediated Politics: Communication in the Future of Democracy* (Cambridge: Cambridge University Press, 2000, forthcoming).

APPENDIX A

Union-Initiated and Other Labor-Based Corporate Campaigns,
1974–1999

Primary Target	Union(s) Participating	Circa	Comments
ABC Television	CWA (NABET)	1998– 1999	Contract dispute over competitiveness and job security; 11-week lockout, which followed 1-day strike during November sweeps affecting Monday Night Football and election night coverage; union called on allies in Democratic Party to decline interviews with ABC News, many did; pickets at ABC News London Bureau; some targeting of parent company Disney; Union Summer participation
Adam's Mark Hotel	AFL–CIO, Denver Federation of Labor	1995– 1998	Purchase of former Radisson Hotel, dismissal of union workers, and refusal to recognize previous contracts led to 3-year boycott; ended when Mayor intervened because labor threatened to picket hotel if Denver selected for 2000 Democratic National Convention
AHL/ Argenbright Security	SEIU	1998–	Initially component an O' Hare Airport organizing campaign; included attacks on lease renewals for airlines (UAL); expanded to organizing drive at several airports, notably LAX, and broadened to incorporate AHL Services (parent company); first use of cyberleaflet; union issued travel advisory regarding airport security provided by company; NLRB complaints
AK Steel Holdings	USWA	1999–	Lockout at Mansfield, Ohio, facility when contract expired; replacement workers; dispute over mandatory overtime; bombings and shootings at trucking companies hauling AK products; city-ordered background checks on some replacement workers; leaflets at United Way dinner where CEO spoke; union filed "taxpayer lawsuit" alleging company no longer met requirements for tax abatement; other litigation; NLRB complaints included two "Bill Johnson's" charges; union letter to shareholders highlighting costs of anti-union activity

311

Primary Target	Union(s) Participating	Circa	Comments
Alaska Air	IAM, AFA	1993–1999	Contract dispute; billboards at Seattle airport, rallies; pickets at 1999 annual meeting; flight attendants developed "CHAOS" tactic (Create Havoc Around Our System) later used elsewhere
Albertson's	UFCW	1984	Victor Kamber brought in to make embarrassing TV spots after back-wage dispute in Albuquerque; attacks using reputation of founder Joe Albertson
		1996–	Multiple off-the-clock claims filed as class action litigation despite contract provisions requiring arbitration; litigation settled 1999; separate NLRB complaint on grievance processing
American Airlines	APFA	1986–1987	Campaign to end two-tier wage system; when union hired Rogers, company claimed act constituted failure to bargain in good faith; brochure attacked company for safety violations, dumping toxic waste, price-fixing
American Home Products	OCAW		Issue was moving jobs to Puerto Rico; IRS code used as campaign weapon; Richard Leonard directed campaign
Aramark	HERE Local 100	1997	Effort to organize food service workers at Smith Barney and Travelers; led union to oppose proposed settlement terms in NOW campaign against Smith Barney
AT&T	CWA	1992	Union wanted card check to ensure role in new technologies, especially AT&T Wireless; campaign included threat to switch thousands of customers to Sprint; instructions on using AT&T credit card in way that company would lose money
Avondale Shipyards	AFL–CIO Metal Trades Department	1993–1999	Contract campaign after workers voted for union; 10-city "Journey for Justice" tour in 1999; one issue was $5.4 million payment from Navy to help company fight the union; $537,000 OSHA fine April 1999 followed by claims of "willful" cover-up of incidents; July 1999 appeals court ordered NLRB to conduct new election; company agreed to neutrality and card check; Litton acquired company and replaced top management; union recognized November 1999

Primary Target	Union(s) Participating	Circa	Comments
Baltimore Gas & Electric	IBEW	1994–	Organizing campaign led to vote against union, then ULPs and NLRB complaint against company; picketed 1998 shareholders meeting; objected to planned merger with Pepco, which killed it because of regulatory requirements
BASF	OCAW	1985–1989	Grew from a dispute in Geismar, Louisiana; Headed by Richard Leonard; involved cooperation between U.S. And South African unions; German parent company intervened at union request
Basic Vegetable	IBT	1999–	Campaign in support of strike when company asked for wage and benefit concessions; IBT won recognition by card check, but when workers began to organize decertification election, union called for NLRB to conduct representation election; attacks on owners as funding right-wing causes; union established The Citizenship Project to forge common ground with Latino activists
Bayou Steel	USWA	1993–1996	Contract dispute and strike; union filed 200+ OSHA complaints; environmental consortium (National Environmental Law Center, USPIRG) alleged violations of Clean Air Act; union hired consulting firm to do environmental audit; pressure through First Chicago Bank, including shareholders resolution at bank's annual meeting; 1995 company filed RICO suit; strike ended 1996; pending RICO and ULPs settled 1997, terms not disclosed
BE&K	UBC	1984–1993	Extensive use of OSHA complaints, especially at International Paper plant in Jay, Maine, where BE&K was maintenance contractor; complaints to customers such as Westvaco; picketing at job sites around country; union produced video "BE&K: The Workers' Enemy"; portrayal of company as major union-buster by providing replacement workers, especially in paper industry at IP and Weyerhauser, including release of internal memo; "truth squad" meeting with community leaders where company planning construction projects
Bell Atlantic	CWA	1995–1996	Major issue in contract negotiation was outsourcing; $5 million TV campaign against outsourcing service and installation; inplant included work-to-rule, refusal of overtime, union T-shirts; two letters to shareholders warning of company's poor performance; also contacts with banks union maintained Internet site

Primary Target	Union(s) Participating	Circa	Comments
Beverly Enterprises	UFCW; SEIU	1983–	Organizing campaign; power analysis showed growth of company depended on leveraging public funds, company had vital regulatory dependencies; multiple white papers using data from state regulatory agencies, graphic imagery; claims of corporate greed and poor patient care; congressional investigations; hundreds of ULPs; shareholder litigation; Medicare fraud allegations settled for $225 million; AFL–CIO involvement through FAST; company sued two locals for defamation; CEO resigned November 1999; February 2000 company agreed to pay $175M and sell 10 nursing homes to settle Medicare fraud case
Blue Cross	AFSCME, CWA, IUE, OPEIU, UAW, UFCW, USWA	1985– 1988	Organizing campaign included neutrality agreement in Massachusetts, but unions lost or withdrew from representation elections
Breed Technologies	PACE	1999–	NAFTA-related dispute over 1997 strike and reinstatement of workers at Custom Trim auto parts *maquiladora* factory in Mexico, letter-writing campaign to president of Mexico; Campaign for Labor Rights participation; union issued report on hazmat practices at company's Florida facilities; possible EPA, SEC involvement; warnings to lenders
Bridgestone-Firestone	United Rubber Workers/IBT	1994– 1996	Strike over downsizing issues; replacement workers; foreign ownership raised as issue; *Running Over the American Dream* white paper; boycott; vigil at "Camp Justice" outside company's U.S. Headquarters in Nashville; "corporate renegade" theme; 1996 TV broadcast and radio spots; flooding of company Web site with protests; hand-billing at retail outlets; sympathy actions in Latin America, Japan
Brown & Root	Texas Building and Construction Trades Council	1983	Rogers retained to plan a possible campaign because company strongly anti-union; public threat seems to have concluded effort

Primary Target	Union(s) Participating	Circa	Comments
Brown & Sharpe	IAM	1982	Company sought team work with union, which objected; Rogers brought in, but eventually fired; targeted Rhode Island Hospital Trust bank, where company president on board, and claimed $40 million withdrawn; strong AFL–CIO support; Senator Chafee also targeted in flyer; 1998 Supreme Court declined to review appellate finding favoring company on 1981 ULP filing
Burlington Northern	BMWE	1993	Company was main focus of union campaign against industry over work rules, pay for commuting time; Rogers involved; pickets in Washington; demonstrations to warn shippers of possible strike; chain-gang theme and workers in prison uniforms
Cagle-Keystone	UFCW	1999–	Part of poultry workers organizing campaign; community petition calling for end to intimidation; petition to NLRB to reinstate fired workers; claim of misuse of tax incentives; Committee of 100 led involvement of community and religious leaders; off-the-clock lawsuit filed February 2000
California Strawberry Workers	UFW	1996–	Multiple targets among growers included Gargiullo Farms, Driscoll, Coastal Berry; active support of AFL–CIO; Monsanto sold Gargiullo to Coastal Berry, which became major target; independent union defeated UFW in 1998 and 1999 votes
Campbell's Soup	FLOC	1984	Rogers; secondary campaign pressuring Campbell's to force contracts on tomato and cucumber growers in Midwest
Carrefour	UFCW	1988–1991	Market-share campaign became organizing campaign at first U.S. "Hypermarket" of French-owned firm; Flag Day rally in parking lot; Vicki Lawrence/Mama campaign; 1989 radio and newspaper ads calling for boycott; union recognized 1991; company left U.S. Market 1993
Carson International	HERE	1989–1992	Element of the larger O'Hare Airport organizing campaign; heavy involvement of Catholic parishes; coalition formed Interfaith Committee on Worker Issues; included inspection tours, demonstrations, petitions, and lobbying of City Council by clergy; Jesse Jackson and Cesar Chavez participated; 1991 company settled ULPs and pledged neutrality; 1992 airport food service contract transferred to Marriott, which recognized union

Primary Target	Union(s) Participating	Circa	Comments
Caterpillar	UAW	1991–1998	Extensive use of "jack-rocks" (nails welded together and sprinkled in company parking lots to cause blowouts); major inside game with T-shirts, rallies, work-to-rule; approximately 1,000 ULPs filed by union, some received on camera by NLRB Regional Director in staged media event; extensive ad campaign—radio, TV, newspapers, billboards; staged rallies as media events; centered in Decatur, Illinois; "Fat Cat" theme; "Road Warriors" pressured dealers at trade shows; shareholder resolutions brought by religious community; OSHA review
Catholic Healthcare West	SEIU	1996–	Attack based on claim company does not adhere to Church teachings, does not meet charitable obligations; attempt to turn Church institutions against one another to pressure religious orders that owned company; National Interfaith Committee for Worker Justice; CEO resigned 1999; union lost recognition vote February 2000
Central Illinois Power	IBEW		Contract campaign centered on inplant tactics, primarily a mass refusal to work overtime
Chiquita Brands	US/Guatemala Labor Education Project (now U.S./Labor and Education Project)	1998–	Organizing campaign for banana workers in Guatemala; Campaign for Labor Rights involvement through US/LEAP; letter-writing campaign directed at U.S. and Guatemalan governments; controversy involving reporting by *Cincinnati Enquirer* corresponded with campaign; tied to banana dispute involving U.S., EU, WTO
Coca-Cola	IBT, IUF	1992–?	International campaign by IUF to replace Guatemalan franchise holder; David Dyson and William Paterson led effort in United States; also campaign by IBT that began over benefits reductions at bottlers and distributors
	IBT	1999–	Product safety problems in Europe corresponded with filing of class action discrimination lawsuit by 1,500 African-American employees; Pepsico encouraged antitrust investigations of Coke in EU; CEO resigned 1999; strike at Minute Maid accompanied by warnings from union on product safety; company accused of "ethnic cleansing" in firing African-American workers; IBT strike in Ohio and West Virginia area March 2000; company included in ecopledge hiring boycott; Jesse Jackson and Joseph Lowry involvement; call for product boycott April 2000, "Ride for Corporate Justice" bus caravan to 2000 annual meeting

Primary Target	Union(s) Participating	Circa	Comments
Colt Industries	UAW		Use of political pressure and boycotts to influence contract negotiations
Columbia/HCA	SEIU	1996–	Organizing campaign in Las Vegas and elsewhere; criminal fraud proceedings with DOJ intervention; whistle-blowers; 1999 activity in Denver included IRS audit, HCFA, and state health department investigations; February 2000 class action lawsuit filed in behalf of hospital volunteers claiming they were used to substitute for regular workers in violation of FLSA
Commercial Real Estate Developers	SEIU	1994–	Justice for Janitors campaign in Washington, other major cities, including blocking bridges into DC with stalled school bus; based on research by David Chu
Consolidated Foods (now Sara Lee)	ACTWU	1982– 1983	Arose from organizing campaign at Hanes subsidiary; election overturned on company charges of ULPs; campaign initiated by two nuns (Sisters of Divine Providence—affiliated with ICCR) through Southerners for Economic Justice, a group set up in 1976 by ACTWU to generate support in the Stevens campaign; Citizens Commission on Justice at Hanes included Bella Abzug, Julian Bond, Gloria Steinem, Studs Terkel, SCLC, NOW, others; ABC Evening News, 60 Minutes investigated but did not air dispute; company agreed to release EEO and occupational injury data
Consolidated Freightways	IBT	1992– 1994	Nonunion side of double-breasted company gaining market share from other union companies; significant shareholders initiatives; effort to impose union-drafted code of conduct
Continental Airlines	ALPA	1983– 1984	CEO Frank Lorenzo used a Chapter 11 filing in 1983 to wipe out existing labor agreements; Kamber Group advised union

Primary Target	Union(s) Participating	Circa	Comments
Continental Tire	USWA, ICEM	1998–1999	Strike in Charlotte, North Carolina, and hiring of replacement workers; series of NLRB complaints arising from ULPs; significant international campaign through ICEM, including "Global Week of Action" with protests at Ford Dealerships and German consulates, and strikes or protests by unions in France, Belgium, and South Africa; ILO complaint filed; ad campaign criticizing parent company; NLRB declared strike was over ULPs, contract settled shortly after
Crown Central Petroleum	OCAW	1996–	Workers locked out over subcontracting issue; environmental issues raised by Texans United and defined as "environmental racism"; allegations of racist handbills; picketing CEO public appearances; NICWJ involvement; NAACP, National Baptist Convention, Environmental Defense Fund, Natural Resources Defense Council, Sierra Club, Coalition of Labor Union Women, National Black Caucus of State Legislators endorsed boycott of Crown products; 1999 Norway's Statoil announced it would not renew contract until dispute resolved; buyout offer from Apex Oil 1999; FBI investigated company allegations of sabotage; company adopted "shareholders rights plan" to try to sustain support; competing buyout offer 2000 from founding family
Cummins Engine	IUOE		Campaign resulted from strike over concessions; union attended annual meeting using proxies from union pension fund, placed on agenda in return for agreement not to demonstrate outside meeting; full-page ad in newspaper day of annual meeting
Del Monte	IUF; US/Guatemala Labor Education Project (now U.S./Labor Education and Action Project)	1999–	Disputes over labor rights, organizing in Guatemala; Campaign for Labor Rights links to Chiquita campaign; company leasing plantations who would become employers; letter-writing campaign to Guatemalan embassy in United States; support from IUF, AFL–CIO, religious and human rights groups; boycott, claims company supported violent intimidation of workers; campaign suspended March 2000 pending negotiations
Delta Air Lines	AFA	1999–	Organizing campaign; attendance at 1999 annual meeting

Primary Target	Union(s) Participating	Circa	Comments
Delta Pride Catfish	UFCW	1990	Contract negotiation, 3-month strike; Mississippi cooperative accused of racism; company had three different CEOs during year of dispute; strike and boycott endorsed by Jesse Jackson, NAACP, SCLC; Congressional Black Caucus intervened; two fish farmers-shareholders charged with trying to bribe union leader to end strike; OSHA complaints about repetitive motion injuries; 1991 company agreed to pay OSHA fine and start safety program
Detroit Newspapers	Newspaper Guild (CWA)	1995–	Contract disputes with six unions at *News* and *Free Press,* which operated under joint operating agreement between Gannett and Knight-Ridder; replacement workers; company filed RICO suit 1995; committee of local religious leaders supported strikers, sympathy pickets from other newspapers; board strategy targeted Rosalyn Carter on Gannett board; letter to Starbucks objecting to instore distribution of *USA Today;* union produced video, published alternative weekly newspaper (suspended 1999), 1997 NLRB found strike arose from ULPs, required reinstatement of workers, ruling appealed
Diamond Walnut	IBT	1991–	Growers' cooperative operated only in California but 40% of sales in Europe; IUF led campaign to deny European market; IBT, Natural Resources Defense Council, Friends of the Earth sued EPA to force company and other users of methyl bromide to label products; 1993 AFL–CIO produced white paper and delivered to Labor Secretary; 1993 Fannie May agreed not to buy nuts from company; Lantos subcommittee held hearings 1992; IBT produced three glossy pamphlets attacking company; Justice for Diamond Walnut Workers Committee published handbills, full-page ad in *New York Times* calling for boycott
(Walt) Disney Company	UNITE	1997–	Sweatshop and child labor issues centered in Haiti, later extended to China; Campaign for Labor Rights involvement; video on Haiti produced by National Labor Committee; 1997 congressional letter from Conyers; company among four focus of 1998 NYC "People's Tribunal on Corporate Crimes Against Humanity"; sweatshop-related shareholders resolution at 1999 annual meeting, 1999 *Working for Disney Is No Fairy Tale* report on Chinese factories

Primary Target	Union(s) Participating	Circa	Comments
Eastern Air Lines	TWU (flight attendants), IAM, ALPA	1986–1991	Campaign targeted Frank Lorenzo after he acquired company and began to shift assets to other Texas Air subsidiaries to circumvent union contracts; had been power-sharing arrangement established by CEO Frank Borman, workers traded wage concessions for 25% of stock; Rogers brought in by TWU flight attendants; Michael Locker analyzed company books for IAM during Borman's tenure (also Randy Barber analyzed pension funds); culminated in 1989 strike that drove company out of business; litigation over bankruptcy, pilots' claims still active 1999
Echlin/Friction Materials	ACTWU, UBC	1987–1988	Organizing campaign led to 1988 NLRB election and 1989 contract
ENI (Ente Nazionale Idrocarburi)	UMWA	1988-1989	Agip mining subsidiary in contract dispute over shift to outsourcing labor; ULPs resolved in company's favor 1989
Family Foods	UFCW	Late 1980s	Targeted customer groups—seniors with claim company took excess pension funds, minorities with claims about hiring and firing practices; company forced out of business
Farah Manufacturing	ACWU	1972–1974	Prototype campaign; boycott; religious group participation; personalized attack on CEO
Farm Fresh	UFCW	1990–1992	Organizing campaign based in Tidewater, Virginia; off-the-clock complaints in class-action lawsuit aided by union and in Labor Department filing; Jesse Jackson rally
Federal Express	ALPA Local	1996	After 1995 work slowdown, company agreed to 5-year contract; local produced plan, known as "Phoenix Plan," to allege safety violations at company as means of pressuring for a better contract; national leaders objected and threatened to cut off funding
Federated Stores	UFCW	1998–	Organizing campaigns at May Company, Macy's, and Bloomingdale's; union wants card check; labor issues raised in development and zoning for San Francisco project

Primary Target	Union(s) Participating	Circa	Comments
Food Lion	UFCW	1985–	Multiple off-the-clock complaints packaged as DOL complaint (settled) and class action private litigation; AFL–CIO involvement through FAST; Kamber; ABC *PrimeTime Live* hidden-camera report extended allegations to poor sanitation; followed by series of "studies" released by union-front Consumers United with Employees alleging poor sanitation and pressure campaign to force FDA action; company sued ABC for fraud and other charges (won, but partially reversed on appeal) and the union and others for RICO (pending)
Frionor A/S	IBT	1994	New Bedford, Massachusetts, fish-processing plant hit with allegations of discrimination, invasion of privacy (video surveillance of workplace); New Bedford Coalition for Justice assisted union—also NOW, National Council of Senior Citizens, National Consumers League, Jesse Jackson, Edward Kennedy; company sued Church Women United for role in campaign after group called on Long John Silver's to boycott products; included newspaper ads in Norway to influence parent company
Frontier Hotel and Casino	HERE	1997	Organizing campaign, part of major push in Las Vegas
GAP	UNITE	1999–	Global Exchange and Campaign for Labor Rights leading much of the campaign, which targets garment production in the U.S. Colony of Saipan; tied to sweatshop movement; Global Exchange threatened in 1999 to expand the campaign to other GAP production in Honduras, Indonesia, Russia, and El Salvador; focus of campus handbills and protests; EEOC and private litigation filed 1999; workers tours; effort for legislation on worker rights in Marianas; call for independent monitoring; vandalism; "strip-in" in Los Angeles when demonstrators said they would rather be naked than wear GAP clothing
General Dynamics	UAW	1984	Sparked by hiring of replacements for 2,200 strikers at Electric Boat Division; AFL–CIO involvement through IUD; among union allies were NOW, Missouri Citizen/Labor Energy Coalition, Sierra Club, Sisters of Loretto, Religious Committee on Labor Relations; company portrayed as antilabor, antitaxpayer

Primary Target	Union(s) Participating	Circa	Comments
General Electric	UE, others	1995–	Contract negotiations in Erie, Pennsylvania, over cost reductions and downsizing; led to "Living Wage Campaign" targeted at GE contractors; base building for 2000 contract cycle; multi-union, international Coordinated Bargaining Committee formed with extensive Web site; globalization is issue; leafletting at 2000 annual meeting; CBC planning meeting in Washington March 2000
Genesis Health Ventures	SEIU	1997–	White papers alleging corporate greed and uneven patient care, built around theme of gambling on Genesis care; newsletter and Web site targeted at Wall Street and shareholders; union testimony filed with Senate Special Committee on Aging; company countered 2000 by posting nursing center "report card" on Web
Goya Foods	UNITE	1999–	Campaign arising from a contract dispute at Hispanic-owned company began after union recognized but no first contract reached; union alleged rat infestation and other unsanitary conditions, OSHA violations; company forced to suspend operations in Miami distribution center for inspection by state and USDA team; busloads of delegates to UNITE national convention staged demonstration at company, joined by local religious leaders; NLRB compliant issued 1999; OSHA hearing on ergonomics 2000
Greyhound Lines	ATU	1983–1992	After 1983 strike, company wanted additional concessions, which led to split between local and international in 1986; striking workers replaced; complaints to Federal Highway Administration about replacement drivers who failed drug tests led to fines

Primary Target	Union(s) Participating	Circa	Comments
Guess?	UNITE	1997–	Part of Los Angeles area organizing campaign; much of campaign spearheaded by Campaign for Labor Rights; tied to sweatshop campaign; company ads claiming sweatshop-free products attacked by DOL as misleading; 1998 company sued union for libel; 1999 wage and hour litigation settled
Gulf & Western	UE		Morse Cutting Tool division; campaign focused on disinvestment policies; campaign headed by Ron Carver
Han Young - Hyundai		1997–	Han Young operates *maquiladora* assembly plant in Mexico for Hyundai; tied to NAFTA dispute; Campaign for Labor Rights involvement
Harper and Row	UAW	1983–1987	Contract dispute eventually resolved after company sold to News Corp.; Rogers assisted union
Hasbro Toys	IBT	1992–1993	Arose from lockout in contract dispute; included call for national boycott, Christmas-time events; lockout ended after union threatened to have Barney character protest
Hilton Hotels	UFCW, AFL–CIO Food and Allied Service Trades Department	1984	Lead company in major Las Vegas organizing initiative; pressure on lenders (Crocker Bank), board of directors; demonstrations and some violence
Hormel	UFCW; Local P-9	1985–1986	Rogers; P-9 vs. UFCW; campaign associated with strike over contract concessions; bitter conflict over acceptance of industry-standard wage structure split labor; involvement of Old Left
Hudson Foods	UFCW	1997–1998	Campaign around OSHA complaints and issue of bathroom breaks; coincided with food poisoning incident at Burger King that led to massive recalls and sale of company to Tyson's and IBP (see also)
IBM	CWA	1999–	Nascent organizing campaign sparked by proposed change in pension plan; personalization; active Web site; leafleting at event honoring CEO; questions raised about company's accounting practices; EEOC investigation of type of pension plan IBM proposed; letter from Senator Jeffords and hearings by his Senate committee; *Disgruntled* e-zine named Alliance@IBM as 1999 Disgruntled Employees of the Year

Primary Target	Union(s) Participating	Circa	Comments
IBP	UFCW	1986	Lockout followed by strike; issue was wage and other concessions; extended to Armand Hammer and Occidental Petroleum as parent company; included protest at National Press Club; focus on exploitation of Asian workers and call on refugee organizations not to place SE Asian refugees with company; extensive OSHA claims; Rep. Lantos held hearings
Ideal Basic Industries	Boilermakers	1984	Union believed producers working to eliminate unions in cement industry; inplant strategy and shareholder initiative
Imerys	PACE, ICEM	2000	Campaign in response to withdrawal of union recognition at U.S. Facilities of French-owned company after merger with nonunion plants
International Paper	UPUI	1983 1987–1988	Rogers planned campaign, but called off after 2 weeks when IP conceded After continued conflict, UPIU brought in Kamber Group, but striking and locked-out Locals insisted on replacement by Rogers; secondary targets included Bank of Boston, Avon
Kaiser Aluminum	USWA	1998–	Strike and campaign over demands for wage concessions and job cuts; replacement workers hired; Washington State Attorney General investigated replacement hiring as possible criminal misdemeanor; lockout after union offered return to work; eight-page ad supplement in Spokane; focus on parent Maxxam's (see also) CEO Charles Hurwitz including picketing at his home and office, claims he is clear-cutting redwoods; union attended annual meeting; product boycotts (asked customers to reduce orders 10%), Pepsi Bottling agreed to stop; meetings with Wall Street analysts; secondary targets included Wells Fargo and other banks; effort to deny company advantageous electric rates from Bonneville Power Administration; Thanksgiving 1998 picketed home of manager; 2000 glossy brochure distributed attacking company as polluter; protest planned at Boeing against use of Kaiser products; 2000 Bradley presidential campaign visit to picket line

Primary Target	Union(s) Participating	Circa	Comments
Kansas City Star	ITU	1983–1984	Contract dispute; campaign substituted for strike; Kamber Group participation; agreement reached after 2 years
K-Mart	UNITE	1993–1996	Organizing drive in Greensboro, North Carolina warehouse; Pulpit Forum (group of local ministers) participated in boycott by urging parishioners to shop elsewhere; sit-ins
	UAW	1999–	Organizing campaign at Ohio and Pennsylvania warehouses; Jobs with Justice involvement; "Seven Days in June" 1999 included 110 events in 38 states coordinated by AFL–CIO; rally at 1999 shareholders meeting with UNITE and Teamster participation; company included in 1999 NYC "People's Tribunal on Corporate Crimes Against Humanity"
Kraft Foods	BCT	1993	No details available
Kulback's Construction	Buffalo, NY, Construction Trades Council	1997	Organizing campaign included picketing worksites and home of CEO and his son; leafleting at NFL game showed rat on sandwich and urged fans to boycott Cracker Barrel restaurants, a company client
Last Radio Group	IAM	1999–	Recognition drive at NYC limousine firm began 1997; company claimed drivers were independent contractors, but NLRB ruled December 1998 that they were employees; Cardinal O'Connor wrote letters to Wall Street firms that were customers urging them to use only unionized firms, several did; U.S. Airways also pledged to use unionized drivers for La Guardia shuttle pickups
Litton Industries	UE	1981–1984	Rogers; response to failure to secure an initial contract after union won NLRB election at a new plant; UE not in AFL–CIO because of its radical politics but did receive assistance from IUD analysis of company's business structure and from some AFL–CIO Locals with Litton contracts; union used "Craypo Report" to argue company was repeat labor law violator, unworthy of federal contracts; ICCR, United Methodist Church, other religious group involvement; shareholder initiatives

Primary Target	Union(s) Participating	Circa	Comments
Liz Claiborne	National Labor Committee	1999–	Part of sweatshop movement; campaign arose from firings at El Salvador contract facility; effort to enforce 1996 company pledge on code of conduct, AIP code; attack on monitoring by Price Waterhouse
Lloyd Noland Hospital	USWA	1984	Impasse on wage concessions led to campaign; targeting of hospital board highlighted by informational picketing at the business of one member, open letter to full board, and full-page newspaper advertisement
Lohr's	IBT		Company was Anheuser-Busch distributor; union attacked A-B to generate pressure for a contract; started referendum on state law allowing distribution monopoly, which led to alliance with tavern owners; St. Louis Councilman held hearing
Louisiana-Pacific	UBC	1983–1984	Company refused to follow national pattern-bargaining agreement; when union struck, company hired replacement workers; consumer boycott organized through 1,800 UBC Locals; letter to State Farm, which was largest shareholder, asking for assistance; rally on Wall Street; Working Assets money market fund wrote letter to company chairman; shareholders actions; state EPAs brought in; union spent $4 million, company $5 million; after campaign company won series of decertification elections

Primary Target	Union(s) Participating	Circa	Comments
LTV	UAW	1987	Dispute over pension benefits when company declared Chapter 11, terminated pensions; inplant strategies and strike
		1995–1996	Union claims new Trico venture ignores company neutrality pledge; union addressed 1996 annual meeting; work-to-contract; complaints to Congress, Pension Benefit Guaranty Corporation
Magruder's Supermarkets	UFCW		"Mini-campaign" after unsuccessful organizing effort and ULPs centered on threat to set up informational pickets at stores and begin publicity campaign; company agreed to card check, and union was recognized
Maintenance Unlimited	SEIU	1998	Campaign for recognition by Seattle maintenance contractor; Justice for Janitors and Union Summer participation
Marriott International	HERE	1998–	Company is major nonunion chain; organizing campaign, especially in San Francisco; union formed alliance with Institutional Shareholder Services, which carried fight against a proposed stock restructuring
Mattel	AFL–CIO, Coalition of Labor Union Women	1995	Company included with Nike and Van Heusen in year-long "Come Shop With Me" campaign that was predecessor of anti-sweatshop movement
	UPIU	1997–	Strike at Ft. Wayne, Indiana, plant ended when company threatened permanent replacements, led into campaign; themes include ties to child labor, sweatshops, attacks on executive compensation; union representatives spoke at annual meeting, Las Vegas Toy Expo; held funeral procession for 8-hour day; 1999 company established code of conduct for all contractors and accepted outside labor practices audit for all; independent audit of Asian factories released 1999
Maxxam	USWA	1999	Campaign includes environmental, health and safety, finance themes; shareholders resolution got 22% support at 1999 annual meeting; ran Metzenbaum and Mikva for the board; supported by CalPERS; Alliance for Sustainable Jobs and Environment (Sierra Club, Friends of the Earth, Teamsters, USWA, UBC) claims Maxxam fight forged its coalition (see also Kaiser Aluminum)

Primary Target	Union(s) Participating	Circa	Comments
McDonalds	UFCW		Centered on introduction of Chicken McNuggets, campaign was off-shoot of effort to organize poultry workers; ended when company sued union
MGM Grand	HERE	1993–1996	Part of Las Vegas organizing campaign; demonstrations and some violence; appeals to shareholders; threats to use union clout in Detroit to oppose company gaming license there
Monfort Beef (ConAgra)	UFCW	1983–1994	Retaliation and organizing campaign; Greeley, Colorado, plant reopened as nonunion 1982, formerly union plant had closed for 2 years; 1983 workers voted nonunion, but 1992 federal court ruled company had committed ULPs influencing that vote and ordered new election; UFCW recognized 1993, then year to get contract; extensive NLRB and OSHA pressure including $1.1 million OSHA fine
Moog Automotive	UAW	1981–1982	Fearing replacement workers if strike, Jerry Tucker of union devised first successful inplant strategies including mass march to complain about safety, refusal of overtime, lunch and break rallies, work-to-rule
Mount Olive Pickles	FLOC	1999–	Similar to Campbell's in that effort to impose contracts on growers; secondary targets include Kroger, Food Lion; union recruiting support from churches, students, minorities; demonstrations at NASCAR event; boycott endorsed by AFL–CIO; some Kroger stores dropped products in 2000
Nestle	IBT	1999	California lock-out during contract dispute sparked campaign; leafleting at NBA game; civil rights lawsuit over replacement workers
New Balance	UNITE	1999–	Union won right to represent distribution employees, but accused company of shifting to temp workers and to China; Web site
New Otani Hotel	HERE	1994–	Effort to force company to accept city-wide labor agreement; contacts with travel agents, Internet postings warning customers away; attack on Japanese owners as World War II war criminals

Primary Target	Union(s) Participating	Circa	Comments
Newport News Shipbuilding	USWA	1999	Campaign associated with strike over pension plan; union filed safety complaints with OSHA and the U.S. Navy claiming replacement workers could not safely handle nuclear fuel rods, other tasks; eventual contract agreement
New York Air	ALPA	1991–1992	Rogers; 8-month campaign for union recognition was unsuccessful; said to have cost union $500,000; AFL–CIO Executive Council advised 102 unions to remove funds from company's financial backers
New York *Daily News*	Newspaper Guild (CWA)	1993	Campaign in the midst of New York newspaper wars by only union at paper without a contract, boycott not supported by other unions; Rogers organized; sought support from local minority and senior citizens groups; personalized attacks on publisher Morton Zuckerman, accused of racism and union-busting, led to secondary targeting of *US News, Atlantic* and his real estate holdings
Nike	UNITE	1992–	Extensive use of surrogates, especially Global Exchange, Press for Change, Campaign for Labor Rights; NOW; focal point of anti-sweatshop campaign; after CEO Phil Knight acceded to demands in 1998, campaign continued unabated; effort to turn Michael Jordan against company; consumer lawsuit alleging false advertising, later dismissed; worker tours; possible Reebok participation; company included in 1999 NYC "People's Tribunal on Corporate Crimes Against Humanity"; German retailers took Nike jerseys off shelves January 2000 after allegations they contained harmful fungicide
Nordstrom	UFCW	1989	Organizing drive; allegations of off-the-clock work; ABC and *60 Minutes* interested at same time, CBS ran a story; employees rejected union

Primary Target	Union(s) Participating	Circa	Comments
NORPAC Food Sales	Oregon Farm Workers Union (PCUN - Pineros y Campesinos Unidos del Noroeste)	1997–	Principal target of recognition campaign is NORPAC, Gardenburger was secondary boycott target because visible in marketplace (especially on college campuses where much of effort centered), also FLAV-R-PAK branded items; Gardenburger ended ties to NORPAC May 1999; Campaign for Labor Rights involvement; includes claims of child labor violations; worker tours and campus organizing packets; January 2000 PCUN called for federal review of state OSHA inspections of farm workplaces
Northern Telecom	CWA	1989	Company decertified five of seven bargaining units between 1984 and 1989 and was moving to replace union with nonunion workers in United States; CWA relied on much stronger Canadian unions to pressure company and conducted campaign in Canada
Northwest Airlines	ALPA	1978	Rogers helped union leverage company's financial backers to force a contract settlement
NYNEX	CWA, IBEW	1988–1989	Contract negotiation; objectives were card check and neutrality; inside game included red T-shirts, tapping, work-to-rule, marching in to work *en masse*; company claimed at least 60 acts of vandalism or sabotage; unions mobilized state legislature in their support
Obayashi Construction	Kentucky Building and Construction Trades Council	1986	Campaign over hiring nonunion workers to build Toyota plant; Toyota was secondary target; rally at Japanese Embassy in Washington; sheet metal workers union marched in support in Chicago and called for boycott of Toyota; Kamber Group advised union
Ogden/Danly	USWA	1984	Campaign assisted by Kamber Group complemented strike; contract settled 1985, decertification defeated

Primary Target	Union(s) Participating	Circa	Comments
Oregon Steel	USWA	1997–	Strike after contract expiration at Boulder, Colorado, mill; secondary boycott of Wells Fargo Bank including pension fund withdrawal; pressure generated through Union Pacific (major customer), several political bodies that buy steel rail (especially in California); letter to company from Colorado governor; extensive use of Internet, especially Usenet groups, to post anti-company materials; inplant T-shirts with cobra picture and slogan "If provoked we will strike"; union struck, company hired replacement workers; tactics included letters to customers and rallies at their facilities, advertising, direct mail, talk shows, conference calls for Wall Street with USWA analyst Randy Barber to discuss two critical reports he wrote; 1999 shareholders resolutions received 42% to 45% of vote; National Interfaith Committee for Worker Justice; December 1999 company adopted poison pill; February 2000 union and neighbors in North Portland opposed proposed emissions permit; congressional investigation threatened 2000 by James Oberstar, ranking Democrat on House Transportation Committee; company sued BART after decision to stop buying its rail
Overnite Transportation	IBT	1994–	Organizing campaign, also pension fund issue similar to UPS campaign; 1995 parent company Union Pacific targeted including petition to ICC to delay merger with Southern Pacific; 1996, 15 locations accepted unionization, 28 rejected it; 1997 Overnite CEO resigned; strategic use of ULP filings including massive complaint in 1998; 1999 union set up e-mail service to advise customers of impending labor actions at company; company and three managers sued union for libel based on published claim they had been indicted on criminal charges, a reference to issuance of an NLRB complaint; February 1999 union published white paper; series of petitions and votes to decertify union; 1999 strike at unionized facilities after several months of planning; secondary boycott at Bed Bath & Beyond, other customers; 1999 IPO postponed after report by Locker Associates; December 1999 presidential candidate Bill Bradley endorsed strike; IBT president Hoffa took strong personal stake in strike; AFL–CIO provided $500,000 February 2000; company sued union spokesman for defamation, also RICO suit against Hoffa and union for pattern of violent activities; company claimed 95% of picketers were from unionized competitors; TV, radio, newspaper ad glitz April 2000; IBT at Union Pacific 2000 annual meeting; Congressional hearing; Jobs with Justice involvement

Primary Target	Union(s) Participating	Circa	Comments
Perdue Farms	UFCW	1995–1996; 1999–	Centered on Lewiston, North Carolina, facility; part of poultry industry campaign; union found to have forged half of authorization cards for first of two NLRB elections; resumed 1999 with filing of class action off-the-clock litigation; USDA 1999 investigating complaints company short-changed growers
Phelps Dodge	USWA	1983	Private-sector equivalent of PATCO defeat; company broke pattern bargaining, union struck; replacement workers; IUD coordinated campaign; union eventually decertified
		1998–	Second-wave campaign based at Chino mine in New Mexico; SEC involvement; environmental disclosure issue led to white paper, litigation (later dropped), coalition with environmentalists; company-focused Web site established by project of Tides Foundation
Phillips Van Heusen	UNITE	1992–	Organizing campaign in Guatemala; Campaign for Labor Rights involvement through US/GLEP-US/LEAP; Human Rights Watch; tied to sweatshop movement; leafleting at annual meetings, outlets, retailers targeting all PVH brands; after union won vote in December 1998 company closed that factory; worker tours
Pittston Coal	UMWA	1988–1989	Campaign headed by Eddie Burke; established Camp Solidarity in Virginia; secondary boycott against Crestar Bank; extensive shareholder activity; union fined $52 million for contempt of court during 1989 strike, which included use of jack-rocks, rock throwing, gunfire, 4-day occupation of a processing facility
Placer Dome Mining	ICEM	1999–	International campaign against Canadian company following job cuts in South Africa; focus on environmental issues in Philippines, Chile, Peru, Papua New Guinea, and Australia; planning workshop set for 2000

Primary Target	Union(s) Participating	Circa	Comments
Pony Express	IBT	1994–1995	Organizing campaign at company that carried cancelled checks for banks and Federal Reserve Banks; NationsBank was secondary target, hit for red-lining and union opposed merger with Bank South; pressure on Fed to find fault with company revealed in memo during Carey financing scandal; company recognized union 1997
Post/Dedham Transcript	ITU	1984–1986	Campaign substituted for strike; assisted by Rogers; company transferred work 1986; numerous ULP charges filed
Price Chopper	UFCW	1988–1990	$2 million market-share campaign in upstate New York; consumer boycott; attacked Industrial Development Bond support for new facilities
Publix	UFCW	1991–	Campaign to slow growth of nonunion company; by 1999, union was actively trying to organize workers; 1996 series of affirmative action claims through class action litigation—after company settled gender case for $81 million, union filed race case; NLRB complaints; Florida Consumers Federation served as front group
Quincy Farms	UFW	1996–1999	Mushroom workers organizing campaign in Florida; boycott supported by NAACP and local churches; resolved after management change and 68% workers signed union cards; contract reached July 1999
Ravenswood Aluminum	USWA	1990	Personal attacks on Marc Rich using wanted posters; forced congressional investigation into why U.S. Mint did business with Rich; boycott secured pledges from Stroh Brewery, Anheuser-Busch, Miller Brewing, Coca-Cola not to use company's products in their cans
RCA/NBC	NABET (now CWA)	1984	Six-month campaign over contract issues; assisted by Rogers; union gained job security provisions in contract
Restaurant Associates	HERE	1999–	Organizing campaign; secondary target was Metropolitan Opera, which was customer, including demonstration on opening night of season; letters to Met board members and to prominent Met donors; union wants card check, company wants NLRB election

Primary Target	Union(s) Participating	Circa	Comments
Richmark	UNITE	1997	MA curtain-maker was targeted for organizing campaign; after strike, eventually yielded to contract with increased wages, went out of business 1 year later; Jobs with Justice set up Workers Rights Board to pressure company; ULPs filed; state Attorney General intervened in response to claim of illegal take-home work
Rio Tinto	ICEM	1998–	International campaign includes themes of protecting environment and indigenous peoples; Australian union and ICEM issued series of reports (*Rio Tinto: Behind the Façade, Rio Tinto: Tainted Titan*) for distribution to shareholders; extensive online materials; 2000 shareholder resolutions for diversity on board, code of conduct
Ryder	IBT	1992	Carhaulers' contract at issue, but union attacked truck rental and school bus leasing businesses to bring pressure; fly-over at Ryder-sponsored PGA event; compared Ryder to Eastern Air Lines; met with Wall Street analysts and trade press; Jobs with Justice
Santa Fe Gaming	HERE	1995–	Effort to get contract 5 years after pro-union vote; extensive financial analysis by Courtney Alexander of HERE; coalition with major shareholder group seeking dividends helped elect two directors; trying to unseat CEO; conference calls with bond holders, distributed negative report at investor show-and-tell
Sawyer Lumber	PACE	1999–2000	Campaign followed company appeal of 1998 election recognizing union; NLRB complaints over coercion, failure to bargain; congressional involvement; union complaining about federal loans to company; March 2000 rally addressed by local political leaders
SeaFirst Bank	UFCW	1978	Rogers; after union reorganization that brought existing unit into UFCW, company declined to bargain; included legal battle through NLRB and courts
Smithfield Foods	UFCW	1999–	Probably organizing campaign; involvement of SEC to hear complaint of failure to disclose alleged conflicts of interest; USDA pressured company January 2000 over proposed acquisition
Somers Building Maintenance	SEIU	1995–	For building maintenance staff; secondary campaign against Hewlett-Packard, other clients; Justice for Janitors; company says will accept election but union insisting on card check

Primary Target	Union(s) Participating	Circa	Comments
Sprint	CWA	1993–1997	Organizing campaign at nonunion Le Conexion Familiar division with heavily Hispanic workforce; division closed by company 8 days before scheduled election; union used as first test of NAFTA labor side agreement
A. E. Staley	AIW (UPIU)	1993	Rogers; Jerry Tucker; use of inside strategies including extensive sabotage; may be origin of price-fixing charge against ADM; included Pepsi boycott; tied in with Caterpillar and Bridgestone–Firestone campaigns
Starbucks		1993–1998	Organizing campaign for Guatemalan coffee workers; Campaign for Labor Rights involvement through US/GLEP; central issue has been Code of Conduct; 1995 company issued code, 1997 accused of reneging; 1998 adopted new code and US/GLEP ended campaign
		2000	Campaign reemerged with Chicago-area campus demonstrations by Student Alliance to Reform Corporation over working conditions at suppliers
Stemilt Growers, others	UFW, IBT	1996–	Organizing drive among apple workers in Washington State; IBT focused on warehouse workers and UFW on pickers; earlier organizing campaign was probable origin of the Alar scare; 1998 immigrant workers filed complaints in Mexico under NAFTA alleging discrimination, health and safety violations, anti-union activity; Washington Committee on Justice in the Apple Industry included former Governor, state Supreme Court justice; 1997 IBT issued "Ripe for Fairness" white paper; 1999 card check agreement, then union got majority of workers to sign cards, but Stemilt challenged; in related effort NLRB filed charges against Washington Fruit & Produce
J.P. Stevens	ACTWU	1976–1980	First full-scale campaign; Rogers; Michael Locker; shareholder resolutions; attack on banking and lending relationships (especially Metropolitan Life), board interlocks (Manufacturers Hanover Trust, Avon Products)
Sutter Health	SEIU	1997–	Elaborate regulatory attack using multiple federal, state, and local agencies
Texaco	OCAW	1982	Associated with strike over pension benefit changes; Rogers led actions at Texaco and Manufacturers Hanover (Texaco CEO was board member) annual meetings, but then fired because of costs

Primary Target	Union(s) Participating	Circa	Comments
Titan International	USWA	1999–	ULP strike of 1,200 workers led to campaign against tire manufacturer; union contacted shareholders, analysts, lenders; called for resignation of CEO; aggressive OSHA campaign; issued *Bad for Business* white paper 2000 attacking CEO; secondary attack on Harris Bank
Townsend Culinary	UFCW	1999–	Organizing campaign; 1996 workers voted union in, year later voted to decertify; led to NLRB complaint and 1999 court order requiring company to negotiate with union; also class action sexual harassment lawsuit brought by EEOC; letters to CEO from Senator Kennedy, Rep. Bonior
Toys 'R Us	UFCW	1996	Global Exchange and Campaign for Labor Rights have tied company to sweatshop issue, but explicitly avoided boycott call; 1999 company paid DOL fine for child labor violations in United States and agreed to compliance procedures
Tyson's Foods	UFCW	1998–	Dispute centered at Corydon, Indiana, plant, which company acquired when bought Hudson Foods; pegged to strike; strong racial thematic; part of union's long-running Poultry Justice Organizing Campaign (NICWJ), although Corydon plant organized since 1970s; truth squads sent to numerous Tyson plants in organizing effort; targeted in Union Summer 1999; leafleting at shareholders meeting; sign displays at SEC basketball games in Atlanta; secondary boycott aimed at KFC in effort to get it to impose code of conduct on Tyson's, others; Jobs with Justice involvement; endorsed by Jesse Jackson, National Baptist Convention; strike ended March 1999, but other organizing efforts continued; June 1999 union announced back-pay lawsuit; NAFTA tie-in 1999 when Mexico banned imports of meat from Tyson's, IBP, and Conagra; 1999 company initiated environmental awards program for growers; campaign focused in 1999 on deaths and injuries of workers; February 2000 company announced wage practices being audited by DOL; CalPERS contacted shareholders to end dual-class stock structure; $230,000 settlement of wage discrimination claims February 2000
Uniroyal	PACE	1999	Brief campaign after 4-year negotiation failed to produce first contract; media outreach, inside mobilization activities; contacts with outside directors, business partners of CEO; five locals wrote to CEO of KeySpan Energy on whose board Uniroyal CEO served; contract agreed after 1 month, ratified December 1999

Primary Target	Union(s) Participating	Circa	Comments
United Parcel Service	IBT	1996–1997	Year-long preparation before major strike; media strategy included reliance on training rank-and-file to speak; leveraged personalized public contact with drivers; intended as symbol of labor resurgence and timed to $2 million ad campaign for "new" labor movement; effect dampened by Carey financing scandal
US West	CWA	1998	Campaign associated with strike largely over pay for performance, growth into nonunion high-technology sectors; context of industry-wide bargaining; NLRB complaints; newspaper ads singling out company as "renegade" within industry for its poor customer service; union released survey results showing customer support for its bargaining positions; charged company with illegally recruiting strikebreakers in Canada; resolved after 2 weeks
Vencor	SEIU	1995–	Part of larger health care industry campaign; union focused media attention on company decision to evict Medicare patients in favor of private patients; allegations of Medicare fraud; 1998 company fined $300,000 for nursing home violations in Wisconsin; 1999 company filed for bankruptcy protection; March 2000 Department of Justice filed civil fraud claim against company for $1 billion
Wal-Mart	UFCW, UMWA	1992–	Organizing campaign; included "turning" of celebrity vendor Kathie Lee Gifford through the sweatshop issue; for example, took TV cameras into Seo Fashions, a contractor making KLG goods for Wal-Mart; December 1998 rally at company headquarters to protest move into supermarket industry; "Good Neighbor Campaign" asks neighbors to sign cards pledging not to buy groceries from company; FAST report supported attack on company's "Buy American" program, also protest over volume of Chinese-made goods company sells; "War on Women" theme alleges poor treatment of female employees; union stated complaints at 1994 shareholders meeting; company was target of report by National Trust for Historic Preservation attacking urban sprawl, and is centerpiece of antisprawl drive that became theme of Gore presidential campaign; active effort to oppose zoning for stores in new markets; company included in 1999 NYC "People's Tribunal on Corporate Crimes Against Humanity"; company tied in to anti-WTO protests; supercenter zoning denied in Las Vegas January 2000; first U.S. Store unionized by UFCW February 2000, but then company closed the department that had voted in the union; Wal-Mart Litigation Project established on Web

Primary Target	Union(s) Participating	Circa	Comments
Washington Gas Light Company	IUGW	1996	Company sought union-weakening work-rule changes; Rogers' secondary target was Crestar Bank for interlocks and financial support; AFL–CIO, UE, other unions joined boycott and pledged to withdraw $114 million from bank; using old ACORN allegation, A. Phillip Randolph Institute weighed in alleging bank was a major red-liner
Wheeling-Pittsburgh	USWA	1996–1997	Dispute over pension benefits led to 10-month strike and campaign; resolved when company adopted defined-benefits plan; company threatened to close facilities; pressure on principal WHX (parent company) shareholders including Mellon Bank, Merrill Lynch; neutrality agreement
Whole Foods	UFCW	1990–	Organizing campaign began when founder bought store in Berkeley but refused to accept old union contracts; picketing and media attacks
Zurich Insurance	Manufacturing Science Finance (MSF) union	1993–1994	European union ran U.S.-style campaign against company after it decertified union; legal, lobbying, advertising components; company yielded

KEY TO UNION ACRONYMS: ACWU (Amalgamated Clothing Workers Union; later ACTWU, UNITE), ACTWU (Amalgamated Clothing and Textile Workers Union; now UNITE), AFA (Association of Flight Attendants), AFSCME (American Federation of State, County and Municipal Employees), AIW (Allied Industrial Workers—defunct), ALPA (Air Line Pilots Association), APFA (Association of Professional Flight Attendants), ATU (Amalgamated Transit Union), BCT (Bakery, Confectionery and Tobacco Workers International Union), BMWE (Brotherhood of Maintenance of Way Engineers), CWA (Communications Workers of America), FLOC (Farm Labor Organizing Committee), HERE (Hotel Employees and Restaurant Employees International Union), IAM (International Association of Machinists), IBEW (International Brotherhood of Electrical Workers), IBT (International Brotherhood of Teamsters), IUOE (International Union of Operating Engineers), ICEM (International Federation of Chemical, Energy, Mine and General Workers Unions), ITU (International Typographical Union), IUE (International Union of Electronic Workers), IUF (International Union of Food, Agricultural, Hotel, Restaurant, Catering, Tobacco and Allied Workers Associations), IUGW (International Union of Gas Workers), NABET (National Association of Broadcast Employees and Technicians, later merged into CWA), OCAW (Oil, Chemical and Atomic Workers International Union; now merged with UPUI to form PACE), OPEIU (Office and Professional Employees International Union), PACE (Paper, Allied-Industrial, Chemical, and Energy Workers International Union), SEIU (Service Employees International Union), TWU (Transport Workers Union), UAW (United Auto Workers International Union), UBC (United Brotherhood of Carpenters and Joiners), UE (United Electrical, Radio, and Machine Workers of America), UFCW (United Food and Commercial Workers International Union), UFW (United Farm Workers Union), UMWA (United Mine Workers of America), UNITE (Union of Needletrades, Industrial and Textile Employees), UPUI (United Paperworkers International Union; now merged with OCAW to form PACE), and USWA (United Steelworkers Union of America)

METHODOLOGICAL NOTE: The selection of campaigns for inclusion in this table is inevitably subjective. The author has applied three general criteria. The first is that the target of an attack must be a corporation. This obviously excludes electoral campaigns, but it also excludes policy-directed campaigns, such as those opposing NAFTA or the Multilateral Agreement on Investment (MAI), which may feature the same actors and employ the same tactics. The second requires that, to be considered a corporate campaign, an effort must be based on some form of stakeholder analysis, either explicit or implicit, so that one or more key stakeholders of the target corporation is identified and exploited as a point of leverage. This serves to exclude less sophisticated campaigns comprising only general public relations, simple boycotts, or lobbying. The third is that a campaign will always be included if it is explicitly labeled by the engaging party as a *corporate campaign*, unless there is clear reason to exclude it on other grounds. It is also important to note that the time periods and specific years noted here for the beginning and ending points of any given campaign may be approximations and may be unreliable. Campaigns often begin long before they become visible and may continue even after they have dropped from public view.

SOURCES: Appendix A is drawn from a variety of sources, including the several articles in *Labor Research Review* 21 (Chicago: Midwest Center for Labor Research, Fall/Winter 1993); Timothy J. Bartl, *Union Corporate Campaign Tactics: Issues and Examples* (Washington, DC: Labor Policy Association, 1997); Charles R. Perry, *Union Corporate Campaigns* (Philadelphia: Industrial Research Unit, The Wharton School, University of Pennsylvania, 1987); Kate Bronfenbrenner et al., eds., *Organizing to Win: New Research on Union Strategies* (Ithaca, NY: Cornell University Press, 1998); Paul Jarley and Cheryl Maranto, "Union Corporate Campaigns: An Assessment," *Industrial & Labor Relations Review*, Vol. 43, No. 5 (July 1990), pp. 509–510; multiple issues of the *Daily Labor Report*; hundreds of news accounts and news releases; union and other Web sites; and other sources credited elsewhere in this book.

APPENDIX B

Anticorporate Campaigns Launched by Nonlabor Entities, 1989–1999

Primary Target	Group(s) Initiating	Circa	Comments
ARCO	Free Burma Coalition	1995–1998	Web-based campaign; company eventually ceased operations in Burma
Baxter International	ICCR, Health Care Without Harm (coalition led by Greenpeace); SEIU	1998–1999	SEIU pension fund, together with two Catholic orders active in ICCR and Health Care Without Harm (coalition led by Greenpeace), initiated shareholder action to force company to reduce use of PVC materials in packaging; may also be labor-specific objectives; company agreed to end use of vinyl
BP Amoco	Greenpeace	1997–	Campaign to halt offshore oil development on Alaska's North Slope, initially targeting ARCO; interference with drilling activity; Shareholders Against New Exploration formed to question company at annual meetings; shareholder resolution introduced 2000; opposition at FTC to merger of BP with ARCO; joined in lawsuit with Eskimos to stop project; posted online database of institutional shareholders to be used as secondary targets; company included in ecopledge hiring boycott

Primary Target	Group(s) Initiating	Circa	Comments
Chevron	Human Rights Watch, others	1998–	Pressure on company to cease operations in Nigeria; 1999 effort to get House subcommittee on Africa to hold hearings; 2000 lawsuit in San Francisco over alleged human rights violations in Nigeria allowed to proceed
Conoco	Rainforest Action Network		Pressure on company to cease operations in the Amazon region
Dayton-Hudson	Global Exchange	1999	Effort to force retailer to stop selling garments manufactured in Saipan
Detroit Edison	NOW	1998–	Opportunity for female employees, sexual harassment; threat to name company next "Merchant of Shame"; not clear this campaign developed fully, but in 1999 company signed agreement with its unions on a set of "partnership principles" committing company to success of the unions; company agreed October 1999 to settle three class action lawsuits on age and race discrimination; new class action on denial of overtime filed same day; possible union involvement
DuPont	Greenpeace	1992–	Objective to get company to stop using ozone-destroying chemicals; Rogers involved in planning
		2000–	Targeted in genetically modified foods campaign by ICCR; shareholder resolutions
Freeport-McMoRan	Rainforest Action Network, Project Underground	1995–	Effort to force company to stop operations said to threaten indigenous Indonesian tribes, human rights litigation; attacks on financial performance, CEO compensation, and environmental issues; Rio Tinto owns 12% of company and may be connection between campaigns
Georgia-Pacific	Rainforest Action Network		Effort to get company to cease harvesting old-growth timber

Primary Target	Group(s) Initiating	Circa	Comments
Hoechst/ Rhone Poulenc	Fund for the Feminist Majority	1992–	Objective to speed U.S. availability of RU-486, the day after birth control pill; Rogers involved in planning; pressure on U.S. subsidiaries of the two targets, whose joint venture controlled rights and manufacture of RU-486; tied to pro-abortion movement and generated anti-abortion counterattack
Home Depot	Rainforest Action Network, Greenpeace, Natural Resources Defense Council	1998– 1999	Based in objections to selling old-growth wood; floating demonstrations at company's stores; RAN tried to have a chief of the Nuxalk tribe in British Columbia address 1999 annual meeting, but denied; 1999 company agreed to phase out old-growth products; Greenpeace activists later arrested for "reclaiming" lumber they said was stolen from the rain forest
Kimberly Clark	Rainforest Action Network	1998–	Based on claim that company manufactures toilet paper from old-growth timber
MacMillan Bloedel	Rainforest Action Network		Effort to get company to cease harvesting old-growth timber
Mattel	Greenpeace	1999–	Part of campaign to reduce use of PVC; EU imposed ban on selected toys with PVCs; company agreed to switch plastics
Microsoft	Netscape; Sun Microsystems; Oracle; Consumer Project on Technology (Ralph Nader); CWA	1995–	Much of the campaign has been channeled through a virtual group, Net Action; although not initiated by labor, the CWA began an organizing campaign at the company during the campaign and was a partner in Net Action from the outset
Mitsubishi	Rainforest Action Network	1989–	Pressure through U.S. subsidiaries and elsewhere to reduce logging of old-growth timber; noteworthy for daredevil publicity stunts; demonstrations at auto dealers and trade shows, Bank of California (owned by Mitsubishi Bank of Tokyo); two subsidiaries settled

Primary Target	Group(s) Initiating	Circa	Comments
	NOW and Operation PUSH	1996– 1998	Targeted company's U.S. auto plant after filing of private and EEOC sexual harassment charges; 1999 African-American workers sued company and UAW for having ignored discrimination and harassment against them; company agreed to $34 million settlement; race discrimination class action suit filed January 2000
	Natural Resources Defense Council	1999– 2000	Opposition to expansion of salt extraction operations at a facility in Baja California because of effects on sea life; letter-writing campaign to Mexican government; several celebrities involved including Glenn Close, Pierce Brosnan, son of Jacques Cousteau; endorsed February 2000 by SEIU; company withdrew from project March 2000
Mobil	Africa Fund, others	1998–	Pressure on company to cease operations in Nigeria
Monsanto	Greenpeace	1999–	Attempt to dissuade company from engaging in genetic engineering as part of worldwide campaign; 1999 class action lawsuit filed by farmers with backing of Greenpeace; next week company agreed to merge with pharmaceutical firm and spin off agricultural components; targeted in genetically modified foods campaign by ICCR with shareholder resolutions; Greenpeace opposed approval of products by EU March 2000
Nestle	Action for Corporate Accountability; INFACT	1977– 1984; 1988–	Company attacked for distributing infant formula in Third World countries; Edward Kennedy held hearings 1978; 1981 World Health Assembly adopted Code of Marketing for formula; 1984 company signed on; campaign reinstated after group decided company not abiding by code
Occidental Petroleum	Rainforest Action Network	1999–	Effort to force company to stop operations in Andes Mountains; included threat by tribe to walk off side of a mountain as ancestors had done to preserve land; accused of supporting paramilitaries who killed American activists in Colombia; order of Dominican nuns introduced shareholders resolution at 1999 annual meeting; secondary campaign against Fidelity Investments for financing company's Colombian operations; sit-in shut down Gore for President headquarters in New Hampshire during primary week

Primary Target	Group(s) Initiating	Circa	Comments
Pepsico	Free Burma Coalition	1995–1998	Company targeted for doing business in Burma; boycotts urged for restaurant group in United States, campuses; eventually left Burma and sold restaurants
		2000	Targeted in genetically modified foods campaign by ICCR; shareholder resolutions
Philip Morris	INFACT	1993–	Principal target in campaign against tobacco industry; boycott of Kraft Foods (subsidiary); targeting investors; ICCR participation; mass phone-in campaign March 2000; March 2000 issued white paper on company's lobbying and public relations pressure tactics
Shell	Project Underground	1995–	Company targeted for doing business in Nigeria; sparked by death of activist; 1998 wave of campus events in United States and other countries
Siemens	Global 2000, Friends of the Earth	1996–	Objective is to force company to cease upgrading and operating nuclear power facilities in Russia, Eastern Europe, elsewhere; support from Greenpeace; included 1996 Christmas boycott of company's commercial brands
Smith Barney	NOW	1997–1998	Intervention to support sexual harassment claims; HERE intervened as part of its Aramark campaign to oppose settlement favored by NOW leadership; company named first "Merchant of Shame"
Starbucks	US/Guatemala Labor Education Project	1996	US/GLEP is a labor-friendly group, but this campaign appears to have been grounded more firmly in Latin American politics than in a U.S. Labor dispute; focused on environmental and workplace issues of Guatemalan coffee growers
		2000	Threatened campaign over "fair trade coffee" led to immediate change in policy by company; campaign called off
Texaco	International Rivers Network, Committee for the Defense of the Amazon	1996–	Based in objections to company's doing business in Burma and, in a 1999 iteration, to alleged Ecuadorian oil pollution; indigenous tribes suing in U.S. Courts under 18th-century Alien Tort Claims Act; *New York Times* ad and letter to Chevron board timed to disrupt Chevron takeover of Texaco; likely connection to RAN, which earlier pressured Conoco into leaving the region; September 1999 tribes started new advertising campaign attacking company to support their lawsuit

Primary Target	Group(s) Initiating	Circa	Comments
	Rainbow Coalition	1996–1997	Jesse Jackson and others (NOW, NAACP, SCLC, etc.) pressured company to settle race discrimination lawsuit; threatened boycott
Unocal	Free Burma Coalition, National Lawyers Guild	1995–	Effort to force company to cease operations in Burma; supported by OCAW; included effort to revoke corporate charter

METHODOLOGICAL NOTE: The selection of campaigns for inclusion in this table is inevitably subjective. The author has applied three general criteria. The first is that the target of an attack must be a corporation. This obviously excludes electoral campaigns, but also excludes policy-directed campaigns, such as those opposing NAFTA or the Multilateral Agreement on Investment (MAI), which feature the same actors and employ the same tactics. The second requires that, to be considered a corporate campaign, an effort must be based on some form of stakeholder analysis, either explicit or implicit, so that one or more key stakeholders of the target corporation is identified and exploited as a point of leverage. This serves to exclude less sophisticated campaigns comprising only general public relations or lobbying techniques. The third is that a campaign will always be included if it is explicitly labeled by the engaging party as a *corporate campaign* unless there is clear reason to exclude it on other grounds. It is also important to note that the time periods and specific years noted here for the beginning and ending points of any given campaign may be approximations and may be unreliable. Campaigns often begin long before they become visible and may continue even after they have dropped from public view.

SOURCES: Appendix B is drawn primarily from news accounts, news releases, and Internet postings by groups engaged in these various campaigns and their allies, and from other sources credited elsewhere in this book.

INDEX